The Moral Writings of John Dewey

The Moral Writings of John Dewey

edited,
with an introduction and notes,
by

James Gouinlock

Associate Professor of Philosophy, Emory University

HAFNER PRESS
A Division of Macmillan Publishing Co., Inc.
New York

Collier Macmillan Publishers
London

Hafner Press
A Division of Macmillan Publishing Co., Inc.
866 Third Avenue, New York, N.Y. 10022

Collier Macmillan Canada, Ltd.

Library of Congress Catalog Card Number: 75–29826

Printed in the United States of America

printing number
1 2 3 4 5 6 7 8 9 10

Library of Congress Cataloging in Publication Data

Dewey, John, 1859-1952.
   The moral writings of John Dewey.

   Includes bibliographical references and index.
   1. Ethics--Collected works. I. Gouinlock, James.
II. Title.
B945.D41G68 1975   170   75-29826
ISBN 0-02-845370-0

For Barb, Liz, Sue, and Bill

CONTENTS

FOREWORD

An incisive critic once maintained that if any thinker was entitled to be regarded as the national philosopher of American civilization, it was John Dewey. The justification for so characterizing him flowed not only from his commitment to the ideals of American democracy but from his direct and indirect influence upon American cultural thought and educational practice. What may have been true more than a half century ago may not be as apparent today. Dewey has been largely ignored by professional philosophers and although his name is still both invoked and reviled in educational circles, there is little evidence that his major works are read with the care and piety lavished on the great philosophical figures of the past. So, while his commitment to the philosophy of democracy is not denied, its rich and complex implications are rarely explored.

Nonetheless, a persuasive case can be made for the continuing and vital significance of John Dewey's thought not only in the context of the contemporary democratic aspirations of the American republic, but also in understanding the nature of the moral life of human beings as they reflect upon their experience. For Dewey the discipline of philosophy, to the extent that philosophy can be significantly distinguished from inquiries in other fields, is still the quest for wisdom. More technically, it is the normative study of human values. What makes a man a philosopher, as distinct from his historical role as a logician, physicist, biologist or psychologist, is his concern at some point with the nature of the good life and the good society. In all periods philosophers have sought to resolve the conflicts between the inherited traditions of the past and the challenges posed to them by advances of knowledge—or from the shock of the discovery of other cultures. On this view, the philosopher is primarily, but not exclusively, a moralist. He does systematically what the ordinary man and woman do episodically. The philosopher's theoretical concern about cosmology (the nature of the universe), anthropology (the nature of man), and epistemology (the nature and validity of knowledge), according to Dewey, is ultimately derived from his underlying interest in the nature of the good and the right in personal and social life.

Professor Gouinlock's excellent collection of Dewey's writings presents the many-faceted aspects of Dewey's ethical thought. With this collection in hand, students and scholars will more readily acknowledge his substantial contributions to our understanding of the moral life.

Chief among these contributions is his analysis of the nature of the moral experience. Dewey contends that the moral experience does not arise, as is commonly believed, from the confrontation between good and evil or right and wrong. For if the alternatives of action are properly characterized as good and evil, right and wrong, there is really no problem for reflection before us. In such a situation we do not ask the *distinctively* ethical question:

"What shall I do?" which is addressed to the ends of action, not to the technical means of carrying them out. It is only when ends conflict, when the good is opposed to the good, the right to the right, and the good to the right that the perplexities and agonies of moral choice develop. To solve these conflicts we must apply all the resources of human intelligence in exploring the causes and consequences of the options open to us.

The moral decision which is authentic is not merely a matter of words whether in the descriptive or imperative mood. It requires an action of some sort. Such action modifies the objective situation which is the focus of the conflict. But it also modifies the self or personality of the individual who acts. To be sure, the self that we are always limits what we can do but it does not completely determine it. Thinking and resolution can make a difference. The world is still open; to some extent we redetermine events and at the same time reconstitute ourselves. The older we are the more difficult such a reconstruction of self and the world is. The pity of it is that wisdom and the willingness to use it often come too late. This makes the character of the education of the young and the development of habits of reflection crucial for moral conduct.

If ends conflict how do we resolve the conflict? Dewey denies that there is only one overarching end from which the resolutions of all conflicts can be deduced. He maintains that there are a plurality of ends, and that at any given time they enter into the reconstruction of experience which will resolve the given ethical difficulty. The means we use to achieve the reconstructed end are integrated into that end; they become a part of it. The process is one in which we use our intelligence and imagination to discover or enstate the shared interests that will enrich our experience, and to provide the widest social theatre for compatible individual differences.

We solve the conflict of ends in our moral economy by discovering a set of other ends or a large encompassing end within which they can be harmonized. If this is impossible, we seek ends ordered in such a way as to make accessible other ends chosen after reflection, and which reflect the kind of person we want to be. We solve the conflicts of ends among different human beings only if we can discover some shared interests or sensibilities on the basis of which we can live, or live and let live. When this is impossible, we have two objective systems of morality in conflict. The trouble is that in the past human beings have resorted to conflict, not when all other avenues of approach and reconciliation have been undertaken, but at the very outset when incompatible claims are first made. Dewey's moral philosophy is no rose-hued view of human nature. It does not guarantee that all problems can be solved. It offers the best way of solving them *if* they can be solved. And it recognizes the possibility that we may face the stern necessity to fight, if the rational approach is rejected by those who place their faith only in force.

Here then is an ethical philosophy which avoids absolutism without being subjective, and objective without necessarily having universal validity for all times, places and conditions.

No thumbnail sketch or summary, however, can do justice to the subtlety and richness of Dewey's own exposition and analysis. Students will find in Dr. Gouinlock's collection of readings suggestions and observations that will illumine their own moral reflections and decisions. They will also find helpful leads that will aid them in orienting themselves in the study of contemporary ethical issues and movements.

Sidney Hook

PREFACE

At a time when philosophy is looking for renewal and redirection, a fresh examination of the moral writings of John Dewey is highly salutary. The vitality and importance of his philosophy are undiminished. Scholars and students alike will find stimulus, insight, and a solid basis for further inquiry in a careful study of his works.

Contrary to some premature assessments, Dewey's ethical philosophy has not been challenged in any crucial way by recent philosophical analysis.[1] As in any innovative philosophy, there are many ways in which his views could be more carefully formulated, more thoroughly developed, and pertinently criticised. Accordingly, analysis and evaluation are surely welcome. But his ideas are anything but museum pieces. They are sources of genuine understanding and philosophic growth.

Philosophers can learn much from Dewey, but his writings were not addressed primarily to his professional colleagues. He was concerned with the problems of men, and he directed his ideas to all persons who desire a better understanding of the nature of the human situation and its resources for the good. Dewey was extraordinarily successful in attaining such an understanding himself, and he acquired it by undertaking an incisive analysis of fundamental philosophic issues. Viewed in the light of comparable efforts in the history of philosophy, his achievement is outstanding. Indeed, it can hardly be seriously argued that he has any peers among the moral philosophers of this century.

During the last forty years, attention has shifted away from Dewey's humanistic emphasis. Philosophers have been increasingly occupied with exclusively technical issues, most of them relating to moral language. Substantive issues, such as the nature of the good life and the good society, have been slighted.

Since we are beings who must somehow decide what kind of lives to lead, substantive issues cannot long be ignored. So, more recently, there has been a return to them. Their treatment in current philosophic literature emphasizes logical rigor. Conspicuously lacking in this literature is the comprehensive analysis of the nature of man and the world which serves to identify and clarify the possibilities of natural existence.

A *combination* of brilliant analysis with substantive and human wisdom typifies Dewey's writings. This combination would bring welcome refreshment to philosophy today. Regrettably, however, there has not been a convenient and systematic mode of access to Dewey's moral philosophy. He wrote over forty books and seven hundred articles, and hardly any of these is without some contribution to his over-all moral theory. Hence the present book serves a dual purpose. The most important moral writings are collected

1. See below, for example, pp. xlv–xlix, 122, 146.

and organized in a single volume, and Dewey's ideas are made available in convenient form at a time when philosophic thought seems especially receptive to reorientation.

Each of the main divisions in the anthology deals with a distinguishable subject matter. Introductory notes for these divisions and for most of their subsections indicate the place of the selections in the larger context of Dewey's philosophy. Any of the topics, therefore, may be isolated to suit the varied purposes of classroom instruction and selective reading. A comprehensive general introduction specifies the inclusive framework of ideas in which the several topics are placed.

Inasmuch as Dewey's moral thought deals with most of the basic issues in philosophy, this book is appropriate for use not only in courses in ethics, social philosophy, and value theory, but also for general introductions to philosophy. It is well suited to introduce the student to Dewey's philosophy as a whole. Indeed, for almost any course concerned with Dewey's various contributions to philosophy, relevant subject matter in this collection can be found.

Although this volume is suited to many educative purposes, its principal aim is to make it possible for any concerned reader to acquire a grasp of a moral philosophy which is profoundly relevant to the predicaments of modern times.

I want to express my thanks to my friend and colleague, John P. Anton, for giving his close attention to the formulation of the general introduction. I also wish to thank Mr. Edward Quigley for very helpful editorial advice and assistance. Finally, I want to thank Dr. Jo Ann Boydston, Director of The Center for Dewey Studies, for her definitive judgment regarding the authorship of certain chapters in the Dewey and Tufts *Ethics* of 1932.

CREDITS

Grateful acknowledgment is made to the following for permission to reprint materials from the works indicated (selections have been edited to provide uniform spelling and punctuation throughout):

Beacon Press, for John Dewey, *Reconstruction in Philosophy*. Original edition, copyright 1920 by Henry Holt and Company. Enlarged edition, copyright © 1948 by Beacon Press.

The Center for Dewey Studies, Southern Illinois University at Carbondale, for John Dewey and James H. Tufts, *Ethics* (Part III), revised edition. For John Dewey, *Human Nature and Conduct*. For John Dewey, *The Influence of Darwin on Philosophy*. For John Dewey, *Logic: The Theory of Inquiry*. And for John Dewey, *The Public and Its Problems*.

Harvard University Press, for John Dewey, "Authority and Resistance to Social Change," in *Authority and the Individual* (Harvard Tercentenary Publications, 1937). Copyright 1937, 1965 by the President and Fellows of Harvard College.

Holt, Rinehart and Winston, Publishers, for John Dewey and James H. Tufts, *Ethics* (Part II), published by Holt, Rinehart and Winston, Inc. in 1960 as *Theory of the Moral Life*. *Ethics* copyright 1908, 1932 by Holt, Rinehart and Winston, Publishers. Copyright 1936 by John Dewey and James H. Tufts. Copyright © 1960 by Roberta L. Dewey.

The Editors of *Intellect*, for John Dewey, "Democracy and Educational Administration," *School and Society*, XLV (1937).

The Editors of *The Journal of Philosophy*, for John Dewey, "Ethical Subject-Matter and Language," *The Journal of Philosophy*, XLII (1945). And for John Dewey, "Reply to a Letter to Mr. Dewey Concerning John Dewey's Doctrine of Possibility," *The Journal of Philosophy*, XLVI (1949).

Macmillan Publishing Co., Inc. from *Democracy and Education*, by John Dewey. Copyright 1916 by Macmillan Publishing Co., Inc. Renewed 1944 by John Dewey. And for "Philosophy" by John Dewey. Reprinted with permission of the publisher from *Encyclopaedia of the Social Sciences*, Seligman and Johnson, editors. Volume 12, pages 118–128. Copyright 1934, 1962 by Macmillan Publishing Co., Inc.

New York University Press, for John Dewey, "Time and Individuality," from *Time and Its Mysteries* by the James Arthur Foundation, © 1940 by New York University.

G. P. Putnam's Sons, for John Dewey, *Art as Experience*. Copyright 1934 by John Dewey; renewed © 1962 by Roberta L. Dewey. For John Dewey, *Freedom and Culture*. Copyright 1939 by John Dewey; renewed © 1967 by Roberta L. Dewey. For John Dewey, *Individualism Old and New*. Copyright 1929, 1939 by John Dewey; renewed © 1957, 1958 by Roberta L. Dewey. For John Dewey, *Liberalism and Social Action*. Copyright 1935 by John Dewey; renewed © 1962 by Roberta L. Dewey. For John Dewey,

INTRODUCTION

In its fundamental aspect, moral philosophy is concerned with questions of absorbing interest: What is the nature of man? What kind of world does he inhabit? What is man's relationship to the world? And what do the answers to these questions suggest about the good of man? Throughout a philosophic career spanning more than sixty-five years, Dewey addressed himself to these issues. As a result he developed a moral philosophy more comprehensive, innovative, and enlightening than any comparable effort in the last one hundred years.

The concern with man's relation to the universe can take the form of a cosmology which offers speculations about man's role in the cosmic process as a whole. Dewey regarded such speculations as futile and sterile. But this concern can also take the form of inquiry into the *nature* of man in relation to the *nature* of the world: What *kind* of being is man, and what *kind* of world is it which includes human existence? Dewey judged such inquiry to be all important for any philosophy with pretenses of enlightening and enriching human life.

About a century ago, American thinkers began an unusually searching inquiry into this fundamental subject matter, engaging in a systematic reconstruction of the prevailing philosophic traditions. C. S. Peirce, William James, George Santayana, G. H. Mead, and Dewey developed remarkably fecund conceptions relating to the most decisive issues in philosophy: the nature of man, nature, experience, ideas, mind, knowledge, art, society, value, philosophic method. In the judgment of some scholars, it is debatable whether it was James or Dewey who contributed most to this vigorous growth. It is not debatable, however, that it was Dewey more than anyone else who developed the moral implications of these inquiries.

These achievements occurred during a period of unprecedented developments in human knowledge and social change. By the end of the nineteenth century a new revolution in the sciences was well underway. Discoveries were being made especially in the physical and biological sciences which challenged the assumptions of philosophers and the hopes of educated people. Physicists were disposing of the view that the universe was composed of fixed, unchanging material substances related to each other only externally by mechanical action; and Darwin had undermined traditional conceptions of human nature. Scientists were suggesting that man and the world were very much different than had hitherto been supposed, and the assumed privileged position of man in the universe was thought to be diminished to the vanishing point. The shock to human sensibilities was considerable; science itself was widely regarded as being essentially antagonistic to what is most precious in human life. At the same time, the western world was undergoing massive and uncontrolled change from the effects of technology and industrialization. Social, economic, and political structures were (as they still are) volatile and precarious.

In response to these scientific and social changes, and with stimulus from his colleagues, Dewey formulated conceptions which elucidated the fullness and variety of human experience as specific functions of natural processes. In doing so, he presented compelling argument that science and scientific thinking are not alien to human values, but could be used for the greatest good. Presenting radically revised ideas of man, nature, and science, Dewey held that nature can be supportive of human good; and man as a constituent part of nature can achieve an enriched and inherently valuable existence only by understanding how he can function as an organic part of these natural processes. According to these revised conceptions, science and its characteristic methods are not alien to the good life, but essential to it. The method of science is a form of what Dewey calls social intelligence. As embodied in democratic life, social intelligence points the way to a moral ideal which is shareable on the widest possible scale. Dewey was firmly convinced that to make democratic social intelligence a reality in human affairs is the greatest —and perhaps only—possibility for contemporary man to deal effectively with his urgent problems.

Although Dewey was essentially a moral philosopher, he never presented his moral thought as a systematic whole. He was notorious, in fact, for scattering his ideas into various contexts and developing them in connection with a dismaying variety of writings. The result has been most regrettable. Interpretations of Dewey as an ethical philosopher have typically been based on a highly incomplete selection from his work. They have also treated one moral text in isolation from the rest. Most important, many interpretations have been conceived in ignorance of the basic conception of moral philosophy which guided Dewey's efforts. "The Construction of Good,"[1] for example, has been unfailingly misunderstood. Not surprisingly, the results of such scholarship have been superficial, and the present generation of scholars and students are unable to appreciate the achievements and resources of Dewey's philosophy. The present volume attempts to remedy these difficulties by making available a selection of Dewey's moral writings in an integrated and comprehensive form.

Since Dewey never provided an outline of his entire moral philosophy, the

1. Chapter X of *The Quest for Certainty*. See below, pp. 146–56.

following introductory essay will identify the various themes of his thought and show how they are unified in his moral theory.[2]

PART ONE
THE NATURE OF MORAL PHILOSOPHY

Broadly speaking, moral philosophy was for Dewey the attempt to determine the instrumentalities of thought and conduct which have the most significant bearing on the quality of human life. He was inquiring into those conditions of existence which can be employed to enhance the values of life experience. Dewey was not trying to dictate or prescribe values. Rather, he wished both to discover and clarify the ways in which persons could determine their own fulfillment as natural and social beings. The philosophic task —a formidable one—is to enlighten, not to prescribe, human conduct; and the inquiry encompasses all major philosophic issues.

Values—in the sense of actual human interests—already exist in abundance. All persons have a multitude of desires, aversions, hopes, loves, loyalties, and fears, many of them of the keenest sort; and they have an assortment of moral convictions. In any actual situation, a person strives somehow to deal with its real possibilities and limitations in terms of the values—including the moral—which he actually holds. As the human record overwhelmingly attests, success in this activity is rare. The various human values have a precarious existence: they are insecure and transient; they are frustrated, and they are in conflict with one another. Achievement often brings unexpected disappointment; hopes are frequently the product of corrupted sensibilities; and many possibilities for human fulfillment pass unknown or unrecognized.

Given this situation, the role of the philosopher is neither to contrive a wholesale escape from the conditions of human existence nor to lay down rules to which human nature in all its various predicaments must conform. Dewey, rather, wishes to put at the disposal of individuals the knowledge and methods with which they can minimize these liabilities and construct rich and enduring unifications of value. Dewey was profoundly skeptical of any kind of absolutism, no matter how beneficent in intent; he was extremely wary of any attempt to impose an alleged good on individuals. At the same time, he was firm in the belief that it is possible for human beings to make their lives fundamentally worthwhile and to attain a happiness which is neither parasitical, fragile, nor superficial. He believed that failure to achieve such ends is not due to inherent limitations in human nature or natural existence. To gain such ends, men must behave more knowledgeably and intelligently.

2. Several of the themes treated here are examined in greater detail and with extensive documentation in my *John Dewey's Philosophy of Value* (New York: Humanities Press, 1972). (Ed.)

They are capable of doing so, and the philosopher can elucidate assumptions and methods which help to make this possible.

Actual life activity, as Dewey understands it, is found to be inherently satisfactory when the powers of the individual are effectively integrated with his environment so that the entire inclusive process functions harmoniously. The agencies of both individual and environment are united in an ongoing process; initially diverse or impeded values are unified in a reconstructed situation. When conduct is of this sort, the capacities of the individual are liberated and fulfilled. Such activity is a unification of values—what Dewey calls consummatory experience. It is a form of organic interaction of man and nature, and it cannot be achieved without a certain amount of knowledge of how human nature and its environment function together. Further, inasmuch as most ventures involve the various activities of a plurality of persons, consummatory experience requires that the persons involved deliberately act in concert. That is, our social condition makes intelligent cooperation a necessary condition of consummatory value.[3]

Unifications of value can be deliberately achieved only insofar as we have knowledge of their conditions. The achievement of consummatory experience is faciliated by possessing knowledge of man and nature and their organic continuities, knowledge of methods of inquiry into the particulars and possibilities of given situations, and actual means of social cooperation. Dewey as moral philosopher did not dictate choices or ends, but attempted to identify all that is involved in the discrimination, unification, and achievement of value. In doing this, he was led to formulate his ideal of democracy, which incorporates much that is precious in human experience.[4] In proposing this ideal, he offered an object of reflective choice—an object dear to the actual strivings of human nature. But no law of heaven or earth or John Dewey says categorically that we *ought* to choose such an end. It was a liberating venture that Dewey engaged in, in the service of human nature.

Although it is liberating, his moral theory does not imply that individuals should do whatever they might wish. His theory is neither anarchic nor individualistic, for Dewey believed that when nature, society, and human nature are adequately understood, certain unambiguous lessons for conduct become evident. That is, the nature of reality is such that it characteristically rewards certain kinds of character formation and behavior and defeats others. A principle example—that of intelligent cooperation—has just been mentioned, and it will be elaborated later when further examples are presented. It is sufficient now to point out that according to Dewey, we cannot do just as we please

3. See below, pp. 78–82, 187–205.
4. The democratic ideal and its constituents are discussed in Part Three of this essay, and see below, pp. 114–21, 258–65.

with impunity, as if we lived in a void, for the achievement of the intrinsically most satisfying experience demands that the salient features of our
shared experience be profoundly respected. The democratic character and behavior—as Dewey understands them—are best suited to the realities of the
human predicament, and the virtues of democracy can be learned by individuals who are attentive to the lessons of experience.

Although nature provides general lessons, it is neither an inflexible nor a
closed system, conducing only to perfectly definite outcomes. While in the
final analysis nature remains the teacher of wisdom, it admits of change and
reconstruction. The democratic character has the further merit that it is
equipped to deal constructively with the contingencies of existence as these
arise, for the democratic virtues include creative methods of deliberate social
decision and intelligent cooperation.

Regard for the lessons of experience by no means guarantees, of course, a
uniform and enduring moral consensus, unqualified happiness, and the eradi-
cation of evil. These are goals beyond human competence, and a philosopher
cannot reasonably be expected to produce the formulae which would bring an
end to the limitations of being human. But he can enlighten us about the general traits of natural existence so vital to our well-being; and he can also de-
lineate the instrumentalities which can be used to function effectively within
this generic situation. Equally important, he can suggest for our consideration
nature's unrealized and shareable possibilities.

This conception of moral philosophy, therefore, gives no categorical prescription of specific ends or rules of conduct, but consists of an analysis of
man and nature in which the conditions and possibilities of human value are
made perspicuous. Dewey also proposes, in light of just such an analysis,
modes of behavior which would release, enrich, and fulfill human interests.
The determination of these modes is a matter of inquiring how individuals
can function most effectively as constituent parts of more inclusive processes.
In Dewey's favored terminology, it is a problem of discovering how the individual can attain the most satisfactory experience in interaction with his
environment. Noting especially that other human beings are organic parts of
the environment, Dewey concludes that democratic behavior, when it is
widely shared, is the best apparent solution to this problem. When combined
with his well-founded suspicion of all forms of absolutism, this conception
leads to his recommendation that the norms of moral conduct and social action be determined by the very processes of social intelligence.[5]

5. Social intelligence itself can be regarded as a rule of conduct, in that it constitutes a procedure for decision. However, it is not a rule presented as an
   unconditional imperative or law. It is offered as a means to solve actual human
   problems, and its appeal consists in its attractiveness to human values and
   aspirations.

This conception of moral philosophy and the instrumentalities of moral decision are not typical of the Western philosophic tradition. The more usual procedure is to lay down certain ethical standards, rights, or prescriptions which have universal application and are morally absolute and independent of any particular social circumstance. These norms are thought to be products of revelation, intuition, or pure reason; or perhaps they are declared to represent the true or higher will of a benighted mankind. Even utilitarianism declares certain moral principles to be universally justified and unexceptionable. Dewey, by contrast, has no ethical *system*: no invariant standards, rights, or laws to determine moral behavior. He relies, rather, on democratic method and character. He alternately refers to democracy as a way of life and as social method, but either conception implies the other: a democratic individual has certain moral and intellectual habits which are inseparable from the method; and the method is genuinely functional only when such habits are operative.

Given the reliance on democratic social method, it would be a contradiction to prescribe in advance the ends which the method must accomplish. The democratic procedure, however, may seem to admit of too much possibility for conflict and indeterminacy of criteria for adjudicating disputes. The severe moralists of the Western tradition have always found such an approach intolerable. Yet one of the most obvious lessons of history is that even the most conscientious persons cannot persistently reach moral agreement either in theory or practice. Aristotle, Epicurus, Kant, Hume, Nietzsche, Mill, Bradley, and Moore cannot be brought into agreement with each other except by rejecting precisely what is crucial and distinctive in each; and controversies among moral philosophers continue unabated today. In practice we witness at least as much disagreement as we do in theory. Even small groups of individuals united in freely shared enterprises have to make compromises with each other. It is the beginning of wisdom to acknowledge this fact. Those who will not acknowledge it are declaring that their morality alone is legitimate, and they immediately divide mankind into children of light and children of darkness. And inasmuch as no two absolutists entertain quite the same absolutes, there continues to be confusion regarding just who are the children of light. Many people lament the demise of moral absolutes, but Dewey can only applaud. Such absolutes, he argued, simply represent established social bias; they make conflict with other absolutes inevitable; and they preclude intelligent inquiry into the creation of genuinely inclusive goods.

Clearly, however, Dewey's philosophy of social intelligence is itself a moral position with moral presuppositions. For Dewey, these include such notions as regard for the individuality of persons, equal rights and opportunities, impartial justice, and an allegiance to the values of growth, freedom, and shared experience for all. In the abstract—that is, apart from any particular social formation or problem—these are unexceptionable commitments. Yet no conceivable society of human beings can provide these things in equal or unlimited supply and without conflict concerning the nature, priorities, and distributions of all such values. Although individuals may advance any number of claims for power, wealth, security, freedom, pleasure, honor, etc., there is no way to determine a completely harmonious or mutually acceptable adjustment of their claims. It certainly can't be done by a philosopher who respects the fact of moral disagreement. The general moral commitments embodied in democracy can only be worked out in actual social practice, experimentally, and tentatively, with inevitable grievances. Since a democratic group or community takes no policy as final and excludes the interests of no one from continued consideration, it is an ongoing process which inherently possesses the conditions of self-improvement. There is not an antecedently existing ideal good which the group must realize; but it may attempt to create or construct a more inclusive good.

Dewey's ethical theory is clearly something more than a method of *ad hoc* problem solving. His is a "principled" philosophy in that certain enduring values (such as the democratic virtues) are proposed to guide conduct in all situations, and certain ideals of experience are strenuously upheld.[6] Yet it must be remembered that such values in themselves are not specifications for a particular action in a given situation. Human ideals are not established by copying Platonic forms, but by creative social action. Social decisions usually involve the weighing of incompatible interests, and the difficulties with which decision is concerned can't be solved like problems in mathematics. Insofar as problems are addressed by means of social intelligence, they must be analyzed with regard to the specific conditions of a society, and decision is made by the members of that society. Accordingly, a principled philosophy does not necessarily eliminate moral doubt and conflict, and possession of democratic virtues does not ensure that all parties will be led to the same conclusion regarding what to do.[7]

To understand Dewey's moral thought more fully, we must take note of his conception of his own task, and then set forth the conceptions which he advanced to elucidate the nature and conditions of the unification of value.

6. See below, esp. pp. 94–105, 251–58.
7. The fact that social decisions are not entailed by philosophic theory does not mean that philosophers should not propose theoretical or concrete moral ideas. Dewey's analysis of typical ethical concepts is to be found especially in Part II of *Ethics*. This book was a collaboration with James H. Tufts, but Part II was written by Dewey. In *Ethics* Dewey says explicitly that ethical theory is not a means of obviating choice, and he says that his theory is democratic. See excerpts below, pp. 21–22 and 251–52.

   Historically, the closest parallel to Dewey's views is to be found in Aristotle, who holds that choice in particular circumstances should be a function of the moral and intellectual virtues, rather than determined by fixed rule. (*Nicomachean Ethics*, Bk. VI)

PART TWO
DEWEY'S CONCEPTION OF HIS OWN TASK

Modern philosophy has been marked, though in diverse ways, by an explicit assumption of the dualism of man and nature. That is, human nature and physical nature were thought to be separate and essentially unrelated systems, the nature of one having no implication for the nature of the other. Human nature was thought to be confined within an alleged thinking substance. This substance, so it was held, possessed innate faculties of, e.g., thinking, willing, evaluating, each of which acts according to its own innate laws. At the same time, the concepts of nature were reductive: regarded variously (depending on the philosophy) as nothing but matter in motion, a mass of unrelated particulars, or a pure rational structure. What Dewey called the classical tradition, stemming principally from Plato and represented in modern times by rationalism and idealism, posited a realm of static perfection transcending the world of experience, process, and change. Changeless perfection constituted true being, ultimate reality, and ultimate value. It was known only by the unaided reason. Indeed, in the classic tradition, cognition of this domain of absolutes was alone accounted to be knowledge. Process, change, and experience could never yield genuine truth.

From the standpoint of any tradition in modern philosophy, experience was assumed to be subjective: something "in the mind" only. So all the qualities that are experienced are imputed to nature only by mistake. According to subjectivism, there is no ground for supposing that the valued experiences of life, as well as all other experiences, are a function of the organism-environment process. These values are only in the mind. So-called empiricists, believing all ideas to be composites of intrinsically unrelated bits of experience, and regarding experience as subjective, were led to conclude that there can be no knowledge of nature. In neither the classical nor empirical tradition was inquiry thought to be a deliberately active and overt process. It was either a passive accumulation of sensations or an immediate grasp of the structure of reality by reason.

All these conclusions Dewey considered radically mistaken.[8] All of them render every aspect of life and experience unintelligible. If ideas are justified by being descriptively accurate, by explaining how events occur, how they are related, and how they lead to other events under specified conditions, then these philosophic conceptions are all failures. If ideas, in short, are to be functional in human existence, then these philosophies succeeded only in

---

8. He believed the philosophical root of these errors was in the axiomatic assumption (taken from Platonic thought) that the object of rational knowledge, as such, is alone really real. Hence experience, which was not regarded as in any way part of rational knowledge, must be "in" the mind; and the traits of experience and the traits of nature have nothing in common.

creating obscurity. They do nothing to illuminate and strengthen human life—except, perhaps, to provide emotional consolation or to buttress a traditional social order. Contrary to these philosophies, experience is not comprised of atoms of sensation; and the fertile methods of experimental science bear very little resemblance to the epistemologies of either rationalism or empiricism. Moreover, values are the qualitative outcome of knowable and repeatable processes in the natural world. Against the assumptions of subjectivism, unifications of value can be deliberately created by intelligent conduct. The typical theories of modern philosophy existed in spite of the evidence, yet philosophers were not inclined to give up theories just because they were not supported by facts.

That such theories were false or meaningless was not their greatest deficiency. We endure many luxuries, Dewey said. But if consistently entertained, these philosophies simply cannot investigate and identify the genuine possibilities of human nature. They made such inquiry impossible, and they could not in their own terms suggest any of the means by which experience could be enlarged and enriched. Modern philosophy had conceived reality to be divided into separate and non-interacting realms. If, however, human nature and values are functions of processes inclusive of organism and environment, the basic dualism of man and nature must be shown to be nonexistent. If all of the possibilities of shared human conduct have not yet been discovered, the futility of the static absolute in guiding processes of change must be exposed for what it is, and the actual continuities of man and nature made clear and explicit. The result would be that we would know how to live in a way which enriches the intrinsic qualities of experience. Such knowledge simply cannot be achieved on the assumptions of systematic dualism. This was the situation confronting Dewey. Its specific nature will be examined further in Part Three.

A critique of prevailing philosophic traditions would not by itself elucidate the nature of intelligent activity and growth. In scores of articles and in such major books as *Human Nature and Conduct, Experience and Nature, The Public and Its Problems, The Quest for Certainty, Art as Experience, Logic: The Theory of Inquiry,* Dewey explored the functions of man and nature; and in terms of their interaction addressed himself to the major issues in philosophy. Some of his principle conclusions are given in the succeeding section. We shall see the bearing of basic philosophic ideas on moral issues.

PART THREE
DEWEY'S MORAL PHILOSOPHY

The fundamental point of Dewey's philosophic method is that ideas must be tested by their usefulness in explaining and illuminating human experience. This means not only a commitment to experimental method: that is, to the testing of a proposition by what it entails. It means as well an insistence that philosophic conceptions provide as thorough a description and analysis as possible of the salient characteristics of reality. Philosophy had been plagued above all, Dewey believed, by offering conceptions of the nature of the world which omitted the most obvious traits. As a result, the world men find themselves in is very much unlike the world philosophers depict.[9] Finally, the aim of philosophic inquiry is to show the relation of these ideas to human good. Use of this method and pursuit of this aim led Dewey to the following conclusions:

Man in Nature and Society. Utilizing Darwin's theory of biological evolution and following the suggestions in James's psychology, Dewey advanced the notion that human nature is the *outcome* of the interaction of the organism and the environment. Character and behavior, including all such functions as thinking, imagining, feeling, and acting, do not emanate from an original, fixed, and encapsulated essence or self. Rather, they are functions of processes inclusive of organism and environment. What is called the self is an outcome: a dynamic complex of habits forged in life activity. The structure and behavior of human nature are not native, and they are not characteristics of the human organism in itself. Again, the organism is a constituent of an inclusive process. This view is in contrast to the dualistic position, which assumes innate faculties acting according to innate laws. The nature of these laws was thought to be independent of processes external to the mental self. In opposition to the dualistic view, Dewey wrote extensively and most suggestively to characterize mind, language, thinking, inquiry, knowing, valuing, and all habits of activity as products of this inclusive process and carried on by virtue of it. All of these traits of the human are natural functions: they are part and parcel of nature, not a separate substance set over against it.

Acquired or learned behavior Dewey calls habit, which is a conjoint activity of organism and environment. Impulse by itself is not a way of acting. Merely impulsive activity becomes habit only in interaction with surroundings. Habits which are functional are strengthened, while those that are not tend to undergo extinction.

The most important determinant of habits and their distinctive traits is interaction with society: direct human association. Activity is rewarded and punished in various ways by other people, and thereby a certain dynamic complex of habits (or self) is developed. Moreover, the *meaning* of behavior is socially determined. As an educable source of activity, the agent is held

9. See especially Chapter One of *Experience and Nature,* in both the first and Revised editions.

responsible for what he does. His conduct affects other people, who find it agreeable or disagreeable in various ways, and they respond accordingly. Hence behavior is characterized as greedy, rude, cooperative, amiable, vicious, and so forth.

Although interaction with the natural and social environment creates distinctively human nature, the differences between individuals are not exclusively attributable to differences in the environment. Dewey acknowledges variations in native endowment (of biological origin), but whether and in what forms such endowment develops depends upon the environment.

Dewey's rejection of dualism implies a new conception of society. He found untenable the notion that society is merely an aggregate of individuals each of which is a monadic entity acting according to its inherent laws. Classical liberalism had proceeded on the assumption that individuals are fixed and self-sufficient in their nature and as members of society need only to observe rules to ensure that they do no violence to each other. The natural result of such observance would be a collection of essentially separate selves in harmonious equilibrium, where each individual freely enjoyed the fruits of his own labor. These assumptions are in marked contrast to Dewey's view, according to which individuality is constituted and sustained by the social medium, harmony is the outcome of deliberate cooperation, and vital human association is "the greatest of human goods."

Dewey also rejected the theory of philosophical idealism that the individual is a microcosm of the state or of the entire society. The social monism of Rousseau or of the Hegelians envisioned the good of man in terms of an identification with the whole. Hegelians posited an underlying unity of value for the entire society, and one's good consisted in recognizing one's place in this organic whole. Dewey stressed, however, that the individual is not related primarily to the state or to society at large, but to a variety of different groups within a society. He pointed out that if the good is conceived as conformity to one's station in life, the possibility of constructive social reform is implicitly denied. Indeed, by insisting that all human beings conform to a comprehensive order in all phases of life, the monistic view is a philosophic invitation to totalitarianism.

Without going into further detail about Dewey's conception of man as a natural and social being, we can see that the moral implications of his ideas are considerable. If human nature is the product of the inclusive process of organism-environment, so, too, are the values organic to human nature. Accordingly, to discover and achieve the best possibilities of human nature requires knowledge of this process: its limitations, potentialities, and instrumentalities. Discovery of the forms of human good requires extensive inquiries into a wide range of subjects.

The organism-environment process—or to denote it with a single term: *nature*—admits of reconstruction and novelty. This is to say that nature admits of the possibility of producing novel relations and ends, and the possibilities open to human conduct are not defined *a priori*. Thus the forms of conduct and social order hitherto in evidence are not final examples of nature's potentialities; there are possibilities for genuine discovery and innovation regarding human well-being. Yet man is not free to fulfill mere fantasies; he is, after all, a creature of nature, and he must function within what are, in the final analysis, fairly narrow bounds. As Dewey wrote in *Experience and Nature,*

Men move between extremes. They conceive of themselves as gods, or feign a powerful and cunning god as an ally who bends the world to do their bidding and meet their wishes. Disillusionized, they disown the world that disappoints them; and hugging ideals to themselves as their own possession, stand in haughty aloofness apart from the hard course of events that pays so little heed to our hopes and aspirations. But a mind that has opened itself to experience and that has ripened through its discipline knows its own littleness and impotencies; it knows that its wishes and acknowledgments are not final measures of the universe whether in knowledge or in conduct, and hence are, in the end, transient. But it also knows that its juvenile assumption of power and achievement is not a dream to be wholly forgotten. It implies a unity with the universe that is to be preserved. . . .

Fidelity to the nature to which we belong, as parts however weak, demands that we cherish our desires and ideals till we have converted them into intelligence, revised them in terms of the ways and means which nature makes possible.[10]

The moral implications of Dewey's view of man and nature can usefully be contrasted to one or two other views. In Plato's conception, for example, the cosmos has an entirely definite and fixed order, and there is but one formation of human nature and one social order which will function harmoniously with the whole. Any variation from this closely defined system is certain to be disastrous. The modern empiricists, on the other hand, simply had no conception of organic unities of any sort, and they were consequently unable to propose anything but the most meagre possibilities of a human ideal. Such notions as the intelligent construction of value, the unification of the self, and a community of shared experience cannot be conceived in terms of the empiricist philosophy.[11]

10. Revised edition (New York: Dover Publications Inc., 1958), pp. 419–20. (Revised edition was first published in 1929.)
11. Perhaps the greatest contrast to a Platonic conception is found in a philosophy never considered by Dewey: that of Sartre. Sartre evidently holds that nothing in nature provides any lesson whatever for human conduct; nature shows no values prior to choice, teaches no virtue. Choice is completely arbitrary.

Dewey falls within these extremes (in many respects closer to Plato than, say, to Hume). An analysis of the nature of things clearly discloses that certain methods of decision and patterns of behavior tend to be far more rewarding than others. But Dewey places far more reliance on social intelligence than Plato would ever have thought necessary and more reliance on a philosophical analysis of nature than was ever undertaken by the empiricists.

The organic continuity of man and nature suggests a final point of importance: Inasmuch as all experience is the outcome of conjoint processes of man and nature, the traits of experience are traits of nature. All experience is indicative of the nature of nature. Qualities, for example, are not independent properties in an object, and neither are they events within a subject. They are real events in nature existing by virtue of the interaction of subject and object. The crucial point here is that the experience of qualities is experience of nature. We are not confined within our own experience without access to nature. On the contrary, the qualities of events are real and are phases of natural processes. When Dewey speaks of the continuity of experience and nature, he means both that experience is a function of nature and that what is experienced is an objective phase of natural processes. The conditions upon which experienced events depend is determinable by experimental inquiry. In *Experience and Nature* especially, Dewey indicates that nature has a great many traits that have been persistently denied in modern philosophy. The concept of nature must be radically revised when it is understood that experience is continuous with nature, rather than juxtaposed to it. For present purposes it is important to outline Dewey's view regarding the status of value in nature.

Value in Nature. Subjectivism has been a uniform assumption of modern philosophy. According to subjectivism, whatever is experienced, including value, is within the mind and is not an event in the world. The structure of experience is presumably a consequence of mental laws of association, so the connections of experienced events are mental. This doctrine means in addition that the order of events in nature (if it were knowable at all) is independent of the order of experience. When such assumptions are consistently maintained, the occurrence of any value must be completely adventitious as far as nature is concerned; and the process of reconstructing natural processes to create consummatory experience can be neither recognized nor understood. Experience, in brief, cannot be a guide to conduct. When some guide to conduct which transcends experience is sought, the only recourse is to the alleged universal laws known only to reason, and these, too, bear no relation to either the changing processes of nature or the order of experience.

Dewey's analysis of the status of value in nature is not beset with such difficulties. His inquiry begins with an examination of the traits of experience as it actually occurs in life activity. It was stated in Part One (p. xx) that conduct is inherently valuable when there is a felt unity and fulfillment in the interaction of man and nature. It is typical of the course of activity, however, that it is faced with difficulties of various sorts. There are obstacles, frustrations, and ignorance of the constituents of a problem and how to deal with them. There are diverse and conflicting possibilities. When conduct is impeded or interrupted in some way, the situation is what Dewey calls problematic. The individual responds to various features of the situation in an immediate way as promoting or retarding his interests. Dewey usually calls such features "problematic goods."

Problematic goods are a species of value. All value is qualitative: events are valued in some way because their qualities are attractive, repulsive, loveable, hateful, fearful, admirable, and so on. The point is not that an object or person has certain characteristics to which an individual imputes certain valued qualities, adding them on, as it were. Rather, in a given situation events are immediately experienced as valuable in some way. It is a condition of life activity that events are responded to directly as having a bearing on weal or woe. Such experiences are not cases of knowing, not cognitive, but affective, transactions. The process of determining how interactions with problematic goods will function in unifying the situation does, however, involve cognitive transactions; but if the subjectivist hypothesis were true, these cognitive transactions would be pointless.

Problematic goods occur in situations where there is a question of how to proceed. Some specific endeavor or activity is going on, and the nature of this activity determines which elements of the situation will be problematic goods. If, for example, a student is considering how to finance his education, then a loan, a part-time job, or a competition for a scholarship all become problematic goods; but they would not be so classified in a situation in which he is considering which courses to take. Problematic goods are a function of the situation, and as such they are real events of nature.

A characteristic desire of human nature is to resolve such situations in a way which re-establishes integrated activity. One desires to convert the situation from something indeterminate and disunified into a settled and unified condition, one in which a harmonious ongoing process is restored or established.

Situations vary in complexity and difficulty. The matter could be so simple as deciding upon a place to dine, or as formidable as dealing with national social problems. Most human activity takes place on a more intermediate scale. Individuals ally themselves for every purpose under the sun: political, intellectual, artistic, economic, religious, recreational, ecological, educational, and so on. Each group attempts to deal with its characteristic problems in a way which will create unified conduct of the sort appropriate to the interests of the group. Examples of the nature of this process can be found in any activity. Consider a group of students organizing to undertake theatrical productions. The talents, aims, and interests of several people must somehow function together. Every artifact and physical condition which they utilize constitutes an interaction with nature, and all such things and the nature of the individuals involved constitute both resources and limitations. But only in the shared and experimental attempt to unify all these factors can the participants determine what these powers and limits might be. Dewey calls those actions which integrate the activity of the situation "ends-in-view," and he calls the unified situation itself "value proper," or "a consummatory situation." Situations may be more or less consummatory: they may be more or less unified; there may be more or less interest, effort, and ability which is consummated. If the theatrical group succeeds in producing an accomplished performance, calling forth the fullest interests, abilities, and cooperation of all the participants, then an ideal limit of consummatory experience has been approached.

The transformation of the situation from problematic to consummatory involves the reconstruction of natural processes; and the values of the experience are qualities of nature. The transformation requires knowledge of the actual and possible relations of the situation upon which the various values depend. This sort of activity cannot even be characterized within the framework of dualism and subjectivism, and *a priori* absolutes can shed no light on how the situation can be transformed or on what the particular form of the result should be. An adequate theory of the nature of nature is required in order to understand the nature and conditions of consummatory activity.

Science and Value. The continuity of experience and nature implies that values are functions of natural processes. As such they are in principle open to scientific investigation and control as much as any other event in nature. In light of the dominance of the dualistic tradition, to establish this conclusion is a major achievement. There has always been confusion, however, regarding Dewey's convictions about the appropriate functions of science in human conduct. In general terms, the role of scientific inquiry is to determine how individuals can interact with nature in a consummatory way. Science is conceived as an instrument of human liberation and enrichment. Dewey abhors the notion of having scientists rule communities; and he never advocated anything so authoritarian (and logically absurd) as making the "right" human choice follow deductively from scientific propositions. When he writes in *Experience and Nature*, "The serious matter is that philosophies have denied that common experience is capable of developing from within itself methods which will secure direction for itself and will create inherent standards of judgment and value,"[12] he does not mean that normative propositions

12. *Ibid.*, p. 38.

can be deduced from descriptive ones. He simply means that the processes of
human experience, indicative of the order of natural events, are capable of
discerning and achieving consummatory value. We can learn how to liberate
and enrich human existence.

Establishing the continuity of science and value involves more than determining the status of value in nature. It involves as well a clarification of
the nature of science. Modern philosophers and scientists accepted subjectivism; at the same time they contended that a real world beyond experience was the subject matter of science. They thereby maintained the
impossible view that the realm of experience and the realm of science were
wholly divorced from each other: experience has no access to science, and
science provides no knowledge of experience. Dewey, however, provided any
number of analyses to show that scientific ideas are formulated to account
for experienced events, and that the test for the truth of such propositions is
determined in experience. Science does not explain away experience; it specifies the conditions upon which the occurrence of experienced events depends.[13]

Dewey repeatedly drew attention to a crucial characteristic of science: the
hypothetical and predictive nature of its ideas. (In a rather careless selection
of terms, he used the word "idea" to refer indifferently to concepts, definitions, propositions, hypotheses.) Ideas, and not only scientific ideas, he
pointed out, are not summaries of antecedent experience. They are not composites of sensations, and they are not copies of the antecedently existing
structure of reality. Rather, an idea has reference to anticipated events,
forthcoming events. Behaviorally, to possess an idea is to be prepared to
interact with nature in specified ways. Logically, an idea is a tool of inference: it forecasts events which are contingent upon specific occurrences.
Thus an idea (a meaning, a definition, a proposition) is sharply distinguished
from an image. The idea of something specifies its function in natural
processes. The idea of wood, for example, specifies the events that will occur
upon the performance of such operations as sawing, burning, striking, weighing, and so forth. "This is wood" entails "This will float in water, will burn,
will cut with a saw," etc. To determine the truth about a proposition regarding an alleged piece of wood, one does not compare a visual image to antecedent sensations or essences. He performs operations on the alleged wood
to see if predicted events in fact ensue. If they do, the proposition is pro-
visionally judged to be true: an anticipated sequence of events has occurred
in a manner predictable by the idea in question.[14]

13. See below, pp. 123–33.
14. One might conclude that an object before him was wood simply by its visual
    resemblance to wood. In such a case, merely looking at the object *is* a test
    of a proposition about it, but of a rudimentary sort. Further operations
    would have to be undertaken to gain reliable confirmation. Dewey repeatedly
    draws attention to the fact that reliable confirmation requires intersubjective
    testing: verification is a social procedure.

To have an idea is to be prepared to act in certain ways. Thus the importance of having true ideas cannot be underestimated. (To believe that something is wood means it will be acted with as wood. If it is wax instead, action will be unsuccessful.) The difference between truth and error is one of the principle differences between being able to function effectively in nature or not.

To understand Dewey, it is essential to be clear about his conception of how ideas guide conduct. Ideas predict events which result from specific operations. The formulation has reference to future events which are contingent upon present action. The idea of wood, for example, means that if an object is wooden, it will cut in two when sawed, float when immersed in water, burn when placed in fire, etc. Since most natural processes are highly complex, the experimental operations specified by an idea may well involve an elaborate reconstruction of existing circumstances—whether in the laboratory or in worldly affairs.

In the conduct of inquiry, the idea takes the form of a hypothesis. The hypothesis proposes a means of reordering present activity to achieve a specific result. When, for instance, the student is looking for a way to finance his education, he might hypothesize that an appeal to a relative will yield an interest-free loan. In all such inquiry, the formulation of the hypothesis is a creative venture, for it concerns either the introduction of novel relationships or the examination of events not hitherto investigated. The hypothesis is not sheer guesswork, however. It is based on knowledge of more or less similar situations. Any person seeking a solution to any problem would be at a complete loss if every feature of the problem were new to him. Thus, for example, useful hypotheses in biology can only be contrived by someone knowledgeable in biological science.

All problem-solving activity occurs in a given context, or situation. The biologist, say, wants to find a cure for cancer, and he deals with that problematic situation *qua* biologist. All persons deal with problematic situations as an inescapable feature of life experience. The proposed solutions can be formulated as hypotheses: the introduction of certain conditions is necessary to solving these problems. The solution for the biologist is to find a cure for cancer. He formulates hypotheses requiring very precise experimental procedures. A definite form of action for the biologist is specified by the hypotheses: there are certain operations he must undertake in his inquiry. In this altogether straightforward sense, the hypothesis guides conduct, and the hypothesis is confirmed if the subsequent experimental activity does indeed result in the discovery of a cure for cancer. To revert to the example of the student, he confirms his hypothesis if the earnest appeal to his uncle results in a generous loan.

In all such cases the hypothesis proposes a means for solving a problem already at hand: an existing problematic situation. Such ideas direct activity simply by specifying a means to an end. *This* is how Dewey understands ideas to guide conduct. By indicating the way in which situations can be transformed from problematic to consummatory, ideas guide us from the difficulties of the present into a better future. There should be no further grounds for wondering why Dewey held intelligent inquiry to be of such practical importance.

This way of guiding conduct by ideas is clearly distinct from such means as issuing imperatives, claiming knowledge of the eternal forms of perfection, or declaring that propositions about the nature of reality logically entail definite courses of action. Note that the function of ideas as Dewey analyzes them could not have been discerned from within any of the established traditions in philosophy. Empiricists regarded ideas as summaries of antecedent sense data; rationalists regarded them as copies of antecedently existing essences. In neither case is there reference to the future or an awareness of the creative function of ideas. According to the older views, ideas mirror the past; they do not lead to a new future.

Note also that the inquiry into the means of reconstructing a situation is at the same time a means of revising existing valuations. In such inquiry various possibilities for action are imaginatively conceived. Each possibility leads to different objects of desire and aversion; and as inquiry discloses new alternatives, actions that seemed desirable at first may be regarded as unattractive. A plan not evident at the outset may stimulate interests initially dormant. This reconstitution of existing valuations is especially evident in situations where several persons are directly involved. The values, aims, and expected response of others play a critical role in stimulating revised interests in each participant. Accordingly, in a community where full and open communication exists, one finds an essential condition for the growth of new values and forms of behavior.

Ideally, a course of action can be conceived which will reconstitute impractical desires, unite hitherto conflicting or impeded interests, and show the way to consummatory experience. When an imagined course of conduct is sufficient to stimulate restored overt activity, choice occurs. Choice is the response to the values disclosed in creative inquiry.[15] Intelligent and creative inquiry results in a response to the real possibilities of the situation, rather than to a partial or mistaken view; so it also results in a much greater likelihood that conduct will be consummatory.

Intelligent choice is a response to nature's real possibilities; intelligent conduct is deliberate activity in concert with natural processes. In the final analysis, nature determines choice, and nature rewards and punishes. As we understand nature better or worse, our conduct will prosper or suffer. Dewey

15. See below, pp. 70–73, 103–04, 139–44.

emphasizes this in many ways throughout his writings. We must have knowledge of the actual functions of man and nature, and we must develop appropriate instrumentalities of inquiry and decision. Especially in his writings pertaining to education, Dewey stresses the development of habits of experimental inquiry so vital to determining nature's real functions; and coincident with this he insists on the importance of impressing on the young the need to conceive of their conduct as a constituent part of a social medium. Together, these two ideas comprise a recognition that informed and cooperative conduct is necessary to liberate and enrich life activity.

William James frequently lapsed into a kind of pragmatism very much alien to Dewey's experimentalism. James would imply that the truth of a proposition is determined by whether or not we are pleased by believing it to be true. Although Dewey unfailingly referred to James himself in reverential tones, he spoke with a certain contempt for those who tried to evade reality and cling to compensatory or consolatory values. The emotional gratification of indulging in pleasant but unfounded ideas is usually brief, and the cultivation of emotional ways of thinking frustrates the values organic to actual human conduct. Anyone possessing even a modest grasp of his moral philosophy could not confuse Dewey's instrumentalism with the lapses in James's pragmatism.

Instrumentalities of Intelligent Conduct. The value of intelligence and knowledge in conduct needs little elaboration at this point. Dewey conceives intelligence primarily in terms of habits of experimental thought, inquiry, and verification; and these are indispensable for consummatory interaction. In order to deal effectively with a situation, one needs knowledge of its actual agencies: how they function and how they can be acted with. One can bring such knowledge in varying degrees to any situation, but he also has to undertake intelligent inquiry into the possible unifications of the situation.

For any situation one also needs a more general knowledge: an awareness of the value of cultivating particular habits of conduct, and a recognition of how they contribute to the well-being of one's community. The kind of behavior one engages in produces and strengthens his habits, and in the long run the quality of life depends more than anything else on the kind of habits which constitute the self. Consideration of this fact might well be decisive in determining choice. Suppose, for instance, one is involved in a situation where the expression of one's convictions would be highly unpopular. If he were concerned with the immediate situation only, one might follow the policy of safety first and remain silent. If he reflected, however, he might conclude that such a policy would tend to strengthen his cowardly habit, while the consequences of being forthright could be endured for the sake of reinforcing one's courage and integrity. Further reflection would reveal that a life ruled by fear is slavish, while life informed with courage is liberating. These kinds of life are drastically different, and knowledge of this fact may well determine a different choice and a different direction in the formation of character. Further, when action tends to destroy the conditions of a good community, it is not only the interests of others that are sacrificed, but the conditions of one's own good as well. For anyone who has any hope of functioning well as a social being, this, too, is a major consideration.

Habits are not only intellectual methods and moral virtues. All our forms of behavior are habits; so our ability to function in unity with natural processes varies directly with the suitability of our habits. The scholar, the sportsman, the cook and artisan and farmer, the statesman and artist and teacher—all need the appropriate skills to carry on their activities. Intelligent conduct, then, requires more than intelligence and moral virtue; it also requires habits that are forms of mastery. Such habits are most often social habits in the straightforward sense that they include ways of working with others. Most human endeavors of consequence are social; that is, they involve human interaction. Therefore successful behavior must be such that it incorporates the means of acting as a social being. As all such habits are cultivated, one's capacity for consummatory experience is enlarged.

Moral principle is a further instrument of intelligent conduct. Moral principles are the rules of behavior prescribed in religions, philosophies, and cultural traditions; but Dewey argues that principles are not to be regarded as imperatives. Principles are embodiments of much past experience, and as such they provide useful and often wise suggestions for conduct. But in any case they function as hypotheses, not as absolutes. Although keeping promises is a very desirable practice, it is fanatical to demand its observance under every conceivable circumstance.

The greatest means of intelligent conduct, in Dewey's judgment, is an explicitly social process: social intelligence as a method of social decision and action. Further reference to social method will be postponed, however, until attention has been drawn to what Dewey regarded as some of the main constituents of human good.

The Principal Values of Experience. Dewey's observations about the values organic to human nature can perhaps best be summarized by discussing freedom, growth, and shared experience.

As might be expected, the notion of consummatory experience is central.

Indeed, "freedom" is another name for that activity in which the powers of organism and environment are unified in an ongoing process. It is a way in which an individual functions deliberately as part of a whole. Free conduct is also characterized as art.[16] This freedom, Dewey believes, is the same that men struggle for and cherish in political life; but it is more generic than the liberty discussed in political philosophies and praised by contenders for public favor.[17] Freedom can be attained in any mode of activity: in politics, work, play, scholarship, art, and so on. In any kind of situation an individual has operative desires and habits demanding activity of various sorts. These are often frustrated by obstacles; but when the powers of the individual are equal to the problem, the agencies of the situation can be effectively converted into instrumentalities of unified conduct. One's individuality and intelligence find expression in free conduct. If modes of behavior are determined in advance (perhaps regimented by external authority), or if—at the other extreme—they become completely chaotic, then intelligence and individuality have no essential function. In either case, freedom is negated.

Freedom is not, however, a condition in which there are no obstacles to action. Nothing in a situation is a means of conduct unless one knows how it might be used. Hence an environment contains many features which may or may not impede activity depending on whether the agent has the appropriate powers of action. When conduct is art, the habits of the agent are engaged in such a way that the process of transforming the situation is inherently satisfying, and the consequent unified activity is both good in itself and a fulfillment of antecedent effort. Without obstacles to contend with and master, there could be no fulfillment.

A main condition of free activity is the absence of prohibitions over which individuals can exercise no control. Economic, political, or physical limitations might be of this nature. But absence of such prohibitions is not a sufficient condition of freedom. To act freely the individual must have effective powers of action: the habits referred to in the preceding section and the other instrumentalities of intelligent conduct. Such habits do not arise spontaneously, and they are not the awakening of already constituted inner powers; they are a social creation. Yet social arrangements are typically haphazard in respect to the formation of habit. On the other hand, a society can deliberately provide the conditions of freedom. When these conditions are lacking, or impossible to institute, ideals of withdrawal or otherworldliness are typically cultivated.

16. Dewey's best single discussion of freedom is in the article "Philosophies of Freedom," reprinted below, pp. 187–205. For a characterization of conduct as art, see esp. Chapter Nine of *Experience and Nature* (and below pp. 79–82). I have presented an analysis of conduct as art in my *John Dewey's Philosophy of Value*, esp. pp. 150–60. (Ed.)
17. See *Human Nature and Conduct*, Part Four, Section III: "What is Freedom?"

Freedom is not only a social product, but a social way of acting as well. If being free meant being left alone, then very little activity would be free. Each individual in a society functions with other individuals. For each to function effectively (freely), his planning and conduct must be integrated with the planning and conduct of those with whom he is associated. This can only be accomplished by deliberate communication and cooperation. Conflict, frustration, and disappointment mark the experience of anyone who attempts to live as an isolated atom, while freedom is possible only for those who deliberately act as social beings in relation to others who do likewise.

Freedom is not something that one has or has not in a wholesale way, or once and for all. An individual might have the powers of conduct appropriate to one situation, but not to another. An accomplished woodsman is able to carry on effectively in a wilderness; he delights in that situation. His environment is alive with significance. Everything in it is for him a definite instrumentality, and his powers are effectively engaged in the transformation of his problematic situations. Put the same man in, say, a chemistry laboratory, and he is totally at a loss, a slave to his environment. A chemist by contrast is perfectly at home there, but in the wilderness he would be a tenderfoot, with no powers of action. Almost nothing in such an environment is an instrumentality for him, and his existence there would be precarious.

These are extreme cases. Between a tenderfoot and a woodsman are various differences in degree—differences in freedom. As the tenderfoot becomes more accomplished, he attains more freedom.

Freedom is obviously a result, an achievement, rather than something inherently possessed. Habits of intelligence and conduct are the great instrumentalities of freedom. Again, however, these habits will not develop and will have no medium for their exercise without the appropriate social, political, and economic institutions. The precise conditions of freedom in a given historical context must be determined by inquiry.

Dewey's conception of free conduct should be sharply distinguished from other conceptions. He is not referring to some kind of absolute freedom offering infinite possibilities, and he is not advocating a philosophy of following every impulse, just as it sprouts. Human nature does not have infinite possibilities, and nature is by no means equally hospitable to every form of conduct. To be free requires knowledge of what nature affords, and it requires cultivation of definite abilities. Otherwise one is enslaved by his environment, and the dream of freedom becomes fantasy and escapism. Much of the human struggle in the social context is precisely for the establishment of conditions necessary for the development of these liberating powers.

To encapsulate Dewey's moral philosophy in the most illuminating way, it is perhaps best to focus on this notion of freedom. Consider again the example of the woodsman and the tenderfoot. So long as we remain ignorant of human nature and its continuities with natural processes, each of us is a tenderfoot in life experience, and nature makes us pay the price for remaining a tenderfoot. But if we master nature's ways we become woodsmen: nature is made accomplice in human good.

Nature's place in man is no less significant than man's place in nature. Man in nature is man subjected; nature in man, recognized and used, is intelligence and art.[18]

Dewey's aim as a philosopher was to elucidate nature in such a way that we would know how to be free in it, rather than enslaved by it.

The woodsman example is misleading in that activity in the wilderness might well be a solitary affair and therefore not typical of most human undertaking. The activity crucial to human good is social, so learning to be a "woodsman" is in part learning how to function as a social being. One can perform social duties under the direction of external authority, yet if he does so it is unlikely that the duties suit his individuality and possibilities for growth. One acts socially in the fullest sense only when his conduct is determined by explicit consultation with others. This is democratic behavior; and it is also—in Dewey's sense—the freest behavior. As an ideal limit, each individual develops and exercises his own powers *as* a constituent part of an inclusive social process.

When free activity has a persistent temporal development, the process is what Dewey calls growth. When the individual interacts with his environment in a way which succeeds in transforming the problematic into the consummatory, he undergoes a measure of growth. In dealing with the obstacles and limits of a situation, one is either defeated by them or finds new and more effective ways to function with them. The formation of new or augmented functions is growth—growth in habits. Anyone developing such new or enlarged skills is engaged in growth, and he thereby enhances his power of freedom and the attendant consummatory experience. Growth can occur in relation to particular arts, just as it can occur in what the Greeks called the virtues of man *qua* man: intellectual and moral habits. If a person participates in a variety of different kinds of situation, calling for different kinds of behavior, his personality becomes multi-dimensional, richer, and capable of appreciating a greater range of values. One's individuality becomes unified when the developing habits complement and reinforce each other, rather than excluding or conflicting with each other.

Growth is not valuable because it gains an end extrinsic to the process itself. Dewey speaks of the good of activity, the good of growth itself. The

18. *Experience and Nature* (first edition), p. 28.

sort of activity in which growth occurs is precisely that in which a felt unity
of man and nature is achieved. Life need not be a preparation, a repetitious
sequence of valueless means and sometimes valued ends. The ongoing process
which is growth is intrinsically delightful in itself; and when we attend to
present growth we at the same time enhance our powers to deal with and
enjoy future contingencies. "Perfection means perfecting, fulfillment, fulfilling, and the good is now or never." To treat present activities as important
only as a prelude to something else is dreary and self-defeating. Something
earned from activity might or might not make one happy, but such happiness
is notoriously ephemeral. The good should not be conceived as extrinsic to
activity, but as a quality of activity itself. It can be intrinsic to activity,
organic to ongoing experience, and therefore inseparable from one's nature.

In the light of what has already been said, it hardly needs to be mentioned
that growth is a function of social conditions, and, like most activity, typically
carried on in a social medium. The social nature of growth does not mean
that personal individuality is sacrificed. Individuality is not so limited a
matter as functioning independently of social interaction or in opposition to
it. It is a matter of *how* one interacts socially. It is a distinctive way of
acting with others. A society conducive to growth is, indeed, one in which
participation in a wide variety of groups is readily possible.

The development of some of the capacities of human nature may be destructive. Therefore, the capacities most capable of growth as constituents of
a larger whole must be identified. The problem is to determine directions
for growth which can be pursued by anyone without jeopardizing an equal
opportunity for growth for anyone else. The virtues of intelligent cooperation
are certainly of foremost importance in this context.[19] Indeed, the habits
of being democratic have the unique merit of being more effective the more
they are widely practiced by all members of a community. Within the framework of democratic practice, presumably, there is a greater opportunity for
individualized modes of growth than in alternative forms of associated life.

Only in a community which is highly regimented, fragmented, or oppressive could the notion arise that acting as a social being is inherently onerous.
Shared experience is not a necessary evil. Dewey regarded it as the most
precious and deeply satisfying human value. He regarded the quality of
human relationships as the most important ingredient in the good life. The
striving after one kind of vanity and another which distinguishes so much

---

19. The habits Dewey regards as most important in this connection include a
    willingness to submit social issues to the method of social intelligence,
    actively consulting the interests and intentions of others, using experimental
    procedures to determine ways in which situations can be reconstructed, and
    holding one's moral commitments on a provisional basis until the process of
    consultation and inquiry has been concluded.

of human life signifies more than anything else, he believed, the breakdown or absence of profound and enduring human ties.[20]

Shared experience includes shared activity. Many activities are richly satisfying just because they are carried on in a context of intimate association with others. A characteristic of shared experience which distinguishes it from superficial or exploitative relations is that those who share undergo a growth in their own individuality by virtue of the sharing. Thus growth and shared experience are united, and both of these are united with freedom, which is also a social process and enriched because it is social. Freedom, growth, and shared experience come together in the democratic community. Democracy as social method must be examined before the ideal of democracy can be more fully described.

The Necessity of Social Method. Modern moral philosophy has been remarkably individualistic. It is a commonplace that classical liberalism postulated the atomistic individual and conceived society as no more than an aggregate or quantitative sum. Against this conception continental thinkers posed their monistic organicism. But both sides were individualistic—whether explicitly or by implication—in proposing means for arriving at moral judgment. The theories of natural right advanced in early liberalism assumed that these rights are rationally cognized and that the cognitions of all rational beings are identical. Hence, presumably, the need for explicit social experience and consultation never arises. One rational man can declare moral judgments for all the rest without fear of rational disagreement. The idea of the social contract was envisioned in this context; so there was no need for experimental verification to determine just what principles the parties to the contract would agree to. Thus the appeal to contract or agreement was largely, in effect, fictional. The appeal was really to individual reason.

Rousseau's contract is of the same sort, for the general will is independent of what might happen to result from any actual social consultation. Kant's trust in the unaided reason is so complete that moral certainty is regarded as the product of asking *one's self* what can be a universal law for all rational beings: "I do not . . . need any penetrating acuteness in order to discern what I have to do in order that my volition may be morally good. Inexperienced in the course of the world, incapable of being prepared for all its contingencies, I ask myself only: Can I will that my maxim become a universal law?"[21]

20. See below, pp. 119–20.
21. Kant, *Foundations of the Metaphysics of Morals*, edited and translated by Lewis White Beck (Indianapolis: Bobbs-Merrill, 1959), p. 19.

Intuitionists, like G. E. Moore, are also ultimately committed to moral individualism; for moral distinctions are not, for them, the sort of thing that can be determined by social interaction.

To this day, Kantians persist in asking *themselves* what moral principles they should observe. The ideal legislator postulated by the utilitarians is vested with a similar power and responsibility. Hume and Hegel rejected, in their respective ways, such individualistic means of determining the standards of moral conduct; but they could not substitute for them any constructive and liberating function of intelligence. That is, they had no active and deliberate social method.[22]

The individualism of these philosophies was not a product of anarchistic impulses. Philosophically, it stemmed from conceptions of *nature* and *reason* which are today untenable. *Nature* was typically conceived as a perfectly rational and harmonious system, and human affairs contained implicitly a similar harmony. Men needed only to exercise their reason, perceive the inherent natural order appropriate to social existence, and conform themselves to it. This position was at bottom theological and unsupported by any evidence of experience. Dewey's analysis of human nature and value makes it entirely clear that nothing in the nature of things prohibits conflict and clash of values among intelligent persons. The fact of moral disagreement is not essentially mysterious.

The faculty psychology and the epistemology upon which the conception of *reason* rested have been widely discredited. The conception of intelligence as a function of behavior is replacing the notion of an innate faculty inherently possessed of power to know. According to the functional conception, the activity and materials of intelligence are not such that all processes of judgment will be identical. At the same time, the alleged accomplishments of unaided reason have suffered embarrassment, for the claims of rationalism have fallen before the inquiries of experimental science. Immediately pertinent to the moral issue, rationalism—like any individualistic moral theory—suffers fatally from the persistent fact of moral disagreement. That is, it simply has not happened that one person's considered judgment is like another's; and one person cannot be regarded as truly representative of all the rest. Ironically, moral individualism, when consistently adhered to, actually contributes to moral conflict, for its judgments are formed without consultation and they are taken as absolute.

From Dewey's point of view, the obvious first step to take when one is considering how to behave in relation to another is to ask *him* what *he* thinks

22. Marx was not a moral individualist, but he never formulated a social method, believing that in a class society any such method is a fraud and in a classless society unnecessary. He also regarded science as a summary of past events; so the idea of an experimental method of intelligence did not occur to him.

Dewey did not present an account of the moral individualism of modern philosophy in the systematic form summarized above. His analysis often took the form of criticising the generic notion that separate individuals inherently possess a faculty of moral cognition. See, for example, *Human Nature and Conduct*, Part Three, Section II. See also below, pp. 211–18.

about the matter. This elementary point has still to be noticed by Kantians, but it is at least the beginning of the idea of social intelligence. Human beings in situations of life experience readily fall into discord. There is a shared predicament, but a conflict of interest occurs within it. Accordingly, the participants need to arrive at a resolution of the conflict so that shared activity can continue. It is extraordinarily naive to assume that a mutually acceptable settlement to such a situation could be achieved if each party deliberated about the proper course of action in isolation from the rest. Such a procedure would produce heightened conflict and chaos. No doubt each individual has various ideas about what might be done, and they might be very good ideas —worthy of vigorous defense. But in a social method such ideas are presented for examination and qualification by other persons. No one considers himself infallible or morally perfect, and each is ready to listen to what others have to say.

In this kind of social deliberation, as Dewey conceives it, the ideas presented for consideration are not judgments or verdicts such as "This policy is wrong" or "That is the right action to take." What are presented are means for converting the situation from problematic to consummatory. Alternative plans of action are proposed to which individuals might or might not agree. Insofar as it is predicated on the realities of the matter at hand, the formulation of plans of action will take account of the various interests which are functional in the situation. This must be so if the plan is to be relevant to all elements of the problem. Of course, even for those with the most generous concern for the interests of others, there will be disagreement regarding the priorities of different claims. But at least each party is present to determine the bearing of each plan on his interests and to speak in behalf of his favored alternatives. There is by no means an assumption that unanimity will be achieved, but the effort can be made to construct a solution to the situation which will be as widely acceptable as possible. This is social intelligence, or democracy.

A number of observations about the method of social intelligence should be made.

a) Dewey does not conceive of it exclusively or even primarily as a political method. It is a method for dealing with a great variety of situations, but it is most effective in the activities of face-to-face groups. These are relatively small groups, in which all the members are present for shared communication and action. In such associations the habits appropriate for participation in political democracy are developed.

b) As a method of consultation, inquiry, and choice, it is not necessarily democratic in the strict sense of regarding the majority opinion as decisive. Social intelligence can be the means by which those vested with authority are informed of the interests and ideas of those in their charge and by which, in turn, they justify their policies. A family, for instance, could exemplify social intelligence, as could a teacher and students.

c) It is a scientific procedure in that the inquiry into the means of transforming the situation is a matter of determining the actual relationships that could be instituted in the ongoing processes of nature. Just as in scientific inquiry, hypotheses are innovative and experimentally verifiable. As hypotheses (that is, prior to test) they are more or less warranted to the extent that they are founded on the most reliable knowledge available.

d) Like scientific inquiry, social intelligence has no final terminus. Its determinations are experimental and open to revision as the lessons of experience may direct.

e) The method is open to the widest possible participation relevant to a given problem, and the participants possess the rights which are necessary to continue to share fully in the process. This feature of social intelligence encourages an individual to maintain allegiance to the method even when a particular decision is unwelcome.

f) Even when the participants consider as thoroughly as possible the implications of proposed courses of conduct, they have no guarantee that everyone will subscribe to the same one. Two individuals can be equally well aware of the values implied by a given course of conduct, but they need not be equally moved by them, morally or otherwise. This is not to say that individuals are incapable of morality. It is to say, rather, that the determination of what is the moral thing to do is subject to conscientious disagreement.

g) Although agreement on facts does not necessarily produce the same evaluation, a *shared* knowledge of the realities of our circumstances is the first requisite to the formation of a wider moral consensus. A great deal of conduct is predicated on ignorance and misinformation. When information is accurate, thorough, and shared, a major condition for agreement about conduct is achieved. In this connection, recall that nature's rewards and punishments do not occur at random: certain kinds of behavior tend very much to be individual and social assets, and others tend to be liabilities. Shared knowledge of the ways of nature is conducive to shared virtues and loyalties. Dewey was persuaded that through the lessons of experience individuals could learn the merit of the democratic way of life.

h) The effectiveness of social intelligence depends very heavily on the nature of the prevailing culture with its characteristic habits of thought and action. If social intelligence is to become a working reality, the institutions of society must promote and reward it. What form these institutions might take can only be determined by experimental inquiry.

No one can guarantee that social intelligence will always produce human concord and growth, or that it will not be perverted or exploited. But no means of social action has so far been contrived that is immune to these hazards, and none has so far been discovered that has so much promise. It would be ironic, not to say fatuous, for a moral absolutist to complain about disagreements that persist in social intelligence when it is precisely the absolutists who must suffer the embarrassment of completely irreconcilable moral conflicts among themselves. Democracy, as Dewey conceived it, will tend to moral solidarity more than any individualistic approach, while providing the values of growth, freedom, and shared experience as well.

The Ideal of Democracy. Democracy as a way of life incorporates social method, freedom, growth, and shared experience in one.[23] As such it is a most appealing ideal, and it is predicated on the most thorough analysis of the condition of man in nature. Unlike other modes of conduct, it is more effective the more it is universalized. It won't work particularly well for an individual in a group which is not disposed to democratic behavior, for it is an explicitly shared way of acting. It achieves its characteristic values for an entire community.

It is a constructive and enlightened method of social decision and action, much better suited to the problems of men than any of the various forms of absolutism. It is the condition of freedom: a means of persons acting together in a way which unites their powers, rather than setting them in conflict. Freedom in this sense develops and enhances the powers of the individual. That is, democracy is conducive to growth and individuality. As a process wherein the experience of one person enriches that of another and wherein there is cooperative activity, it realizes the values of a community of shared experience. It is well to note that this is an ideal which in all its phases is effected and consummated by intelligence.

There are many difficult issues relating to the theory and practice of social intelligence. There are real questions, for example, concerning the grounds for excluding persons from it. Another problem is to determine what are the political, economic, and social institutions most conducive to its development. Further inquiry is also needed in regard to variations and limitations of the method. Sometimes, for example, social intelligence may well be inappropriate: in certain cultures, under certain economic conditions, or perhaps in the conduct of activities requiring unusual discipline, authority, or expertise. These are matters for investigation and experiment. It is entirely in accordance with Dewey's conception of the human situation that no philosophy can resolve such problems with finality. The moral dilemmas of mankind will persist, and the most that a philosopher can do is make the nature of the predicament clear and in light of this analysis indicate what appear to be the instrumentalities best suited to the attainment of the richest values which nature affords. This is what Dewey undertakes with his inclusive philosophy of social intelligence.

23. See below, pp. 258–65.

PART FOUR
CONCLUDING REMARKS

In the contemporary world, philosophic styles come come and go rather quickly, and one or another of them monopolizes attention for a comparatively brief duration. Reputations may be deservedly short-lived. The greatest achievements, however, are recognized not only by interest which endures, but also by their power to stimulate fresh insight and accomplishment in succeeding generations. Dewey's philosophy is certainly of the latter kind. He is not a philosopher of a day, or of a decade, or of a generation. He examined the situation of man with fundamental insight into the problems at issue. He developed a methodology which was powerful in liberating philosophy from the blind alleys of its own traditions and in directing it to constructive tasks. His inclusive conception of man and nature is generic to the many phenomena of experience which had formerly been assumed to be independent of each other. Accordingly, his philosophy must be judged among the principle intellectual achievements of the modern world. Although interest in his work will wax and wane, the resources of his thought are so plentiful that they will be continually rediscovered and will generate philosophic renewal.

The scope and significance of Dewey's philosophy are such that his thinking is pertinent to nearly all of the intellectual and practical controversies of the present day. A variety of them could be selected in order to illustrate this relevance, but such an endeavor would be inappropriate here. Even if attention were confined to the exclusively technical studies of current philosophy, a survey of the bearing of Dewey's analyses on them would exceed the limits of this essay. It is left to the reader to judge such matters for himself. Some unusually vital issues, however, cannot be left aside, for attention to them will indicate the continuing strength of Dewey's philosophy.

Three issues will be considered. The first concerns moral language. In the last forty years moral philosophers have been preoccupied with the theory that moral language is meaningless. This is the so-called noncognitivist theory of ethical language, and it has been thought by many to strike at the root of the sort of moral inquiry in which Dewey was engaged.

The second issue focuses essentially on the aims and methods of moral philosophy. Recently a major work on the topic of justice appeared.[24] Its reception in the philosophic community has been impressive. It is remarkably different from Dewey's philosophy in its methods and conclusions, and a brief comparison of the two positions will permit a better evaluation of Dewey's point of view.

24. John Rawls, *A Theory of Justice* (Cambridge: Harvard University Press, 1971).

Finally, an attempt will be made to distinguish the most important lesson of Dewey's philosophy for the contemporary world.

Noncognitivism in ethics is not derived from a theory of value. It is based upon an analysis of language. A. J. Ayer, in one of the earlier and more influential treatments of this subject, declares,

What we are denying is that the suggested reduction of ethical to non-ethical statements is consistent with the conventions of our actual language. . . . Our contention is simply that, in our language, sentences which contain normative ethical symbols are not equivalent to sentences which express . . . empirical propositions of any kind.[25]

Most of the controversy on this issue centers on the question of what is the *de facto* "logic" of moral words in the English language. Ayer's contention, like that of the other noncognitivists, is that these words refer to nothing at all; they are meaningless.[26]

According to this analysis, those who claim that moral expressions are meaningful simply do not understand their own language. If the attempt is made to *stipulate* a meaning, the proposed meaning can be denied without committing a contradiction in language. If, for example, someone stipulates that he will use "good" to mean "pleasant," there would be no contradiction in language to *deny* that good is pleasant. There is no contradiction because in correct English usage "good" does *not* mean "pleasant." Any moral assertions made with stipulative definitions can be denied in the same manner. That is, for instance, there is no contradiction in saying kindness is not good or stealing is not wrong. Those who attempt to formulate definitions of moral terms are said to commit the so-called naturalistic fallacy.

It has been almost universally assumed that if the noncognitivist analysis is valid, ethics ceases to be a legitimate intellectual discipline: moral judgments like "You ought to keep your promises," "Love is good," or "Killing is wrong" are meaningless. Dewey indulged extensively in the use of moral language in his writing, and inasmuch as he was deeply concerned with determining the means by which individuals could discriminate the better from the worse, his efforts would seemingly come to naught if moral claims had no meaning.

25. A. J. Ayer, *Language, Truth and Logic* (New York: Dover Publications, n.d.), p. 105. (This book was originally published in 1936.)
26. If words have no meaning, they entail nothing. When nothing is entailed, nothing can be verified; so propositions containing moral language are said to be unverifiable. "Unverifiable" and "meaningless" are logically equivalent.

The truth of the matter is, however, that the outcome of the disputes about the logic of moral expressions is essentially irrelevant to Dewey's undertaking. That is, the final import of his work is not affected one way or the other by the controversy. There are two reasons for this. First, all that Dewey has to say could be reformulated in such a way that the occasions for committing the alleged naturalistic fallacy need never arise. Second, even if the fallacy were committed, its nature is such that it does not affect Dewey's essential aims.

Consider the first point. The information which Dewey wished to convey in his moral philosophy could be communicated without the use of moral language. The sort of inquiry which is fundamental to understanding the resources and potentialities of human existence can be carried on most effectively without the use of moral language. The analysis of human nature, experience, intelligence, society, and value as functions of natural processes requires no such expressions. If moral words are not used, they are not used fallaciously.

Just as this basic philosophic inquiry can proceed without a distinctively moral vocabulary, the discourse of concrete moral situations can do likewise.[27] In this context, a crucial requirement for discriminating and unifying the values of any situation is that the persons in it have a clear awareness of the nature of their circumstances. Specifically, they must know the constituents and instrumentalities of their problem, including the values, aims, and abilities of the persons themselves. They must consider various plans of action and be fully aware of the implications of each of them for the interests of all concerned. This information must be accurate, thorough, and shared. The language used to communicate it must be as clear as possible. The language would be descriptive, and the statements of proposed plans of action would take the form of verifiable hypotheses. (See above, pp. xxxiii–xxxiv.) When these conditions are satisfied, the action taken is as enlightened as it could be under the circumstances. Moral language needn't be used in this process at any of its stages, and it is difficult to see how the introduction of moral words could improve the nature of the process.

If moral words *were* used, Dewey would insist that their meaning be specifiable in descriptive language. A person who could not say what he meant in that manner would not be engaged in moral discourse, but in obscurantism, sentimentality, or emotional appeal. If one says, for example, "Edwards is a good man," he must be able to specify what he means by "good." He might mean "kind, generous, trustworthy, intelligent, and impartial." If one says "Edwards is a better man than Jackson," he might mean that Edwards displays more of these qualities than Jackson. In concrete situations, the point of such utterances is precisely to impart such

27. See below, pp. 167–74.

factual information about Edwards and Jackson; so the allegedly meaning-less moral language could be dropped completely. If one is wondering how to respond to or participate with Edwards or Jackson, this and similar information is what is essential to his decision, while the word "good," if left unexplained, would be little help, or possibly a hindrance.

The point of these examples is not to say how "good" is to be defined. It is to suggest that such words are not indispensable to moral discourse. In a given situation, descriptive language will do—not just as well—but better in facilitating enlightened conduct. Suppose that Edwards and Jackson were candidates for political office. Certainly a characterization of them simply as good (or, say, just) would be an affront to intelligence.

The propositions of greatest importance for human well-being are hypotheses specifying the conditions of inherently satisfying activity. Assuredly nothing is lost if explicitly moral words are not used in them. The use of moral language is not going to make anyone wiser, more virtuous, or more sensitive to human values.

Propositions referring to the conditions of consummatory experience do not require moral language to perform the function of guiding activity. As we saw in Part Three, hypotheses guide conduct simply by indicating the means of transforming problematic situations. Moreover, conduct is affected by any idea having reference to objects of desire and aversion. If a person is told there is a crocodile in the lake in which he intends to swim, his intentions are radically altered by this information. The values of nature do not have to be denoted by moral words in order to be affective; but in order to discern and achieve these values, it is necessary for discourse to be as clear as possible. The moral functions of discourse recommended by Dewey are to elucidate and to inform, not to command or exhort. The moral functions of language are best fulfilled when it is an instrument of full and accurate communication and for making unambiguous inferences. A productive inquiry into language, indeed, would be concerned primarily with determining how it can best perform these functions in situations of practical activity.

Of course, doing without moral expressions would be awkward and inconvenient. This difficulty could be remedied by using such expressions with frankly stipulative definitions. Dewey formulated a great many of them. The charge that he thereby committed the naturalistic fallacy is inconsequential. That is, the nature of the fallacy does not affect his philosophy. This was the second point to consider in relation to the controversy about moral language.

The naturalistic fallacy is harmless—and even desirable—so long as stipulative definitions are made with full candor and publicity. With carefully specified meanings, such language would be an effective instrument of communication and inference. So long as it was undertaken in a wholly forthright way, there could hardly be any serious objection to this procedure. When Dewey says "Shared experience is good," it might not be a contradiction in our language to say "Shared experience is not good." But Dewey *means* "Shared experience is something most people find intrinsically valuable." If we know what he means, it is of no consequence that he conveyed his meaning by way of an alleged misuse of language. The question at issue here is this: What damage is done in committing the naturalistic fallacy? In the final analysis, the charge of naturalistic fallacy means that there has been a deviation from standard English usage. That is, it is alleged that one has not used moral vocabulary in the accepted manner. It is difficult to see what importance there is in such an objection, unless one also holds the view that we must always be bound by the way things have been done in the past. Any given proposal for change in usage might well be challenged on the grounds that it was either obscure or pointless, and certainly Dewey himself would oppose any change that was of that nature. That sort of objection is wholly inappropriate, however, when the new usage is both carefully specified and indicative of verifiable characteristics of natural processes.

In brief, then, the charge of committing the naturalistic fallacy turns out to be altogether harmless. Dewey could readily admit to it, but have nothing to apologize for. His concern was to contrive a means of transmitting facts and ideas about the conditions of human value as clearly as possible, and committing the naturalistic fallacy might be one good way of doing this! It is evident that his philosophy is not touched in any essential way by this sort of criticism.[28]

The main stimuli to the growth of noncognitivism may well have been a distaste for obscurantism and a fear of moral absolutism. Much moralizing is sheer rhetoric, and exposure of it is welcome. The threat of absolutism is more subtle: If moral discourse were thought to specify precisely and unconditionally what actions ought to be performed or what objects were of value, then it would also be regarded as a menace to liberal values. Clearly, however, no such threat is posed if moral discourse is used to enlighten and liberate, rather than to prescribe. To be sure, the information imparted by such discourse reconstructs in some measure the intentions of the agent, but it does not constitute a negation of choice. The intentions which are affected are, after all, those of the agent. *He* acts according to *his* valuation of the situation. Dewey and the noncognitivists have common cause in opposition to empty talk, but Dewey went far beyond them in conceiving instrumentalities of enlightened and enriched conduct.

To revert to the thesis that the dispute about noncognitivism is irrelevant,

28. A genuinely relevant criticism would take the form of charging that his distinctions in fact fail to fulfill the functions for which they were proposed. No one has attempted this sort of criticism.

it can be safely concluded that the value of Dewey's moral philosophy would be unaltered if all the specifically moral words in it were replaced with descriptive predicates. We would learn just as much from it, and perhaps more clearly. Noncognitivism stirred up an amazing furor, but the time may not be far off when philosophers will be puzzled that the controversy was thought to be so significant. When all is said and done, the noncognitivists' claim against Dewey is that he did not observe the conventions of language. Although even this charge could have been circumvented, it is true that he was in fact guilty of such nonconformity. But this fact does not diminish the significance of his moral philosophy. If anything, it is a credit to it.

It is important to recognize the irrelevance of noncognitivism, for attention can then be turned to determining the resources of Dewey's philosophy for understanding the problems of men and dealing with them. What is at issue here is more than Dewey's philosophy, as such. His *way* of philosophizing can be undertaken by anyone; so this enlightening and liberating inquiry can be carried forward without any qualm that its legitimacy or importance is challenged by "ordinary language" philosophy.

The most important difference between Dewey's moral philosophy and the theory of justice of John Rawls is in their conception of the locus of moral authority. For Dewey, it is in social intelligence; for Rawls it lies in the judgment of beings who do not in fact exist, but are theoretical constructs of that author's mind. From Rawls' point of view, the actual interests, expectations, and moral commitments of real human beings are essentially irrelevant in determining solutions to moral problems; and it is not as a distinctive and individualized person that one is qualified to participate in moral deliberation. It is entirely possible, then, that "justice" will ignore or demand a sacrifice of the interests of a great many persons, including fully conscientious persons, and without their even being consulted. In Rawls' conception, such an eventuality would be forestalled by taking measures in all institutions of society to ensure that the people will embrace the principles of justice already established in accordance with the required procedure.

Rawls' highly detailed theory formulates criteria in terms of which inequalities are minimized, and certain forms of human exploitation could never under any circumstances be justified. He conceives of what he calls "the original position," in which free, equal, and rational beings determine the principles of justice by which all real human beings are forever morally bound. These postulated beings have no prior moral commitments, and each is concerned with his own private interests exclusively. Yet in no *specific* sense do they know their own interests, for each deliberates behind what Rawls calls "the veil of ignorance": none has any information about himself which identifies him as a distinctive person in any way whatsoever. Thus the interests of those in the original position are in no way distinctive or individualized, and it is accordingly assumed that they would reach complete agreement. Each party to the original position chooses his principles, which become the universal principles of justice, without any knowledge of time, place, or circumstance, and without consulting any real living beings about what are their actual aims, interests, or judgments. Each is conceived to have a general knowledge of human nature and society; but this knowledge is, in fact, theory formulated on these matters by Rawls himself.

The principles arrived at in the original position are presumed to be identical with those which are determined in "our considered judgments," as Rawls says, but just who "our" refers to is not made clear. Supposedly it refers to any rational person; but no survey of rational persons is undertaken to verify the claim. In an extremely sophisticated way, Rawls' method is individualistic in the sense mentioned in Part Three, and subject to all the liabilities of that approach.

What is presented is a system of justice in which all fundamental moral judgments are determined independently of any or all actual situations. In contending with the latter, individuals need only investigate empirical circumstances in order to make the appropriate deductions from the first principles. As noted, the only characteristics of human nature that are morally relevant in the determination of conduct are those that are congruent with the postulated nature of those in the original position. A just society would, among other things, be so ordered that the individuals in it would develop in such a way that their moral nature conforms to that of the original position. From the perspective of Dewey's thinking, this prescription for a just society is an invitation to totalitarianism: When individuals don't conform to a model which is, after all, a product of the mind of one philosopher, society must be reconstituted so that they do.

An obvious issue in respect to Rawls' view is whether the individuals in the original position would indeed choose the principles he supposes, and a substantial body of literature has emerged to contend that Rawls has not really made his case. He has succeeded in creating a great deal of controversy; he has not succeeded in creating anything like a consensus regarding the theory of justice. This is a particularly instructive development, for it reveals the persistence of disagreement regarding moral norms. What, then, would follow for actual human conduct? Either individuals who do not subscribe to the principles must be forced to conform to them, or the methodology of making the postulated beings of the original position the moral judge of everyone else must be viewed with great suspicion.

It is the latter alternative which suggests the most fundamental issue. Rawls defines what he takes to be the ideal conditions of moral judgment,

but such a definition cannot be undertaken without entertaining crucial assumptions regarding what is indeed ideal. And Rawls' case for his ideal is
very thin. It is far from evident why these unreal beings—so unlike actual
persons—should constitute the norm for moral behavior. It is far from
evident why the most basic moral issues should be removed from the competence of the flesh-and-blood people for whom the moral principles are
contrived. As indicated, Rawls is concerned that criteria be formulated in
terms of which certain kinds of exploitation are always morally anathema;
but this prohibition is achieved by divesting actual persons of their participation in moral decision. Although judgment regarding just what constitutes
exploitation is by no means uniform, it is always possible that social intelligence will result in some form of exploitation in any given instance of its
use. Dewey, however, would much prefer to put his faith in social method
becoming progressively more enlightened and vigorous than run the risks of
vesting absolute moral authority in a source which is at once esoteric, elitist,
and divorced from human nature.

If Rawls presented his ideas as proposals, as one of the possible means of
ordering society, then his suggestions might be congenially entertained. (After
all, there are many persons who already detest exploitation, and they can
give reasons for opposing it which are persuasive to real people.) But this
is not the spirit with which Rawls offers his theory. In a dangerously misleading use of terms, he characterizes his conception as democratic,[29] when
what in effect is advocated is a highly authoritarian and absolutistic moral
method.

Since the time when Nietzsche announced the death of God, we often hear
that we are undergoing a crisis of value. This crisis is evidenced in the
phenomenon of moralists from many sectors advancing a truly remarkable
array of schemes for salvation: stoical despair, aesthetic withdrawal, subjective romanticism, mysticism, self-conscious courage, grasping at religious
belief, unrestrained hedonism, drugs. Judging by the frenetic pace of the
transition from one scheme to another, none of them has been particularly
satisfactory.

In Dewey's judgment, the philosophic basis for such developments lay in
radically mistaken conceptions of man and nature, where nature was conceived as alien and valueless, and reason was thought to have application
only to the quantitative structure of things. Experience, conceived as subjective, could not be considered evidential of the continuities of natural
processes. The very possibility of conduct as art, enriching and enriched
by nature, was precluded by these conceptions, as was the possibility of *shared*

29. Rawls, *op. cit.*, Section 13.

experience. These ideas provided a rationale for the extremes of retreat into the inner life or the soulless embrace of gross materialism.

Dewey believed, however, that the main problem lay, not in philosophy, but in social practice. The radical dislocations brought about by the developing industrial life destroyed traditional bonds and loyalties and created conditions of work which were both highly impersonal and prohibitive of the consummatory interaction of man and nature. Social institutions were inappropriate to the values of growth, freedom, and shared experience. A predictable reaction to these conditions was to look backward, to wish for a restoration of old beliefs and practices. Failure in this essentially futile task is followed by withdrawal into irrational schemes of salvation.

But nature needn't be something from which we must be saved, and human nature needn't be something from which we crave release. Philosophy can elucidate the predicaments and possibilities of nature and thereby aid social intelligence in the reconstruction of the prevailing conditions of existence. Dewey writes,

Poetry, art, religion are precious things. They cannot be maintained by lingering in the past and futilely wishing to restore what the movement of events in science, industry and politics has destroyed. They are an out-flowering of thought and desires that unconsciously converge into a disposition of imagination as a result of thousands and thousands of daily episodes and contact. They cannot be willed into existence or coerced into being. . . . But while it is impossible to retain and recover by deliberate volition old sources of religion and art that have been discredited, it is possible to expedite the development of the vital sources of a religion and art that are yet to be. Not indeed by action aimed directly at their production, but by substituting faith in the active tendencies of the day for dread and dislike of them, and by the courage of intelligence to follow whither social and scientific changes direct us. We are weak today in ideal matters because intelligence is divorced from aspiration. The bare force of circumstance compels us onwards in the daily detail of our beliefs and acts, but our deeper thoughts and desires turn backwards. When philosophy shall have co-operated with the course of events and made clear and coherent the meaning of the daily detail, science and emotion will interpenetrate, practice and imagination will embrace. Poetry and religious feeling will be the unforced flowers of life. To further this articulation and revelation of the meanings of the current course of events is the task and problem of philosophy in days of transition.[30]

30. *Reconstruction in Philosophy*, Enlarged Edition (Boston: Beacon Press, 1948), pp. 212–13. Dewey's "religion" is primarily a religion of shared experience. See below, pp. 114–21, and "The Religion of Shared Experience," by John

It is often noted that intelligence has a corrosive effect. It exposes illusion and prejudice for what they are, leaving human aspirations without foundation or direction. When intelligence performs this merely negative function, it becomes the object of hate and contempt. In the modern world intelligence has suffered much in this way, and many persons have accordingly been lured by various forms of irrationalism. If intelligence is to be embraced in human conduct, it must be shown that it can be the great instrument of the enhancement of life. More than any other thinker in the modern world, Dewey is to be credited with showing that intelligence is indeed such an instrument.

Intelligence is far removed from dogmatism. Dewey has no kinship with doctrinaire philosophies and moral finalities. His advocacy of intelligence and his faith in the possibilities of human nature constitute a recognition that the responsibility for continued inquiry and social effort is shared by all. Much of the man and the philosophy is captured in the following remarks, on which it is fitting to close:

... Dewey was hopeful of scientific methods because they help you to find out something you didn't know before. Surprisingly enough, in view of our present fashion today of regarding science and knowledge as the source of all our evils, this struck him as a good thing. He was convinced we don't know enough yet, not nearly enough, especially about human affairs, about wisdom. It's easy to feel that way about other people—most of us do. But Dewey felt it about himself. Unlike most intellectuals, he was not even sure he knew what other people need better than they do themselves. Far too intelligent to to be an intellectual, he thought you might find out more about what people need by asking them, by talking it over with them. They know where the shoe pinches better than you do.

This respect for the experience of other men, this willingness to learn from them what they have found out, above all, to learn by working with them, is the very core of John Dewey the man, and it is the core of his philosophy as well. From the point of view of assorted absolutists—chancellors, commissars, or cardinals—who already know all the answers, this has been Dewey's inforgiveable sin. He hadn't found The Truth, and he actually thought that other men were as likely to discover more of it as he or you or I. He had a curious, faintly old-fashioned faith, that men can really hope to learn something of wisdom by working together on their common problems. . . .

The best way of honoring Dewey is to work on Dewey's problems—to reconstruct his insights, to see, if need be, farther than Dewey saw. If it may be given to us to see farther, it will be largely because he pointed out to us

Herman Randall, Jr., in *The Philosopher of the Common Man* (New York: G. P. Putnam's Sons, 1940), edited by Sidney Ratner.

where to look. In that way, you and I can be really working with Dewey, as he always wanted us to do, and sharing in that enjoyed meaning that was, and is, and will continue to be John Dewey.[31]

James Gouinlock

Atlanta, Georgia
April 16, 1975

---

31. John Herman Randall, Jr., "John Dewey, 1859–1952," remarks made at a memorial meeting in tribute to John Dewey held by the Department of Philosophy of Columbia University. Printed in *The Journal of Philosophy*, Vol. L, No. 1 (January, 1953), pp. 5–13. Quotation is from pp. 11–13.

The Moral Writings of John Dewey

The
Nature
of
Moral
Philosophy

1

The first selection below provides Dewey's understanding of the sources and functions of philosophy. He regards philosophic reflection as originating in the need to elucidate the modes of thought and action that prevail in a given culture. Philosophers are those who articulate, clarify, and integrate the distinctive moral and scientific beliefs. The resulting formulations are intended not simply to provide a comprehensive view of the world but, more importantly, to determine the relevance of this view to human problems and aspirations. Clearly, Dewey regards philosophy as primarily a moral enterprise, stimulated by the varied problems of human endeavor and directed to the enlightenment of further thought and conduct. The first article also displays his conviction that it is mistaken to assume that there can be universal or ultimately conclusive solutions to the problems of men. This conviction should not be misunderstood, however: an approximation to a community of·shared beliefs and values is not beyond the potentialities of human nature.

PHILOSOPHY[1]

Definitions of philosophy are usually made from the standpoint of some system of philosophy and reflect its special point of view. For the purposes of this account the difficulty may be avoided by defining philosophy from the point of view of its historical role within human culture. Since the survey is confined to western civilization, the origin of European philosophy in Greece supplies the natural beginning. For not only does the name "philosophy" come from Greek thought, but also the explicit consciousness of what is denoted by the term. . . .

The reason for the primacy of Greek thought is not accidental, nor is it for the most part a mere matter of chronological priority. On the contrary, the reason for it is an essential part of a definition of philosophy from the cultural point of view. For Greece was a ground for exhibiting and proving most of the difficulties and predicaments that arise in the collective relation of man to nature and fellow man. This condition would not of itself have generated philosophy without the extraordinary capacity of the Greek mind for observation and statement. An explanation of this fact would here be irrelevant and perhaps impossible. Such is not the case, however, with respect to the traits of Greek culture that called forth the reflections that initiated western philosophy: these exhibit in striking fashion the typical conflicts of collective human experience. Consequently, in spite of the limitations of the Greek world in space and time, Greek traits form the very stuff out of which philosophy is made. Greece, and especially Athens, was an intellectual looking glass in which the western world became conscious of its essential problems. The Greek origins of the European philosophical tradition dispose completely of the notion that philosophical problems evolve in the consciousness of lonely though brilliant thinkers. These origins prove that such problems are formulations of complications existing in the material of collective experience, provided that experience is sufficiently free, exposed to change and subjected to attempts at deliberate control to present in typical form the basic difficulties with which human thought has to reckon.

It was probably natural that interest in physical nature should have predominated in the adventurous, seafaring, trading Greek colonists, especially as their political life was borrowed. In Athens, however, cosmology was definitely subordinated to moral and political interests. Throughout Greece generally, with the exception of Sparta, civic matters were adjusted through the medium of discussion. Athens was moreover a pure democracy in that all citizens rather than a delegated body took part in public affairs. Party conflict was rife and changes in type of government were frequent. The situation was expressed, on the intellectual side, in consciousness of a number of problems defined in terms of antitheses. There were, for example, the problems of stability versus change, of harmony and order versus conflict, of reason (represented by discussion and consultation with a view to persuasion) versus force. Intermingled with these were other questions brought to the fore by the traveling scholars called sophists. . . . Disputes regarding the role assumed by these men evoked such further antitheses as tradition versus innovation, the relations between custom and conscious thought, between nature and culture, between nature and art. . . .

Socrates, the initiator of Athenian philosophic reflection, deliberately strove to limit theoretical discussion to moral and political subjects. Apparently the direct stimulus to his conversations on these topics came from the sophists. His primary question was whether the various forms of social excellence, the "virtues," which command recognition by others, can be taught and if so how. Consideration of this theme led him to consideration of the relation of the various virtues to one another and to their unity in understanding, or rational insight. Since rational insight was found by him to be practically nonexistent among politicians, among the poets, who were the acknowledged moral teachers of the community, as well as among the sophists, his teaching came to its climax in a demand for the pursuit of understanding or wisdom.

The philosophical tradition of the western world did not originate because of a mere taste for abstract speculation or yet because of pure interest in knowledge divorced from application to conduct. On the contrary, wisdom, in its material and goal, was something more than science even though it was not possible without science. It was science enlisted in the service of conduct, first communal, or civic, and then personal. Most of the distinctive traits of philosophy through the ages are intimately connected with this fact. The connection is not external or due to the accident of its origin in Greece, but is intrinsic. The Greeks brought to consciousness three problems that are bound to emerge whenever civilization becomes reflectively turned back upon itself: What are the place and role of knowledge and reason in the conduct of life? What are the constitution and structure of knowledge and reason by virtue of which they can perform the assigned function? And, growing out of this question, what is the constitution of nature, of the universe, which renders possible and guarantees the conceptions of knowledge and of good that are reached? Upon the whole, in course of time, philosophy began with the last question, and this fact often disguises the initial problem as to the guidance of life and conduct. But the tie that unites the seemingly most remote speculations with this issue has never been completely cut.

The problem of the organization and direction of personal and community conduct was still uppermost with Plato, although he took steps which led to an apparent relegation of that issue to a secondary position, a fact that has frequently caused his modern interpreters to place him in a perspective foreign to his own intent. Instead of excluding or neglecting speculations about the constitution of nature in formulating the end of the organized state and individual, he asserted that the problem of the end and of good can be solved only when the inquiry is extended to include the totality of things and when the final conclusion is reached by understanding the constitution of nature. This latter problem, moreover, can be solved only as the problem of the structure and method of knowledge is solved. Thus the ethico-political problem was widened to include cosmology and logic. Dialectic became central, not merely auxiliary, in the philosophic scheme, for it was the means by which insight into the good was to be attained. By reason of the place of the good in the structure of the universe this fact instituted a necessary connection between logic and metaphysics.

Because of the inherent relation set up by Plato between cosmology, science (especially mathematics), logic, and political ethics, his fundamental distinctions, such as those between being and becoming, reality and appearance, form and matter, whole and part, or universal and particular, were not presented by him as detached intellectual distinctions. While he defines philosophy as desiderated science of the whole, he defines it also as the legislative science, or science of the state, since social organization is the form in which man is most directly concerned with the whole. . . .

It is evident that the interpenetration which, in the case of Plato, gave meaning to philosophy as the search for wisdom could not long be maintained in the form in which he set it forth. Philosophy was in a condition of unstable equilibrium with respect to the various factors contained in it. To Plato it seemed still possible, at least as an intellectual and moral aspiration, to reform and preserve the city-state. The fact that Aristotle was a tutor of Alexander the Great indicates that the failure of this dream was imminent and consequently a redistribution of the constituents of the whole inevitable. . . .

Subsequent to the dissolution of Greece, during the time of the supremacy of Rome in politics, of Alexandria and oriental beliefs in religion, the values assigned by Aristotle became as unreal to his successors as the Platonic social aspirations had been to Aristotle. During the period which Gilbert Murray describes as "failure of nerve," the chief interest of thinkers was in the supernatural. There ensued of necessity a period of acute metaphysical speculation with all phenomena arranged and interpreted in hierarchical descent from supreme being, a reality unattainable by way of scientific thought but capable of being at least occasionally grasped in mystic intuition. Thus neo-Platonism effected a further distinctive redistribution of the constituents of philosophic reflection, because of a new center of dominant value. Thinkers in Rome, more removed from oriental influence, translated philosophy into a practical direction of conduct, a tendency common to stoic, Epicurean and skeptic schools. The domination of western European life by the Roman church introduced another factor, and from the time of St. Augustine through the twelfth century there was a systematic distribution of metaphysical, logical, cosmological and ethical factors worked out on the basis of the supremacy of the values characteristic of religious faith.

The purpose of the foregoing is not to sketch, even in outline, the history of philosophic thought, but to suggest the features that have always been characteristic of philosophy, and to indicate that cultural causes have produced the main changes in the direction and content of philosophic systems. If the movement of modern philosophy were followed, its tendencies would be seen to be connected with the new values that emerged with the revival of scholarship in the Renaissance, and especially with the growth of the natural sciences and the secularization of interest that mark recent centuries. Such a historical survey shows the necessity of defining philosophy from the standpoint of value, since the changes of philosophy are all inherently bound up with problems that arise when new emphases and new redistributions in the significance of values take place. For example, it is as certain as anything can be that if science, at present a dominant interest, were to become subordinated to some value that may emerge in the future, there will be produced a new set of problems and hence of philosophies.

The connection of philosophies and of change in the aim and method of philosophizing with changes in culture and social organization, which bring about redistributions of collective valuations and prestige, makes it possible to explain the fact that each system has a definition of philosophy couched in its own terms. For each philosophy is in effect, if not in avowed intent, an interpretation of man and nature on the basis of some program of comprehensive aims and policies. The generality and comprehensiveness claimed for philosophy have their origin in this fact. Each system has of necessity an exclusive aspect, often expressing itself in a controversial way, because it is, implicitly, a recommendation of certain types of value as normative in the direction of human conduct. . . .

. . . While philosophies have not as a rule been presented in an especially satisfactory form, they have aimed at appeal and persuasion more general and more moving than those of the specialized sciences. They have striven to bring about adoption of certain basic attitudes, not merely to convey information. . . .

The connection of philosophy with conflicts of ends and values serves to explain two criticisms frequently brought against the enterprise of philosophy. One of them points to the diverging and controversial character of philosophy in contrast with the definite trend toward unity in the sciences. If, however, valuation enters into philosophy, divergence is inevitable. It could not be eliminated except by attainment of a complete consensus as to universal ends and methods. If those who hold up different values as the directive aims of life were to agree with one another in their interpretations of existence, it would be a sure sign of insincerity. Relativists and absolutists, radicals and conservatives, spiritualists and materialists, differ primarily in their systems of value, and their strictly intellectual differences follow logically. How can those who believe in the necessity of a transcendent source of authority agree with those who believe that the seat of authority is and should be in the process and operations of actual experience? In spite of conflicts, philosophy serves the purpose of clarifying the source of opposition and the problems attendant upon it; while with respect to some problems articulation and clarification are more significant than formal solution.

The other indictment of philosophy, that it mills around among the same problems without settling any of them, may be met, on the basis of the relation of philosophy to value, by pointing out that no phase of culture can settle the problems that arise in and for another phase of culture. General problems regarding aims and the means appropriate to their realization arise in every type of social life. They have formal features in common, and these are stated in philosophical generalizations. But in actual content they differ, and hence they have to be dealt with in the terms both of the science and of the dominant practical tendencies of each period. Only if social institutions and the culture attending them were wholly static would it be possible to carry over completely the solutions or even the methods of one epoch into the conditions of another.

A striking illustration of the formal constancy of certain problems along with tremendous change in content is found in the question of the relation between the individual and the universal. Conflicts between the individual and the total order of which he is a part are bound to arise in every complex and changing culture. Wherever reflection is free and energetic, these conflicts will be generalized and will take conceptual form as the problem of the relation of universal and particular. In this conceptual form they will have a certain independent dialectical career of their own. But the state of knowledge and the state of institutions are the variables of the formal relationship, and they will inevitably color the meaning of the problem. One has only, for example, to contrast Greek, mediaeval and contemporary culture with respect to the knowledge of nature bearing upon this problem and with respect to the political and economic conditions that determine the actual status of individuals, to see how constancy of the problem in formal terms is compatible with great variability in content, so that the issue must be approached from a new point of view, never repeated in subsequent history. . . .

. . . When once the principles underlying beliefs and valuations have received formal statement, the resulting concepts obtain a certain independent intellectual existence of their own and are capable of having their own career without reference to the cultural conditions of their origin. This secondary and derived existence is accentuated when, as so often happens, professional teachers are the chief guardians and representatives of philosophy. . . .

In addition to the definite services of philosophy in generating ideas that inspire and direct thinking in the physical and social fields, philosophy exercises a third and rather indirect and vague function. Although few philosophers have found a significant aesthetic form of expression for their ideas, when expression is judged by the criterion of literature, nevertheless philosophy performs for some exactly the same office that the fine arts perform for others. There is a kind of music of ideas that appeals, apart from any question of empirical verification, to the minds of thinkers, who derive an emotional satisfaction from an imaginative play synthesis of ideas obtainable by them in no other way. The objective side of this phenomenon is the role of philosophy in bringing to a focus of unity and clarity the ideas that are at work in a given period more or less independently of one another, in separate cultural streams. Much of the culture characteristic of the eighteenth century is summed up for all subsequent history in the Enlightenment, and the Enlightenment is definitely a philosophical synthesis. The same is true of the romanticism of the nineteenth century, especially in Germany. It applies also to the vogue, during the latter part of the nineteenth century, of the idea of universal evolution. The significance of such synthesizing ideas is more or less independent of the question of verifiability. The human mind, taken collectively, experiences the need of holding itself together, and during periods of rapid influx of new materials and the inception of new and diverging tendencies, accomplishes this task by means of comprehensive speculative ideas.

On the other hand, the failure from the standpoint of verifiability of these adventures in synthesis is one cause, and a rather large cause, of the comparative eclipse of philosophy in recent days. If such ventures were frankly offered as imaginative, without claiming objective truth, it is probable that the reaction against philosophy provoked by them (and largely in proportion to their previous vogue) would not occur. The positive cause which accounts for the recent comparative decline of the prestige of philosophy is found, however, in the tremendous multiplication of specialized knowledge and in the irreconcilable divergences among social tendencies characteristic of the present time. Uncertainty in the position of religion, due to its affiliation with a supernaturalism that is discredited from the standpoint of natural science; the enormous mass of specialized detail in science; sharp conflicts between movements in politics and economic life, between tradition and innovation, have often forced philosophy into either taking sides and becoming the intellectual partisan of a particular movement, or else withdrawing completely from the field of vital common experience and becoming itself another technical mode of specialization. The recent general revival of formalism in philosophical thought is probably to be accounted for on this basis. Judging from past history, this divided and crippled state of philosophy is a transitional phenomenon, preliminary to the appearance of comprehensive even if rival formulations, as subject matter is better digested and the lines of cleavage in social movements become more articulate. From the standpoint of culture philosophy is a perennial adventure of the human spirit.

PHILOSOPHY AND CIVILIZATION[2]

In the historic role of philosophy, the scientific factor, the element of correctness, of verifiable applicability, has a place, but it is a negative one. The meanings delivered by confirmed observation, experimentation and calculation, scientific facts and principles, serve as tests of the values which tradition transmits and of those which emotion suggests. Whatever is not compatible with them must be eliminated in any sincere philosophizing.

This fact confers upon scientific knowledge an incalculably important office in philosophy. But the criterion is negative; the exclusion of the inconsistent is far from being identical with a positive test which demands that only what has been scientifically verifiable shall provide the entire content of philosophy. It is the difference between an imagination that acknowledges its responsibility to meet the logical demands of ascertained facts, and a complete abdication of all imagination in behalf of a prosy literalism.

Finally, it results from what has been said that the presence and absence of native-born philosophies is a severe test of the depth of unconscious tradition and rooted institutions among any people, and of the productive force of their culture. For the sake of brevity, I may be allowed to take our own case, the case of civilization in the United States. Philosophy, we have been saying, is a conversion of such culture as exists into consciousness, into an imagination which is logically coherent and is not incompatible with what is factually known. But this conversion is itself a further movement of civilization; it is not something performed upon the body of habits and tendencies from without, that is, miraculously. If American civilization does not eventuate in an imaginative formulation of itself, if it merely rearranges the figures already named and placed—in playing an inherited European game—that fact is itself the measure of the culture which we have achieved. A deliberate striving for an American Philosophy as such would be only another evidence of the same emptiness and impotency. There is energy and activity, among us, enough and to spare. Not an inconsiderable part of the vigor that once went into industrial accomplishment now finds its way into science; our scientific "plant" is coming in its way to rival our industrial plants. Especially in psychology and the social sciences an amount of effort is putting forth which is hardly equaled in any one other part of the world. He would be a shameless braggart who claimed that the result is as yet adequate to the activity. What is the matter? It lies, I think, with our lack of imagination in generating leading ideas. Because we are afraid of speculative ideas, we do, and do over and over again, an immense amount of dead, specialized work in the region of "facts." We forget that such facts are only data; that is, are only fragmentary, uncompleted meanings, and unless they are rounded out into complete ideas—a work which can only be done by hypotheses, by a free imagination of intellectual possibilities—they are as helpless as are all maimed things and as repellent as are needlessly thwarted ones.

Please do not imagine that this is a plea in disguise for any particular type of philosophizing. On the contrary, any philosophy which is a sincere outgrowth and expression of our own civilization is better than none, provided it speaks the authentic idiom of an enduring and dominating corporate experience. If we are really, for instance, a materialistic people, we are at least materialistic in a new fashion and on a new scale. I should welcome then a consistent materalistic philosophy, if only it were sufficiently bold. For in the degree in which, despite attendant esthetic repulsiveness, it marked the coming to consciousness of a group of ideas, it would formulate a coming to self-consciousness of our civilization. Thereby it would furnish ideas, supply an intellectual polity, direct further observations and experiments, and organize their results on a grand scale. As long as we worship science and are afraid of philosophy we shall have no great science; we shall have a lagging and halting continuation of what is thought and said elsewhere. As far as any plea is implicit in what has been said, it is, then, a plea for the casting off of that intellectual timidity which hampers the wings of imagination, a plea for speculative audacity, for more faith in ideas, sloughing off a cowardly reliance upon those partial ideas to which we are wont to give the name of facts. I have given to philosophy a more humble function than that which is often assigned it. But modesty as to its final place is not incompatible with boldness in the maintenance of that function, humble as it may be. A combination of such modesty and courage affords the only way I know of in which the philosopher can look his fellowman in the face with frankness and with humanity.

THE METHOD AND AIMS OF PHILOSOPHY[3]

Philosophic ideas are tested by determining their efficacy in clarifying the events of life experience, from the immediately qualitative to the refined processes of knowing and evaluating. Philosophy elucidates not just selected aspects of reality, but all of its characteristic traits and continuities. Such analysis is necessary for any philosophy that would be relevant to the moral strivings of mankind. Dewey contends that philosophic ideas which render any phase of experience unintelligible must be discarded, rather than be given the axiomatic status they have enjoyed in many philosophic systems. It is primarily on this basis that he insists that the traits of experience are evidential of the nature of the real world.

This consideration of method may suitably begin with the contrast between gross, macroscopic, crude subject-matters in primary experience and the refined, derived objects of reflection. The distinction is one between what is experienced as the result of a minimum of incidental reflection and what is experienced in consequence of continued and regulated reflective inquiry. For derived and refined products are experienced only because of the intervention of systematic thinking. The objects of both science and philosophy obviously belong chiefly to the secondary and refined system. But at this point we come to a marked divergence between science and philosophy. For the natural sciences not only draw their material from primary experience, but they refer it back again for test. Darwin began with the pigeons, cattle and plants of breeders and gardeners. Some of the conclusions he reached were so contrary to accepted beliefs that they were condemned as absurd, contrary to commonsense, etc. But scientific men, whether they accepted his theories or not, employed his hypotheses as directive ideas for making new observations and experiments among the things of raw experience—just as the metallurgist who extracts refined metal from crude ore makes tools that are then set to work to control and use other crude materials. An Einstein working by highly elaborate methods of reflection, calculates theoretically certain results in the deflection of light by the presence of the sun. A technically equipped expedition is sent to South Africa so that by means of experiencing a thing—an eclipse—in crude, primary, experience, observations can be secured to compare with, and test the theory implied in, the calculated result.

The facts are familiar enough. They are cited in order to invite attention to the relationship between the objects of primary and of secondary or reflective experience. That the subject-matter of primary experience sets the problems and furnishes the first data of the reflection which constructs the secondary objects is evident; it is also obvious that test and verification of the latter is secured only by return to things of crude or macroscopic experience—the sun, earth, plants and animals of common, everyday life. But just what role do the objects attained in reflection play? Where do they come in? They *explain* the primary objects, they enable us to grasp them with *understanding*, instead of just having sense-contact with them. But how?

Well, they define or lay out a path by which return to experienced things is of such a sort that the meaning, the significant content, of what is experienced gains an enriched and expanded force because of the path or method by which it was reached. Directly, in immediate contact it may be just what is was before—hard, colored, odorous, etc. But when the secondary objects, the refined objects, are employed as a method or road for coming at them, these qualities cease to be isolated details; they get the meaning contained in a whole system of related objects; they are rendered continuous with the rest of nature and take on the import of the things they are now seen to be continuous with. The phenomena observed in the eclipse tested and, as far as they went, confirmed Einstein's theory of deflection of light by mass. But that is far from being the whole story. The phenomena themselves got a far-reaching significance they did not previously have. Perhaps they would not even have been noticed if the theory had not been employed as a guide or road to observation of them. But even if they had been noticed, they would have been dismissed as of no importance, just as we daily drop from attention hundreds of perceived details for which we have no intellectual use. But approached by means of theory these lines of slight deflection take on a significance as large as that of the revolutionary theory that lead to their being experienced.

This empirical method I shall call the *denotative* method. That philosophy is a mode of reflection, often of a subtle and penetrating sort, goes without saying. The charge that is brought against the nonempirical method of philosophizing is not that it depends upon theorizing, but that it fails to use refined, secondary products as a path pointing and leading back to something in primary experience. The resulting failure is threefold.

First, there is no verification, no effort even to test and check. What is even worse, secondly, is that the things of ordinary experience do not get enlargement and enrichment of meaning as they do when approached through the medium of scientific principles and reasonings. This lack of function reacts, in the third place, back upon the philosophic subject-matter in itself. Not tested by being employed to see what it leads to in ordinary experience and what new meanings it contributes, this subject-matter becomes arbitrary, aloof—what is called "abstract" when that word is used in a bad sense to designate something which exclusively occupies a realm of its own without contact with the things of ordinary experience.

As the net outcome of these three evils, we find that extraordinary phenomenon which accounts for the revulsion of many cultivated persons from any form of philosophy. The objects of reflection in philosophy, being reached by methods that seem to those who employ them rationally mandatory are taken to be "real" in and of themselves—and supremely real. Then it becomes an insoluble problem why the things of gross, primary experience, should be what they are, or indeed why they should be at all. The refined objects of reflection in the natural sciences, however, never end by rendering the subject-matter from which they are derived a problem; rather, when used to describe a path by which some goal in primary experience is designated or denoted, they solve perplexities to which that crude material gives rise but which it cannot resolve of itself. They become means of control, of enlarged use and enjoyment of ordinary things. They may generate new problems, but these are problems of the same sort, to be dealt with by further use of the same methods of inquiry and experimentation. The problems to which empirical method gives rise afford, in a word, opportunities for more investigations yielding fruit in new and enriched experiences. But the problems to which nonempirical method gives rise in philosophy are blocks to inquiry, blind alleys; they are puzzles rather than problems, solved only by calling the original material of primary experience, "phenomenal," mere appearance, mere impressions, or by some other disparaging name.

Thus there is here supplied, I think, a first-rate test of the value of any philosophy which is offered us: Does it end in conclusions which, when they are referred back to ordinary life-experiences and their predicaments, render them more significant, more luminous to us, and make our dealings with them more fruitful? Or does it terminate in rendering the things of ordinary experience more opaque than they were before, and in depriving them of having in "reality" even the significance they had previously seemed to have? Does it yield the enrichment and increase of power of ordinary things which the results of physical science afford when applied in everyday affairs? Or does it become a mystery that these ordinary things should be what they are; and are philosophic concepts left to dwell in separation in some technical realm of their own? It is the fact, I repeat, that so many philosophies terminate in conclusions that make it necessary to disparage and condemn primary experience, leading those who hold them to measure the sublimity of their "realities" as philosophically defined by remoteness from the concerns of daily life, which leads cultivated common sense to look askance at philosophy.

These general statements must be made more definite. We must illustrate the meaning of empirical method by seeing some of its results in contrast with those to which nonempirical philosophies conduct us. We begin by noting that "experience" is what James called a double-barreled word. . . . Like its congeners, life and history, it includes *what* men do and suffer, *what* they strive for, love, believe and endure, and also *how* men act and are acted upon, the ways in which they do and suffer, desire and enjoy, see, believe, imagine—in short, processes of *experiencing*. "Experience" denotes the planted field, the sowed seeds, the reaped harvests, the changes of night and day, spring and autumn, wet and dry, heat and cold, that are observed, feared, longed for; it also denotes the one who plants and reaps, who works and rejoices, hopes, fears, plans, invokes magic or chemistry to aid him, who is downcast or triumphant. It is "double-barreled" in that it recognizes in its primary integrity no division between act and material, subject and object, but contains them both in an unanalyzed totality. "Thing" and "thought," as James says in the same connection, are single-barreled; they refer to products discriminated by reflection out of primary experience. . . .

One illustration out of the multitude available follows. It is taken almost at random, because it is both simple and typical. To illustrate the nature of experience, what experience really is, an author writes: "When I look at a chair, I say I experience it. But what I actually experience is only a very few of the elements that go to make up a chair, namely the color that belongs to the chair under these particular conditions of light, the shape which the chair displays when viewed from this angle, etc." Two points are involved in any such statement. One is that "experience" is reduced to the traits connected with the *act of experiencing*, in this case the act of seeing. Certain patches of color, for example, assume a certain shape or form in connection with qualities connected with the muscular strains and adjustments of seeing. These qualities, which define the act of seeing when it is made an object of reflective inquiry, *over against what is seen*, thus become the chair itself for immediate or direct experience. Logically, the chair disappears and is replaced by certain qualities of sense attending the act of vision. There is no longer any other object, much less the chair which was bought, that is placed in a room and that is used to sit in, etc. If we ever get back to this total chair, it will not be the chair of direct experience, of use and enjoyment, a thing with its own independent origin, history and career; it will be only a complex of directly "given" sense qualities as a core, plus a surrounding cluster of other qualities revived imaginatively as "ideas."

The other point is that, even in such a brief statement as that just quoted, there is compelled recognition of an *object* of experience which is infinitely other and more than what is asserted to be alone experienced. There is the *chair* which is looked at; the *chair displaying* certain colors, the *light* in which they are displayed; the angle of vision implying reference to an organism that possesses an optical apparatus. Reference to these *things* is compulsory, because otherwise there would be no meaning assignable to the sense qualities—which are, nevertheless, affirmed to be the sole data experienced. It would be hard to find a more complete recognition, although an unavowed one, of the fact that in reality the account given concerns only a selected portion of the actual experience, namely that part which defines the act of experiencing, to the deliberate omission, *for the purpose of the inquiry in hand,* of *what* is experienced.

The instance cited is typical of all "subjectivism" as a philosophic position. Reflective analysis of one element in actual experience is undertaken; its result is then taken to be primary; as a consequence the subject-matter of actual experience from which the analytic result was derived is rendered dubious and problematic, although it is assumed at every step of the analysis. Genuine empirical method sets out from the actual subject-matter of primary experience, recognizes that reflection discriminates a new factor in it, the *act* of seeing, makes an object of that, and then uses that new object, the organic response to light, to regulate, when needed, further experiences of the subject-matter already contained in primary experience.

The topics just dealt with, segregation of physical and mental objects, will receive extended attention in the body of this volume. . . . As respects *method*, however, it is pertinent at this point to summarize our results. Reference to the primacy and ultimacy of the material of ordinary experience protects us, in the first place, from creating artificial problems which deflect the energy and attention of philosophers from the real problems that arise out of actual subject-matter. In the second place, it provides a check or test for the conclusions of philosophic inquiry; it is a constant reminder that we must replace them, as secondary reflective products, in the experience out of which they arose, so that they may be confirmed or modified by the new order and clarity they introduce into it, and the new significantly experienced objects for which they furnish a method. In the third place, in seeing how they thus function in further experiences, the philosophical results themselves acquire empirical value; they are what they contribute to the common experience of man, instead of being curiosities to be deposited, with appropriate labels, in a metaphysical museum.

There is another important result for philosophy of the use of empirical method which, when it is developed, introduces our next topic. Philosophy, like all forms of reflective analysis, takes us away, for the time being, from the things had in primary experience as they directly act and are acted upon, used and enjoyed. Now the standing temptation of philosophy, as its course abundantly demonstrates, is to regard the results of reflection as having, in and of themselves, a reality superior to that of the material of any other mode of experience. The commonest assumption of philosophies, common even to philosophies very different from one another, is the assumption of the identity of objects of knowledge and ultimately real objects. The assumption is so deep that it is usually not expressed; it is taken for granted as something so fundamental that it does not need to be stated. A technical example of the view is found in the contention of the Cartesian school— including Spinoza—that emotion as well as sense is but confused thought which when it becomes clear and definite or reaches its goal is *cognition*. That esthetic and moral experience reveal traits of real things as truly as does intellectual experience, that poetry may have a metaphysical import as well as science, is rarely affirmed, and when it is asserted, the statement is likely to be meant in some mystical or esoteric sense rather than in a straightforward everyday sense.

Suppose however that we start with no presuppositions save that what is experienced, since it is a manifestation of nature, may, and indeed, must be used as testimony of the characteristics of natural events. Upon this basis, reverie and desire are pertinent for a philosophic theory of the true nature of things; the possibilities present in imagination that are not found in observation, are something to be taken into account. The features of objects reached by scientific or reflective experiencing are important, but so are all the phenomena of magic, myth, politics, painting, and penitentiaries. The phenomena of social life are as relevant to the problem of the relation of the individual and universal as are those of logic; the existence in political organization of boundaries and barriers, of centralization, of interaction across boundaries, of expansion and absorption, will be quite as important for metaphysical theories of the discrete and the continuous as is anything derived from chemical analysis. The existence of ignorance as well as of wisdom, of error and even insanity as well as of truth will be taken into account.

That is to say, nature is construed in such a way that all these things, since they are actual, are naturally possible; they are not explained away into mere "appearance" in contrast with reality. Illusions are illusions, but the occurrence of illusions is not an illusion, but a genuine reality. What is really "in" experience extends much further than that which at any time is *known*. From the standpoint of knowledge, objects must be distinct; their traits must be explicit; the vague and unrevealed is a limitation. Hence, whenever the habit of identifying reality with the object of knowledge as such prevails, the obscure and vague are explained away. It is important for philosophic theory to be aware that the distinct and evident are prized and why they are. But it is equally important to note that the dark and twilight abound. For in any object of primary experience there are always potentialities which are not explicit; any object that is overt is charged with possible consequences that are hidden; the most overt act has factors which are not explicit. Strain thought as far as we may and not all consequences can be foreseen or made an express or known part of reflection and decision. In the face of such empirical facts, the assumption that nature in itself is all of the same kind, all distinct, explicit and evident, having no hidden possibilities, no novelties or obscurities, is possible only on the basis of a philosophy which at some point draws an arbitrary line between nature and experience.

In the assertion (implied here) that the great vice of philosophy is an arbitrary "intellectualism," there is no slight cast upon intelligence and reason. By "intellectualism" as an indictment is meant the theory that all experiencing is a mode of knowing, and that all subject-matter, all nature, is, in principle, to be reduced and transformed till it is defined in terms identical with the characteristics presented by refined objects of science as such. The assumption of "intellectualism" goes contrary to the facts of what is primarily experienced. For things are objects to be treated, used, acted upon and with, enjoyed and endured, even more than things to be known. They are things *had* before they are things cognized.

The isolation of traits characteristic of objects known, and then defined as the sole ultimate realities, accounts for the denial to nature of the characters which make things lovable and contemptible, beautiful and ugly, adorable and awful. It accounts for the belief that nature is an indifferent, dead mechanism; it explains why characteristics that are the valuable and valued traits of objects in actual experience are thought to create a fundamentally troublesome philosophical problem. Recognition of their genuine and primary reality does not signify that no thought and knowledge enter in when things are loved, desired and striven for; it signifies that the former are subordinate, so that the genuine problem is how and why, to what effect, things thus experienced are transformed into objects in which cognized traits are supreme and affectional and volitional traits incidental and subsidiary.

"Intellectualism" as a sovereign method of philosophy is so foreign to the facts of primary experience that it not only compels recourse to nonempirical method, but it ends in making knowledge, conceived as ubiquitous, itself inexplicable. If we start from primary experience, occurring as it does chiefly in modes of action and undergoing, it is easy to see what knowledge contributes—namely, the possibility of intelligent administration of the elements of doing and suffering. We are about something, and it is well to know what we are about, as the common phrase has it. To be intelligent in action and in suffering (enjoyment too) yields satisfaction even when conditions cannot be controlled. But when there is possibility of control, knowledge is the sole agency of its realization. Given this element of knowledge in primary experience, it is not difficult to understand how it may develop from a subdued and subsidiary factor into a dominant character. Doing and suffering, experimenting and putting ourselves in the way of having our sense and nervous system acted upon in ways that yield material for reflection, may reverse the original situation in which knowing and thinking were subservient to action-under-going. And when we trace the genesis of knowing along this line, we also see that knowledge has a function and office in bettering and enriching the subject-matters of crude experience. We are prepared to understand what we are about on a grander scale, and to undestand what happens even when we seem to be the hapless puppets of uncontrollable fate. But knowledge that is ubiquitous, all-inclusive and all-monopolizing, ceases to have meaning in losing all context; that it does not appear to do so when made supreme and self-sufficient is because it is literally impossible to exclude that context of noncognitive but experienced subject-matter which gives what is *known* its import. . . .

What empirical method exacts of philosophy is two things: First, that refined methods and products be traced back to their origin in primary experience, in all its heterogeneity and fullness; so that the needs and problems out of which they arise and which they have to satisfy be acknowledged. Secondly, that the secondary methods and conclusions be brought back to the things of ordinary experience, in all their coarseness and crudity, for verification. In this way, the methods of analytic reflection yield materials which form the ingredients of a method of designation, denotation, in philosophy. A scientific work in physics or astronomy gives a record of calculations and deductions that were derived from past observations and experiments. But it is more than a record; it is also an indication, an assignment, of further observations and experiments to be performed. No scientific report would get a hearing if it did not describe the apparatus by means of which experiments were carried on and results obtained; not that apparatus is worshipped, but because this procedure tells other inquirers how they are to go to work to get results which will agree or disagree in their experience with those previously arrived at, and thus confirm, modify and rectify the latter. The recorded scientific result is in effect a *designation* of a method to be followed and a *prediction* of what will be found when specified observations are set on foot. That is all a philosophy can be or do. In the chapters that follow I have undertaken a revision and reconstruction of the conclusions, the reports, of a number of historic philosophic systems, in order that they may be usable methods by which one may go to his own experience, and, discerning what is found by use of the method, come to understand better what is already within the common experience of mankind.

There is a special service which the study of philosophy may render. Empirically pursued it will not be a study of philosophy but a study, by means of philosophy, of life-experience. But this experience is already overlaid and saturated with the products of the reflection of past generations and bygone ages. It is filled with interpretation, classifications, due to sophisticated thought, which have become incorporated into what seems to be fresh, naïve empirical material. It would take more wisdom than is possessed by the wisest historic scholar to track all of these absorbed borrowings to their original sources. If we may for the moment call these materials prejudices (even if they are true, as long as their source and authority is unknown), then philosophy is a critique of prejudices. These incorporated results of past reflection, welded into the genuine materials of firsthand experience, may become organs of enrichment if they are detected and reflected upon. If they are not detected, they often obfuscate and distort. Clarification and emancipation follow when they are detected and cast out; and one great object of philosophy is to accomplish this task. . . .

I am loath to conclude without reference to the larger liberal humane value of philosophy when pursued with empirical method. The most serious indictment to be brought against nonempirical philosophies is that they have cast a cloud over the things of ordinary experience. They have not been content to rectify them. They have discredited them at large. In casting aspersion upon the things of everyday experience, the things of action and affection and social intercourse, they have done something worse than fail to give these affairs the intelligent direction they so much need. It would not matter much if philosophy had been reserved as a luxury of only a few thinkers. We endure many luxuries. The serious matter is that philosophies have denied that common experience is capable of developing from within itself methods which will secure direction for itself and will create inherent standards of judgment and value. No one knows how many of the evils and deficiencies that are pointed to as reasons for flight from experience are themselves due to the disregard of experience shown by those peculiarly reflective. To waste of time and energy, to disillusionment with life that attends every deviation from concrete experience must be added the tragic failure to realize the value that intelligent search could reveal and mature among the things of ordinary experience. I cannot calculate how much of current cynicism, indifference and pessimism is due to these causes in the deflection of intelligence they have brought about. It has even become in many circles a sign of lack of sophistication to imagine that life is or can be a fountain of cheer and happiness. Philosophies no more than religions can be aquitted of responsibility for bringing this result to pass. The transcendental philosopher has probably done more than the professed sensualist and materialist to obscure the potentialities of daily experience for joy and for self-regulation. . . .

MORAL PHILOSOPHY AND LIFE EXPERIENCE[4]

Generically, values—or goods—are whatever events are liked, prized, cherished, etc., or the reverse. A crucial requirement for enriching and unifying the values of experience is for individuals to understand the ways in which different types of life activity condition one another (for example, the economic and the religious). Likewise, it is essential to understand the continuities between different phases of experience— such as the problematic and the cognitive—which occur in any activity. Fundamental to all such understanding is a conception of man and nature that makes these relations clear and subject to intelligent direction. The discernment of these vital relations Dewey here calls criticism. The philosopher's distinctive moral function is not to prescribe values, but to provide the assumptions in terms of which the discrimination and construction of values can be carried on most effectively. "Love of wisdom" is devoted to "opening and enlarging of the ways of nature in man"; that is, to discovering the means "of administering the unfinished processes of existence so that frail goods shall be substantiated, secure goods be extended, and the precarious promises of good that haunt experienced things be more liberally fulfilled."[5]

These remarks are preparatory to presenting a conception of philosophy; namely, that philosophy is inherently criticism, having its distinctive position among various modes of criticism in its generality; a criticism of criticisms, as it were. . . .

. . . Of immediate values as such, values which occur and which are possessed and enjoyed, there is no theory at all; they just occur, are enjoyed, possessed; and that is all. The moment we begin to discourse about these values, to define and generalize, to make distinctions in kinds, we are passing beyond value-objects themselves; we are entering, even if only blindly, upon an inquiry into causal antecedents and causative consequents, with a view to appraising the "real," that is the eventual, goodness of the thing in question. We are criticizing, not for its own sake, but for the sake of instituting and perpetuating more enduring and extensive values.

. . . Philosophy is and can be nothing but this critical operation and function become aware of itself and its implications, pursued deliberately and systematically. It starts from actual situations of belief, conduct and appre-

ciative perception which are characterized by immediate qualities of good
and bad, and from the modes of critical judgment current at any given time
in all the regions of value; these are its data, its subject-matter. These values,
criticisms, and critical methods, it subjects to further criticism as comprehensive and consistent as possible. The function is to regulate the further appreciation of goods and bads; to give greater freedom and security in those acts
of direct selection, appropriation, identification and of rejection, elimination,
destruction which instate and which exclude objects of belief, conduct and
contemplation. . . .

In traditional discussion the fact is overlooked that the subject-matter of
belief is a good, since belief means assimilation and assertion. It is overlooked that its immediate goodness is both the obstacle to reflective examination and the source of its necessity. The "true" is indeed set up along with
the good and the beautiful as a transcendent good, but the role of empirical
good, of value, in the sweep of ordinary beliefs is passed by. The counterpart
of this error, which isolates the subject-matter of intellect from the scope of
values and valuations, is a corresponding isolation of the subject-matter of
esthetic contemplation and immediate enjoyment from judgment. Between
these two realms, one of intellectual objects without value and the other
of value-objects without intellect, there is an equivocal mid-country in which
moral objects are placed, with rival claimants striving to annex them either
to the region of purely immediate goods (in this case termed pleasures) or
to that of purely rational objects. Hence the primary function of philosophy
at present is to make it clear that there is no such difference as this division
assumes between science, morals, and esthetic appreciation. All alike exhibit
the difference between immediate goods casually occurring and immediate
goods which have been reflectively determined by means of critical inquiry.
If bare liking is an adequate determinant of values in one case, it is in the
others. If intelligence, criticism, is required in one, it is in the others. If
the end to be attained in any case is an enhanced and purified immediate
appreciative, experienced object, so it is in the others. All cases manifest the
same duality and present the same problem; that of embodying intelligence
in action which shall convert casual natural goods, whose causes and effects
are unknown, into goods valid for thought, right for conduct and cultivated
for appreciation.

Philosophic discourse partakes both of scientific and literary discourse.
Like literature, it is a comment on nature and life in the interest of a more
intense and just appreciation of the meanings present in experience. Its business is reportorial and transcriptive only in the sense in which the drama
and poetry have that office. Its primary concern is to clarify, liberate and
extend the goods which inhere in the naturally generated functions of experience. It has no call to create a world of "reality" de novo, nor to delve
into secrets of Being hidden from common sense and science. It has no stock

of information or body of knowledge peculiarly its own; if it does not always become ridiculous when it sets up as a rival of science, it is only because a particular philosopher happens to be also, as a human being, a prophetic man of science. Its business is to accept and to utilize for a purpose the best available knowledge of its own time and place. And this purpose is criticism of beliefs, institutions, customs, policies with respect to their bearing upon good. This does not mean their bearing upon *the* good, as something itself attained and formulated in philosophy. For as philosophy has no private score of knowledge or of methods for attaining truth, so it has no private access to good. As it accepts knowledge of facts and principles from those competent in inquiry and discovery, so it accepts the goods that are diffused in human experience. It has no Mosaic nor Pauline authority of revelation entrusted to it. But it has the authority of intelligence, of criticism of these common and natural goods. . . .

. . . What especially makes necessary a generalized instrument of criticism, is the tendency of objects to seek rigid noncommunicating compartments. It is natural that nature, variegatedly qualified, should exhibit various trends when it achieves experience of itself, so that there is a distribution of emphasis such as are designated by the adjectives scientific, industrial, political, religious, artistic, educational, moral and so on,

But however natural from the standpoint of causation may be the institutionalizing of these trends, their separation effects an isolation which is unnatural. Narrowness, superficiality, stagnation follow from lack of the nourishment which can be supplied only by generous and wide interactions. Goods isolated as professionalism and institutionalization isolate them, petrify; and in a moving world solidification is always dangerous. Resistant force is gained by precipitation, but no one thing gets strong enough to defy everything. Overspecialization and division of interests, occupations and goods create the need for a generalized medium of intercommunication, of mutual criticism through all-around translation from one separated region of experience into another. Thus philosophy as a critical organ becomes in effect a messenger, a liaison officer, making reciprocally intelligible voices speaking provincial tongues, and thereby enlarging as well as rectifying the meanings with which they are charged. . . .

THE SCOPE OF MORAL PHILOSOPHY[6]

In the eighteenth century, the word Morals was used in English literature with a meaning of broad sweep. It included all the subjects of distinctively humane import, all of the social disciplines as far as they are intimately connected with the life of man and as they bear upon the interests of humanity. The pages that follow are intended as a contribution . . . to Morals thus conceived. . . .

Were it not for one consideration, the volume might be said to be an essay in continuing the tradition of David Hume. But it happens that in the usual interpretation of Hume, he is treated simply as a writer who carried philosophical skepticism to its limit. There is sufficient ground in Hume for this way of looking at his work. But it is one-sided. No one can read the introductory remarks with which he prefaced his two chief philosophical writings without realizing that he had also a constructive aim. To a considerable extent local and temporal controversies incident to the period in which he wrote led to an excessive emphasis on the skeptical import of his conclusions. He was so anxious to oppose certain views current and influential in his own day that his original positive aim got obscured and overlaid as he proceeded. In a period in which these other views were themselves dim and unimportant his thought might well have taken a happier turn.

His constructive idea is that a knowledge of human nature provides a map or chart of all humane and social subjects, and that with this chart in our possession we can find our way intelligently about through all the complexities of the phenomena of economics, politics, religious beliefs, etc. Indeed, he went further, and held that human nature gives also the key to the sciences of the physical world, since when all is said and done they are also the products of the workings of the human mind. It is likely that in enthusiasm for a new idea, Hume carried it too far. But there is to my mind an inexpugnable element of truth in his teachings. Human nature is at least a contributing factor to the *form* which even natural science takes, although it may not give the key to its *content* in the degree which Hume supposed.

But in the social subjects, he was on safer ground. Here at least we are in the presence of facts in which human nature is truly central and where a knowledge of human nature is necessary to enable us to thread our way through the tangled scene. If Hume erred in his use of his key, it was because he failed to note the reaction of social institutions and conditions upon the ways in which human nature expresses itself. He saw the part played by the structure and operations of our common nature in shaping social life. He failed to see with equal clearness the reflex influence of the latter upon the shape which a plastic human nature takes because of its social environment. He emphasized habit and custom, but he failed to see that custom is essentially a fact of associated living whose force is dominant in forming the habits of individuals. . . .

REFLECTIVE MORALITY AND CHOICE[7]

Realization that the need for reflective morality and for moral theories grows out of conflict between ends, responsibilities, rights, and duties defines the service which moral theory may render, and also protects the student from false conceptions of its nature. The difference between customary and reflective morality is precisely that definite precepts, rules, definitive injunctions and prohibitions issue from the former, while they cannot proceed from the latter. Confusion ensues when appeal to rational principles is treated as if it were merely a substitute for custom, transferring the authority of moral commands from one source to another. Moral theory can (i) generalize the types of moral conflicts which arise, thus enabling a perplexed and doubtful individual to clarify his own particular problem by placing it in a larger context; it can (ii) state the leading ways in which such problems have been intellectually dealt with by those who have thought upon such matters; it can (iii) render personal reflection more systematic and enlightened, suggesting alternatives that might otherwise be overlooked, and stimulating greater consistency in judgment. But it does not offer a table of commandments in a catechism in which answers are as definite as are the questions which are asked. It can render personal choice more intelligent, but it cannot take the place of personal decision, which must be made in every case of moral perplexity. Such at least is the standpoint of the discussions which follow; the student who expects more from moral theory will be disappointed. The conclusion follows from the very nature of reflective morality; the attempt to set up ready-made conclusions contradicts the very nature of reflective morality.

1. *Encyclopaedia of the Social Sciences* XII (New York: The Macmillan Company, 1934), pp. 118–28.

2. *Philosophy and Civilization* (New York: Minton, Balch and Company, 1931), pp. 10–12.

3. *Experience and Nature*, 2d ed. rev. (Chicago: Open Court Publishing Company, 1929). Selections are taken from the facsimile edition by Dover Publications (New York: 1958), pp. 3–8, 16–23, 36–37, 38–39. Heading provided by the editor. All subsequent selections from *Experience and Nature* are taken from the Dover edition.

4. *Ibid.*, pp. 398, 403–04, 406–08, 409–10. Heading provided by the editor.

5. *Ibid.*, pp. 76–77.

6. *Human Nature and Conduct,* foreword to the Modern Library edition (New York: Random House, n.d.), pp. v–vii. Heading provided by the editor. *Human Nature and Conduct* was first published by Henry Holt and Company (New York: 1922). All further selections will be from the Modern Library edition.

7. *Ethics*, rev. ed. (New York: Henry Holt and Company, 1932), pp. 175–76. Written by Dewey and James H. Tufts, this book was characterized by the authors as "throughout a joint work." Nevertheless, each of them individually assumed responsibility for writing specific chapters. The present selection and all those subsequent to it from the *Ethics* were written by Dewey. Heading provided by the editor.

Man,
Nature,
and
Society

2

*The four articles reprinted in this section summarize many of Dewey's
views concerning human nature as a functional constituent of more inclusive natural processes. As noted in the introduction to this anthology,
elucidating the continuities of man, nature, and society is crucial to the
process of deliberately enriching life experience.*

*All of the continuities of man and nature are understood in terms of
a fundamental conception derived from the theory of biological evolution: the living organism and its environment together constitute an
inclusive functional system, or process. This view stands in radical contrast to the antecedent theories, which regarded human nature as a
fixed and self-enclosed system, and likewise the external world. The
nature of each system was thought to be utterly independent of the
nature of the other. These conceptions render wholly opaque the genuine
possibilities of human nature to function in a creative and consummatory way. The biological point of view replaces the dualistic view.
While Darwinism was being greeted with nearly universal dismay,
Dewey discovered it to be the richest source of ideas for human benefit. A specimen of his conclusions on this topic is provided in the first
article below.*

*The second article offers Dewey's summary account of the revolution
in the view of the world created by recent physical theory. His intention is to indicate the implications of physical theory for the nature of
human individuation.*

*In the third article he is again contending for the continuities of
natural and human processes. It is only in social interaction that human
beings develop mind, rational discourse, and instrumentalities of inference. With the emergence of these functions, nature becomes mean-*

ingful and variable: novel traits of nature emerge in this context. Social interaction is the condition of bringing nature to its greatest fruition.

Dewey was repeatedly engaged in analyzing the social determinants of human nature. The abiding concern with the importance of the social continues in the fourth selection, which is a summary account of his contention that human nature is socially constituted. A sound, healthy, and productive individuality is the creature of society, just as is a fragmented and destructive individual. Like Plato and Aristotle, Dewey regards the community as the source of human excellence. Accordingly, knowledge of the conditions of a good society is the most precious knowledge. When individuals function in ways that destroy community, they destroy not only the good of others, but the conditions of their own good as well.[1]

THE INFLUENCE OF DARWINISM ON PHILOSOPHY[2]

I

That the publication of the *Origin of Species* marked an epoch in the development of the natural sciences is well known to the layman. That the combination of the very words origin and species embodied an intellectual revolt and introduced a new intellectual temper is easily overlooked by the expert. The conceptions that had reigned in the philosophy of nature and knowledge for two thousand years, the conceptions that had become the familiar furniture of the mind, rested on the assumption of the superiority of the fixed and final; they rested upon treating change and origin as signs of defect and unreality. In laying hands upon the sacred ark of absolute permanency, in treating the forms that had been regarded as types of fixity and perfection as originating and passing away, the *Origin of Species* introduced a mode of thinking that in the end was bound to transform the logic of knowledge, and hence the treatment of morals, politics, and religion.

No wonder, then, that the publication of Darwin's book, a half-century ago, precipitated a crisis. The true nature of the controversy is easily concealed from us, however, by the theological clamor that attended it. The vivid and popular features of the anti-Darwinian row tended to leave the impression that the issue was between science on one side and theology on the other. Such was not the case—the issue lay primarily within science itself, as Darwin himself early recognized. The theological outcry he discounted from the start, hardly noticing it save as it bore upon the "feelings of his female relatives." But for two decades before final publication he contemplated the possibility of being put down by his scientific peers as a fool or as crazy; and he set, as the measure of his success, the degree in which he should affect three men of science: Lyell in geology, Hooker in botany, and Huxley in zoology.

Religious considerations lent fervor to the controversy, but they did not provoke it. Intellectually, religious emotions are not creative but conservative. They attach themselves readily to the current view of the world and consecrate it. They steep and dye intellectual fabrics in the seething vat of emotions; they do not form their warp and woof. There is not, I think, an instance of any large idea about the world being independently generated by religion. Although the ideas that rose up like armed men against Darwinism owed their intensity to religious associations, their origin and meaning are to be sought in science and philosophy, not in religion.

II

Few words in our language foreshorten intellectual history as much as does the word species. The Greeks, in initiating the intellectual life of Europe, were impressed by characteristic traits of the life of plants and animals; so impressed indeed that they made these traits the key to defining nature and to explaining mind and society. And truly, life is so wonderful that a seemingly successful reading of its mystery might well lead men to believe that the key to the secrets of heaven and earth was in their hands. The Greek rendering of this mystery, the Greek formulation of the aim and standard of knowledge, was in the course of time embodied in the word species, and it controlled philosophy for two thousand years. To understand the intellectual face-about expressed in the phrase "Origin of Species," we must, then, understand the long-dominant idea against which it is a protest.

Consider how men were impressed by the facts of life. Their eyes fell upon certain things slight in bulk, and frail in structure. To every appearance, these perceived things were inert and passive. Suddenly, under certain circumstances, these things—henceforth known as seeds or eggs or germs—begin to change, to change rapidly in size, form, and qualities. Rapid and extensive changes occur, however, in many things—as when wood is touched by fire. But the changes in the living thing are orderly; they are cumulative; they tend constantly in one direction; they do not, like other changes, destroy or consume, or pass fruitless into wandering flux; they realize and fulfill. Each successive stage, no matter how unlike its predecessor, preserves its net effect and also prepares the way for a fuller activity on the part of its successor. In living beings, changes do not happen as they seem to happen elsewhere, any which way; the earlier changes are regulated in view of later results. This progressive organization does not cease till there is achieved a true final term, a τελὸs, a completed, perfected end. This final form exercises in turn a plenitude of functions, not the least noteworthy of which is production of germs like those from which it took its own origin, germs capable of the same cycle of self-fulfilling activity.

But the whole miraculous tale is not yet told. The same drama is enacted to the same destiny in countless myriads of individuals so sundered in time, so severed in space, that they have no opportunity for mutual consultation and no means of interaction. As an old writer quaintly said, "things of the same kind go through the same formalities"—celebrate, as it were, the same ceremonial rites.

This formal activity which operates throughout a series of changes and holds them to a single course; which subordinates their aimless flux to its own perfect manifestation; which, leaping the boundaries of space and time, keeps individuals distant in space and remote in time to a uniform type of structure and function: this principle seemed to give insight into the very nature of reality itself. To it Aristotle gave the name, εἶδος. This term the scholastics translated as *species*.

The force of this term was deepened by its application to everything in the universe that observes order in flux and manifests constancy through change. From the casual drift of daily weather, through the uneven recurrence of seasons and unequal return of seed time and harvest, up to the majestic sweep of the heavens—the image of eternity in time—and from this to the unchanging pure and contemplative intelligence beyond nature lies one unbroken fulfillment of ends. Nature as a whole is a progressive realization of purpose strictly comparable to the realization of purpose in any single plant or animal.

The conception of εἶδος, species, a fixed form and final cause, was the central principle of knowledge as well as of nature. Upon it rested the logic of science. Change as change is mere flux and lapse; it insults intelligence. Genuinely to know is to grasp a permanent end that realizes itself through changes, holding them thereby within the metes and bounds of fixed truth. Completely to know is to relate all special forms to their one single end and good: pure contemplative intelligence. Since, however, the scene of nature which directly confronts us is in change, nature as directly and practically experienced does not satisfy the conditions of knowledge. Human experience is in flux, and hence the instrumentalities of sense-perception and of inference based upon observation are condemned in advance. Science is compelled to aim at realities lying behind and beyond the processes of nature, and to carry on its search for these realities by means of rational forms transcending ordinary modes of perception and inference.

There are, indeed, but two alternative courses. We must either find the appropriate objects and organs of knowledge in the mutual interactions of changing things; or else, to escape the infection of change, we *must* seek them in some transcendent and supernal region. The human mind, deliberately, as it were, exhausted the logic of the changeless, the final, and the transcendent, before it essayed adventure on the pathless wastes of generation and transformation. We dispose all too easily of the efforts of the schoolmen to interpret nature and mind in terms of real essences, hidden forms, and occult faculties, forgetful of the seriousness and dignity of the ideas that lay behind. We dispose of them by laughing at the famous gentleman who accounted for the fact that opium put people to sleep on the ground it had a dormitive faculty. But the doctrine, held in our own day, that knowledge of the plant that yields the poppy consists in referring the peculiarities of an individual to a type, to a universal form, a doctrine so firmly established that any other method of knowing was conceived to be unphilosophical and unscientific, is a survival of precisely the same logic. This identity of conception in the scholastic and anti-Darwinian theory may well suggest greater sympathy for what has become unfamiliar as well as greater humility regarding the further unfamiliarities that history has in store.

Darwin was not, of course, the first to question the classic philosophy of nature and of knowledge. The beginnings of the revolution are in the physical science of the sixteenth and seventeenth centuries. When Galileo said: "It is my opinion that the earth is very noble and admirable by reason of so many and so different alterations and generations which are incessantly made therein," he expressed the changed temper that was coming over the world; the transfer of interest from the permanent to the changing. When Descartes said: "The nature of physical things is much more easily conceived when they are beheld coming gradually into existence, than when they are only considered as produced at once in a finished and perfect state," the modern world became self-conscious of the logic that was henceforth to control it, the logic of which Darwin's *Origin of Species* is the latest scientific achievement. Without the methods of Copernicus, Kepler, Galileo, and their successors in astronomy, physics, and chemistry, Darwin would have been helpless in the organic sciences. But prior to Darwin the impact of the new scientific method upon life, mind, and politics, had been arrested, because between these ideal or moral interests and the inorganic world intervened the kingdom of plants and animals. The gates of the garden of life were barred to the new ideas; and only through this garden was there access to mind and politics. The influence of Darwin upon philosophy resides in his having conquered the phenomena of life for the principle of transition, and thereby freed the new logic for application to mind and morals and life. When he said of species what Galileo had said of the earth, *e pur se muove*, he emancipated, once for all, genetic and experimental ideas as an organon of asking questions and looking for explanations.

III

The exact bearings upon philosophy of the new logical outlook are, of course, as yet, uncertain and inchoate. We live in the twilight of intellectual transition. One must add the rashness of the prophet to the stubbornness of the partisan to venture a systematic exposition of the influence upon philosophy of the Darwinian method. At best, we can but inquire as to its general bearing—the effect upon mental temper and complexion, upon that body of half-conscious, half-instinctive intellectual aversions and preferences which determine, after all, our more deliberate intellectual enterprises. In this vague inquiry there happens to exist as a kind of touchstone a problem of long historic currency that has also been much discussed in Darwinian literature. I refer to the old problem of design *versus* chance, mind *versus* matter, as the causal explanation, first or final, of things.

As we have already seen, the classic notion of species carried with it the idea of purpose. In all living forms, a specific type is present directing the earlier stages of growth to the realization of its own perfection. Since this purposive regulative principle is not visible to the senses, it follows that it must be an ideal or rational force. Since, however, the perfect form is gradually approximated through the sensible changes, it also follows that in and through a sensible realm a rational ideal force is working out its own ultimate manifestation. These inferences were extended to nature: (*a*) She does nothing in vain; but all for an ulterior purpose. (*b*) Within natural sensible events there is therefore contained a spiritual causal force, which as spiritual escapes perception, but is apprehended by an enlightened reason. (*c*) The manifestation of this principle brings about a subordination of matter and sense to its own realization, and this ultimate fulfillment is the goal of nature and of man. The design argument thus operated in two directions. Purposefulness accounted for the intelligibility of nature and the possibility of science, while the absolute or cosmic character of this purposefulness gave sanction and worth to the moral and religious endeavors of man. Science was underpinned and morals authorized by one and the same principle, and their mutual agreement was eternally guaranteed.

This philosophy remained, in spite of skeptical and polemic outbursts, the official and the regnant philosophy of Europe for over two thousand years. The expulsion of fixed first and final causes from astronomy, physics, and chemistry had indeed given the doctrine something of a shock. But, on the other hand, increased acquaintance with the details of plant and animal life operated as a counterbalance and perhaps even strengthened the argument from design. The marvelous adaptations of organisms to their environment, of organs to the organism, of unlike parts of a complex organ—like the eye— to the organ itself; the foreshadowing by lower forms of the higher; the preparation in earlier stages of growth for organs that only later had their functioning—these things were increasingly recognized with the progress of botany, zoology, paleontology, and embryology. Together, they added such prestige to the design argument that by the late eighteenth century it was, as approved by the sciences of organic life, the central point of theistic and idealistic philosophy.

The Darwinian principle of natural selection cut straight under this philosophy. If all organic adaptations are due simply to constant variation and the elimination of those variations which are harmful in the struggle for existence that is brought about by excessive reproduction, there is no call for a prior intelligent causal force to plan and preordain them. Hostile critics charged Darwin with materialism and with making chance the cause of the universe.

Some naturalists, like Asa Gray, favored the Darwinian principle and attempted to reconcile it with design. Gray held to what may be called design on the installment plan. If we conceive the "stream of variations" to be itself tempted to reconcile it with design. Gray held to what may be called design the first to be selected. In that case, variation, struggle, and selection simply define the mechanism of "secondary causes" through which the "first cause" acts; and the doctrine of design is none the worse off because we know more of its *modus operandi*.

Darwin could not accept this mediating proposal. He admits or rather he asserts that it is "impossible to conceive this immense and wonderful universe including man with his capacity of looking far backwards and far into futurity as the result of blind chance or necessity."[*] But nevertheless he holds that since variations are in useless as well as useful directions, and since the latter are sifted out simply by the stress of the conditions of struggle for existence, the design argument as applied to living beings is unjustifiable; and its lack of support there deprives it of scientific value as applied to nature in general. If the variations of the pigeon, which under artificial selection give the pouter pigeon, are not preordained for the sake of the breeder, by what logic do we argue that variations resulting in natural species are predesigned?[†]

IV

So much for some of the more obvious facts of the discussion of design *versus* chance, as causal principles of nature and of life as a whole. We brought up this discussion, you recall, as a crucial instance. What does our touchstone indicate as to the bearing of Darwinian ideas upon philosophy? In the first place, the new logic outlaws, flanks, dismisses—what you will— one type of problems and substitutes for it another type. Philosophy forswears inquiry after absolute origins and absolute finalities in order to explore specific values and the specific conditions that generate them.

Darwin concluded that the impossibility of assigning the world to chance as a whole and to design in its parts indicated the insolubility of the question. Two radically different reasons, however, may be given as to why a problem is

[*]*Life and Letters*, Vol. I., p. 282; cf. 285.
[†]*Life and Letters*, Vol. II., pp. 146, 170, 245; Vol. I., pp. 283–84.
See also the closing portion of his "Variations of Animals and Plants under Domestication."

insoluble. One reason is that the problem is too high for intelligence; the other
is that the question in its very asking makes assumptions that render the question meaningless. The latter alternative is unerringly pointed to in the celebrated
case of design *versus* chance. Once admit that the sole verifiable or fruitful
object of knowledge is the particular set of changes that generate the object of
study together with the consequences that then flow from it, and no intelligible
question can be asked about what, by assumption, lies outside. To assert—
as is often asserted—that specific values of particular truth, social bonds and
forms of beauty, if they can be shown to be generated by concretely knowable conditions, are meaningless and in vain; to assert that they are justified
only when they and their particular causes and effects have all at once been
gathered up into some inclusive first cause and some exhaustive final goal,
is inellectual atavism. Such argumentation is reversion to the logic that
explained the extinction of fire by water through the formal essence of
aqueousness and the quenching of thirst by water through the final cause of
aqueousness. Whether used in the case of the special event or that of life as
a whole, such logic only abstracts some aspect of the existing course of events
in order to reduplicate it as a petrified eternal principle by which to explain
the very changes of which it is the formalization.

When Henry Sidgwick casually remarked in a letter that as he grew older
his interest in what or who made the world was altered into interest in what
kind of a world it is anyway, his voicing of a common experience of our own
day illustrates also the nature of that intellectual transformation effected by
the Darwinian logic. Interest shifts from the wholesale essence back of special
changes to the question of how special changes serve and defeat concrete
purposes; shifts from an intelligence that shaped things once for all to the
particular intelligences which things are even now shaping; shifts from an
ultimate goal of good to the direct increments of justice and happiness that
intelligent administration of existent conditions may beget and that present
carelessness or stupidity will destroy or forgo.

In the second place, the classic type of logic inevitably set philosophy
upon proving that life *must* have certain qualities and values—no matter
how experience presents the matter—because of some remote cause and
eventual goal. The duty of wholesale justification inevitably accompanies all
thinking that makes the meaning of special occurrences depend upon something that once and for all lies behind them. The habit of derogating from
present meanings and uses prevents our looking the facts of experience in the
face; it prevents serious acknowledgment of the evils they present and serious
concern with the goods they promise but do not as yet fulfill. It turns thought
to the business of finding a wholesale transcendent remedy for the one and
guarantee for the other. One is reminded of the way many moralists and
theologians greeted Herbert Spencer's recognition of an unknowable energy
from which welled up the phenomenal physical processes without and the

conscious operations within. Merely because Spencer labeled his unknowable energy "God," this faded piece of metaphysical goods was greeted as an important and grateful concession to the reality of the spiritual realm. Were it not for the deep hold of the habit of seeking justification for ideal values in the remote and transcendent, surely this reference of them to an unknowable absolute would be despised in comparison with the demonsrations of experience that knowable energies are daily generating about us precious values.

The displacing of this wholesale type of philosophy will doubtless not arrive by sheer logical disproof, but rather by growing recognition of its futility. Were it a thousand times true that opium produces sleep because of its dormitive energy, yet the inducing of sleep in the tired, and the recovery to waking life of the poisoned, would not be thereby one least step forwarded. And were it a thousand times dialctically demonstrated that life as a whole is regulated by a transcendent principle to a final inclusive goal, none the less truth and error, health and disease, good and evil, hope and fear in the concrete, would remain just what and where they now are. To improve our education, to ameliorate our manners, to advance our politics, we must have recourse to specific conditions of generation.

Finally, the new logic introduces responsibility into the intellectual life. To idealize and rationalize the universe at large is after all a confession of inability to master the courses of things that specifically concern us. As long as mankind suffered from this impotency, it naturally shifted a burden of responsibility that it could not carry over to the more competent shoulders of the transcendent cause. But if insight into specific conditions of value and into specific consequences of ideas is possible, philosophy must in time become a method of locating and interpreting the more serious of the conflicts that occur in life, and a method of projecting ways for dealing with them: a method of moral and political diagnosis and prognosis.

The claim to formulate *a priori* the legislative constitution of the universe is by its nature a claim that may lead to elaborate dialectic developments. But it is also one that removes these very conclusions from subjection to experimental test, for, by definition, these results make no differences in the detailed course of events. But a philosophy that humbles its pretensions to the work of projecting hypotheses for the education and conduct of mind, individual and social, is thereby subjected to test by the way in which the ideas it propounds work out in practice. In having modesty forced upon it, philosophy also acquires responsibility.

Doubtless I seem to have violated the implied promise of my earlier remarks and to have turned both prophet and partisan. But in anticipating the direction of the transformations in philosophy to be wrought by the Darwinian genetic and experimental logic, I do not profess to speak for any save those who yield themselves consciously or unconsciously to this logic. No one can fairly deny that at present there are two effects of the Darwinian mode of thinking. On the one hand, there are many making sincere and vital efforts to revise our traditional philosophic conceptions in accordance with its demands. On the other hand, there is as definitely a recrudescence of absolutistic philosophies; an assertion of a type of philosophic knowing distinct from that of the sciences, one which opens to us another kind of reality from that to which the sciences give access; an appeal through experience to something that essentially goes beyond experience. This reaction affects popular creeds and religious movements as well as technical philosophies. The very conquest of the biological sciences by the new ideas has led many to proclaim an explicit and rigid separation of philosophy from science.

Old ideas give way slowly; for they are more than abstract logical forms and categories. They are habits, predispositions, deeply engrained attitudes of aversion and preference. Moreover, the conviction persists—though history shows it to be a hallucination—that all the questions that the human mind has asked are questions that can be answered in terms of the alternatives that the questions themselves present. But in fact intellectual progress usually occurs through sheer abandonment of questions together with both of the alternatives they assume—an abandonment that results from their decreasing vitality and a change of urgent interest. We do not solve them: we get over them. Old questions are solved by disappearing, evaporating, while new questions corresponding to the changed attitude of endeavor and preference take their place. Doubtless the greatest dissolvent in contemporary thought of old questions, the greatest precipitant of new methods, new intentions, new problems, is the one effected by the scientific revolution that found its climax in the *Origin of Species*.

TIME AND INDIVIDUALITY[3]

The Greeks had a saying "Count no man happy till after his death." The adage was a way of calling attention to the uncertainties of life. No one knows what a year or even a day may bring forth. The healthy become ill; the rich poor; the mighty are cast down; fame changes to obloquy. Men live at the mercy of forces they cannot control. Belief in fortune and luck, good or evil, is one of the most widespread and persistent of human beliefs. Chance has been deified by many peoples. Fate has been set up as an overlord to whom even the Gods must bow. Belief in a Goddess of Luck is in ill repute among pious folk but their belief in providence is a tribute to the fact no individual controls his own destiny.

The uncertainty of life and one's final lot has always been associated with mutability, while unforeseen and uncontrollable change has been linked with time. Time is the tooth that gnaws; it is the destroyer; we are born only to die and every day brings us one day nearer death. This attitude is not confined to the ignorant and vulgar. It is the root of what is sometimes called the instinctive belief in immortality. Everything perishes in time but men are unable to believe that perishing is the last word. For centuries poets made the uncertainty which time brings with it the theme of their discourse—read Shakespeare's sonnets. Nothing stays; life is fleeting and all earthly things are transitory.

It was not then for metaphysical reasons that classic philosophy maintained that change and consequently time, are marks of inferior reality, holding that true and ultimate reality is immutable and eternal. Human reasons, all too human, have given birth to the idea that over and beyond the lower realm of things that shift like the sands on the seashore there is the kingdom of the unchanging, of the complete, the perfect. The grounds for the belief are couched in the technical language of philosophy, but the cause for the grounds is the heart's desire for surcease from change, struggle, and uncertainty. The eternal and immutable is the consummation of mortal man's quest for certainty.

It is not strange then that philosophies which have been at odds on every other point have been one in the conviction that the ultimately real is fixed and unchanging, even though they have been as far apart as the poles in their ideas of its constitution. The idealist has found it in a realm of rational ideas; the materialist in the laws of matter. The mechanist pins his faith to eternal atoms and to unmoved and unmoving space. The teleologist finds that all change is subservient to fixed ends and final goals, which are the one steadfast thing in the universe, conferring upon changing things whatever meaning and value they possess. The typical realist attributes to unchanging essences a greater degree of reality than belongs to existences; the modern mathematical realist finds the stability his heart desires in the immunity of the realm of possibilities from vicissitude. Although classic rationalism looked askance at experience and empirical things because of their continual subjection to alteration, yet strangely enough traditional sensational empiricism relegated time to a secondary role. Sensations appeared and disappeared but in their own nature they were as fixed as were Newtonian atoms—of which indeed they were mental copies. Ideas were but weakened copies of sensory impressions and had no inherent forward power and application. The passage of time dimmed their vividness and caused their decay. Because of their subjection to the tooth of time, they were denied productive force.

In the late eighteenth and the greater part of the nineteenth centuries appeared the first marked cultural shift in the attitude taken toward change. Under the names of indefinite perfectability, progress, and evolution, the movement of things in the universe itself and of the universe as a whole began to take on a beneficent instead of a hateful aspect. Not every change was regarded as a sign of advance but the general trend of change, cosmic and social, was thought to be toward the better. Aside from the Christian idea of a millennium of good and bliss to be finally wrought by supernatural means, the Golden Age for the first time in history was placed in the future instead of at the beginning, and change and time were assigned a benevolent role.

Even if the new optimism was not adequately grounded, there were sufficient causes for its occurrence as there are for all great changes in intellectual climate. The rise of new science in the seventeenth century laid hold upon general culture in the next century. Its popular effect was not great, but its influence upon the intellectual elite, even upon those who were not themselves engaged in scientific inquiry, was prodigious. The enlightenment, the *éclairissement*, the *Aufklärung*—names which in the three most advanced countries of Europe testified to the widespread belief that at last light had dawned, that dissipation of the darkness of ignorance, superstition, and bigotry was at hand, and the triumph of reason was assured—for reason was the counterpart in man of the laws of nature which science was disclosing. The reign of law in the natural world was to be followed by the reign of law in human affairs. A vista of the indefinite perfectibility of man was opened. It played a large part in that optimistic theory of automatic evolution which later found its classic formulation in the philosophy of Herbert Spencer. The faith may have been pathetic but it has its own nobility.

At last, time was thought to be working on the side of the good instead of as a destructive agent. Things were moving to an event which was divine, even if far off.

This new philosophy, however, was far from giving the temporal an inherent position and function in the constitution of things. Change was working on the side of man but only because of *fixed* laws which governed the changes that take place. There was hope in change just because the laws that govern it do not change. The locus of the immutable was shifted to scientific natural law, but the faith and hope of philosophers and intellectuals were still tied to the unchanging. The belief that "evolution" is identical with progress was based upon trust in laws which, being fixed, worked automatically toward the final end of freedom, justice, and brotherhood, the natural consequences of the reign of reason.

Not till the late nineteenth century was the doctrine of the subordination of time and change seriously challenged. Bergson and William James, animated by different motives and proceeding by different methods, then installed change at the very heart of things. Bergson took his stand on the primacy of life and consciousness, which are notoriously in a state of flux. He assimilated that which is completely real in the natural world to them, conceiving the static as that which life leaves behind as a deposit as it moves on. From this point of view he criticized mechanistic and teleological theories on the ground that both are guilty of the same error, although from opposite points. Fixed laws which govern change and fixed ends toward which changes tend are both the products of a backward look, one that ignores the forward movement of life. They apply only to that which life has produced and has then left behind in its ongoing vital creative course, a course whose behavior and outcome are unpredictable both mechanically and from the standpoint of ends. The intellect is at home in that which is fixed only because it is done and over with, for intellect is itself just as much a deposit of past life as is the matter to which it is congenial. Intuition alone articulates in the forward thrust of life and alone lays hold of reality.

The animating purpose of James was, on the other hand, primarily moral and artistic. It is expressed, in his phrase, "block universe," employed as a term of adverse criticism. Mechanism and idealism were abhorrent to him because they both hold to a closed universe in which there is no room for novelty and adventure. Both sacrifice individuality and all the values, moral and aesthetic, which hang upon individuality, for according to absolute idealism, as to mechanistic materialism, the individual is simply a part determined by the whole of which he is a part. Only a philosophy of pluralism, of genuine indetermination, and of change which is real and intrinsic gives significance to individuality. It alone justifies struggle in creative activity and gives opportunity for the emergence of the genuinely new.

It was reserved, however, for the present century to give birth to the out-and-out assertion in systematic form that reality *is* process, and that laws as well as things develop in the processes of unceasing change. The modern Heraclitean is Alfred North Whitehead, but he is Heraclitus with a change. The doctrine of the latter, while it held that all things flow like a river and that change is so continuous that a man cannot step into the same river even once (since it changes as he steps), nevertheless also held that there is a fixed order which controls the ebb and flow of the universal tide.

My theme, however, is not historical, nor is it to argue in behalf of any one of the various doctrines regarding time that have been advanced. The purpose of the history just roughly sketched is to indicate that the nature of time and change has now become in its own right a philosophical problem of the first importance. It is of time as a problem that I wish to speak. The aspect of the problem that will be considered is the connection of time with individuality, as the latter is exemplified in the living organism and especially in human beings.

Take the account of the life of any person, whether the account is a biography or an autobiography. The story begins with birth, a temporal incident; it extends to include the temporal existence of parents and ancestry. It does not end with death, for it takes in the influence upon subsequent events of the words and deeds of the one whose life is told. Everything recorded is an historical event; it is something temporal. The individual whose life history is told, be it Socrates or Nero, St. Francis or Abraham Lincoln, is an extensive event; or, if you prefer, it is a course of events each of which takes up into itself something of what went before and leads on to that which comes after. The skill, the art, of the biographer is displayed in his ability to discover and portray the subtle ways, hidden often from the individual himself, in which one event grows out of those which preceded and enters into those which follow. The human individual is himself a history, a career, and for this reason his biography can be related only as a temporal event. That which comes later explains the earlier quite as truly as the earlier explains the later. Take the individual Abraham Lincoln at one year, at five years, at ten years, at thirty years of age, and imagine everything later wiped out, no matter how minutely his life is recorded up to the date set. It is plain beyond the need of words that we then have not his biography but only a fragment of it, while the significance of that fragment is undisclosed. For he did not just exist in a time which externally surrounded him, but time was the heart of his existence.

Temporal seriality is the very essence, then, of the human individual. It is impossible for a biographer in writing, say the story of the first thirty years of the life of Lincoln, not to bear in mind his later career. Lincoln as an individual is a history; any particular event cut off from that history ceases to be a part of his life an an individual. As Lincoln is a particular development in time, so is every other human individual. Individuality is the uniqueness of the history, of the career, not something given once for all at the beginning which then proceeds to unroll as a ball of yarn may be unwound. Lincoln made history. But it is just as true that he made himself as an individual in the history he made.

I have been speaking about human individuality. Now an important part of the problem of time is that what is true of the human individual does not seem to be true of physical individuals. The common saying "as like as two peas" is a virtual denial to one kind of vegetable life of the kind of individuality that marks human beings. It is hard to conceive of the individuality of a given pea in terms of a unique history or career; such individuality as it appears to possess seems to be due in part to spatial separateness and in part to peculiarities that are externally caused. The same thing holds true of lower forms of animal life. Most persons would resent denial of some sort of unique individuality to their own dogs, but would be slow to attribute it to worms, clams, and bees. Indeed, it seems to be an exclusive prerogative of the romantic novelist to find anything in the way of a unique career in animal lives in general.

When we come to inanimate elements, the prevailing view has been that time and sequential change are entirely foreign to their nature. According to this view they do not have careers; they simply change their relations in space. We have only to think of the classic conception of atoms. The Newtonian atom, for example, moved and was moved, thus changing its position in space, but it was unchangeable in its own being. What it was at the beginning or without any beginning it is always and forever. Owing to the impact of other things it changes its direction and velocity of motion so that it comes closer and further away from other things. But all this was believed to be external to its own substantial being. It had no development, no history, because it had no potentialities. In itself it was like a God, the same yesterday, today, and forever. Time did not enter into its being either to corrode or to develop it. Nevertheless, as an ultimate element it was supposed to have some sort of individuality, to be itself and not something else. Time, in physical science, has been simply a measure of motion in space.

Now, this apparently complete unlikeness in kind between the human and the physical individual is a part of the problem of time. Some philosophers have been content to note the difference and to make it the ground for affirming a sheer dualism between man and other things, a ground for assigning to man a spiritual being in contrast with material things. Others, fewer in numbers, have sought to explain away the seeming disparity, holding that the apparent uniqueness of human individuality is specious, being in fact the effect of the vast number of physical molecules, themselves complex, which make up his being, so that what looks like genuine temporal change or development is really but a function of the number and complexity of changes of constituent fixed elements. Of late, there have been a few daring souls who have held that temporal quality and historical career are a mark of everything, including atomic elements, to which individuality may be attributed.

I shall mention some of the reasons from the side of physical science that have led to this third idea. The first reason is the growing recognition that scientific objects are purely relational and have nothing to do with the intrinsic qualities of individual things and nothing to say about them. The meaning of this statement appears most clearly in the case of scientific laws. It is now a commonplace that a physical law states a correlation of changes or of ways and manners of change. The law of gravitation, for example, states a relation which holds between bodies with respect to distance and mass. It needs no argument to show that distance is a relation. Mass was long regarded as an inherent property of ultimate and individual elements. But even the Newtonian conception was obliged to recognize that mass could be defined only in terms of inertia and that inertia could be defined only in terms, on the one hand, of the resistance it offered to the impact of other bodies, and, on the other hand, of its capacity to exercise impact upon them, impact being measured in terms of motion with respect to acceleration. The idea that mass is an inherent property which caused inertia and momentum was simply a holdover from an old metaphysical idea of force. As far as the findings of science are concerned, independent of the intrusion of metaphysical ideas, mass is inertia-momentum and these are strictly measures and relations. The discovery that mass changes with velocity, a discovery made when minute bodies came under consideration, finally forced surrender of the notion that mass is a fixed and inalienable possession of ultimate elements or individuals, so that time is now considered to be their fourth dimension.

It may be remarked incidentally that the recognition of the relational character of scientific objects completely eliminates an old metaphysical issue. One of the outstanding problems created by the rise of modern science was due to the fact that scientific definitions and descriptions are framed in terms in which qualities play no part. Qualities were wholly superfluous. As long as the idea persisted (an inheritance from Greek metaphysical science) that the business of knowledge is to penetrate into the inner being of objects, the existence of qualities like colors, sounds, etc., was embarrassing. The usual way of dealing with them is to declare that they are merely subjective, existing only in the consciousness of individual knowers. Given the old idea that the purpose of knowledge (represented at its best in science) is to penetrate into the heart of reality and reveal its "true" nature, the conclusion was a logical one. The discovery that the objects of scientific knowledge are purely relational shows that the problem is an artificial one. It was "solved" by the discovery that it needed no solution, since fulfillment of the function and business of science compels disregard of qualities. Using the older language, it was seen that so-called primary qualities are no more inherent properties of ultimate objects than are so-called secondary qualities of odors, sounds, and colors, since the former are also strictly relational; or, as Locke stated in his moments of clear insight, are "retainers" of objects in their connections with other things. The discovery of the nonscientific because of the empirically unverifiable and unnecessary character of absolute space, absolute motion, and absolute time gave the final *coup de grâce* to the traditional idea that solidity, mass, size, etc., are inherent possessions of ultimate individuals. . . .

As long as scientific knowledge was supposed to be concerned with individuals in their own intrinsic nature, there was no way to bridge the gap between the career of human individuals and that of physical individuals, save by holding that the seeming fundamental place of development and hence of time in the life histories of the former is only seeming or specious. The unescapable conclusion is that as human individuality can be understood only in terms of time as fundamental reality, so for physical individuals time is not simply a measure of predetermined changes in mutual positions, but is something that enters into their being. Laws do not "govern" the activity of individuals. They are a formulation of the frequency-distributions of the behavior of large numbers of individuals engaged in interactions with one another.

This statement does not mean that physical and human individuality are identical, nor that the things which appear to us to be nonliving have the distinguishing characteristic of organisms. The difference between the inanimate and the animate is not so easily wiped out. But it does show that there is no fixed gap between them. The conclusion which most naturally follows, without indulging in premature speculations, is that the principle of a developing career applies to all things in nature, as well as to human beings —that they are born, undergo qualitative changes, and finally die, giving place to other individuals. The idea of development applied to nature involves differences of forms and qualities as surely as it rules out absolute breaches of continuity. The differences between the amoeba and the human organism are genuinely there even if we accept the idea of organic evolution of species. Indeed, to deny the reality of the differences and their immense significance would be to deny the very idea of development. To wipe out differences because of denial of complete breaks and the need for intervention of some outside power is just as surely a way to deny development as is assertion of gaps which can be bridged only by the intervention of some supernatural force. It is then in terms of development, or if one prefers the more grandiose term, evolution, that I shall further discuss the problem of time.

The issue involved is perhaps the most fundamental one in philosophy at the present time. Are the changes which go on in the world simply external redistributions, rearrangements in space of what previously existed, or are they genuine qualitative changes such as apparently take place in the physiological development of an organism, from the union of ovum and sperm to maturity, and as apparently take place in the personal life career of individuals? When the question is raised, certain misapprehensions must be first guarded against. Development and evolution have historically been eulogistically interpreted. They have been thought of as necessarily proceeding from the lower to the higher, from the relatively worse to the relatively better. But this property was read in from outside moral and theological preoccupations. The real issue is that stated above: Is what happens simply a spatial rearrangement of what existed previously or does it involve something qualitatively new? From this point of view, cancer is as genuinely a physiological development as is growth in vigor; criminals as well as heroes are a social development; the emergence of totalitarian states is a social evolution out of constitutional states independently of whether we like or approve them.

If we accept the intrinsic connection of time with individuality, they are not mere redistributions of what existed before.

Since it is a *problem* I am presenting, I shall assume that genuine transformations occur, and consider its implications. First and negatively, the idea (which is often identified with the essential meaning of evolution) is excluded that development is a process of unfolding what was previously implicit or latent. Positively it is implied that potentiality is a category of existence, for development cannot occur unless an individual has powers or capacities that are not actualized at a given time. But it also means that these powers are not unfolded from within, but are called out through interaction with other things. While it is necessary to revive the category of potentiality as a characteristic of individuality, it has to be revived in a different form from that of its classic Aristotelian formulation. According to that view, potentialities are connected with a *fixed* end which the individual endeavors by its own nature or essence to actualize, although its success in actualization depended upon the cooperation of external things and hence might be thwarted by the "accidents" of its surroundings—as not every acorn becomes a tree and few if any acorns become the typical oak.

When the idea that development is due to some indwelling end which tends to control the series of changes passed through is abandoned, potentialities must be thought of in terms of consequences of interactions with other things. Hence potentialities cannot be *known* till *after* the interactions have occurred. There are at a given time unactualized potentialities in an individual because and in as far as there are in existence other things with which it has not yet interacted. Potentialities of milk are known today, for example, that were not known a generation ago, because milk has been brought into interaction with things other than organisms, and hence now has other than furnishing nutriment consequence. It is now predicted that in the future human beings will be wearing clothes made of glass and that the clothes will be cleaned by throwing them into a hot furnace. Whether this particular prediction is fulfilled or not makes no difference to its value as an illustration. Every new scientific discovery leads to some mode of technology that did not previously exist. As things are brought by new procedures into new contacts and new interactions, new consequences are produced and the power to produce these new consequences is a recognized potentiality of the thing in question. The idea that potentialities are inherent and fixed by relation to a predetermined end was a product of a highly restricted state of technology. . . .

. . . I said earlier that the traditional idea of progress and evolution was based upon belief that the fixed structure of the universe is such as automatically brings it about. This optimistic and fatalistic idea is now at a discount. It is easy in the present state of the world to deny all validity whatever to the idea of progress, since so much of the human world seems bent on demonstrating the truth of the old theological doctrine of the fall of man. But the real conclusion is that, while progress is not inevitable, it is up to men as individuals to bring it about. Change is going to occur anyway, and the problem is the control of change in a given direction. The direction, the quality of change, is a matter of individuality. Surrender of individuality by the many to some one who is taken to be a superindividual explains the retrograde movement of society. Dictatorships and totalitarian states, and belief in the inevitability of this or that result coming to pass are, strange as it may sound, ways of denying the reality of time and the creativeness of the individual. Freedom of thought and of expression are not mere rights to be claimed. They have their roots deep in the existence of individuals as developing careers in time. Their denial and abrogation is an abdication of individuality and a virtual rejection of time as opportunity. . . .

SOCIAL AS A CATEGORY[4]

There are at the present time a considerable number of persons who habitually employ the social as a principle of philosophic reflection and who assign it a force equal and even superior to that ascribed the physical, vital and mental. There are others, probably a greater number, who decline to take "social" seriously as a category of description and interpretation for purposes of philosophy, and who conceive any attempt so to take it as involving a confusion of anthropology and sociology with metaphysics. The most they would concede is that cultural material may throw light on the genesis and history of human beliefs about ultimate subject-matter. But it is asserted that it is but a case of the familiar genetic fallacy, the confusion of the history of belief with the nature of that believed, to assign to such an account a place anywhere except within the history of human culture. Such a situation solicits attention; and I desire to state as far as time permits what is the intent of those who attribute genuine philosophic import to the idea of the social.

A start may be conveniently made by noting that associated or conjoint behavior is a universal characteristic of all existences. Knowledge is in terms of related objects and unless it is supposed that relations are a subjective intrusion, or that, *a la* Hume, only *ideas* are associated, relation as the nerve of science correlates with association among things. This fact being noted, we observe that the qualities of associated things are displayed only in association, since in interactions alone are potentialities released and actualized. Furthermore, the manifestation of potentialities varies with the manner and range of association. This statement is only a formal way of calling attention to the fact that we characterize an element, say hydrogen, not only, as the name implies, in terms of its water-forming potentiality but ultimately in terms of consequences effected in a whole range of modes of conjoint behavior.*

These considerations being premised, attention fastens upon the fact that the more numerous and varied the forms of association into which anything enters, the better basis we have for describing and understanding it, for the more complex is an association the more fully are potentialities released for

---

*In case there is objection to the use of the conceptions of potentiality and actualization, it may be pointed out that the same facts may be stated, though as it seems to me more awkwardly, by saying that things in different modes of association occasion different effects and that our knowledge of them is adequate in the degree in which it includes a broad range of effects due to a variety of associated operations.

observation. Since things present themselves to us in such fashion that narrower and wider ranges, simpler and more complex ones, are readily distinguished, it would appear that metaphysical description and understanding is demarcated as that which has to do with the widest and fullest range of associated activity. And I remark that if the phrase "degrees of reality" can be given an empirically intelligible meaning, that meaning would seem to depend upon following out the line of thought thus suggested.* In short, there appears to be a fairly straight road to the conclusion that a just gauge of the adequacy of any philosophic account of things is found in the extent to which that account is based upon taking things in the widest and most complex scale of associations open to observation.

In making this statement I am not unaware that the opposite method has been pursued and is still recommended by philosophers in good repute: namely, a method based on predilection for ultimate and unattached simples, called by various writers essences, data, etc. The question of whether we should begin with the simple or the complex appears to me the most important problem in philosophic method at the present time, cutting under, for example, the traditional distinctions of real and ideal. Or, if it be said that while perforce we are compelled psychologically and practically to begin with the complex but that *philosophy* begins only when we have come upon simples, the problem of method still remains. Are these simples isolated and self-sufficient, or are they the results of intellectual analysis, themselves intellectual rather than existential in quality, and therefore of value only in the degree in which they afford us means of arriving at a better understanding of the complex wholes with which we began? Time forbids consideration of this fundamental question. I content myself with observing that the hypothesis that ultimate and detached simples are the only reals for philosophy seems to be the sole logical alternative to the position that the wider and more complex the range of associated interaction with which we deal the more fully is the nature of the object of philosophic thought revealed to us. Hence, the issue as to method reduces itself to the question whether isolated simples can be asserted without self-contradiction to be ultimate and self-sufficient on their own account. Those who do not accept them as the real, appear committed to the position herein stated.

While the fact of association and of range of associations as determining "degrees of reality" gives us our starting point, it gives *only* a starting point for discussing the value of "social" as a philosophic category. For by the social as a distinctive mode of association is denoted specifically human forms of grouping, and these according to the findings of science appear only late in time. Hence, the objection which readily occurs to mind. The

---

*It is perhaps worth while in passing to note also that such concepts as "levels" and "emergence" seem to be most readily definable upon the basis of this consideration.

view that "social" in its characteristically human sense is an important category is met with the retort that, on the contrary, it is but a highly special case of association and as such is restricted in significance, humanly interesting of course, but a matter of detail rather than of an important principle. My introductory remarks were intended as an anticipatory reply to such an objection. Association barely by itself is a wholly formal category. It acquires content only by considering the different forms of association which constitute the material of experience. Thus, while it is admitted that society, in the human sense, is a form of association that is restricted in its space-time manifestation, it cannot be placed in contrast with association in general. Its import can be determined not by comparing it with association in its generic formal sense, but only by comparing and contrasting it with other special types of association.

This fact gives what has been said regarding the importance of range and complexity of association as a philosophic measure its special import. If reference to association is to be anything more than a ceremonial and barren act of deference, if it is to be used in any enterprise of philosophic description and understanding, it indicates the necessity of study and analysis of the different modes of association that present themselves in experience. And the implication of our argument is that in such a comparison of definite types of association, the social, in its human sense, is the richest, fullest and most delicately subtle of any mode actually experienced. There is no need to go through the form of discovering, as if for the first time, the different typical modes which are to be compared and contrasted. They have been made familiar enough in the course of thought. Aside from social, whose thoroughgoing admission still awaits adequate acknowledgment, they are the physical, the vital or organic, and the mental. The gist of our problem consists in deciding which of these forms presents the broader and fuller range of associations. Association in general is but a highly abstract notation of what is formally common to the special modes.

Before coming, however, to this affair of comparison, which constitutes the main topic of this paper, it will be well to clear the ground of certain notions which led to misconstruction and depreciation of the meaning of "social" as a category. A moment ago I referred to the facts of association as they are actually displayed in human life. The reference implied that social facts are themselves natural facts. This implication goes against preconceptions engendered by the common opposition of the physical and the social sciences; by the tacit identification, in other words of the natural sciences with the purely physical. As far as this idea lingers in the back of the head, social and natural are oppositional conceptions; the attempt to find a key by which to read the cipher of nature in the social is then immediately felt to be absurd; this feeling then operates to effect the contemptuous dismissal of the "social." Denial of opposition between the social and natural is, however, an important element of the *meaning* of "social" as a category; and if anyone is interested in finding out the intent of those who would employ "social" as a philosophic category, that one should begin by asking himself what are the implications of the current separation of natural and social sciences, and whether upon reflection he is willing to stand by them. A denial of the separation is not only possible to a sane mind, but is demanded by any methodological adoption of the principle of continuity, and also, as will be indicated later, by social phenomena themselves. Upon the hypothesis of continuity—if that is to be termed a hypothesis which cannot be denied without self-contradiction—the social, in spite of whatever may be said regarding the temporal and spatial limitation of its manifestations, furnishes philosophically the inclusive category. . . .

In now turning to the main point, the social as a ranking philosophic category, because it is indicative of the widest and richest range of association empirically accessible (and no apology is offered for basing philosophy upon the empirically manifest rather than upon the occult), it is necessary to point out a certain ambiguity of language which, because of brevity of exposition, necessarily attaches to our statement. Social *phenomena* are not of themselves, of course, equivalent to social as a *category*. The latter is derived from the former by means of an intellectual analysis which determines what is their distinctive character. Now I am not here dealing with the important and eventually imperative problem of the category *of* the social, or the determination of the characteristics which constitute the distinguishing nature of the social, but rather with social phenomena *en gross* as comprehending, for philosophic analysis, physical, organic and mental phenomena in a mode of association in which the latter take on new properties and exercise new functions. In other words, I am here implying that social phenomena do as a matter of fact manifest *something* distinctive, and that that something affords the key to a naturalistic account of phenomena baffling philosophic interpretation when it is left out of account. To those who accept this view, the burden of proof as to the value of "social" as a metaphysical category lies upon those who habitually treat its worth as trivial. For what do *they* mean by social phenomena? If social phenomena are not an exemplification upon the widest and most intricate scale of the generic trait of associated behavior or interaction, what do they signify? I see but one kind of answer open to them, covering two alternatives: Either social phenomena are anomalous, an excrescence or intrusion, supervening in an accidental and meaningless way upon other phenomena, or else they have no distinctive import, being in reality *nothing but* physical, vital or psychological phenomena. Does not each of these views contradict the observable traits of social phenomena?

Upon a *prima facie* view, social phenomena take up and incorporate within themselves things associated in the narrower way which we term the physical. It gives a ludicrous result to think of social phenomena merely as lying on top of physical phenomena; such a notion is negated by the most casual observation of the facts. What would social phenomena be without the physical factor of land, including all the natural resources (and obstacles) and forms of energy for which the word "land" stands? What would social phenomena be without the tools and machines by which physical energies are utilized? Or what would they be without physical appliances and apparatus, from clothes and houses to railways, temples and printing presses? No, it is not the social which is a superficial category. The view of those is superficial who fail to see that in the social the physical is taken up into a wider and more complex and delicate system of interactions so that it takes on new properties by release of potentialities previously confined because of absence of full interaction.

The same consideration applies to the inclusion within the social of the vital or organic. The members of society are living human beings with the characteristics of living creatures; but as these enter into distinctively human associations their strictly organic properties are modified and even transformed. Certain physiological factors of sex, of procreation, immaturity and need of care, are assuredly implicated in the functions expressed in family life. But however great the role of animal lust, there is something more in any family association than bare physiological factors. The fact of transformation of the purely organic by inclusion within the scope of human association is so obvious—note the significant case of change of cries into speech—that it has indeed led to belief in the intrusive intervention of unnatural and supernatural factors in order to account for the differences between the animal and the human. The disjunction between the assertion that the human is the merely animal and the assertion that an extraneous force is obtruded is not, however, exhaustive. There remains an alternative which is most fully confirmed by empirical fact, namely that the difference is made when new potentialities are actualized, when the range of interactions that delimits the notion of the organic is taken up into the wider and more subtly complex association which forms human society.

Since traits derived from the physical mode have been admitted into philosophy, since materialism in other words is at least grudgingly admitted into philosophic companionship, and since organic philosophies, framed on the pattern of vital phenomena, upon conceptions of species, development and purpose, are freely admitted, it seems arbitrary, to say the least, to exclude the social from the role of a legitimate category.

That the mental has a recognized claim to serve as a category of description and interpretation of natural existence is evident in the very existence of idealistic philosophies. There are those who deny the ability of these theories to execute their claim, just as there are those who deny the capacity of the physical and vital to make good. But thought, as well as matter and life, is at least admitted to rank as a respectable figure in the gallery of categories.

Now of the mental as of the physical and organic it may be said that it operates as an included factor within social phenomena, since the mental is empirically discernible only where association is manifested in the form of participation and communication. It would therefore appear legitimate to adopt as a hypothesis worthy of being tried out the idea that the ulterior meaning of the mental as well as of the physical and vital is revealed in this form of associational interaction. The implication is not they have no describable *existence* outside the social, but that in as far as they appear and operate outside of that large interaction which forms the social they do not reveal that full force and import with which it is the traditional business of philosophy to occupy itself. . . .

. . . The state of philosophic discussion exhibits a dilemma, or rather a trilemma. The mental is viewed (i) as a mysterious intrusion occurring in some unaccountable way in the order of nature; (ii) as illusory, or, in current language, as an epiphenomenon; and (iii) as ontological, whether as a section of being on the same level with the physical section, or as the Being of which so-called physical things are but disguised forms or "appearances." It may be argued that the persistence of the problem and of these widely opposed modes of solution is itself strongly indicative that some factor of the situation, the one which is the key to understanding, has been omitted. In any case, the persistence of these unreconcilable conceptions is a challenge to search for something which will eliminate the scandal of such sharp antagonisms in interpretation. Now when we turn to the social, we find *communication* as an existential occurrence involved in all distinctively communal life, and we find that communication effects meaning and understanding as conditions of unity or agreement in conjoint behavior. We find, that is, meaning where it is not an anomaly nor an accidentally supervening quality but a constitutive ingredient of existential events. That is, we find meaning as a describable, verifiable empirical phenomenon whose genesis, modes and consequences can be concretely examined and traced. It presents itself not as an intrusion, nor as an accidental and impotent iridescence, nor as the reduplication of a structure already inhering in antecedent existence, but as an additive quality realized in the process of wider and more complex interaction of physical and vital phenomena; and having a distinctive and concretely verifiable office in sustaining and developing a distinctive kind of observable facts, those namely which are termed social. We do not then have to resort to purely metaphysical and dialectical considerations, adopted *ad hoc,* in order to "save" the reality and importance of the mental. The realm of meanings, of mind, is at home, securely located and anchored in an empirically observable order of existence. And this order stands in genetic continuity with physical and vital phenomena, being, indeed, these phenomena taken up into and incorporated within a wider scope of associated interactions. We do not have to read back the mental into the antecedent physical, much less resort to the desperate measure of making it so all-inclusive that the physical is treated as a disguised and illusory "appearance" of the mental. The social affords us an observable instance of a "realm of mind" objective to an individual, by entering into which as a participating member organic activities are transformed into acts having a mental quality. . . .

. . . Report, communication, is not a bare emission of thoughts framed and completed in private soliloquy or solipsistic observation. The entire operation of individual experimentation and soliloquizing has been influenced at every point by reference to the social medium in which their results are to be set forth and responded to. Indeed what has been said is an understatement. It is not simply that the characteristic findings of thought cannot pass into knowledge save when framed with reference to social submission and adoption, but that language and thought in their relation to signs and symbols are inconceivable save as ways of achieving concerted action. . . .

. . . It is the historic claim of philosophy that it occupies itself with the ideal of wholes and the whole. It is submitted that either the whole is manifested in concretely empirical ways, and in ways consonant with infinite variety, or else the whole is but a dialectical speculation. I do not say that the social as we know it *is* the whole, but I do emphatically suggest that it is the widest and richest manifestation of the whole accessible to our observation. As such it is at least the proper point of departure for any more imaginative construings of the whole one may wish to undertake. . . .

THE UNITY OF THE HUMAN BEING[5]

I make no apology for starting out by saying that we have no words that are prepared in advance to be fit for framing and expressing sound and tested ideas about the unity of the human being, the wholeness of the self. If we ask an economist "What is money?" the proper official reply is that it is a medium of exchange. The answer does not stand in the way of a great deal of money being accumulated by using it to obstruct the processes of exchange. Similarly, we say that words are a means of communicating ideas. But upon some subjects—and the present one falls in this class—the words at our disposal are largely such as to *prevent* the communication of ideas. The words are so loaded with associations derived from a long past that instead of being tools for thought, our thoughts become subservient tools of words.

The meanings of such words as soul, mind, self, unity, even body, are hardly more than condensed epitomes of mankind's agelong efforts at interpretation of its experience. These efforts began when man first emerged from the state of the anthropoid ape. The interpretations which are embodied in the words that have come down to us are the products of desire and hope, of chance circumstance and ignorance, of the authority exercised by medicine men and priests as well as of acute observation and sound judgment.

Physicists had in the beginning a like problem. They are solving it by the invention of technical terms and a technical language. Symbols have, in principle, only the meanings that are put upon them because of special inquiries engaged in. It will be a long time before anything of this sort will be accomplished for human beings. To expel traditional meanings and replace them by ideas that are products of controlled inquiries is a slow and painful process.

Doubtless advance is possible, and will be made, by invention of words that are not charged with the debris of man's past experience. But it is also possible that this process cannot be carried with safety as far as it can be with physical things. Our technical terms might easily represent such artificial constructions that they would fail to help us in dealings with human beings—with the John Smiths and Susan Joneses with whom we rub elbows in daily life.

The words in which I try to communicate ideas to you are, then, at best, but means of stimulating personal observation and reflection. This statement holds even of the phrase "the unity of the human being." At first, the words have only a meaning derived from a contrast effect. The idea of man as an integral whole is projected against a background of beliefs about man which are chiefly of emotional origin and force; against belief in a dualism that was the expression of religious and moral institutions and traditions.

The phrase "unity of man" has at first, accordingly, a negative meaning. It expresses a way of *not* talking about soul *and* body, body *and* mind. The word "unity" is a protest against the canonized dualism expressed in the presence of the word "and." Nevertheless, the split expressed in this word is so engrained in our emotional and intellectual habits that no sooner have we consciously rejected it in one form than it recurs in another. The dualism is found today even among those who have abandoned its earlier manifestations. It is shown in separations made between the structural and the functional; between the brain and the rest of the body; between the central nervous system and the vegetative nervous system and viscera; and most fundamentally, between the organism and the environment. For the first of each of these pairs of terms—structure, brain, organism—retains something of the isolation and alleged independence that used to belong to the "soul" and the "mind" and later to "consciousness."

While it is necessary to advance from the negative meaning of the phrase "the unity of man" the idea of unity also has its perils. For it has taken on associations during centuries of philosophic discussion that make it a dangerous word. It has become almost an invitation to set an abstraction in place of concrete phenomena. You and I can easily think of comprehensive systems—psychiatric, therapeutic, philosophical and psychological—suggested in the first place by undoubted facts, which under the protecting shield of the idea of unity, have been built up so as to force the facts, disguising and distorting them. At the present time there is a revulsion against the endless splitting up of human beings into bits. It is going on with respect to cells, structures and organs, sensations, ideas, reflexes; and with respect to atoms and electrons. The phrase "unity of man" is a protest against analysis of man into separate ultimate elements, as well as against the traditional split into body and soul. But it is easier, much easier, to set up the idea of unity in a vague way, than it is to translate it into definite facts.

"Unity of the human being" only indicates, at best, a point of view, and the point of view has no meaning save as it is used as a vantage point from which to observe and interpret actual phenomena.

We often hear such phrases as the unity of a family, the unity of a nation. These phrases stand for something. Yet in the history of social and political speculation, men have allowed the words to take the bit in their teeth and run away from inquiry into the actual facts to which they refer. These instances of the use of "unity" may, however provide a suggestion from which it is safe to set out. Whatever else the unity is or is not, it at least means the way in which a number of different persons and things work together toward a common end. This *working together* exists in action, operation, not as a static object or collection of objects. It is this kind of unity that seems to me to give the clew to understanding the unity of the human being.

We can recognize and identify a man as a single object, a numerical unit, by observation which marks out boundaries, as we note that the bounded object moves as a whole. In that way you recognize me as a single object standing here on the stage before you. That is the way in which we recognize a rock, tree or house as a single object, as a unity and whole. But that which makes a rock a single whole is the interaction of swarms of molecules, atoms, and electrons; its unity is an affair of the way elements work together. The boundaries by which we mark off a human being as a unit are very different from the energies and organization of energies that make *him* a *unified human being*. We can observe the boundaries at a single moment. We can grasp the unity only, so to speak, longitudinally—only as something that goes on in a stretch of time. It is not found in any number of cross-sectional views.

Nevertheless, if we could look into the minds of our neighbors, I think we should not be much surprised to find in them quite frequently the notion that a man exists within the boundaries which are visible, tangible, and observable. In a word, the man is identified with what is underneath his skin. We incline to suppose that we would know all about him if we could find out everything that is happening in his brain and other parts of his nervous system: in his glands, muscles, viscera, heart and lungs and so on.

Now up to a certain point we are on the right track, provided we emphasize sufficiently the interaction, the working together, of all these diverse processes. We can get a better idea of the unity of the human being as we know more about all these processes and the way they work together, as they check, and stimulate one another and bring about a balance. But the one positive point I wish to present is that while this is necessary it is not enough. We must observe and understand these internal processes and their interactions from the standpoint of their interaction with what is going on outside the skin—with that which is called the *environment*—if we are to obtain a genuine conception of the unity of the human being.

Our attitude with respect to this matter is a strange mixture. In special points we take for granted the inclusion of the conditions and energies that are outside the boundaries set by the skin. No one supposes for a moment that there can be respiration without the surrounding air; or that the lungs are anything more than organs of interaction with what is outside the body. No one thinks of separating the processes of digestion from connection with foodstuffs derived by means of other organs from the environment. We know that eye, ear and hand, and somatic musculature, are concerned with objects and events outside the boundaries of the body. These things we take for granted so regularly and unconsciously that it seems foolish to mention them. Physiologists at least recognize that what is true of breathing and digestion holds also of the circulation of fluids that goes on entirely within the body, although the connection of these processes with environing conditions is a stage more indirect. The structure and processes of the central nervous system do not have that immediate connection with the outside world that the peripheral neural structures have.

Yet an authority upon the anatomy and physiology of the nervous system recently used these words: "Every movement is the result of the messages which pass from the central mass of nerve cells to the muscles, and the outgoing messages are varied according to the reports submitted by the sense organs. These show what is happening in the world outside, and the nervous system must evolve a plan of action appropriate to the occasion."*

That movements affected by the muscles have to do, directly and indirectly, with activities of seeking, defense, and taking possession of energies of the outside world is obvious. The central nervous system has the function of evolving the plans and procedures that take effect in dealing with outside conditions as they are reported through sense organs—and I suppose it would be admitted that these reports vary, depending upon what the body was doing previously in connection with outside conditions.

In other words, with respect to every special set of organic structures and processes, we take it for granted that things beyond the body are in-

*N. Adrian, *Harvard Tercentenary Publications*, vol. I, p. 4.

volved in interaction with those inside the body, and that we cannot understand the latter in isolation. I did not give the quotation from Dr. Adrian because it presented a novel revelation. Actually, it states a fact so generally recognized as to be a commonplace. The strangeness of the mixture of which I spoke consists in the fact that while we recognize the involvement of conditions external to the body in all organic processes, when they are taken one by one, we often fail to recognize and act upon the idea as an inclusive principle by which to understand the unity of man and the disorders which result from disruption of this unity.

Whole philosophical systems have been built up, for example, by treating thinking, especially in so-called abstract ideas, as having no connection with the activities the body executes in the environment in use and enjoyment of the conditions it presents. There is many a mathematician who would be shocked if he were told that his constructions had anything to do with activities carried on in the environment. Yet we know that neural structures and processes developed in control and use of the environment are the organs of all thinking. Even some who call themselves behaviorists, who pride themselves on their strictly scientific attitude, have identified the behavior about which they talk with the behavior of the nervous system in and by itself. Having, for example, identified thought with language—a position for which much may be said—they go on to locate language in the vocal cords, ignoring the transaction of communication in which, directly and indirectly, other human beings take part. It may even be that on occasion physicians think of diseases, and even psychical disorders, as something that goes on wholly inside the body, so that they treat what goes on outside as, at most, an external cause rather than a constituent and interacting factor in the disease.

At all events, there is a good deal of description and interpretation in many fields in which the structural and static lord it over the active and functioning. Whenever we find this to be the case we may be sure that some structure of the body has been described and interpreted in isolation from its connection with an activity in which an environment plays an integral part.

On the other hand, when physicians proceed to regulate the diet, sleep and exercise of patients, when they inquire into and give advice about their habits, they are dealing with the "use of the self" in its active functional connection with the outside world. What, then, I am urging is simply the systematic and constant projection of what is here involved into all our observations, judgments and generalizations about the unity and the breakdowns of unity of human beings. For its implications are that all beliefs and practices which gratuitously split up the unity of man have their final root in the separation of what goes on inside the body from integrated interaction with what goes on outside.

This abstract principle becomes concrete as soon as one thinks not of environment in general, but of the human environment—that which is formed by contacts and relations with our human fellows. Psychiatrists have made us familiar with disturbances labeled "withdrawal from reality." They have pointed out the role of this withdrawal in many pathological occurrences. What are these withdrawals but cases of the interruption or cessation of "the active operative presence of environing conditions in the activities of a human being"? What are the resulting pathological phenomena but evidences that the self loses its integrity *within itself* when it loses integration with the medium in which it lives?

It is only necessary to think of those mild instances of withdrawal, forming ordinary daydreaming and fantasy building, to appreciate that the environment which is involved is human or social. When a person builds up not only a systematized delusion of wealth but engages in a daydream in which he has come into possession of a large sum of money, it is not the physical money he is thinking of, but the prestige and power it gives him over his fellows. If a fantasy becomes habitual and controlling, it brings about, sooner or later, retraction from even the physical environment. But these withdrawals from physical surroundings originate in disturbances of relationship with the human environment. They go back to such things as pettings and coddlings, personal rejections, failure to win recognition and approvals, fear of those in authority, frustration of hope and desire by social conditions.

We may then anticipate a time when our entire traditional psychology will be looked upon as extraordinarily one-sided in its exclusive concern with actions and reactions of human beings with their physical surroundings to the neglect of interpersonal relationships. We have, to be sure, reached a point where we have chapters and books entitled "social psychology." But we are far from having reached the point in which it is seen that the whole difference between animal and human psychology is constituted by the transforming effect exercised upon the former by intercourse and association with other persons and groups of persons. For, apart from unconditioned reflexes, like the knee jerk, it may be questioned whether there is a single human activity or experience which is not profoundly affected by the social and cultural environment. Would we have any intellectual operations without the language which is a social product? As for our emotional life, permit me to cite two passages written by a physician: "Contact with human beings is the stimulus that elicits emotional and visceral reactions. It is not the clatter of railways and motors, this 'fast hurrying age in which we live' so often spoken of; it is rather the pride, the envy, the ambition, the rage, the disappointment, the defeat that develop in purely human relations that stir the viscera"; and again: "There is an immense amount of hokum uttered about the psychological tensions caused by our swiftly moving era, as though the telephone, the radio, and the electric refrigerator were instruments that could swerve the viscera. The emotional life does not actually hinge on machinery but on the type of response to living situations, situations that for the most part are created by human contacts."*

I do not believe I am going beyond the implications of these passages when I say that the operation of "living situations created by human contacts" is the only intelligible ground upon which we can distinguish between what we call the *higher* and the *lower* (the physical on one side and the ideal and "spiritual" on the other) in human experience. The occurrence of a sensation, for example, may be described as an interaction between certain neural processes and certain vibrations. The principle involved here is the same in animals and in man. But the *significance* of a quality of red depends upon the part it plays in the customary uses and enjoyments of the social group of which a person is a member. To a bull, its presense is a purely physiological stimulus. For a child, it may be that a dress, worn perhaps only on a festal occasion or a ribbon worn for adornment in the presence of others, is that which fixes the significance of red. When we wait in an automobile for a traffic light to turn, red is still a physiological stimulus. But it has its *significance* in terms of adaptation of the behavior of individuals to one another. The emotional import of red in a red, white and blue flag to a patriotic American citizen is surely not native in physiological structure.

Examples do not *prove* the principle laid down. But I do believe that reflection upon these and similar cases will show that the only verifiable basis we have for marking off the experiences that have practical, emotional and intellectual significance from those which do not is the influence of cultural and social forces upon internal physiological processes.

At least, what I have said is a challenge to produce any instance of an experience having so-called ideal or even "spiritual" meaning that cannot be accounted for on this ground. Otherwise we must have recourse to the old division between soul and body. Take the case of those who revolt against the old dualism, and who because of their revolt imagine they must throw away and deny the existence of all phenomena that go by the names of "higher," intellectual and moral. Such persons exist. They suppose they are not scientific unless they reduce everything to the exclusively somatic and physiological. This procedure is a conspicuous instance of what must happen when observation, description and interpretation of human events are confined to what goes on under the skin to the exclusion of their integrated interaction with environmental conditions, particularly the environment formed by other human beings. Knowledge of strictly somatic organs and processes is certainly necessary for scientific understanding of "higher" phenomena. But only half-way science neglects and rules out the other factor.

We may reject the traditional dualism. In my conviction we should reject it. We cannot be scientific save as we seek for the physiological, the physical

*Houston, *The Art of Treatment*, pp. 348–49; p. 450.

factor in every emotional, intellectual and volitional experience. As more is known of this factor, more intellectual capital and more resources of control are at our command. In the case of the physician especially is it so true as to be a truism, that the more anatomical, chemical and immunological information he has, the better prepared is he for his work. And it is also true that our knowledge of social relations and their effects upon native and original physiological processes is scanty and unorganized in comparison with the physical knowledge at command.

But in view of the role played by human contacts and relations in developing and sustaining the emotional and intellectual quality of human experience on one side, and in bringing disturbance and disorder into it on the other, this fact is all the more reason for devoting constant attention to the as yet relatively unknown factor in the case of every human being who comes under observation. This need cannot be met by knowledge of even the most up-to-date scientific psychology which now exists. For, unfortunately, this psychology suffers for the most part from exactly the one-sided concern in question: the failure to take into account the operations and effects of relationships between human beings. . . .

We cannot understand the conditions that produce unity in the human being and conditions that generate disruptions of this unity until the study of the relations of human beings to one another is as alert, as unremitting and as systematic as the study of strictly physiological and anatomical processes and structures has been in the past. The plea is not for any remission on the side of the latter. But we need to recover from the impression, now widespread, that the essential problem is solved when chemical, immunological, physiological and anatomical knowledge is sufficiently obtained. We cannot understand and employ this knowledge until it is placed integrally in the context of what human beings do to one another in the vast variety of their contacts and associations. Until the study is undertaken in this spirit, neglect will continue to breed and so support belief in the soul, and in mental processes supposed to be wholly independent of the organism and of somatic conditions. The consequences produced by this belief will not be confined to errors of theory. The practical outcome is division and conflict in action where unity and cooperation of social effort are urgently required.

I may rephrase what I have said by saying that the fine old saying "A sound mind in a sound body" can and should be extended to read "A sound human being in a sound human environment." The mere change in wording is nothing. A change in aims and methods of working in that direction would mean more than any of us can estimate. Is there anything in the whole business of politics, economics, morals, education—indeed in any profession —save the construction of a proper human environment that will serve, by its very existence, to produce sound and whole human beings, who in turn will maintain a sound and healthy human environment? . . .

1. The relations of man to nature and society are developed most thoroughly and systematically in *Experience and Nature* and *Human Nature and Conduct*. My own *John Dewey's Philosophy of Value* deals extensively with Dewey's analysis of these relations—*Ed*.

2. One of a course of public lectures on "Charles Darwin and His Influence on Science," given at Columbia University in the winter and spring of 1909. Reprinted from *The Influence of Darwin on Philosophy and Other Eassys in Contemporary Thought* (New York: Henry Holt and Company, 1910), pp. 1–19.

3. Dewey's contribution to *Time and Its Mysteries*, series II (New York: New York University Press, 1940).

4. *The Monist* XXXVIII (April 1928): pp. 161–77; reprinted as "The Inclusive Philosophic Idea" in *Philosophy and Civilization*.

5. An address delivered before the College of Physicians in St. Louis, April 21, 1937. Published in *Intelligence in the Modern World: John Dewey's Philosophy*, edited and with an introduction by Joseph Ratner (New York: The Modern Library, 1939), pp. 817–34.

Value
and
Nature

3

Determining the status of value in nature is crucial to Dewey's moral philosophy. Unless this issue is treated adequately, the assumptions are lacking that would clarify the deliberate discernment, criticism, and realization of value. The more we know of values as functions of natural processes involving both organism and environment, the more capable we are of using intelligence to convert situations of difficulty and frustration into consummatory experiences: the unification of values, or— as Dewey named it—the construction of good.

Dewey contends that the many forms of withdrawal or retreat from human endeavor have been a consequence of human incapacity to function effectively with nature, inclusive of society. Failure in earthly aspiration leads to a quest for certainty in an alleged transcendent realm, accessible only to intuition of some form. This flight from the precarious conditions of nature means that the possibilities of natural existence go unheeded and uncultivated. With the rise of experimental science, the development of an adequate conception of human nature in nature, and the clarification of the status of value in nature, this quest and its allied theory of knowledge are rendered wholly dubious.

One of Dewey's briefest accounts of the quest for certainty is provided in the first selection. Subsequent selections set forth some of his analyses of value. Regrettably, he never succeeded in employing a consistent terminology in denoting distinctions about value.[1] His unswerving intention, however, was to signify those phases of activity which are crucial in converting the natural processes of any situation into a coherent unity of meaning and value. This, the consummatory phase of experience, is not an instance of a fixed and final good but is the creation of an intrinsic good out of a unique combination of elements in ongoing experience.

BEFORE INTELLIGENCE BECOMES EFFECTIVE[2]

. . . Of the older philosophies, framed before experimental knowing had made any significant progress, it may be said that they made a definite separation between the world in which man thinks and knows and the world in which he lives and acts. In his needs and in the acts that spring from them, man *was* a part of the world, a sharer in its fortunes, sometimes willingly, sometimes perforce; he was exposed to its vicissitudes and at the mercy of its irregular and unforeseeable changes. By acting in and upon the world he made his earthly way, sometimes failing, sometimes achieving. He was acted upon by it, sometimes carried forward to unexpected glories and sometimes overwhelmed by its disfavor.

Being unable to cope with the world in which he lived, he sought some way to come to terms with the universe as a whole. Religion was, in its origin, an expression of this endeavor. After a time, a few persons with leisure and endowed by fortune with immunity from the rougher impacts of the world, discovered the delights of thought and inquiry. They reached the conclusion that through rational thought they could rise above the natural world in which, with their body and those mental processes that were connected with the body, they lived. In striving with the inclemencies of nature, suffering its buffetings, wresting sustenance from its resources, they were parts of Nature. But in knowledge, true knowledge which is rational, occupied with objects that are universal and immutable, they escaped from the world of vicissitude and uncertainty. They were elevated above the realm in which needs are felt and laborious effort imperative. In rising above this world of sense and time, they came into rational communion with the divine which was untroubled and perfect mind. They became true participants in the realm of ultimate reality. Through knowledge, they were without the world of chance and change, and within the world of perfect and unchanging Being.

How far this glorification by philosophers and scientific investigators of a life of knowing, apart from and above a life of doing, might have impressed the popular mind without adventitious aid there is no saying. But external aid came. Theologians of the Christian Church adopted this view in a form adapted to their religious purposes. The perfect and ultimate reality was God; to know Him was eternal bliss. The world in which man lived and acted was a world of trials and troubles to test and prepare him for a higher destiny. Through thousands of ways, including histories and rites, with symbols that engaged the emotions and imagination, the essentials of the doctrine of classic philosophy filtered its way into the popular mind.

It would be a one-sided view which held that this story gives the entire account of the elevation of knowing and its object above practical action and its objects. A contributing cause was found in the harshness, cruelties and tragic frustrations of the world of action. Were it not for its brutalities and failures, the motive for seeking refuge in a higher realm of knowledge would have been lacking. It was easy and, as we say, "natural" to associate these evils with the fact that the world in which we act is a realm of change. The generic fact of change was made absolute and the source of all the troubles and defects of the world in which we directly live. At the very best, good and excellence are insecure in a world of change; good can be securely at home only in a realm of fixed unchanging substance. When the source of evil was once asserted to reside in the inherent deficiencies of a realm of change, responsibility was removed from human ignorance, incapacity and insusceptibility. It remained only to change our own attitude and disposition, to turn the soul from perishable things toward perfect Being. In this idea religion stated in one language precisely what the great philosophic tradition stated in another. . . .

THE STATUS OF VALUES IN NATURE[3]

Human experience in the large, in its coarse and conspicuous features, has for one of its most striking features preoccupation with direct enjoyment, feasting and festivities; ornamentation, dance, song, dramatic pantomime, telling yarns and enacting stories. In comparison with intellectual and moral endeavor, this trait of experience has hardly received the attention from philosophers that it demands. Even philosophers who have conceived that pleasure is the sole motive of man and the attainment of happiness his whole aim, have given a curiously sober, drab, account of the working of pleasure and the search for happiness. Consider the utilitarians how they toiled, spun and wove, but who never saw man arrayed in joy as the lilies of the field. Happiness was to them a matter of calculation and effort, of industry guided by mathematical bookkeeping. The history of man shows however that man takes his enjoyment neat, and at as short range as possible.

Direct appropriations and satisfactions were prior to anything but the most elementary and exigent prudence, just as the useful arts preceded the sciences. The body is decked before it is clothed. While homes are still hovels, temples and palaces are embellished. Luxuries prevail over necessities except when necessities can be festally celebrated. Men make a game of their fishing and hunting, and turn to the periodic and disciplinary labor of agriculture only when inferiors, women and slaves, cannot be had to do the work. Useful labor is, whenever possible, transformed by ceremonial and ritual accompaniments, subordinated to art that yields immediate enjoyment; otherwise it is attended to under the compulsion of circumstance during abbreviated surrenders of leisure. For leisure permits of festivity, in revery, ceremonies and conversation. The pressure of necessity is, however, never wholly lost, and the sense of it led men, as if with uneasy conscience at their respite from work, to impute practical efficacy to play and rites, endowing them with power to coerce events and to purchase the favor of rulers of events.

But it is possible to magnify the place of magical exercise and superstitious legend. The primary interest lies in staging the show and enjoying the spectacle, in giving play to the ineradicable interest in stories which illustrate the contingencies of existence combined with happier endings for emergencies than surrounding conditions often permit. It was not conscience that kept men loyal to cults and rites, and faithful to tribal myths. So far as it was not routine, it was enjoyment of the drama of life without the latter's liabilities that kept piety from decay. Interest in rites as means of influencing the course of things, and the cognitive or explanation office of myths were hardly more than an embroidery, repeating in pleasant form the pattern which inexpugnable necessities imposed upon practice. When rite and myth are spontaneous rehearsal of the impact and career of practical needs and doings, they must also seem to have practical force. The political significance of July Fourth, 1776, is perhaps renewed by the juvenile celebrations of Independence Day, but this effect hardly accounts for the fervor of the celebration. Any excuse serves for a holiday and the more the holiday is decked out with things that contrast with the pressure of workaday life while re-enacting its form, the more a holiday it is. The more unrestrained the play of fancy the greater the contrast. The supernatural has more thrills than the natural, the customary; holidays and holy-days are indistinguishable. Death is an occasion for a wake, and mourning is acclaimed with a board of funeral meats.

Reflected upon, this phase of experience manifests objects which are final. The attitude involved in their appreciation is esthetic. The operations entering into their production is fine art, distinguished from useful art. It is dangerous however to give names, especially in discourse that is far aloof from the things named—direct enjoyment of the interplay of the contingent and the effective, purged of practical risks and penalties. Esthetic, fine art, appreciation, drama have a eulogistic flavor. We hesitate to call the penny dreadful of fiction artistic, so we call it debased fiction or a travesty on art. Most sources of direct enjoyment for the masses are not art to the cultivated, but perverted art, an unworthy indulgence. Thus we miss the point. A passion of anger, a dream, relaxation of the limbs after effort, swapping of jokes, horseplay, beating of drums, blowing of tin whistles, explosion of firecrackers and walking on stilts, have the same quality of immediate and absorbing finality that is possessed by things and acts dignified by the title of esthetic. For man is more preoccupied with enhancing life than with bare living; so that a sense of living when it attends labor and utility is borrowed not intrinsic, having been generated in those periods of relief when activity was dramatic.

To say these things is only to say that man is naturally more interested in consummations than he is in preparations; and that consummations have first to be hit upon spontaneously and accidentally—as the baby gets food and all of us are warmed by the sun—before they can be objects of foresight, invention and industry. Consciousness so far as it is not dull ache and torpid comfort is a thing of the imagination. The extensions and transformations of existence generated in imagination may come at last to attend work so as to make it significant and agreeable. But when men are first at the height of business, they are too busy to engage either in fancy or reflective inquiry. At the outset the hunt was enjoyed in the feast, or in the calm moments of shaping spears, bows and arrows. Only later was the content of these experiences carried over into hunting itself, so that even its dangers might be savored. Labor, through its structure and order, lends play its pattern and plot; play then returns the loan with interest to work, in giving it a sense of beginning, sequence and climax. As long as imagined objects are satisfying, the logic of drama, of suspense, thrill and success, dominates the logic of objective events. Cosmogonies are mythological not because savages indulge in defective scientific explanations, but because objects of imagination are consummatory in the degree in which they exuberantly escape from the pressure of natural surroundings, even when they reenact its crises. The congenial is first form of the consistent. . . .

The other most self-evident thing in experience is useful labor and its coercive necessity. As direct appreciative enjoyment exhibits things in their consummatory phase, labor manifests things in their connections of things with one another, in efficiency, productivity, furthering, hindering, generating, destroying. From the standpoint of enjoyment a thing is what it directly does for us. From that of labor a thing is what it will do to other things— the only way in which a tool or an obstacle can be defined. Extraordinary and subtle reasons have been assigned for belief in the principle of causation. Labor and the use of tools seem, however, to be a sufficient empirical reason: indeed, to be the only empirical events that can be specifically pointed to in this connection. They are more adequate grounds for acceptance of belief in causality than are the regular sequences of nature or than a category of reason, or the alleged fact of will. The first thinker who proclaimed that every event is effect of something and cause of something else, that every particular existence is both conditioned and condition, merely put into words the procedure of the workman, converting a mode of practice into a formula. External regularity is familiar, customary, taken for granted, not thought of, embodied in thoughtless routine. Regularity, orderly sequence, in productive labor presents itself to thought as a controlling principle. Industrial arts are the typeforms of experience that bring to light the sequential connections of things with one another.

In contrast, the enjoyment (with which suffering is to be classed) of things is a declaration that natural existences are not mere passageways to another passageway, and so on *ad infinitum*. Thinkers interested in esthetic experience are wont to point out the absurdity of the idea that things are good or valuable only for something else; they dwell on the fact vouchsafed by esthetic appreciation that there are things that have their goodness or value in themselves, which are not cherished for the sake of anything else. These philosophers usually confine this observation however to human affairs isolated from nature, which they interpret exclusively in terms of labor, or causal connections. But in every event there is something obdurate, self-sufficient, wholly immediate, neither a relation nor an element in a relational whole, but terminal and exclusive. Here, as in so many other matters, materialists and idealists agree in an underlying metaphysics which ignores in behalf of relations and relational systems, those irreducible, infinitely plural, undefinable and indescribable qualities which a thing must *have* in order to be, and in order to be capable of becoming the subject of relations and a theme of discourse. Immediacy of existence is ineffable. But there is nothing mystical about such ineffability; it expresses the fact that of direct existence it is futile to say anything to one's self and impossible to say anything to another. Discourse can but intimate connections which if followed out may lead one to *have* an existence. Things in their immediacy are unknown and unknowable, not because they are remote or behind some impenetrable veil of sensation of ideas, but because knowledge has no concern with them. For knowledge is a memorandum of conditions of their appearance, concerned, that is, with sequences, coexistences, relations. Immediate things may be *pointed to* by words, but not described or defined. Description when it occurs is but a part of a circuitous method of pointing or denoting; index to a starting point and road which if taken may lead to a direct and ineffable presence. To the empirical thinker, immediate enjoyment and suffering are the conclusive exhibition and evidence that nature has its finalities as well as its relationships. . . .[4]

Dewey considers the Greek conception of nature and the related theory of value, together with their demise in modern thought. (Ed.)

. . . The sole notability, intelligibility, of nature was conceived to reside in objects that were ends, since they set limits to change. Changing things were not capable of being known on the basis of relationship to one another, but only on the basis of their relationship to objects beyond change, because marking its limit, and immediately precious. The terminal objects lent changing objects the properties which made them knowable; such stability of character as they possessed was derived from the form of the end-objects toward which they moved. Hence an inherent appetition or nisus toward these terminal and static objects was attributed to them. The whole scheme of cosmic change was a vehicle for attaining ends possessed of properties which caused them to be objects of attraction of all lesser things, rendering the latter uneasy and restless until they attained the end-object which constitutes their real nature. Thus an immediate contemplative possession and enjoyment of objects, dialectically ordered, was interpreted as defining both true knowledge and the highest end and good of nature. A doctrine of morals, of what is better in reflective choice, was thus converted into a metaphysics and science of Being, the moral aspect being disguised to the modern mind by the fact that the highest good was conceived esthetically, instead of in the social terms which upon the whole dominate modern theories of morality.

The doctrine that objects as ends are the proper objects of science, because they are the ultimate forms of real being, met its doom in the scientific revolution of the seventeenth century. Essences and forms were attacked as occult; "final causes" were either wholly denied or relegated to a divine realm too high for human knowledge. The doctrine of natural ends was displaced by a doctrine of designs, ends-in-view, conscious aims constructed and entertained in individual minds independent of nature. Descartes, Spinoza and Kant are, upon this matter at least, in agreement with Bacon, Hume and Helvetius. The imputation to natural events of cosmic appetition toward ends, the notion that their changes were to be understood as efforts to reach a natural state of rest and perfection, were indicated as the chief source of sterility and fantasy in science; the syllogistic logic connected with the doctrine was discarded as verbal, polemical, and at its best irrelevant to the subtle operations of nature; purpose and contingency were alike relegated to the purely human and personal; nature was evacuated of qualities and became a homogeneous mass differentiated by differences of homogeneous motion in a homogeneous space. Mechanical relations, which Greek thought had rejected as equivalent to the chaotic reign of pure accident, became the head cornerstone of the conception of law, of uniformity and order. If ends were recognized at all, it was only under the caption of design, and design was defined as conscious aim rather than as objective order and architechtonic form. Wherever the influence of modern physics penetrated, the classic theory became remote, faded, factitious, with its assertion that natural changes are inherent movements toward objects which are their fulfillments or perfections, so that the latter are true objects of knowledge, supplying the forms or characters under which alone changes may be known. With the decay of this doctrine, departed also belief in cosmic qualitative differences and kinds, so that of necessity quality and immediacy had no recourse, expelled from objective nature, save to take refuge in personal consciousness.

Is this reversal of classic theories of existence inevitable? Must belief in ends involved in nature itself be surrendered, or be asserted only by means of a roundabout examination of the nature of knowledge which starting from conscious intent to know, finally infers that the universe is a vast, nonnatural fulfillment of a conscious intent? Or is there an ingredient of truth in ancient metaphysics which may be extracted and reaffirmed? Empirically, the existence of objects of direct grasp, possession, use and enjoyment cannot be denied. Empirically, things are poignant, tragic, beautiful, humorous, settled, disturbed, comfortable, annoying, barren, harsh, consoling, splendid, fearful; are such immediately and in their own right and behalf. If we take advantage of the word esthetic in a wider sense than that of application to the beautiful and ugly, esthetic quality, immediate, final or self-enclosed, indubitably characterizes natural situations as they empirically occur. These traits stand in themselves on precisely the same level as colors, sounds, qualities of contact, taste and smell. Any criterion that finds the latter to be ultimate and "hard" data will, impartially applied, come to the same conclusion about the former. *Any* quality as such is final; it is at once initial and terminal; just what it is as it exists. It may be referred to other things, it may be treated as an effect or as a sign. But this involves an extraneous extension and use. It takes us beyond quality in its immediate qualitativeness. If experienced things are valid evidence, then nature in having qualities within itself has what in the literal sense must be called ends, terminals, arrests, enclosures.

It is dangerous to venture at all upon the use of the word "ends" in connection with existential processes. Apologetic and theological controversies cluster about it and affect its signification. Barring this connotation, the word has an almost inexpugnable honorific flavor, so that to assert that nature is characterized by ends, the most conspicuous of which is the life of mind, seems like engaging in a eulogistic, rather than empirical account of nature. Something much more neutral than any such implication is, however, meant. We constantly talk about things coming or drawing to a close; getting ended, finished, done with, over with. It is a commonplace that no *thing* lasts forever. We may be glad or we may be sorry but that is wholly a matter of the kind of history which is being ended. We may conceive the end, the close, as due to fulfillment, perfect attainment, to satiety, or to exhaustion, to dissolution, to something having run down or given out. Being an end may be indifferently an ecstatic culmination, a matter-of-fact consummation, or a deplorable tragedy. Which of these things a closing or terminal object is, has nothing to do with the property of being an end.

The genuine implications of natural ends may be brought out by considering beginnings instead of endings. To insist that nature is an affair of beginnings is to assert that there is no one single and all-at-once beginning of everything. It is but another way of saying that nature is an affair *of* affairs, wherein each one, no matter how linked up it may be with others, has its *own* quality. It does not imply that every beginning marks an advance or improvement; as we sadly know accidents, diseases, wars, lies and errors, begin. Clearly the fact and idea of beginning is neutral, not eulogistic; temporal, not absolute. And since wherever one thing begins something else ends, what is true of beginnings is true of endings. Popular fiction and drama show the bias of human nature in favor of happy endings, but by being fiction and drama they show with even greater assurance that unhappy endings are natural events.

To minds inured to the eulogistic connotation of ends, such a neutral interpretation of the meaning of ends as has just been set forth may seem to make the doctrine of ends a matter of indifference. If ends are only endings or closings of temporal episodes, why bother to call attention to ends at all, to say nothing of framing a theory of ends and dignifying it with the name of natural teleology? In the degree, however, in which the mind is weaned from partisan and egocentric interest, acknowledgment of nature as a scene of incessant beginnings and endings, presents itself as the source of philosophic enlightenment. It enables thought to apprehend causal mechanisms and temporal finalities as phases of the same natural processes, instead of as competitors where the gain of one is the loss of the other. Mechanism is the order involved in an historic occurrence, capable of definition in terms of the order which various histories sustain to each other. Thus it is the instrumentality of control of any particular termination since a sequential order involves the last term.

The traditional conception of natural ends was to the effect that nature does nothing in vain; the accepted meaning of this phrase was that every change is for the sake of something which does not change, occurring in its behalf. Thus the mind started with a ready-made list of good things or perfections which it was the business of nature to accomplish. Such a view may verbally distinguish between something called efficient causation and something else called final causation. But in effect the distinction is only between the causality of the master who contents himself with uttering an order and the efficacy of the servant who actually engages in the physical work of execution. It is only a way of attributing ultimate causality to what is ideal and mental—the directive order of the master—while emancipating it from the supposed degradation of physical labor in carrying it out, as well as avoiding the difficulties of inserting an immaterial cause within the material realm. But in a legitimate account of ends as endings, all directional order resides in the sequential order. This no more occurs for the sake of the end than a mountain exists for the sake of the peak which is its end. A musical phrase has a certain close, but the earlier portion does not therefore exist for the sake of the close as if it were something which is done away with when the close is reached. And so a man is not an adult until after he has been a boy, but childhood does not exist for the sake of maturity.

By the nature of the case, causality, however it be defined, consists in the sequential order itself and not in a last term which as such is irrelevant to causality, although it may, of course be, in addition, an initial term in another sequential order. The view held—or implied—by some "mechanists," which treats an initial term as if it had an inherent generative force which it somehow emits and bestows upon its successors, is all of a piece with the view held by teleologists which implies that an end brings about its own antecedents. Both isolate an event from the history in which it belongs and in which it has its character. Both make a factitiously isolated position in a temporal order a mark of true reality, one theory selecting initial place and the other final place. But in fact causality is another name for the sequential order itself; and since this is an order of a history having a beginning and end, there is nothing more absurd than setting causality over against either initiation or finality.

The same considerations permit a naturalistic interpretation of the ideas of dynamic and static. Every end is as such static; this statement is but a truism; changing into something else, a thing is obviously transitive, not final. Yet the thing which is a close of one history is always the beginning of another, and in this capacity the thing in question is transitive or dynamic. This statement also is tautology, for dynamic does not mean possessed of "force" or capable of emitting it so as to stir up other things and set them in motion; it means simply change in a connected series of events. The traditional view of force points necessarily to something transcendental, because outside of events, whether called God or Will or The Unknowable. So the traditional view of the static points to something fixed and rigid, incapable of change, and therefore also outside the course of things and consequently nonempirical. Empirically, however, there is a history which is a succession of histories, and in which any event is at once both beginning of one course and close of another; is both transitive and static. The phrase constantly in our mouths, "state of affairs," is accurately descriptive, although it makes sheer nonsense in both the traditional spiritual and mechanistic theories. There are no changes that do not enter into an affair, *res*, and there is no affair that is not bounded and thereby marked off as a state or condition. When a state of affairs is perceived, the perceiving-of-a-state-of-affairs is a further state of affairs. Its subject-matter is a thing in the idiomatic sense of thing, *res*, whether a solar system, a stellar constellation, or an atom, a diversified and more or less loose interconnection of events, falling within boundaries sufficiently definite to be capable of being approximately traced. Such is the unbiased evidence of experience in gross, and such in effect is the conclusion of recent physics as far as a layman can see. For this reason, and not because of any unique properties of a separate kind of existence, called psychic or mental, every situation or field of consciousness is marked by initiation, direction or intent, and consequence or import. What is unique is not these traits, but the property of awareness or perception. Because of this property, the initial stage is capable of being judged in the light of its probable course and consequence. There is anticipation. Each successive event being a stage in a serial process is both expectant and commemorative. What is more precisely pertinent to our present theme, the terminal outcome when anticipated (as it is when a moving cause of affairs is perceived) becomes an end-in-view, an aim, purpose, a prediction usable as a plan in shaping the course of events. In classic Greek thought, the perception of ends was simply an esthetic contemplation of the forms of objects in which natural processes were completed. In most modern thought, it is an arbitrary creation of private mental operations guided by personal desire, the theoretical alternative being that they are finite copies of the fulfilled intentions of an infinite mind. In empirical fact, they are projections of possible consequences; they are ends-in-view. The in-viewness of ends is as much conditioned by antecedent natural conditions as is perception of *contemporary* objects external to the organism, trees and stones, or whatever. That is, natural processes must have actually terminated in specifiable consequences, which give those processes definition and character, before ends can be mentally entertained and be the objects of striving desire. In so far, we must side with Greek thought. But empirical ends-in-view are distinguished in two important respects from ends as they are conceived in classic thought. They are not objects of contemplative possession and use, but are intellectual and regulative means, degenerating into reminiscences or dreams unless they are employed as plans within the state of affairs. And when they are attained, the objects which they inform are conclusions and fulfillments; *only* as these objects are the consequence of prior reflection, deliberate choice and directed effort are they fulfillments, conclusions, completions, perfections. A natural end which occurs without the intervention of human art is a terminus, a de facto boundary, but it is not entitled to any such honorific status of completions and realizations as classic metaphyics assigned them.

When we regard conscious experience, that is to say, the *object* and *qualities* characteristic of conscious life, as a natural end, we are bound to regard *all* objects impartially as distinctive ends in the Aristotelian sense. We cannot pick or choose; when we do pick and choose we are obviously dealing with practical ends—with objects and qualities that are deemed worthy of selection by reflective, deliberate choice. These "ends" are not the less natural, if we have an eye to the continuity of experienced objects with other natural occurrences, but they are not ends without the intervention of a special affair, reflective survey and choice. But popular thought, in accord with the Greek tradition, picks and chooses among all ends those which it likes and honors, at the same time ignoring and implicitly denying the act of choice. Like those who regard a happy escape from a catastrophe as a providential intervention, neglecting all who have not escaped, popular teleology regards *good* objects as natural ends, *bad* objects and qualities being regarded as mere accidents or incidents, regrettable mechanical excess or defect. Popular teleology like Greek metaphysics, has accordingly been apologetic, justificatory of the beneficence of nature; it has been optimistic in a complacent way. . . .

By "ends" we also mean ends-in-view, aims, things viewed after deliberation as worthy of attainment and as evocative of effort. They are formed
from objects taken in their immediate and terminal qualities; objects once
having occurred as endings, but which are not now in existence and which
are not likely to come into existence save by an action which modifies surroundings. Classic metaphysics is a confused union of these two senses of
ends, the primarily natural and the secondarily natural, or practical, moral.
Each meaning is intelligible, grounded, legitimate in itself. But their mixture is one of the Great Bads of philosophy. For it treats as natural ends
apart from reflection just those objects that are worthy and excellent to reflective choice. Popular teleology has unknowingly followed the leadings that
controlled Greek thought; spiritualistic quasi-theological metaphysics has consciously adopted the latter's point of view.

The features of this confused metaphysics are: first, elimination from the
status of natural ends of all objects that are evil and troublesome; secondly,
the grading of objects selected to constitute natural ends into a fixed, unchangeable hierarchical order. Objects that possess and import qualities of
struggle, suffering and defeat are regarded not as ends, but as frustrations of
ends, as accidental and inexplicable deviations. Theology has resorted to an
act of original sin to make their occurrence explicable, Greek metaphysics
resorted to the presence in nature of a recalcitrant, obdurate, factor. To this
provincially exclusive view of natural termini, popular teleology adds a ranking of objects according to which some are more completely ends than others,
until there is reached an object which is only end, never eventful and temporal—*the* end. The hierarchy is explicit in Greek thought: first, and lowest
are vegetative ends, normal growth and reproduction; second in rank, come
animal ends, locomotion and sensibility; third in rank, are ideal and rational
ends, of which the highest is blissful contemplative possession in thought of
all the forms of nature. In this gradation, each lower rank while an *end* is
also means or preformed condition of higher ends. Empirical things, things
of useful arts, belonging to the second class but, affected by an adventitious
mixture of thought, are ultimately instrumentalities potential for the life of
pure rational possession of ideal objects. Modern teleologies are much less
succinct and definite, they agree however in the notion of rows of inferior
ends which prepare for and culminate in something which is *the* end.

Such a classificatory enterprise is naturally consoling to those who enjoy
a privileged status, whether as philosophers, as saints or scholars, and who
wish to justify their special status. But its consoling apologetics should not
blind us to the fact that to think of objects as more or less ends is nonsense.
They either have immediate and terminal quality; or they do not: quality as
such is absolute, not comparative. A thing may be of some shade of blue when
compared with some quality that is wanted and striven for; but its blue is

not itself more nor less blue than blueness, and so with the quality of being
terminal and absorbing. Objects may be more or less absorptive and arresting
and thus possess degrees of intensity with respect to finality. But this difference of intensity is not, save as subject to reflective choice, a distinction in
rank or class of finality. It applies to different toothaches as well as to different objects of thought; but it does not apply, inherently, to the difference
between a toothache and an ideal object—save that a thing like a toothache
is often possessed of greater intensity of finality. If we follow the clew of the
latter fact, we shall probably conclude that search for pure and unalloyed
finality carries us to inarticulate sensation and overwhelming passion. For
such affairs are the best instances of things that are complete in themselves
with no outleadings. . . .

. . . The things that are most precious, that are final, being just the things
that are unstable and most easily changing, seem to be different in kind from
good, solid, old-fashioned substance. Matter has turned out to be nothing
like as lumpy and chunky as unimaginative prejudice conceived it to be. But
as compared with the changes of immediate qualities it seems in any case
solid and substantial; a fact which accounts, I suppose, for the insertion of
an immaterial sort of substance, after the analogy of matter-substance, underneath mental affairs. But when it is recognized that the latter are eventual and
consummatory to highly complicated interactions of natural events, their
transiency becomes itself intelligible; it is no ground of argument for a
radical difference from the physical, the latter being also resolvable into a
character of the course of events. While "consciousness" as the conspicuous
and vivid presence of immediate qualities and of meanings, is alone of direct
worth, things not immediately present, whose intrinsic qualities are not directly had, are primary from the standpoint of control. For just because the
things that are directly had are both precious and evanescent, the only thing
that can be thought of is the conditions under which they are had. The common, pervasive and repeated *is* of superior rank from the standpoint of safeguarding and buttressing the having of terminal qualities. Directly we can
do nothing with the latter save have, enjoy and suffer them. So reflection is
concerned with the order which conditions, prevents and secures their occurrence. The irony of many historic systems of philosophy is that they have so
inverted the actualities of the case. The general, recurrent and extensive has
been treated as the worthy and superior kind of Being; the immediate, inten-
sive, transitory, and qualitatively individualized taken to be of importance
only when it is imputed to something ordinary, which is all the universal can
denotatively mean. In truth, the universal and stable are important because
they are the instrumentalities, the efficacious conditions, of the occurrence of
the unique, unstable and passing. . . .

Recent philosophy has witnessed the rise of a theory of value. Value as it
usually figures in this discussion marks a desperate attempt to combine the

obvious empirical fact that objects are qualified with good and bad, with philosophic deliverances which, in isolating man from nature, qualitative individualities from the world, render this fact anomalous. The philosopher erects a "realm of values" in which to place all the precious things which are extruded from natural existence because of isolations artificially introduced. Poignancy, humor, zest, tragedy, beauty, prosperity and bafflement, although rejected from a nature which is identified with mechanical structure, remain just what they empirically are, and demand recognition. Hence they are gathered up into the realm of values, contradistinguished from the realm of existence. Then the philosopher has a new problem with which to wrestle: What is the relationship of these two "worlds?" Is the world of value that of ultimate and transcendent Being from which the world of existence is a derivation or a fall? Or is it but a manifestation of human subjectivity, a factor somehow miraculously supervening upon an order complete and closed in physical structure? Or are there scattered at random through objective being, detached subsistences as "real" as are physical events, but having no temporal dates and spatial locations, and yet at times and places miraculously united with existences?

Choice among such notions of value is arbitrary, because the problem is arbitrary. When we return to the conceptions of potentiality and actuality, contingency and regularity, qualitatively diverse individuality, with which Greek thought operated, we find no room for a theory of values separate from a theory of nature. Yet if we are to recur to the Greek conceptions, the return must be a return with a difference. It must surrender the identification of natural ends with good and perfection; recognizing that a natural end, apart from endeavor expressing choice, has no intrinsic eulogistic quality, but is the boundary which writes "Finis" to a chapter of history inscribed by a moving system of energies. Failure by exhaustion as well as by triumph may constitute an end; death, ignorance, as well as life, are finalities.

Again, the return must abandon the notion of a predetermined limited number of ends inherently arranged in an order of increasing comprehensiveness and finality. It will have to recognize that natural termini are as infinitely numerous and varied as are the individual systems of action they delimit; and that since there is only relative, not absolute, impermeability and fixity of structure, new individuals with novel ends emerge in irregular procession. It must recognize that limits, closures, ends are experimentally or dynamically determined, presenting, like the boundaries of political individuals or states, a moving adjustment of various energy-systems in their cooperative and competitive interactions, not something belonging to them of their own right. Consequently, it will surrender the separation in nature from each other of contingency and regularity, the hazardous and the assured; it will avoid that relegation of them to distinct orders of Being which is characteristic of the classic tradition. It will note that they intersect everywhere; that

it is uncertainty and indeterminateness that create the need for and the sense
of order and security; that whatever is most complete and liberal in being
and possession is for that very reason most exposed to vicissitude, and most
needful of watchful safeguarding art. . . .

THE NATURE OF AIMS[5]

Our problem now concerns the nature of ends, that is ends-in-view or aims.
The essential elements in the problem have already been stated. It has been
pointed out that the ends, objectives, of conduct are those foreseen consequences which influence present deliberation and which finally bring it to rest
by furnishing an adequate stimulus to overt action. Consequently ends arise
and function within action. They are not, as current theories too often imply,
things lying beyond activity at which the latter is directed. They are not
strictly speaking ends or termini of action at all. They are terminals of deliberation, and so turning points *in* activity. Many opposed moral theories agree
however in placing ends beyond action, although they differ in their notions
of what the ends are. The utilitarian sets up pleasure as such an outside-and-
beyond, as something necessary to induce action and in which it terminates.
Many harsh critics of utilitarianism have however agreed that there is some
end in which action terminates, a final goal. They have denied that pleasure
is such an outside aim, and put perfection or self-realization in its place. The
entire popular notion of "ideals" is infected with this conception of some
fixed end beyond activity at which we should aim. According to this view
ends-in-themselves come before aims. We have a moral aim only as our purpose coincides with some end-in-itself. We *ought* to aim at the latter whether
we actually do or not.

When men believed that fixed ends existed for all normal changes in nature,
the conception of similar ends for men was but a special case of a general
belief. If the changes in a tree from acorn to full-grown oak were regulated by
an end which was somehow immanent of potential in all the less perfect forms,
and if change was simply the effort to realize a perfect or complete form,
then the acceptance of a like view for human conduct was consonant with
the rest of what passed for science. Such a view, consistent and systematic,
was foisted by Aristotle upon western culture and endured for two thousand
years. When the notion was expelled from natural science by the intellectual
revolution of the seventeenth century, logically it should also have disappeared from the theory of human action. But man is not logical and his
intellectual history is a record of mental reserves and compromises. He hangs
on to what he can in his old beliefs even when he is compelled to surrender
their logical basis. So the doctrine of fixed ends-in-themselves, at which
human acts are—or should be—directed and by which they are regulated if
they are regulated at all, persisted in morals and was made the cornerstone

of orthodox moral theory. The immediate effect was to dislocate moral from natural science, to divide man's world as it never had been divided in prior culture. One point of view, one method and spirit animated inquiry into natural occurrences; a radically opposite set of ideas prevailed about man's affairs. Completion of the scientific change begun in the seventeenth century thus depends upon a revision of the current notion of ends of action as fixed limits and conclusions.

In fact, ends are ends-in-view or aims. They arise out of natural effects or consequences which in the beginning are hit upon, stumbled upon so far as any purpose is concerned. Men *like* some of the consequences and *dislike* others. Henceforth (or till attraction and repulsion alter) attaining or averting similar consequences are aims or ends. These consequences constitute the meaning and value of an activity as it comes under deliberation. Meantime of course imagination is busy. Old consequences are enhanced, recombined, modified in imagination. Invention operates. Actual consequences, that is effects which have happened in the past, become possible future consequences of acts still to be performed. This operation of imaginative thought complicates the relation of ends to activity, but it does not alter the substantial fact: Ends are foreseen consequences which arise in the course of activity and which are employed to give activity added meaning and to direct its further course. They are in no sense ends *of* action. In being ends of *deliberation* they are redirecting pivots *in* action.

Men shoot and throw. At first this is done as an "instinctive" or natural reaction to some situation. The result when it is observed gives a new meaning to the activity. Henceforth men in throwing and shooting think of it in terms of its outcome; they act intelligently or have an end. Liking the activity in its acquired meaning, they not only "take aim" when they throw instead of throwing at random, but they find or make targets at which to aim. This is the origin and nature of "goals" of action. They are ways of defining and deepening the meaning of activity. Having an end or aim is thus a characteristic of *present activity*. It is the means by which an activity becomes adapted when otherwise it would be blind and disorderly, or by which it gets meaning when otherwise it would be mechanical. In a strict sense an end-in-view is a *means* in present action; present action is not a means to a remote end. Men do not shoot because targets exist, but they set up targets in order that throwing and shooting may be more effective and significant. . . .

When ends are regarded as literally ends to action rather than as directive stimuli to present choice they are frozen and isolated. It makes no difference whether the "end" is a "natural" good like health or a "moral" good like honesty. Set up as complete and exclusive, as demanding and justifying action as a means to itself, it leads to narrowness; in extreme cases fanaticism, inconsiderateness, arrogance and hypocrisy. Joshua's reputed success in getting the sun to stand still to serve his desire is recognized to have involved a miracle. But moral theorists constantly assume that the continuous course of events can be arrested at the point of a particular object; that men can plunge with their own desires into the unceasing flow of changes, and seize upon some object as their end irrespective of everything else. The use of intelligence to discover the object that will best operate as a releasing and unifying stimulus in the existing situation is discounted. One reminds one's self that one's end is justice or charity or professional achievement or putting over a deal for a needed public improvement, and further questionings and qualms are stilled. . . .

Why have men become so attached to fixed, external ends? Why is it not universally recognized that an end is a device of intelligence in guiding action, instrumental to freeing and harmonizing troubled and divided tendencies? The answer is virtually contained in what was earlier said about rigid habits and their effect upon intelligence. Ends are, in fact, literally endless, forever coming into existence as new activities occasion new consequences. "Endless ends" is a way of saying that there are no ends—that is no fixed self-enclosed finalities. While, however, we cannot actually prevent change from occurring we can and do regard it as evil. We strive to retain action in ditches already dug. We regard novelties as dangerous, experiments as illicit and deviations as forbidden. Fixed and separate ends reflect a projection of our own fixed and noninteracting compartmental habits. We see only consequences which correspond to our habitual courses. As we have said, men did not begin to shoot because there were ready-made targets to aim at. They made things into targets by shooting at them, and then made special targets to make shooting more significantly interesting. But if generation after generation were shown targets they had had no part in constructing, if bows and arrows were thrust into their hands, and pressure were brought to bear upon them to keep them shooting in season and out, some wearied soul would soon propound to willing listeners the theory that shooting was unnatural, that man was naturally wholly at rest, and that targets existed in order that men might be forced to be active; that the duty of shooting and the virtue of hitting are externally imposed and fostered, and that otherwise there would be no such thing as a shooting-activity—that is, morality.

The doctrine of fixed ends not only diverts attention from examination of consequences and the intelligent creation of purpose, but, since means and ends are two ways of regarding the same actuality, it also renders men careless in their inspection of existing conditions. An aim not framed on the basis of a survey of those present conditions which are to be employed as means of its realization simply throws us back upon past habits. We then do not do what we intended to do but what we have got used to doing, or else we thrash about in a blind ineffectual way. The result is failure. Discouragement follows, assuaged perhaps by the thought that in any case the end is too ideal, too noble and remote, to be capable of realization. We fall back on the consoling thought that our moral ideals are too good for this world and that we must accustom ourselves to a gap between aim and execution. Actual life is then thought of as a compromise with the best, an enforced second or third best, a dreary exile from our true home in the ideal, or a temporary period of troubled probation to be followed by a period of unending attainment and peace. At the same time, as has been repeatedly pointed out, persons of a more practical turn of mind accept the world "as it is," that is as past customs have made it to be, and consider what advantages for themselves may be extracted from it. They form aims on the basis of existing habits of life which may be turned to their own private account. They employ intelligence in framing ends and selecting and arranging means. But intelligence is confined to manipulation; it does not extend to construction. It is the intelligence of the politician, administrator and professional executive—the kind of intelligence which has given a bad meaning to a word that ought to have a fine meaning, opportunism. For the highest task of intelligence is to grasp and realize genuine opportunity, possibility.

Roughly speaking, the course of forming aims is as follows. The beginning is with a wish, an emotional reaction against the present state of things and a hope for something different. Action fails to connect satisfactorily with surrounding conditions. Thrown back upon itself, it projects itself in an imagination of a scene which if it were present would afford satisfaction. This picture is often called an aim, more often an ideal. But in itself it is a fancy which may be only a phantasy, a dream, a castle in the air. In itself it is a romantic embellishment of the present; at its best it is material for poetry or the novel. Its natural home is not in the future but in the dim past or in some distant and supposedly better part of the present world. Every such idealized object is suggested by something actually experienced, as the flight of birds suggests the liberation of human beings from the restrictions of slow locomotion on dull earth. It becomes an aim or end only when it is worked out in terms of concrete conditions available for its realization, that is in terms of "means." . . .

ENDS-IN-VIEW AND UNIFICATIONS OF VALUE[6]

This emphasis upon the function of needs and conflicts as the controlling factor in institution of ends and values does not signify that the latter are themselves negative in content and import. While they are framed with reference to a negative factor, deficit, want, privation, and conflict, their function is positive, and the resolution effected by performance of their function is positive. To attempt to gain an end *directly* is to put into operation the very conditions that are the source of the experienced trouble, thereby strengthening them and at most changing the outward form in which they manifest themselves. Ends-in-view framed with a negative *reference* (i.e., to some trouble or problem) are means which inhibit the operation of conditions producing the obnoxious result; they enable positive conditions to operate as resources and thereby to effect a result which is, in in the highest possible sense, positive in content. The content of the end as an object *held in view* is intellectual or methodological; the content of the attained outcome or the end *as consequence* is existential. It is positive in the degree in which it marks the doing-away of the need and conflict that evoked the *end-in-view*. The negative factor operates as a condition of forming the appropriate *idea* of an end; the idea when acted upon determines a positive outcome.

The attained end or consequence is always an organization of activities, where organization is a coordination of all activities which enter as factors. The *end-in-view* is that particular activity which operates as a coordinating factor of all other subactivities involved. Recognition of the end as a coordination or unified organization of activities, and of the end-in-view as the special activity which is the means of effecting this coordination, does away with any appearance of paradox that seems to be attached to the idea of a temporal continuum of activities in which each successive stage is equally end and means. The *form* of an attained end or consequence is always the same: that of adequate coordination. The content or involved matter of each successive result differs from that of its predecessors; for, while it is a *reinstatement* of a unified ongoing action, after a period of interruption through conflict and need, it is also an *enactment* of a new state of affairs. It has the qualities and properties appropriate to its being the consummatory resolution of a previous state of activity in which there was a peculiar need, desire, and end-in-view. In the continuous temporal process of organizing activities into a coordinated and coordinating unity, a constituent activity is both an end and a means: an end, in so far as it is temporally and relatively a close; a means, in so far as it provides a condition to be taken into account in further activity. . . .

It must also be noted that *activity* and *activities*, as these words are employed in the foregoing account, involve, like any actual behavior, existential materials, as breathing involves air; walking, the earth; buying and selling, commodities; inquiry, things investigated, etc. No human activity operates in a vacuum; it acts in the world and has materials upon which and through which it produces results. On the other hand, no material—air, water, metal, wood, etc.—is *means* save as it is employed in some human activity to accomplish something. When "organization of activities" is mentioned, it always includes within itself organization of the materials existing in the world in which we live. That organization which is the "final" value for each concrete situation of valuation thus forms part of the existential conditions that have to be taken into account in further formation of desires and interests or valuations. . . .

UNIFIED VALUE: CONSUMMATORY EXPERIENCE[7]

Experience occurs continuously, because the interaction of live creature and environing conditions is involved in the very process of living. Under conditions of resistance and conflict, aspects and elements of the self and the world that are implicated in this interaction qualify experience with emotions and ideas so that conscious intent emerges. Oftentimes, however, the experience had is inchoate. Things are experienced but not in such a way that they are composed into *an* experience. There is distraction and dispersion; what we observe and what we think, what we desire and what we get, are at odds with each other. We put our hands to the plow and turn back; we start and then we stop, not because the experience has reached the end for the sake of which it was initiated but because of extraneous interruptions or of inner lethargy.

In contrast with such experience, we have *an* experience when the material experienced runs its course to fulfillment. Then and then only is it integrated within and demarcated in the general stream of experience from other experiences. A piece of work is finishd in a way that is satisfactory; a problem receives its solution; a game is played through; a situation, whether that of eating a meal, playing a game of chess, carrying on a conversation, writing a book, or taking part in a political campaign, is so rounded out that its close is a consummation and not a cessation. Such an experience is a whole and carries with it its own individualizing quality and self-sufficiency. It is *an* experience.

Philosophers, even empirical philosophers, have spoken for the most part of experience at large. Idiomatic speech, however, refers to experiences each of which is singular, having its own beginning and end. For life is no uniform uninterrupted march or flow. It is a thing of histories, each with its own plot, its own inception and movement toward its close, each having its own particular rhythmic movement; each with its own unrepeated quality pervading it throughout. A flight of stairs, mechanical as it is, proceeds by individualized steps, not by undifferentiated progression, and an inclined plane is at least marked off from other things by abrupt discreteness.

Experience in this vital sense is defined by those situations and episodes that we spontaneously refer to as being "real experiences"; those things of which we say in recalling them, "that *was* an experience." It may have been something of tremendous importance—a quarrel with one who was once an intimate, a catastrophe finally averted by a hair's breadth. Or it may have been something that in comparison was slight—and which perhaps because of its very slightness illustrates all the better what is to be an experience. There is that meal in a Paris restaurant of which one says "that *was* an experience." It stands out as an enduring memorial of what food may be. Then there is that storm one went through in crossing the Atlantic—the storm that seemed in its fury, as it was experienced, to sum up in itself all that a storm can be, complete in itself, standing out because marked out from what went before and what came after.

In such experiences, every successive part flows freely, without seam and without unfilled blanks, into what ensues. At the same time there is no sacrifice of the self-identity of the parts. A river, as distinct from a pond, flows. But its flow gives a definiteness and interest to its successive portions greater than exist in the homogeneous portions of a pond. In an experience, flow is from something to something. As one part leads into another and as one part carries on what went before, each gains distinctness in itself. The enduring whole is diversified by successive phases that are emphases of its varied colors.

Because of continuous merging, there are no holes, mechanical junctions, and dead centers when we have *an* experience. There are pauses, places of rest, but they punctuate and define the quality of movement. They sum up what has been undergone and prevent its dissipation and idle evaporation. Continued acceleration is breathless and prevents parts from gaining distinction. In a work of art, different acts, episodes, occurrences melt and fuse into unity, and yet do not disappear and lose their own character as they do so—just as in a genial conversation there is a continuous interchange and blending, and yet each speaker not only retains his own character but manifests it more clearly than is his wont.

An experience has a unity that gives it its name, *that* meal, that storm, that rupture of friendship. The existence of this unity is constituted by a single *quality* that pervades the entire experience in spite of the variation of its constituent parts. This unity is neither emotional, practical, nor intellectual, for these terms name distinctions that reflection can make within it. In discourse *about* an experience, we must make use of these adjectives of interpretation. In going over an experience in mind *after* its occurrence, we may find that one property rather than another was sufficiently dominant so that it characterizes the experience as a whole. There are absorbing inquiries and speculations which a scientific man and philosopher will recall as "experiences" in the emphatic sense. In final import they are intellectual. But in their actual occurrence they were emotional as well; they were purposive and volitional. Yet the experience was not a sum of these different characters; they were lost in it as distinctive traits. No thinker can ply his occupation save as he is lured and rewarded by total integral experiences that are intrinsically worth while. Without them he would never know what it is really to think and would be completely at a loss in distinguishing real thought from the spurious article. Thinking goes on in trains of ideas, but the ideas form a train only because they are much more than what an analytic psychology calls ideas. They are phases, emotionally and practically distinguished, of a developing underlying quality; they are its moving variations, not separate and independent like Locke's and Hume's so-called ideas and impressions, but are subtle shadings of a pervading and developing hue.

We say of an experience of thinking that we reach or draw a conclusion. Theoretical formulation of the process is often made in such terms as to conceal effectually the similarity of "conclusion" to the consummating phase of every developing integral experience. These formulations apparently take their cue from the separate propositions that are premises and the proposition that is the conclusion as they appear on the printed page. The impression is derived that there are first two independent and ready-made entities that are then manipulated so as to give rise to a third. In fact, in an experience of thinking, premises emerge only as a conclusion becomes manifest. The experience, like that of watching a storm reach its height and gradually subside, is one of continuous movement of subject-matters. Like the ocean in the storm, there are a series of waves; suggestions reaching out and being broken in a clash, or being carried onward by a cooperative wave. If a conclusion is reached, it is that of a movement of anticipation and cumulation, one that finally comes to completion. A "conclusion" is no separate and independent thing; it is the consummation of a movement.

Hence *an* experience of thinking has its own esthetic quality. It differs from those experiences that are acknowledged to be esthetic, but only in its materials. The material of the fine arts consists of qualities; that of experience having intellectual conclusion are signs or symbols having no intrinsic quality of their own, but standing for things that may in another experience be qualitatively experienced. The difference is enormous. It is one reason why the strictly intellectual art will never be popular as music is popular. Nevertheless, the experience itself has a satisfying emotional quality because it possesses internal integration and fulfillment reached through ordered and organized movement. This artistic structure may be immediately felt. In so far, it is esthetic. What is even more important is that not only is this quality a significant motive in undertaking intellectual inquiry and in keeping it honest, but that no intellectual activity is an integral event (is *an* experience), unless it is rounded out with this quality. Without it, thinking is inconclusive. In short, esthetic cannot be sharply marked off from intellectual experience since the latter must bear an esthetic stamp to be itself complete.

The same statement holds good of a course of action that is dominantly practical, that is, one that consists of overt doings. It is possible to be efficient in action and yet not have a conscious experience. The activity is too automatic to permit of a sense of what it is about and where it is going, It comes to an end but not to a close or consummation in consciousness. Obstacles are overcome by shrewd skill, but they do not feed experience. There are also those who are wavering in action, uncertain, and inconclusive like the shades in classic literature. Between the poles of aimlessness and mechanical efficiency, there lie those courses of action in which through successive deeds there runs a sense of growing meaning conserved and accumulating toward an end that is felt as accomplishment of a process. Successful politicians and generals who turn statesmen like Caesar and Napoleon have something of the showman about them. This of itself is not art, but it is, I think, a sign that interest is not exclusively, perhaps not mainly, held by the result taken by itself (as it is in the case of mere efficiency), but by it as the outcome of a process. There is interest in completing an experience. The experience may be one that is harmful to the world and its consummation undesirable. But it has esthetic quality.

The Greek identification of good conduct with conduct having proportion, grace, and harmony, the *kalon-agathon,* is a more obvious example of distinctive esthetic quality in moral action. One great defect in what passes as morality is its anesthetic quality. Instead of exemplifying wholehearted action, it takes the form of grudging piecemeal concessions to the demands of duty. But illustrations may only obscure the fact that any practical activity will, provided that it is integrated and moves by its own urge to fulfillment, have esthetic quality.

A generalized illustration may be had if we imagine a stone, which is rolling down hill, to have an experience. The activity is surely sufficiently "practical." The stone starts from somewhere, and moves, as consistently as conditions permit, toward a place and state where it will be at rest—toward an end. Let us add, by imagination, to these external facts, the ideas that it looks forward with desire to the final outcome; that it is interested in the things it meets on its way, conditions that accelerate and retard its movement with respect to their bearing on the end; that it acts and feels toward them according to the hindering or helping function it attributes to them; and that the final coming to rest is related to all that went before as the culmination of a continuous movement. Then the stone would have an experience, and one with esthetic quality.

If we turn from this imaginary case to our own experience, we shall find much of it is nearer to what happens to the actual stone than it is to anything that fulfills the conditions fancy just laid down. For in much of our experience we are not concerned with the connection of incident with what went before and what comes after. There is no interest that controls attentive rejection or selection of what shall be organized into the developing experience. Things happen, but they are neither definitely included nor decisively excluded; we drift. We yield according to external pressure, or evade and compromise. There are beginnings and cessations, but no genuine initiations and concludings. One thing replaces another, but does not absorb it and carry it on. There is experience, but so slack and discursive that it is not *an* experience. Needless to say, such experiences are anesthetic.

Thus the nonesthetic lies within two limits. At one pole is the loose succession that does not begin at any particular place and that ends—in the sense of ceasing—at no particular place. At the other pole is arrest, constriction, proceeding from parts having only a mechanical connection with one another. There exists so much of one and the other of these two kinds of experience that unconsciously they come to be taken as norms of an experience. Then, when the esthetic appears, it so sharply contrasts with the picture that has been formed of experience that it is impossible to combine its special qualities with the features of the picture, and the esthetic is given an outside place and status. The account that has been given of experience dominantly intellectual and practical is intended to show that there is no such contrast involved in having an experience; that, on the contrary, no experience of whatever sort is a unity unless it has esthetic quality.

The enemies of the esthetic are neither the practical nor the intellectual. They are the humdrum; slackness of loose ends; submission to convention in practice and intellectual procedure. Rigid abstinence, coerced submission, tightness on one side and dissipation, incoherence and aimless indulgence on the other, are deviations in opposite directions from the unity of an experience. Some such considerations perhaps induced Aristotle to invoke the "mean proportional" as the proper designation of what is distinctive of both virtue and the esthetic. He was formally correct. "Mean" and "proportion" are, however, not self-explanatory, nor to be taken over in a prior mathematical sense, but are properties belonging to an experience that has a developing movement toward its own consummation.

I have emphasized the fact that every integral experience moves toward a close, an ending, since it ceases only when the energies active in it have done their proper work. This closure of a circuit of energy is the opposite of arrest, of *stasis*. Maturation and fixation are polar opposites. Struggle and conflict may be themselves enjoyed, although they are painful, when they are experienced as means of developing an experience; members in that they carry it forward, not just because they are there. . . .

CONVERTING NATURAL SEQUENCES INTO CONSUMMATIONS[8]

The source of . . . error lies in the habit of calling by the name of means things that are not means at all; things that are only external and accidental antecedents of the happening of something else. Similarly things are called ends that are not ends save accidentally, since they are not fulfillments, consummatory, of means, but merely last terms closing a process. Thus it is often said that a laborer's toil is the means of his livelihood, although except in the most tenuous and arbitrary way it bears no relationship to his real living. Even his wage is hardly an end or consequence of his labor. He might —and frequently does—equally well or ill—perform any one of a hundred other tasks as a condition of receiving payment. The prevailing conception of instrumentality is profoundly vitiated by the habit of applying it to cases like the above, where, instead of an operation of means, there is an enforced necessity of doing one thing as a coerced antecedent of the occurrence of another thing which is wanted.

Means are always at least causal conditions; but causal conditions are means only when they possess an added qualification; that namely, of being freely used, because of perceived connection with chosen consequences. To entertain, choose and accomplish anything as an end or consequence is to be committed to a like love and care for whatever events and acts are its means. Similarly, consequences, ends, are at least effects; but effects are not ends unless thought has perceived and freely chosen the conditions and processes that are their conditions. The notion that means are menial, instrumentalities servile, is more than a degradation of means to the rank of coercive and external necessities. It renders all things upon which the name of end is bestowed accompaniments of privilege, while the name of utility becomes an apologetic justification for things that are not portions of a good and reasonable life. Livelihood is at present not so much the consequence of a wage earner's labor as it is the effect of other causes forming the economic regime, labor being merely an accidental appendage of these other causes.

Paints and skill in manipulative arrangement are means of a picture as end, because the picture is *their* assemblage and organization. Tones and susceptibility of the ear when properly interacting are the means of music, because they constitute, make, are music. A disposition of virtue is a means to a certain quality of happiness because it is a constituent of that good, while such happiness is means in turn to virtue, as the sustaining of good in being. Flour, water, yeast are means of bread because they are ingredients of bread; while bread is a factor *in* life, *not* just *to* it. A good political constitution, honest police system, and competent judiciary, are means of the prosperous life of the community because they are integrated portions of that life. Science is an instrumentality of and for art because it is the intelligent factor *in* art. The trite saying that a hand is not a hand except as an organ of the living body—except as a working coordinated part of a balanced system of activities—applies untritely to all things that are means. The connection of means–consequences is never one of bare succession in time, such that the element that is means is past and gone when the end is instituted. An active process is strung out temporarily, but there is a deposit at each stage and point entering cumulatively and constitutively into the outcome. A genuine instrumentality *for* is always an organ *of* an end. It confers continued efficacy upon the object in which it is embodied.

The traditional separation between some things as mere means and others as mere ends is a reflection of the insulated existence of working and leisure classes, of production that is not also consummatory, and consummation that is not productive. This division is not a *merely* social phenomenon. It embodies a perpetuation upon the human plane of a division between need and satisfaction belonging to brute life. And this separation expresses in turn the mechanically external relationship that exists in nature between situations of disturbed equilibrium, of stress, and strain, and achieved equilibrium. For in nature, outside of man, except when events eventuate in "development" or "evolution" (in which a cumulative carrying forward of consequences of past histories in new efficiencies occurs) antecedent events are external transitive conditions of the occurrence of an event having immediate and static qualities. To animals to whom acts have no meaning, the change in the environment required to satisfy needs has no significance on its own account; such change is a mere incident of egocentric satisfactions. This physically external relationship of antecedents and consequents is perpetuated; it continues to hold true of human industry wherever labor and its materials and products are externally enforced necessities for securing a living. Because Greek industry was so largely upon this plane of servile labor, all industrial activity was regarded by Greek thought as a *mere* means, an extraneous necessity. Hence satisfactions due to it were conceived to be the ends or goods of purely animal nature in isolation. With respect to a truly human and rational life, they were not ends or goods at all, but merely "means," that is to say, external conditions that were antecedently enforced requisites of the life conducted and enjoyed by free men, especially by those devoted to the acme of freedom, pure thinking. As Aristotle asserted, drawing a just conclusion from the assumed premises, there are classes of men who are necessary materials of society but who are not integral parts of it. And he summed up the whole theory of the external and coerced relationship of means and ends when he said in this very connection that: "When there is one thing that is means and another thing that is end, there is *nothing common* between them, except in so far as the one, the means, produces, and the other, the end, receives the product."[9]

It would thus seem almost self-evident that the distinction between the instrumental and the final adopted in philosophic tradition as a solving word presents in truth a problem, a problem so deep-seated and far-reaching that it may be said to be *the* problem of experience. For all the intelligent activities of men, no matter whether expressed in science, fine arts, or social relationships, have for their task the conversion of causal bonds, relations of succession, into a connection of means–consequence, into meanings. When the task is achieved the result is art: and in art everything is common between means and ends. Whenever so-called means remain external and servile, and so-called ends are enjoyed objects whose further causative status is unperceived, ignored or denied, the situation is proof positive of limitations of art. Such a situation consists of affairs in which the problem has *not* been solved; namely that of converting physical and brute relationships into connections of meanings characteristic of the possibilities of nature. . . .

1. Chapter III of my *John Dewey's Philosophy of Value* sorts out the substantive and verbal distinctions that Dewey employed—*Ed.*
2. *The Quest for Certainty* (New York: Minton, Balch and Company, 1929). This excerpt is reprinted from the paperback edition by G. P. Putnam's Sons (New York: Capricorn Books, 1960), pp. 291–93. Heading provided by the editor.
3. *Experience and Nature*, pp. 78–81, 84–86, 94–106, 115–16, 394–96. Heading provided by the editor.
4. In saying that immediate experience cannot be described, Dewey's point is that denoting or describing a quality necessarily creates a new experience with its own quality, and so on. Any qualitative experience is altered in the attempt to characterize it—*Ed.*
5. *Human Nature and Conduct*, pp. 207–10, 211, 214–17.
6. *Theory of Valuation* (Chicago: University of Chicago Press, 1939), pp. 48–50. Heading provided by the editor.
7. *Art as Experience* (New York: Minton, Balch and Company, 1934). This excerpt is reprinted from the paperback edition by G. P. Putnam's Sons (New York: Capricorn Books, 1958), pp. 35–41. Heading provided by the editor. Subsequent selections from *Art as Experience* are also taken from the Capricorn Books edition.
8. *Experience and Nature*, pp. 366–70. Heading provided by the editor.
9. Dewey refers to book VII, chapter 8 of Aristotle's *Politics*—*Ed.*

Human Nature and Value

4

Human nature and nature function as an inclusive process. Accordingly, the determination of the status of value in nature is a task inherently incapable of completion until the self is examined in a way to discern its crucial functions in respect to value. In this section, Dewey's main assumptions about human nature and the values organic to it are presented. The first selection concerns the nature of habit, the principal constituent of human nature. Habit, Dewey argues, is a function of organism and environment together. It is in terms of habit that Dewey accounts for all the distinctive functions of human behavior, at once dispensing with the various forms of psychology which account for human powers merely by postulating an inherent faculty which possesses and wields them. Ideas, for example, are habits in that they are anticipations of the experience which is contingent upon specific modes of behavior. Thinking is the collective activity of habits and impulse functioning with a specific problematic environment.

Dewey's analyses of behavior are voluminous; so the first selection is barely introductory. The subject matter is of greatest importance, however, for habits may be conducive to an enhanced functioning of the self or be detrimental to it. Therefore, the determination of the constituents of specific habits is at the same time the discovery of the means of the formation of a self capable of functioning more effectively and harmoniously with its environment.

HABIT[1]

Habits may be profitably compared to physiological functions, like breathing, digesting. The latter are, to be sure, involuntary, while habits are acquired. But important as is this difference for many purposes, it should not conceal the fact that habits are like functions in many respects, and especially in requiring the cooperation of organism and environment. Breathing is an affair of the air as truly as of the lungs; digesting an affair of food as truly as of tissues of stomach. Seeing involves light just as certainly as it does the eye and optic nerve. Walking implicates the ground as well as the legs; speech demands physical air and human companionship and audience as well as vocal organs. We may shift from the biological to the mathematical use of the word function and say that natural operations like breathing and digesting, acquired ones like speech and honesty, are functions of the surroundings as truly as of a person. They are things done *by* the environment by means of organic structures or acquired dispositions. The same air that under certain conditions ruffles the pool or wrecks buildings, under other conditions purifies the blood and conveys thought. The outcome depends upon what air acts upon. The social environment acts through native impulses and speech and moral habitudes manifest themselves. There are specific good reasons for the usual attribution of acts to the person from whom they immediately proceed. But to convert this special reference into a belief of exclusive ownership is as misleading as to suppose that breathing and digesting are complete within the human body. To get a rational basis for moral discussion we must begin with recognizing that functions and habits are ways of using and incorporating the environment in which the latter has its say as surely as the former.

We may borrow words from a context less technical than that of biology and convey the same idea by saying that habits are arts. They involve skill of sensory and motor organs, cunning or craft, and objective materials. They assimilate objective energies, and eventuate in command of environment. They require order, discipline, and manifest technique. They have a beginning, middle and end. Each stage marks progress in dealing with materials and tools, advance in converting material to active use. We should laugh at any one who said that he was master of stone working, but that the art was cooped up within himself and in no wise dependent upon support from objects and assistance from tools.

In morals we are however quite accustomed to such a fatuity. Moral dispositions are thought of as belonging exclusively to a self. The self is thereby isolated from natural and social surroundings. A whole school of morals flourishes upon capital drawn from restricting morals to character and then separating character from conduct, motives from actual deeds. Recognition of the analogy of moral action with functions and arts uproots the causes which have made morals subjective and "individualistic." It brings morals to earth, and if they still aspire to heaven it is to the heavens *of* the earth, and not to another world. Honesty, chastity, malice, peevishness, courage, triviality, industry, irresponsibility are not private possessions of a person. They are working adaptations of personal capacities with environing forces. All virtues and vices are habits which incorporate objective forces. They are interactions of elements contributed by the makeup of an individual with elements supplied by the outdoor world. They can be studied as objectively as physiological functions, and they can be modified by change of either personal or social elements.

If an individual were alone in the world, he would form his habits (assuming the impossible, namely, that he would be able to form them) in a moral vacuum. They would belong to him alone, or to him only in reference to physical forces. Responsibility and virtue would be his alone. But since habits involve the support of environing conditions, a society or some specific group of fellowmen, is always accessory before and after the fact. . . .

It is a significant fact that in order to appreciate the peculiar place of habit in activity we have to betake ourselves to bad habits, foolish idling, gambling, addiction to liquor and drugs. When we think of such habits, the union of habit with desire and with propulsive power is forced upon us. When we think of habits in terms of walking, playing a musical instrument, typewriting, we are much given to thinking of habits as technical abilities existing apart from our likings and as lacking in urgent impulsion. We think of them as passive tools waiting to be called into action from without. A bad habit suggests an inherent tendency to action and also a hold, command over us. It makes us do things we are ashamed of, things which we tell ourselves we prefer not to do. It overrides our formal resolutions, our conscious decisions. When we are honest with ourselves we acknowledge that a habit has this power because it is so intimately a part of ourselves. It has a hold upon us because we are the habit.

Our self-love, our refusal to face facts, combined perhaps with a sense of a possible better although unrealized self, leads us to eject the habit from the thought of ourselves and conceive it as an evil power which has somehow overcome us. We feed our conceit by recalling that the habit was not deliberately formed; we never intended to become idlers or gamblers or roués. And how can anything be deeply ourselves which developed accidentally, without set intention? These traits of a bad habit are precisely the things which are most instructive about all habits and about ourselves. They teach us that all habits are affections, that all have projectile power, and that a predisposition formed by a number of specific acts is an immensely more intimate and fundamental part of ourselves than are vague, general, conscious choices. All habits are demands for certain kinds of activity; and they constitute the self. In any intelligible sense of the word will, they *are* will. They form our effective desires and they furnish us with our working capacities. They rule our thoughts, determining which shall appear and be strong and which shall pass from light into obscurity.

We may think of habits as means, waiting, like tools in a box, to be used by conscious resolve. But they are something more than that. They are active means, means that project themselves, energetic and dominating ways of acting. We need to distinguish between materials, tools and means proper. Nails and boards are not strictly speaking means of a box. They are only materials for making it. Even the saw and hammer are means only when they are employed in some actual making. Otherwise they are tools, or potential means. They are actual means only when brought in conjunction with eye, arm and hand in some specific operation. And eye, arm and hand are, correspondingly, means proper only when they are in active operation. And whenever they are in action they are cooperating with external materials and energies. Without support from beyond themselves the eye stares blankly and the hand moves fumblingly. They are means only when they enter into organization with things which independently accomplish definite results. These organizations are habits. . . .

The word habit may seem twisted somewhat from its customary use when employed as we have been using it. But we need a word to express that kind of human activity which is influenced by prior activity and in that sense acquired; which contains within itself a certain ordering or systematization of minor elements of action; which is projective, dynamic in quality, ready for overt manifestation; and which is operative in some subdued subordinate form even when not obviously dominating activity. Habit even in its ordinary usage comes nearer to denoting these facts than any other word. If the facts are recognized we may also use the words attitude and disposition. But unless we have first made clear to ourselves the facts which have been set forth under the name of habit, these words are more likely to be misleading than is the word habit. For the latter conveys explicitly the sense of operativeness, actuality. Attitude and, as ordinarily used, disposition suggest something latent, potential, something which requires a positive stimulus outside themselves to become active. If we perceive that they denote positive forms of action which are released merely through removal of some counter-acting "inhibitory" tendency, and then become overt, we may employ them instead of the word habit to denote subdued, nonpatent forms of the latter.

In this case, we must bear in mind that the word disposition means predisposition, readiness to act overtly in a specific fashion whenever opportunity is presented, this opportunity consisting in removal of the pressure due to the dominance of some overt habit; and that attitude means some special case of a predisposition, the disposition waiting as it were to spring through an opened door. While it is admitted that the word habit has been used in a somewhat broader sense than is usual, we must protest against the tendency in psychological literature to limit its meaning to repetition. This usage is much less in accord with popular usage than is the wider way in which we have used the word. It assumes from the start the identity of habit with routine. Repetition is in no sense the essence of habit. Tendency to repeat acts is an incident of many habits but not of all. A man with the habit of giving way to anger may show his habit by a murderous attack upon someone who has offended. His act is nonetheless due to habit because it occurs only once in his life. The essence of habit is an acquired predisposition to *ways* or modes of response, not to particular acts except as, under special conditions, these express a way of behaving. Habit means special sensitiveness or accessibility to certain classes of stimuli, standing predilections and aversions, rather than bare recurrence of specific acts. It means will. . . .

Habits as organized activities are secondary and acquired, not native and original. They are outgrowths of unlearned activities which are part of man's endowment at birth. The order of topics followed in our discussion may accordingly be questioned. Why should what is derived and therefore in some sense artificial in conduct be discussed before what is primitive, natural and inevitable? Why did we not set out with an examination of those instinctive activities upon which the acquisition of habits is conditioned?

The query is a natural one, yet it tempts to flinging forth a paradox. In conduct the acquired is the primitive. Impulses although first in time are never primary in fact; they are secondary and dependent. The seeming paradox in statement covers a familiar fact. In the life of the individual, instinctive activity comes first. But an individual begins life as a baby, and babies are dependent beings. Their activities could continue at most for only a few hours were it not for the presence and aid of adults with their formed habits. And babies owe to adults more than procreation, more than the continued food and protection which preserve life. They owe to adults the opportunity to express their native activities in ways which have meaning. Even if by some miracle original activity could continue without assistance from the organized skill and art of adults, it would not amount to anything. It would be mere sound and fury.

In short, the *meaning* of native activities is not native; it is acquired. It depends upon interaction with a matured social medium. In the case of a tiger or eagle, anger may be identified with a serviceable life-activity, with attack and defense. With a human being it is as meaningless as a gust of wind on a mud puddle apart from a direction given it by the presence of other persons, apart from the responses they make to it. It is a physical spasm, a blind dispersive burst of wasteful energy. It gets quality, significance, when it becomes a smoldering sullenness, an annoying interruption, a peevish irritation, a murderous revenge, a blazing indignation. And although these phenomena which have a meaning spring from original native reactions to stimuli, yet they depend also upon the responsive behavior of others. They and all similar human displays of anger are not pure impulses; they are habits formed under the influence of association with others who have habits already and who show their habits in the treatment which converts a blind physical discharge into a significant anger.

After ignoring impulses for a long time in behalf of sensations, modern psychology now tends to start out with an inventory and description of instinctive activities. This is an undoubted improvement. But when it tries to explain complicated events in personal and social life by direct reference to these native powers, the explanation becomes hazy and forced. It is like saying the flea and the elephant, the lichen and the redwood, the timid hare and the ravening wolf, the plant with the most inconspicuous blossom and the plant with the most glaring color are alike products of natural selection. There may be a sense in which the statement is true; but till we know the specific environing conditions under which selection took place we really know nothing. And so we need to know about the social conditions which have educated original activities into definite and significant dispositions before we can discuss the psychological element in society. This is the true meaning of social psychology. . . .

In the case of the young it is patent that impulses are highly flexible starting points for activities which are diversified according to the ways in which they are used. Any impulse may become organized into almost any disposition according to the way it interacts with surroundings. Fear may become abject cowardice, prudent caution, reverence for superiors or respect for equals; an agency for credulous swallowing of absurd superstitions or for wary skepticism. A man may be chiefly afraid of the spirits of his ancestors, of officials, of arousing the disapproval of his associates, of being deceived, of fresh air, or of Bolshevism. The actual outcome depends upon how the impulse of fear is interwoven with other impulses. This depends in turn upon the outlets and inhibitions supplied by the social environment. . . .

In discussing habit and impulse we have repeatedly met topics where reference to the work of thought was imperative. Explicit consideration of the place and office of intelligence in conduct can hardly begin otherwise than by gathering together these incidental references and reaffirming their significance. The stimulation of reflective imagination by impulse, its dependence upon established habits, and its effect in transforming habit and regulating impulse forms, accordingly, our . . . [next] theme.

Habits are conditions of intellectual efficiency. They operate in two ways upon intellect. Obviously, they restrict its reach, they fix its boundaries. They are blinders that confine the eyes of mind to the road ahead. They prevent thought from straying away from its imminent occupation to a landscape more varied and picturesque but irrelevant to practice. Outside the scope of habits, thought works gropingly, fumbling in confused uncertainty; and yet habit made complete in routine shuts in thought so effectually that it is no longer needed or possible. The routineer's road is a ditch out of which he cannot get, whose sides enclose him, directing his course so thoroughly that he no longer thinks of his path or his destination. All habit-forming involves the beginning of an intellectual specialization which if unchecked ends in thoughtless action. . . .

Habit is however more than a restriction of thought. Habits become negative limits because they are first positive agencies. The more numerous our habits the wider the field of possible observation and foretelling. The more flexible they are, the more refined is perception in its discrimination and the more delicate the presentation evoked by imagination. The sailor is intel- lectually at home on the sea, the hunter in the forest, the painter in his studio, the man of science in his laboratory. These commonplaces are universally recognized in the concrete; but their significance is obscured and their truth denied in the current general theory of mind. For they mean nothing more or less than that habits formed in process of exercising biological aptitudes are the sole agents of observation, recollection, foresight and judgment: a mind or consciousness or soul in general which performs these operations is a myth.

The doctrine of a single, simple and indissoluble soul was the cause and the effect of failure to recognize that concrete habits are the means of knowl- edge and thought. Many who think themselves scientifically emancipated and who freely advertise the soul for a superstition, perpetuate a false notion of what knows, that is, of a separate knower. Nowadays they usually fix upon consciousness in general, as a stream or process or entity; or else, more specifically upon sensations and images as the tools of intellect. Or some- times they think they have scaled the last heights of realism by adverting grandiosely to a formal knower in general who serves as one term in the knowing relation; by dismissing psychology as irrelevant to knowledge and logic, they think to conceal the psychological monster they have conjured up.

Now it is dogmatically stated that no such conceptions of the seat, agent or vehicle will go psychologically at the present time. Concrete habits do all the perceiving, recognizing, imagining, recalling, judging, conceiving and reasoning that is done. "Consciousness," whether as a stream or as special sensations and images, expresses functions of habits, phenomena of their formation, operation, their interruption and reorganization. . . .

We need to discriminate between the physical and the moral question. The former concerns what *has* happened, and how it happened. To consider this question is indispensable to morals. Without an answer to it we cannot tell what forces are at work nor how to direct our actions so as to improve con- ditions. Until we know the conditions which have helped form the characters we approve and disapprove, our efforts to create the one and do away with the other will be blind and halting. But the moral issue concerns the future. It is prospective. To content ourselves with pronouncing judgments of merit and demerit without reference to the fact that our judgments are themselves facts which have consequences and that their value depends upon *their* consequences, is complacently to dodge the moral issue, perhaps even to indulge ourselves in pleasurable passion just as the person we condemn once indulged himself. The moral problem is that of modifying the factors which now influence future results. To change the working character or will of another we have to alter objective conditions which enter into his habits. Our own schemes of judgment, of assigning blame and praise, of awarding punishment and honor, are part of these conditions.

In practical life, there are many recognitions of the part played by social factors in generating personal traits. One of them is our habit of making social classifications. We attribute distinctive characteristics to rich and poor, slum dweller and captain of industry, rustic and suburbanite, officials, politicians, professors, to members of races, sets and parties. These judgments are usually too coarse to be of much use. But they show our practical awareness that personal traits are functions of social situations. When we generalize this perception and act upon it intelligently we are committed by it to recognize that we change character from worse to better only by changing conditions—among which, once more, are our own ways of dealing with the one we judge. We cannot change habit directly: that notion is magic. But we can change it indirectly by modifying conditions, by an intelligent selecting and weighting of the objects which engage attention and which influence the fulfillment of desires. . . .

THE NATURE AND CONDITIONS OF GROWTH[2]

When an individual develops more and more powers of acting effectively with his environment—that is, as he develops and refines habits—he is engaged in what Dewey calls growth. Growth is the process by which an individual is increasingly able to engage his energies with his environment in a manner that creates consummatory experience. The activity of growth is itself one of the greatest goods of human existence, enriching all phases of experience. By contrast, we impoverish experience by longing for an end believed to exist independently of activity.

The first selection is from a work devoted to philosophy of art. The discussion places the esthetic and artistic within the context of the process of growth.

Life itself consists of phases in which the organism falls out of step with the march of surrounding things and then recovers unison with it—either through effort or by some happy chance. And, in a growing life, the recovery is never mere return to a prior state, for it is enriched by the state of disparity and resistance through which it has successfully passed. If the gap between organism and environment is too wide, the creature dies. If its activity is not enhanced by the temporary alienation, it merely subsists. Life grows when a temporary falling out is a transition to a more extensive balance of the energies of the organism with those of the conditions under which it lives. . . .

. . . The world is full of things that are indifferent and even hostile to life; the very processes by which life is maintained tend to throw it out of gear with its surroundings. Nevertheless, if life continues and if in continuing it expands, there is an overcoming of factors of opposition and conflict; there is a transformation of them into differentiated aspects of a higher powered and more significant life. The marvel of organic, of vital, adaptation through expansion (instead of by contraction and passive accommodation) actually takes place. Here in germ are balance and harmony attained through rhythm. Equilibrium comes about not mechanically and inertly but out of, and because of, tension.

There is in nature, even below the level of life, something more than mere flux and change. Form is arrived at whenever a stable, even though moving, equilibrium is reached. Changes interlock and sustain one another. Wherever there is this coherence there is endurance. Order is not imposed from without but is made out of the relations of harmonious interactions that energies bear to one another. Because it is active (not anything static because foreign to what goes on) order itself develops. It comes to include within its balanced movement a greater variety of changes.

Order cannot but be admirable in a world constantly threatened with disorder—in a world where living creatures can go on living only by taking advantage of whatever order exists about them, incorporating it into themselves. In a world like ours, every living creature that attains sensibility welcomes order with a response of harmonious feeling whenever it finds a congruous order about it.

For only when an organism shares in the ordered relations of its environment does it secure the stability essential to living. And when the participation comes after a phase of disruption and conflict, it bears within itself the germs of a consummation akin to the esthetic.

The rhythm of loss of integration with environment and recovery of union not only persists in man but becomes conscious with him; its conditions are material out of which he forms purposes. Emotion is the conscious sign of a break, actual or impending. The discord is the occasion that induces reflection. Desire for restoration of the union converts mere emotion into interest in objects as conditions of realization of harmony. With the realization, material of reflection is incorporated into objects as their meaning. Since the artist cares in a peculiar way for the phase of experience in which union is achieved, he does not shun moments of resistance and tension. He rather cultivates them, not for their own sake but because of their potentialities, bringing to living consciousness an experience that is unified and total. In contrast with the person whose purpose is esthetic, the scientific man is interested in problems, in situations wherein tension between the matter of observation and of thought is marked. Of course he cares for their resolution. But he does not rest in it; he passes on to another problem using an attained solution only as a stepping stone from which to set on foot further inquiries.

The difference between the esthetic and the intellectual is thus one of the place where emphasis falls in the constant rhythm that marks the interaction of the live creature with his surroundings. The ultimate matter of both emphases in experience is the same, as is also their general form. The odd notion that an artist does not think and a scientific inquirer does nothing else is the result of converting a difference of tempo and emphasis into a difference in kind. The thinker has his esthetic moment when his ideas cease to be mere ideas and become the corporate meanings of objects. The artist has his problems and thinks as he works. But his thought is more immediately embodied in the object. Because of the comparative remoteness of his end, the scientific worker operates with symbols, words and mathematical signs. The artist does his thinking in the very qualitative media he works in, and the terms lie so close to the object that he is producing that they merge directly into it.

The live animal does not have to project emotions into the objects experienced. Nature is kind and hateful, bland and morose, irritating and comforting, long before she is mathematically qualified or even a congeries of "secondary" qualities like colors and their shapes. Even such words as long and short, solid and hollow, still carry to all, but those who are intellectually specialized, a moral and emotional connotation. The dictionary will inform any one who consults it that the early use of words like sweet and bitter was not to denote qualities of sense as such but to discriminate things as favorable and hostile. How could it be otherwise? Direct experience comes from nature and man interacting with each other. In this interaction, human energy gathers, is released, dammed up, frustrated and victorious. There are rhythmic beats of want and fulfillment, pulses of doing and being withheld from doing.

All interactions that effect stability and order in the whirling flux of change are rhythms. There is ebb and flow, systole and diastole; ordered change. The latter moves within bounds. To overpass the limits that are set is destruction and death, out of which, however, new rhythms are built up. The proportionate interception of changes establishes an order that is spatially, not merely temporally patterned: like the waves of the sea, the ripples of sand where waves have flowed back and forth, the fleecy and the black-bottomed cloud. Contrast of lack and fullness, of struggle and acheivement, of adjustment after consummated irregularity, form the drama in which action, feeling, and meaning are one. The outcome is balance and counterbalance. These are not static nor mechanical. They express power that is intense because measured through overcoming resistance. Environing objects avail and counteravail.

There are two sorts of possible worlds in which esthetic experience would not occur. In a world of mere flux, change would not be cumulative; it would not move toward a close. Stability and rest would have no being. Equally is it true, however, that a world that is finished, ended, would have no traits of suspense and crisis, and would offer no opportunity for resolution. Where everything is already complete, there is no fulfillment. We envisage with pleasure Nirvana and a uniform heavenly bliss only because they are projected upon the background of our present world of stress and conflict. Because the actual world, that in which we live, is a combination of movement and culmination, of breaks and re-unions, the experience of a living creature is capable of esthetic quality. The live being recurrently loses and reëstablishes equilibrium with his surroundings. The moment of passage from disturbance into harmony is that of intensest life. In a finished world, sleep and waking could not be distinguished. In one wholly perturbed, conditions could not even be struggled with. In a world made after the pattern of ours, moments of fulfillment punctuate experience with rhythmically enjoyed intervals.

Inner harmony is attained only when, by some means, terms are made with the environment. When it occurs on any other than an "objective" basis, it is illusory—in extreme cases to the point of insanity. Fortunately for variety in experience, terms are made in many ways—ways ultimately decided by selective interest. Pleasures are not to be despised in a world full of pain. But happiness and delight are a different sort of thing. They come to be through a fulfillment that reaches to the depths of our being—one that is an adjustment of our whole being with the conditions of existence. In the process of living, attainment of a period of equilibrium is at the same time the initiation of a new relation to the environment, one that brings with it potency of new adjustments to be made through struggle. The time of consummation is also one of beginning anew. Any attempt to perpetuate beyond its term the enjoyment attending the time of fulfillment and harmony constitutes withdrawal from the world. Hence it marks the lowering and loss of vitality. But, through the phases of perturbation and conflict, there abides the deep-seated memory of an underlying harmony, the sense of which haunts life like the sense of being founded on a rock.

Most mortals are conscious that a split often occurs between their present living and their past and future. Then the past hangs upon them as a burden; it invades the present with a sense of regret, of opportunities not used, and of consequences we wish undone. It rests upon the present as an oppression, instead of being a storehouse of resources by which to move confidently forward. But the live creature adopts its past; it can make friends with even its stupidities, using them as warnings that increase present wariness. Instead of trying to live upon whatever may have been achieved in the past, it uses past successes to inform the present. Every living experience owes its richness to what Santayana well calls "hushed reverberations.". . .

To the being fully alive, the future is not ominous but a promise; it surrounds the present as a halo. It consists of possibilities that are felt as a possession of what is now and here. In life that is truly life, everything overlaps and merges. But all too often we exist in apprehensions of what the future may bring, and are divided within ourselves. Even when not over-anxious, we do not enjoy the present because we subordinate it to that which is absent. Because of the frequency of this abandonment of the present to the past and future, the happy periods of an experience that is now complete because it absorbs into itself memories of the past and anticipations of the future, come to constitute an esthetic ideal. Only when the past ceases to trouble and anticipations of the future are not perturbing is a being wholly united with his environment and therefore fully alive. Art celebrates with peculiar intensity the moments in which the past reënforces the present and in which the future is a quickening of what now is.

GROWTH AND VALUE[3]

No matter what the present success in straightening out difficulties and harmonizing conflicts, it is certain that problems will recur in the future in a new form or on a different plane. Indeed every genuine accomplishment instead of winding up an affair and enclosing it as a jewel in a casket for future contemplation, complicates the practical situation. It effects a new distribution of energies which have henceforth to be employed in ways for which past experience gives no exact instruction. Every important satisfac-tion of an old want creates a new one; and this new one has to enter upon an experimental adventure to find its satisfaction. From the side of what has gone before achievement settles something. From the side of what comes after, it complicates, introducing new problems, unsettling factors. There is something pitifully juvenile in the idea that "evolution," progress, means a definite sum of accomplishment which will forever stay done, and which by an exact amount lessens the amount still to be done, disposing once and for all of just so many perplexities and advancing us just so far on our road to a final stable and unperplexed goal. Yet the typical nineteenth-century, mid-Victorian conception of evolution was precisely a formulation of such a consummate juvenilism. . . .

In any case, however, arguments about pessimism and optimism based upon considerations regarding fixed attainment of good and evil are mainly literary in quality. Man continues to live because he is a living creature not because reason convinces him of the certainty or probability of future satis-factions and achievements. He is instinct with activities that carry him on. Individuals here and there cave in, and most individuals sag, withdraw and seek refuge at this and that point. But man as man still has the dumb pluck of the animal. He has endurance, hope, curiosity, eagerness, love of action. These traits belong to him by structure, not by taking thought. Memory of past and foresight of future convert dumbness to some degree of articulate-ness. They illumine curiosity and steady courage. Then when the future arrives with its inevitable disappointments as well as fulfillments, and with new sources of trouble, failure loses something of its fatality, and suffering yields fruit of instruction not of bitterness. Humility is more demanded at our moments of triumph than at those of failure. For humility is not a caddish self-depreciation. It is the sense of our slight inabilty even with our best intelligence and effort to command events; a sense of our dependence upon forces that go their way without our wish and plan. Its purport is not to relax effort but to make us prize every opportunity of present growth. In morals, the infinitive and the imperative develop from the participle, present tense. Perfection means perfecting, fulfillment, fulfilling, and the good is now or never. . . .

. . . Some philosophers define religious consciousness as beginning where moral and intellectual consciousness leave off. In the sense that definite purposes and methods shade off of necessity into a vast whole which is incapable of objective presentation this view is correct. But they have falsified the conception by treating the religious consciousness as something that comes *after* an experience in which striving, resolution and foresight are found. To them morality and science are a striving; when striving ceases a moral holiday begins, an excursion beyond the utmost flight of legitimate thought and endeavor. But there is a point in *every* intelligent activity where effort ceases; where thought and doing fall back upon a course of events which effort and reflection cannot touch. There is a point *in* deliberate action where definite thought fades into the ineffable and undefinable—into emotion. If the sense of this effortless and unfathomable whole comes only in alternation with the sense of strain in action and labor in thought, then we spend our lives in oscillating between what is cramped and enforced and a brief transitory escape. The function of religion is then caricatured rather than realized. Morals, like war, is thought of as hell, and religion, like peace, as a respite. The religious experience is a reality in so far as in the midst of effort to foresee and regulate future objects we are sustained and expanded in feebleness and failure by the sense of an enveloping whole. Peace in action, not after it, is the contribution of the ideal to conduct.

Over and over again, one point has recurred for criticism—the subordination of activity to a result outside itself. Whether that goal be thought of as pleasure, as virtue, as perfection, as final enjoyment of salvation, is secondary to the fact that the moralists who have asserted fixed ends have in all their differences from one another agreed in the basic idea that present activity is but a means. We have insisted that happiness, reasonableness, virtue, perfecting, are, on the contrary, parts of the present significance of present action. Memory of the past, observation of the present, foresight of the future are indispensable. But they are indispensable *to* a present liberation, an enriching growth of action. Happiness is fundamental in morals only because happiness is not something to be sought for, but is something now attained, even in the midst of pain and trouble, whenever recognition of our ties with nature and with fellowmen releases and informs our action. Reasonableness is a necessity because it is the perception of the continuities that take action out of its immediateness and isolation into connection with the past and future.

Perhaps the criticism and insistence have been too incessant. They may have provoked the reader to reaction. He may readily concede that orthodox theories have been one-sided in sacrificing the present to future good, making of the present but an onerous obligation or a sacrifice endured for future gain. But why, he may protest, go to an opposite extreme and make the future but a means to the significance of the present? Why should the power of foresight and effort to shape the future, to regulate what is to happen, be slighted? Is not the effect of such a doctrine to weaken putting forth of endeavor in order to make the future better than the present? Control of the future may be limited in extent, but it is correspondingly precious; we should jealously cherish whatever encourages and sustains effort to that end. To make little of this possibility, in effect, it will be argued, is to decrease the care and endeavor upon which progress depends.

Control of the future is indeed precious in exact proportion to its difficulty, its moderate degree of attainability. Anything that actually tends to make that control less than it now is would be a movement backward into sloth and triviality. But there is a difference between future improvement as a result and as a direct aim. To make it an aim is to throw away the surest means of attaining it, namely attention to the full use of present resources in the present situation. Forecast of future conditions, scientific study of past and present in order that the forecast may be intelligent, are indeed necessities. Concentration of intellectual concern upon the future, solicitude for scope and precision of estimate characteristic of any well-conducted affair naturally give the impression that their animating purpose is control of the future. But thought about future happenings is the only way we can judge the present; it is the only way to appraise its significance. Without such projection, there can be no projects, no plans for administering present energies, overcoming present obstacles. Deliberately to subordinate the present to the future is to subject the comparatively secure to the precarious, exchange resources for liabilities, surrender what is under control to what is, relatively, incapable of control.

The *amount* of control which will come into existence in the future is not within control. But such an amount as turns out to be practicable accrues only in consequence of the best possible management of present means and obstacles. Dominating *intellectual* preoccupation with the future is the way by which efficiency in dealing with the present is attained. It is a way, not a goal. And, upon the very most hopeful outlook, study and planning are more important in the meaning, the enrichment of content, which they add to present activity than is the increase of external control they effect. Nor is this doctrine passivistic in tendency. What sense is there in increased external control except to increase the intrinsic significance of living? The future that is foreseen is a future that is sometime to be a present. Is the value of *that* present also to be postponed to a future date, and so on indefinitely? Or, if the good we are struggling to attain in the future is one to be actually realized when that future becomes present, why should not the good of *this* present be equally precious? And is there, again, any intelligent way of modifying the future except to attend to the full possibilities of the present? Scamping the present in behalf of the future leads only to rendering the future less manageable. It increases the probability of molestation by future events.

Remarks cast in this form probably seem too much like a logical manipulation of the concepts of present and future to be convincing. Building a house is a typical instance of an intelligent activity. It is an activity directed by a plan, a design. The plan is itself based upon a foresight of future uses. This foresight is in turn dependent upon an organized survey of past experiences and of present conditions, a recollection of former experiences of living in houses and an acquaintance with present materials, prices, resources, etc. Now if a legitimate case of subordination of present to regulation of the future may anywhere be found, it is in such a case as this. For a man usually builds a house for the sake of the comfort and security, the "control," thereby afforded to future living rather than just for the fun—or the trouble—of building. If in such a case inspection shows that, after all, intellectual concern with the past and future is for the sake of directing present activity and giving it meaning, the conclusion may be accepted for other cases.

Note that the present activity is the only one really under control. The man may die before the house is built, or his financial conditions may change, or he may need to remove to another place. If he attempts to provide for all contingencies, he will never do anything; if he allows his attention to be much distracted by them, he won't do well in his present planning and execution. The more he considers the future uses to which the house will probably be put, the better he will do his present job which is the activity of building. Control of future living, such as it may turn out to be, is wholly dependent upon taking his present activity, seriously and devotedly, as an end, not a means. And a man has his hands full in doing well what now needs to be done. Until men have formed the habit of using intelligence fully as a guide to present action they will never find out how much control of future contingencies is possible. As things are, men so habitually scamp present action in behalf of future "ends" that the facts for estimating the extent of the possibility of reduction of future contingencies have not been disclosed. What a man *is* doing limits both his direct control and his responsibility. We must not confuse the act of building with the house when built. The latter *is* a means, not a fulfillment. But it is such only because it enters into a new activity which is present not future. Life is continuous. The act of building in time gives way to the acts connected with a domicile. But everywhere the good, the fulfillment, the meaning of activity, resides in a present made possible by judging existing conditions in their connections.

If we seek for an illustration on a larger scale, education furnishes us with a poignant example. As traditionally conducted, it strikingly exhibits a subordination of the living present to a remote and precarious future. To prepare, to get ready, is its keynote. The actual outcome is lack of adequate preparation, of intelligent adaptation. The professed exaltation of the future turns out in practice a blind following of tradition, a rule of thumb muddling along from day to day; or, as in some of the projects called industrial education, a determined effort on the part of one class of the community to secure *its* future at the expense of another class. If education were conducted as a process of fullest utilization of present resources, liberating and guiding capacities that are now urgent, it goes without saying that the lives of the young would be much richer in meaning than they are now. It also follows that intelligence would be kept busy in studying all indication of power, all obstacles and perversions, all products of the past that throw light upon present capacity, and in forecasting the future career of impulse and habit now active—not for the sake of subordinating the latter but in order to treat them intelligently. As a consequence whatever fortification and expansion of the future that is possible will be achieved—as it is now dismally unattained. . . .

Except as the outcome of arrested development, there is no such thing as a fixed, ready-made finished self. Every living self causes acts and is itself caused in return by what it does. All voluntary action is a remaking of self, since it creates new desires, instigates to new modes of endeavor, brings to light new conditions which institute new ends. Our personal identity is found in the thread of continuous development which binds together these changes. In the strictest sense, it is impossible for the self to stand still; it is becoming, and becoming for the better or the worse. It is in the *quality* of becoming that virtue resides. We set up this and that end to be reached, but *the* end is growth itself. To make an end a final goal is but to arrest growth. Many a person gets morally discouraged because he has not attained the object upon which he set his resolution, but in fact his moral status is determined by his movement in that direction, not by his possession. If such a person would set his thought and desire upon the *process* of evolution instead of upon some ulterior goal, he would find a new freedom and happiness. It is the next step which lies within our power.

It follows that at each point there is a distinction between an old, an accomplished self, and a new and moving self, between the static and the dynamic self. The former aspect is constituted by habits already formed. Habit gives facility, and there is always a tendency to rest on our oars, to fall back on what we have already achieved. For that is the easy course; we are at home and feel comfortable in lines of action that run in the tracks of habits already established and mastered. Hence, the old, the habitual self, is likely to be treated as if it were *the* self; as if new conditions and new demands were something foreign and hostile. We become uneasy at the idea of initiating new courses; we are repelled by the difficulties that attend entering upon them; we dodge assuming a new responsibility. We tend to favor the old self and to make its perpetuation the standard of our valuations and the end of our conduct. In this way, we withdraw from actual conditions and their requirements and opportunities; we contract and harden the self.

The growing, enlarging, liberated self, on the other hand, goes forth to meet new demands and occasions, and readapts and remakes itself in the process. It welcomes untried situations. The necessity for choice between the interests of the old and of the forming, moving, self is recurrent. It is found at every stage of civilization and every period of life. The civilized man meets it as well as the savage; the dweller in the slums as well as the person in cultivated surroundings; the "good" person as well as the "bad." For everywhere there is an opportunity and a need to go beyond what one has been, beyond "himself," if the self is identified with the body of desires, affections, and habits which has been potent in the past. Indeed, we may say that the good person is precisely the one who is most conscious of the alternative, and is the most concerned to find openings for the newly forming or growing self; since no matter how "good" he has been, he becomes "bad" (even though acting upon a relatively high plane of attainment) as soon as he fails to respond to the demand for growth. Any other basis for judging the moral status of the self is conventional. In reality, direction of movement, not the plane of attainment and rest, determines moral quality. . . .

. . . Happiness is a matter of the disposition we actively bring with us to meet situations, the qualities of mind and heart with which we greet and interpret situations. Even so it is not directly an *end* of desire and effort, in the sense of an end-in-view purposely sought for, but is rather an end-product, a necessary accompaniment, of the character which is interested in objects that are enduring and intrinsically related to an outgoing and expansive nature. . . .

Happiness as distinct from pleasure is a condition of the self. There is a difference between a tranquil pleasure and tranquility of mind; there is contentment with external circumstances because they cater to our immediate enjoyment, and there is contentment of character and spirit which is maintained in adverse circumstances. A criterion can be given for marking off mere transient gratification from true happiness. The latter issues from objects which are enjoyable in themselves but which also reinforce and enlarge the other desires and tendencies which are sources of happiness; in a pleasure there is no such harmonizing and expanding tendency. There are powers within us whose exercise creates and strengthens objects that are enduring and stable while it excludes objects which occasion those merely transient gratifications that produce restlessness and peevishness. Harmony and readiness to expand into union with other values is a mark of happiness. Isolation and liability to conflict and interference are marks of those states which are exhausted in being pleasurable. . . .

UNIFICATION OF THE SELF[4]

The process of growth is also a process of personal unification. Ideally, the individual develops habits that are complementary and reinforcing, rather than cultivating habits that involve the pursuit of conflicting values. (For example, honesty and avarice are incompatible; honesty and amiability are mutually supporting.) This sort of unification facilitates as well the harmonious functioning of impulse, desire, imagination, and intelligence in all modes of behavior. An integrated self engaged in unifying the values of the environment is the result. As subsequent sections will indicate in various ways, this is fundamentally a social phenomenon.

Now the thing which is closest to us, the means within our power, is a habit. Some habit impeded by circumstances is the source of the projection of the end. It is also the primary means in its realization. The habit is propulsive and moves anyway toward some end, or result, whether it is projected as an end-in-view or not. The man who can walk does walk; the man who can talk does converse—if only with himself. How is this statement to be reconciled with the fact that we are not always walking and talking; that our habits seem so often to be latent, inoperative? Such inactivity holds only of *overt*, visibly obvious operation. In actuality each habit operates all the time of waking life; though, like a member of a crew taking his turn at the wheel, its operation becomes the dominantly characteristic trait of an act only occasionally or rarely.

The habit of walking is expressed in what a man sees when he keeps still, even in dreams. The recognition of distances and directions of things from his place at rest is the obvious proof of this statement. The habit of locomotion is latent in the sense that it is covered up, counteracted, by a habit of seeing which is definitely at the fore. But counteraction is not suppression. Locomotion is a potential energy, not in any metaphysical sense, but in the physical sense in which potential energy as well as kinetic has to be taken account of in any scientific description. Everything that a man who has the habit of locomotion does and thinks he does and thinks differently on that account. This fact is recognized in current psychology, but is falsified into an association of sensations. Were it not for the continued operation of all habits in every act, no such thing as character could exist. There would be simply a bundle, an untied bundle at that, of isolated acts. Character is the interpenetration of habits. If each habit existed in an insulated compartment and operated without affecting or being affected by others, character would not exist. That is, conduct would lack unity, being only a juxtaposition of disconnected reactions to separated situations. But since environments overlap, since situations are continuous and those remote from one another contain like elements, a continuous modification of habits by one another is constantly going on. A man may give himself away in a look or a gesture. Character can be read through the medium of individual acts.

Of course interpenetration is never total. It is most marked in what we call strong characters. Integration is an achievement rather than a datum. A weak, unstable, vacillating character is one in which different habits alternate with one another rather than embody one another. The strength, solidity of a habit is not its own possession but is due to reinforcement by the force of other habits which it absorbs into itself. Routine specialization always works against interpenetration. Men with "pigeonhole" minds are not infrequent. Their diverse standards and methods of judgment for scientific, religious, political matters testify to isolated compartmental habits of action. Character that is unable to undergo successfully the strain of thought and effort required to bring competing tendencies into a unity, builds up barriers between different systems of likes and dislikes. The emotional stress incident to conflict is avoided not by readjustment but by effort at confinement. Yet the exception proves the rule. Such persons are successful in keeping different ways of reacting apart from one another in consciousness rather than in action. Their character is marked by stigmata resulting from this division.

The mutual modification of habits by one another enables us to define the nature of the moral situation. It is not necessary nor advisable to be always considering the interaction of habits with one another, that is to say the effect of a particular habit upon character—which is a name for the total interaction. Such consideration distracts attention from the problem of building up an effective habit. A man who is learning French, or chess playing or engineering has his hands full with his particular occupation. He would be confused and hampered by constant inquiry into its effect upon character. He would resemble the centipede who by trying to think of the movement of each leg in relation to all the others was rendered unable to travel. At any given time, certain habits must be taken for granted as a matter of course. Their operation is not a matter of moral judgment. They are treated as technical, recreational, professional, hygienic or economic or esthetic rather than moral. To lug in morals, or ulterior effect on character at every point, is to cultivate moral valetudinarianism or priggish posing. Nevertheless any act, even that one which passes ordinarily as trivial, may entail such consequences for habit and character as upon occasion to require judgment from the standpoint of the whole body of conduct. It then comes under moral scrutiny. To know when to leave acts without distinctive moral judgment and when to subject them to it is itself a large factor in morality. The serious matter is that this relative pragmatic, or intellectual, distinction between the moral and nonmoral, has been solidified into a fixed and absolute distinction, so that some acts are popularly regarded as forever within and others forever without the moral domain. From this fatal error recognition of the relations of one habit to others preserves us. For it makes us see that character is the name given to the working interaction of habits, and that the cumulative effect of insensible modifications worked by a particular habit in the body of preferences may at any moment require attention. . . .

. . . Selfhood (except as it has encased itself in a shell of routine) is in process of making, and . . . any self is capable of including within itself a number of inconsistent selves, of unharmonized dispositions. Even a Nero may be capable upon occasion of acts of kindness. It is even conceivable that under certain circumstances he may be appalled by the consequences of cruelty, and turn to the fostering of kindlier impulses. A sympathetic person is not immune to harsh arrogances, and he may find himself involved in so much trouble as a consequence of a kindly act, that he allows his generous impulses to shrivel and henceforth governs his conduct by the dictates of the strictest worldly prudence. Inconsistencies and shiftings in character are the commonest things in experience. Only the hold of a traditional conception of the singleness and simplicity of soul and self blinds us to perceiving what they mean: the relative fluidity and diversity of the constituents of selfhood. There is no one ready-made self behind activities. There are complex, unstable, opposing attitudes, habits, impulses which gradually come to terms with one another, and assume a certain consistency of configuration, even though only by means of a distribution of inconsistencies which keeps them in watertight compartments, giving them separate turns or tricks in action.

Many good words get spoiled when the word self is prefixed to them: Words like pity, confidence, sacrifice, control, love. The reason is not far to seek. The word self infects them with a fixed introversion and isolation. It implies that the act of love or trust or control is turned back upon a self which already is in full existence and in whose behalf the act operates. Pity fulfills and creates a self when it is directed outward, opening the mind to new contacts and receptions. Pity for self withdraws the mind back into itself, rendering its subject unable to learn from the buffetings of fortune. Sacrifice may enlarge a self by bringing about surrender of acquired possessions to requirements of new growth. Self-sacrifice means a self-maiming which asks for compensatory pay in some later possession or indulgence. Confidence as an outgoing act is directness and courage in meeting the facts of life, trusting them to bring instruction and support to a developing self. Confidence which terminates in the self means a smug complacency that renders a person obtuse to instruction by events. Control means a command of resources that enlarges the self; self-control denotes a self which is contracting, concentrating itself upon its own achievements, hugging them tight, and thereby estopping the growth that comes when the self is generously released, a self-conscious moral athleticism that ends in a disproportionate enlargement of some organ. . . .

The release of some portion of the stock of impulses is an opportunity, and not an end. In its origin it is the product of chance; but it affords imagination and invention *their* chance. The moral correlate of liberated impulse is not immediate activity, but reflection upon the way in which to use impulse to renew disposition and reorganize habit. Escape from the clutch of custom gives an opportunity to do old things in new ways, and thus to construct new ends and means. Breach in the crust of the cake of custom releases impulses; but it is the work of intelligence to find the ways of using them. There is an alternative between anchoring a boat in the harbor till it becomes a rotting hulk and letting it loose to be the sport of every contrary gust. To discover and define this alternative is the business of mind, of observant, remembering, contriving disposition.

Habit as a vital art depends upon the animation of habit by impulse; only this inspiriting stands between habit and stagnation. But art, little as well as great, anonymous as well as that distinguished by titles of dignity, cannot be improvised. It is impossible without spontaneity, but it is not spontaneity. Impulse is needed to arouse thought, incite reflection and enliven belief. But only thought notes obstructions, invents tools, conceives aims, directs technique, and thus converts impulse into an art which lives in objects. Thought is born as the twin of impulse in every moment of impeded habit. But unless it is nurtured, it speedily dies, and habit and instinct continue their civil warfare. There is instinctive wisdom in the tendency of the young to ignore the limitations of the environment. Only thus can they discover their own power and learn the differences in different kinds of environing limitations. But this discovery when once made marks the birth of intelligence; and with its birth comes the responsibilty of the mature to observe, to recall, to forecast. Every moral life has its radicalism; but this radical factor does not find its full expression in direct action but in the courage of intelligence to go deeper than either tradition or immediate impulse goes. . . .

These facts give us the key to the old controversy as to the respective places of desire and reason in conduct. It is notorious that some moralists have deplored the influence of desire; they have found the heart of strife between good and evil in the conflict of desire with reason, in which the former has force on its side and the latter authority. But reasonableness is in fact a quality of an effective relationship among desires rather than a thing opposed to desire. It signifies the order, perspective, proportion which is achieved, during deliberation, out of a diversity of earlier incompatible preferences. Choice is reasonable when it induces us to act reasonably; that is, with regard to the claims of each of the competing habits and impulses. This implies, of course, the presence of a comprehensive object, one which coordinates, organizes and functions each factor of the situation which gave rise to conflict, suspense and deliberation. This is as true when some "bad" impulses and habits enter in as when approved ones require unification. We have already seen the effects of choking them off, of efforts at direct suppression. Bad habits can be subdued only by being utilized as elements in a new, more generous and comprehensive scheme of action, and good ones be preserved from rot only by similar use.

The nature of the strife of reason and passion is well stated by William James. The cue of passion, he says in effect, is to keep imagination dwelling upon those objects which are congenial to it, which feed it, and which by feeding it intensify its force, until it crowds out all thought of other objects. An impulse or habit which is strongly emotional magnifies all objects that are congruous with it and smothers those which are opposed whenever they present themselves. A passionate activity learns to work itself up artificially— as Oliver Cromwell indulged in fits of anger when he wanted to do things that his conscience would not justify. A presentiment is felt that if the thought of contrary objects is allowed to get a lodgment in imagination, these objects will work and work to chill and freeze out the ardent passion of the moment.

The conclusion is not that the emotional, passionate phase of action can be or should be eliminated in behalf of a bloodless reason. More "passions," not fewer, is the answer. To check the influence of hate there must be sympathy, while to rationalize sympathy there are needed emotions of curiosity, caution, respect for the freedom of others—dispositions which evoke objects which balance those called up by sympathy, and prevent its degeneration into maudlin sentiment and meddling interference. Rationality, once more, is not a force to evoke against impulse and habit. It is the attainment of a working harmony among diverse desires. "Reason" as a noun signifies the happy cooperation of a multitude of dispositions, such as sympathy, curiosity, exploration, experimentation, frankness, pursuit—to follow things through —circumspection, to look about at the context, etc., etc. The elaborate systems of science are born not of reason but of impulses at first slight and flickering; impulses to handle, move about, to hunt, to uncover, to mix things separated and divide things combined, to talk and to listen. Method is their effectual organization into continuous dispositions of inquiry, development and testing. It occurs after these acts and because of their consequences. Reason, the rational attitude, is the resulting disposition, not a ready-made antecedent which can be invoked at will and set into movement. The man who would intelligently cultivate intelligence will widen, not narrow, his life of strong impulses while aiming at their happy coincidence in operation. . . .

GROWTH AND UNIFICATION ARE SOCIAL[5]

. . . It is not easy to exaggerate the extent to which we now pass from one kind of nurture to another as we go from business to church, from science to the newspaper, from business to art, from companionship to politics, from home to school. An individual is now subjected to many conflicting schemes of education. Hence habits are divided against one another, personality is disrupted, the scheme of conduct is confused and disintegrated. But the remedy lies in the development of a new morale which can be attained only as released impulses are intelligently employed to form harmonious habits adapted to one another in a new situation. A laxity due to decadence of old habits cannot be corrected by exhortations to restore old habits in their former rigidity. Even though it were abstractly desirable it is impossible. And it is not desirable because the inflexibility of old habits is precisely the chief cause of their decay and disintegration. Plaintive lamentations at the prevalence of change and abstract appeals for restoration of senile authority are signs of personal feebleness, of inability to cope with change. . . .

. . . Students of politics are familiar with a check and balance theory of the powers of government. There are supposed to be independent separate functions, like the legislative, executive, judicial, administrative, and all goes well if each of these checks all the others and thus creates an ideal balance. There is a philosophy which might well be called the check and balance theory of experience. Life presents a diversity of interests. Left to themselves, they tend to encroach on one another. The ideal is to prescribe a special territory for each till the whole ground of experience is covered, and then see to it each remains within its own boundaries. Politics, business, recreation, art, science, the learned profession, polite intercourse, leisure, represent such interests. Each of these ramifies into many branches: business into manual occupations, executive positions, bookkeeping, railroading, banking, agriculture, trade and commerce, etc., and so with each of the others. An ideal education would then supply the means of meeting these separate and pigeon-holed interests. And when we look at the schools, it is easy to get the impression that they accept this view of the nature of adult life, and set for themselves the task of meeting its demands. Each interest is acknowledged as a kind of fixed institution to which something in the course of study must correspond. The course of study must then have some civics and history politically and patriotically viewed; some utilitarian studies; some science; some art (mainly literature of course); some provision for recreation; some moral education; and so on. And it will be found that a large part of current agitation about schools is concerned with clamor and controversy about the due meed of recognition to be given to each of these interests, and with struggles to secure for each its due share in the course of study; or, if this does not seem feasible in the existing school system, then to secure a new and separate kind of schooling to meet the need. In the multitude of educations education is forgotten.

The obvious outcome is congestion of the course of study, over-pressure and distraction of pupils, and a narrow specialization fatal to the very idea of education. But these bad results usually lead to more of the same sort of thing as a remedy. When it is perceived that after all the requirements of a full life experience are not met, the deficiency is not laid to the isolation and narrowness of the teaching of the existing subjects, and this recognition made the basis of reorganization of the system. No, the lack is something to be made up for by the introduction of still another study, or, if necessary, another kind of school. And as a rule those who object to the resulting over-crowding and consequent superficiality and distraction, usually also have recourse to a merely quantitative criterion: the remedy is to cut off a great many studies as fads and frills, and return to the good old curriculum of the three R's in elementary education and the equally good and equally old-fashioned curriculum of the classics and mathematics in higher education.

The situation has, of course, its historic explanation. Various epochs of the past have had their own characteristic struggles and interests. Each of these great epochs has left behind itself a kind of cultural deposit, like a geologic stratum. These deposits have found their way into educational institutions in the form of studies, distinct courses of study, distinct types of schools. With the rapid change of political, scientific, and economic interests in the last century, provisions had to be made for new values. Though the older courses resisted, they have had at least in this country to retire their pretensions to a monopoly. They have not, however, been reorganized in content and aim; they have only been reduced in amount. The new studies, representing the new interests have not been used to transform the method and aim of all instruction; they have been injected and added on. The result is a conglomerate, the cement of which consists in the mechanics of the school program or time table. Thence arises the scheme of values and standards of value which we have mentioned.

This situation in education represents the divisions and separations which obtain in social life. The variety of interests which should mark any rich and

balanced experience have been torn asunder and deposited in separate institutions with diverse and independent purposes and methods. Business is
business, science is science, art is art, politics is politics, social intercourse
is social intercourse, morals is morals, recreation is recreation, and so on.
Each possesses a separate and independent province with its own peculiar
aims and ways of proceeding. Each contributes to the others only externally
and accidentally. All of them together make up the whole of life by just
apposition and addition. What does one expect from business save that it
should furnish money, to be used in turn for making more money and for
support of self and family, for buying books and pictures, tickets to con-
certs which may afford culture, and for paying taxes, charitable gifts and
other things of social and ethical value? How unreasonable to expect that
the pursuit of business should be itself a culture of the imagination, in
breadth and refinement; that it should directly, and not through the money
which it supplies, have social service for its animating principle and be conducted as an enterprise in behalf of social organization! The same thing is
to be said, *mutatis mutandis,* of the pursuit of art or science or politics or
religion. Each has become specialized not merely in its appliances and its
demands upon time, but in its aim and animating spirit. Unconsciously,
our course of studies and our theories of the educational values of studies
reflect this division of interests.

The point at issue in a theory of educational value is then the unity or
integrity of experience. How shall it be full and varied without losing unity
of spirit? How shall it be one and yet not narrow and monotonous in its
unity? Ultimately, the question of values and a standard of values is the
moral question of the organization of the interests of life. Educationally, the
question concerns that organization of schools, materials, and methods which
will operate to achieve breadth and richness of experience. How shall we
secure breadth of outlook without sacrificing efficiency of execution? How
shall we secure the diversity of interests, without paying the price of isolation? How shall the individual be rendered executive *in* his intelligence
instead of at the cost of his intelligence? How shall art, science, and politics
reinforce one another in an enriched temper of mind instead of constituting
ends pursued at one another's expense? How can the interests of life and
the studies which enforce them enrich the common experience of men instead
of dividing men from one another? . . .

To view institutions as enemies of freedom, and all conventions as slaveries,
is to deny the only means by which positive freedom in action can be secured. A general liberation of impulses may set things going when they have
been stagnant, but if the released forces are on their way to anything they
do not know the way nor where they are going. Indeed, they are bound to
be mutually contradictory and hence destructive—destructive not only of

the habits they wish to destroy but of themselves, of their own efficacy. Convention and custom are necessary to carrying forward impulse to any happy conclusion. A romantic return to nature and a freedom sought within the individual without regard to the existing environment finds its terminus in chaos. Every belief to the contrary combines pessimism regarding the actual with an even more optimistic faith in some natural harmony or other—a faith which is a survival of some of the traditional metaphysics and theologies which professedly are to be swept away. Not convention but stupid and rigid convention is the foe. And, as we have noted, a convention can be reorganized and made mobile only by using some other custom for giving leverage to an impulse. . . .

. . . There are an indefinite number of original or instinctive activities, which are organized into interests and dispositions according to the situations to which they respond. To increase the creative phase and the humane quality of these activities is an affair of modifying the social conditions which stimulate, select, intensify, weaken and coordinate native activities. The first step in dealing with it is to increase our detailed scientific knowledge. We need to know exactly the selective and directive force of each social situation; exactly how each tendency is promoted and retarded. Command of the physical environment on a large and deliberate scale did not begin until belief in gross force and entities was abandoned. Control of physical energies is due to inquiry which establishes specific correlations between minute elements. It will not be otherwise with social control and adjustment. Having the knowledge we may set hopefully at work upon a course of social invention and experimental engineering. A study of the educative effect, the influence upon habit, of each definite form of human intercourse, is prerequisite to effective reform. . . .

. . . The office of reflection we have seen to be the formation of a judgment of value in which particular satisfactions are placed as integral parts of conduct as a consistent harmonious whole. If values did not get in one another's way, if, that is, the realization of one desire were not incompatible with that of another, there would be no need of reflection. We should grasp and enjoy each thing as it comes along. Wisdom, or as it is called on the ordinary plane, prudence, sound judgment, is the ability to foresee consequences in such a way that we form ends which grow into one another and reinforce one another. Moral folly is the surrender of the greater good for the lesser; it is snatching at one satisfaction in a way which prevents us from having others and which gets us subsequently into trouble and dissatisfaction.

Up to this point we have passed over social conditions which affect the development of wise and prudent attitudes of mind. But it is clear that the education which one receives, not so much the formal schooling as the influence of the traditions and institutions of the community in which one lives, and the habits of one's associates, are a profound influence. The simplest illustration is that of a spoiled child. The person who is encouraged to yield to every desire as it arises, the one who receives constantly the help of others in getting what he wants when he wants it, will have to possess extraordinary intellectual powers if he develops a habit of reflective valuation. What is true on this personal scale is true on a wide social scale. The general social order may be such as to put a premium upon the kind of satisfaction which is coarse, gross, "materialistic," and upon attitudes which are in impatient haste to grab any seeming nearby good. This state of affairs is characteristic of many phases of American life today. Love of power over others, of display and luxury, of pecuniary wealth, is fostered by our economic regime. Goods that are more ideal, esthetic, intellectual values, those of friendship which is more than a superficial comradeship, are forced into subordination. The need of fostering the reflective and contemplative attitudes of character is therefore the greater. Above all, there is the need to remake social conditions so that they will almost automatically support fuller and more enduring values and will reduce those social habits which favor the free play of impulse unordered by thought, or which make men satisfied to fall into mere routine and convention. The great bulwark of wisdom in judging values is a just and noble social order. . . .

THE INDIVIDUAL, THE ASSOCIATED, AND THE SOCIAL[6]

One of the abiding concerns of philosophers has been to determine the rightful relation of individual to society. As the following selection makes clear, Dewey regards the traditional problem as misconceived. The growth of human nature is conditional upon a variety of personal interactions, and the self is neither a discrete monadic entity nor a creature of society as a whole. Accordingly, the question of what belongs to the individual and what belongs to society is, as such, in vain. The genuine problem concerns the manner in which individuals are related to various groups, which are themselves interrelated in diverse ways. What is individual must be specified by its function in a given context.

. . . We have to qualify our approximate notion of an individual as being that which acts and moves as a unitary thing. We have to consider not only its connections and ties, but the consequences with respect to which it acts and moves. We are compelled to say that for some purposes, for some results, the tree is the individual, for others the cell, and for a third, the forest or the landscape. Is a book or a leaf or a folio or a paragraph, or a printer's em *the* individual? Is the binding or the contained thought that which gives individual unity to a book? Or are all of these things definers of an individual according to the consequences which are relevant in a particular situation? Unless we betake ourselves to the stock resort of common sense, dismissing *all* questions as useless quibbles, it seems as if we could not determine an individual without reference to differences made as well as to antecedent and contemporary connections. If so, an individual, whatever else it is or is not, is not just the spatially isolated thing our imagination inclines to take it to be.

Such a discussion does not proceed upon a particularly high nor an especially deep level. But it may at least render us wary of any definition of an individual which operates in terms of separateness. A *distinctive* way of behaving in conjunction and *connection* with other distinctive ways of acting, not a self-enclosed way of acting, independent of everything else, is that toward which we are pointed. Any human being is in one respect an association, consisting of a multitude of cells each living its own life. And as the activity of each cell is conditioned and directed by those with which it interacts, so the human being whom we fasten upon as individual *par excellence* is moved and regulated by his associations with others; what he does and what the consequences of his behavior are, what his experience consists of, cannot even be described, much less accounted for, in isolation.

But while associated behavior is, as we have already noted, a universal law, the fact of association does not of itself make a society. This demands . . . perception of the consequences of a joint activity and of the distinctive share of each element in producing it. Such perception creates a common interest; that is, concern on the part of each in the joint action and in the contribution of each of its members to it. Then there exists something truly social and not merely associative. But it is absurd to suppose that a society does away with the traits of its own constituents so that it can be set over against them. It can only be set over against the traits which they and their like present in some *other* combination. A molecule of oxygen in water may act in certain respects differently than it would in some other chemical union. But *as* a constituent of water it acts as water does as long as water is water. The only intelligible distinction which can be drawn is between the behaviors of oxygen in *its* different relations, and between those of water in *its* relations to various conditions, not between that of water and the oxygen which is conjoined with hydrogen in water.

A single man when he is joined in marriage is different in that connection to what he was as single or to what he is in some other union, as a member, say, of a club. He has new powers and immunities, new responsibilities. He can be contrasted with *himself* as he behaves in other connections. He may be compared and contrasted with his wife in their distinctive roles within the union. But *as* a member of the union he cannot be treated as antithetical to the union in which he belongs. *As* a member of the union, his traits and acts are evidently those which he possesses in virtue of it, while those of the integrated association are what they are in virtue of his status in the union. The only reason we fail to see this, or are confused by the statement of it, is because we pass so easily from the man in one connection to the man in some other connection, to the man not as husband but as businessman, scientific investigator, church-member or citizen, in which connections his acts and their consequences are obviously different to those due to union in wedlock.

A good example of the fact and of the current confusion as to its interpretation is found in the case of associations known as limited liability joint-stock companies. A corporation as such is an integrated collective mode of action having powers, rights, duties and immunities different from those of its singular members *in their other connections.* Its different constituents have also diverse statuses—for example, the owners of stock from the officers and directors in certain matters. If we do not bear the facts steadily in mind, it is easy—as frequently happens—to create an artificial problem. Since the corporation can do things which its individual members, *in their many relationships outside of their connections in the corporation,* cannot do, the problem is raised as to the relation of the corporate collective union to that of individuals *as such.* It is forgotten that as members of the corporation the individuals themselves are different, have different characteristics, rights and duties, than they would possess if they were not its members and different from those which they possess in other forms of conjoint behavior. But what the individuals may do legitimately *as* members of the corporation in their respective corporate roles, the corporation does, and vice versa. A collective unity may be taken *either* distributively *or* collectively, but when taken collectively it is the union of its distributive constituents, and when taken distributively, it is a distribution of and within the collectivity. It makes nonsense to set up an antithesis between the distributive phase and the collective. An individual cannot be opposed to the association of which he is an integral part nor can the association be set against its integrated members.

But groups may be opposed to one another, and individuals may be opposed to one another; and an individual as a member of different groups may be divided within himself, and in a true sense have conflicting selves, or be a relatively disintegrated individual. A man may be one thing as a church member and another thing as a member of the business community. The difference may be carried as if in watertight compartments, or it may become such a division as to entail internal conflict. In these facts we have the ground of the common antithesis set up between society and the individual. Then "society" becomes an unreal abstraction and "*the* individual" an equally unreal one. Because *an* individual can be disassociated from this, that and the other grouping, since he need not be married, or be a church-member or a voter, or belong to a club or scientific organization, there grows up in the mind an image of a residual individual who is not a member of any association at all. From this premise, and from this only, there develops the unreal question of how individuals come to be united in societies and groups: *the* individual and *the* social are now opposed to each other, and there is the problem of "reconciling" them. Meanwhile, the genuine problem is that of adjusting groups and individuals to one another.

The unreal problem becomes particularly acute . . . in times of rapid social change, as when a newly forming industrial grouping with its special needs and energies finds itself in conflict with old established political institutions and their demands. Then it is likely to be forgotten that the actual problem is one of reconstruction of the ways and forms in which men unite in associated activity. The scene presents itself as the struggle of the individual as such to liberate himself from society as such and to claim his inherent or "natural" self-possessed and self-sufficing rights. When the new mode of economic association has grown strong and exercises an overweening and oppressive power over other groupings, the old fallacy persists. The problem is now conceived as that of bringing individuals as such under the control of society as a collectivity. It should still be put as a problem of readjusting social relationships; or, from the distributive side, as that of securing a more equable liberation of the powers of all individual members of all groupings.

. . . One reason for the comparative sterility of discussion of social matters is because so much intellectual energy has gone into the supposititious problem of the relations of individualism and collectivism at large, wholesale, and because the image of the antithesis infects so many specific questions. Thereby thought is diverted from the only fruitful questions, those of investigation into factual subject-matter, and becomes a discussion of concepts. The "problem" of the relation of the concept of authority to that of freedom, or personal rights to social obligations, with only a subsumptive illustrative reference to empirical facts, has been substituted for inquiry into the *consequences* of some particular distribution, under given conditions, of specific freedoms and authorities, and for inquiry into what altered distribution would yield more desirable consequences.

. . . The question of what transactions should be left as far as possible to voluntary initiative and agreement and what should come under the regulation of the public is a question of time, place and concrete conditions that can be known only by careful observation and reflective investigation. For it concerns consequences; and the nature of consequences and the ability to perceive and act upon them varies with the industrial and intellectual agencies which operate. A solution, or distributive adjustment, needed at one time is totally unfitted to another situation. That social "evolution" has been either from collectivism to individualism or the reverse is sheer superstition. It has consisted in a continuous redistribution of social integrations on the one hand and of capacities and energies of individuals on the other. Individuals find themselves cramped and depressed by absorption of their potentialities in some mode of association which has been institutionalized and become dominant. They may think they are clamoring for a purely personal liberty, but what they are doing is to bring into being a greater liberty to share in other associations, so that more of their individual potentialities will be released and their personal experience enriched. Life has been impoverished, not by a predominance of "society" in general over individuality, but by a domination of one form of association, the family, clan, church, economic institutions, over other actual and possible forms. On the other hand, the problem of exercising "social control" over individuals is in its reality that of regulating the doings and results of some individuals in order that a larger number of individuals may have a fuller and deeper experience. Since both ends can be intelligently attained only by knowledge of actual conditions in their modes of operation and their consequences, it may be confidently asserted that the chief enemy of a social thinking which would count in public affairs is the sterile and impotent, because totally irrelevant, channels in which so much intellectual energy has been expended.

. . . Political theories have shared in the absolutistic character of philosophy generally. By this is meant something much more than philosophies of the Absolute. Even professedly empirical philosophies have assumed a certain finality and foreverness in their theories which may be expressed by saying that they have been nonhistorical in character. They have isolated their subject-matter from its connections, and any isolated subject-matter becomes unqualified in the degree of its disconnection. In social theory dealing with human nature, a certain fixed and standardized "individual" has been postulated, from whose assumed traits social phenomena could be deduced. Thus Mill says in his discussion of the logic of the moral and social sciences: "The laws of the phenomena of society are, and can be, nothing but the laws of the actions and passions of human beings united together in the social state. Men, however, in a state of society are still men; their actions and passions are obedient to the laws of *individual* human nature."* Obviously what is ignored in such a statement is that "the actions and passions" of individual men are in the concrete what they are, their beliefs and purposes included, because of the social medium in which they live; that they are influenced throughout by contemporary and transmitted culture, whether in conformity or protest. What is generic and the same everywhere is at best the organic structure of man, his biological makeup. While it is evidently important to take this into account, it is also evident that none of the *distinctive* features of *human* association can be deduced from it. Thus, in spite of Mill's horror of the metaphysical absolute, his leading social conceptions

*J. S. Mill, *Logic*, Book VI, ch. 7, sec. 1. Italics mine.

were, logically, absolutistic. Certain social laws, normative and regulative, at all periods and under all circumstances of proper social life were assumed to exist. . . .

GROWTH, SHARED EXPERIENCE, AND COMMUNITY[7]

It is not possible to read very far in Dewey without remarking his reverential feeling for shared experience. Calling it "the greatest of human goods" and reserving religious metaphors for reference to it alone[8] he centers his religious devotion on the ideal of the democratic community. In Reconstruction in Philosophy *he wrote, "And when the emotional force, the mystic force one might say, of communication, of the miracle of shared life and shared experience is spontaneously felt, the hardness and crudeness of contemporary life will be bathed in the light that never was on land or sea."[9]*

A sense of community is evidently something more than immediately shared experience. It is an awareness that our experience and effort are continuous with those of others, and with nature. The sense of organic connection with the whole functions in Dewey's experience in the same manner that a sense of union with God functions in the experience of the orthodox. Clearly, however, Dewey's religion permits intelligent analysis and action in a way that theism cannot.

Personal growth can occur only in the context of shared experience, and best of all in the democratic community. The samplings below intimate some of Dewey's valuation of shared experience and community.

An explanatory comment regarding the first of the following excerpts: Dewey rejects the notion that there is a will or substantial self which performs actions, with the actions being incidental to the essential selfhood. In the same way, there is not a self which possesses interests; rather, the self is interests (as well as other functions). Accordingly, any act of self is an act of interest. The word "self" in "self-interest" is pleonastic. Any act of self seeks reward; so there is no difference between the so-called selfish person and the unselfish in the fact that a satisfaction of interest is sought. The difference between them is in the nature of the object of interest—in what is inherently satisfying. The object of interest is not the mythical self, but an activity which fulfills interest. Such activity may be exclusive of the interests of others or supportive of them. In this distinction we find the real difference between selfishness and unselfishness; and we also find the ground of growth, shared experience, and community without sacrifice of interest —indeed, with massive fulfillment of interest.

Now the prestige that once attached to the "instinct" of self-love has not wholly vanished. The case is still worth examination. In its "scientific" form, start was taken from an alleged instinct of self-preservation, characteristic of man as well as of other animals. From this seemingly innocuous assumption, a mythological psychology burgeoned. Animals, including man, certainly perform many acts whose consequence is to protect and preserve life. If their acts did not upon the whole have this tendency, neither the individual nor the species would long endure. The acts that spring from life also in the main conserve life. Such is the undoubted fact. What does the statement amount to? Simply the truism that life is life, that life is a continuing activity as long as it is life at all. But the self-love school converted the fact that life tends to maintain life into a separate and special force which somehow lies back of life and accounts for its various acts. An animal exhibits in its life-activity a multitude of acts of breathing, digesting, secreting, excreting, attack, defense, search for food, etc., a multitude of specific responses to specific stimulations of the environment. But mythology comes in and attributes them all to a nisus for self-preservation. Thence it is but a step to the idea that all conscious acts are prompted by self-love. This premise is then elaborated in ingenious schemes, often amusing when animated by a cynical knowledge of the "world," tedious when of a would-be logical nature, to prove that every act of man, including his apparent generosities, is a variation played on the theme of self-interest.

The fallacy is obvious. Because an animal cannot live except as it is alive, except, that is, as its acts have the result of sustaining life, it is concluded that all its acts are instigated by an impulse to self-preservation. Since all acts affect the well-being of their agent in one way or another, and since when a person becomes reflective he prefers consequences in the way of weal to those of woe, therefore all his acts are due to self-love. In actual substance, one statement says that life is life; and the other says that a self is a self. One says that special acts are acts of a living creature and the other that they are acts of a self. In the biological statement the concrete diversity between the acts of say a clam and of a dog are covered up by pointing out that the acts of each tend to self-preservation, ignoring the somewhat important fact that in one case it is the life of a clam and in the other the life of a dog which is continued. In morals, the concrete differences between a Jesus, a Peter, a John and a Judas are covered up by the wise remark that after all they are all selves and all act as selves. In every case, a result or "end" is treated as an actuating cause.

The fallacy consists in transforming the (truistic) fact of acting *as* a self into the fiction of acting always *for* self. Every act, truistically again, tends to a certain fulfillment or satisfaction of some habit which is an undoubted element in the structure of character. Each satisfaction is qualitatively what it is because of the disposition fulfilled in the object attained, treachery or loyalty, mercy or cruelty. But theory comes in and blankets the tremendous diversity in the quality of the satisfactions which are experienced by pointing out that they are all satisfactions. The harm done is then completed by transforming this artificial unity of result into an original love of satisfaction as the force that generates all acts alike. Because a Nero and a Peabody both get satisfaction in acting as they do it is inferred that the satisfaction of each is the same in quality, and that both were actuated by love of the same objective. In reality the more we concretely dwell upon the common fact of fulfillment, the more we realize the difference in the kinds of selves fulfilled. In pointing out that both the north and the south poles are poles we do not abolish the difference of north from south; we accentuate it. . . .

The discussion points to the conclusion that neither egoism nor altruism nor any combination of the two is a satisfactory principle. Selfhood is not something which exists apart from association and intercourse. The relationships which are produced by the fact that interests are formed in this social environment are far more important than are the adjustments of isolated selves. To a large extent, the emphasis of theory upon the problem of adjustment of egoism and altruism took place in a time when thought was decidedly individualistic in character. Theory was formed in terms of individuals supposed to be naturally isolated; social arrangements were considered to be secondary and artificial. Under such intellectual conditions, it was almost inevitable that moral theory should become preoccupied with the question of egoistic *versus* altruistic motivation. Since the prevailing individualism was expressed in an economic theory and practice which taught that each man was actuated by an exclusive regard for his own profit, moralists were led to insist upon the need of some check upon this ruthless individualism, and to accentuate the supremacy in *morals* (as distinct from business) of sympathy and benevolent regard for others. The ultimate significance of this appeal is, however, to make us realize the fact that regard for self and regard for others are both of them secondary phases of a more normal and complete interest: regard for the welfare and integrity of the social groups of which we form a part.

The family, for example, is something other than one person, plus another, plus another. It is an enduring form of association in which the members of the group stand from the beginning in relations to one another, and in which each member gets direction for his conduct by thinking of the whole group and his place in it, rather than by an adjustment of egoism and altruism. Similar illustrations are found in business, professional, and political associations. From the moral standpoint, the test of an industry is whether it serves the community as a whole, satisfying its needs effectively and fairly, while also providing the means of livelihood and personal development to the individuals who carry it on. This goal could hardly be reached, however, if the businessman (a) thought exclusively of furthering his own interests; (b) of acting in a benevolent way toward others; or (c) sought some compromise between the two. In a justly organized social order, the very relations which persons bear to one another demand of the one carrying on a line of business the kind of conduct which meets the needs of others, while they also enable him to express and fulfill the capacities of his own being. Services, in other words, would be reciprocal and cooperative in their effect. We trust a physician who recognizes the social import of his calling and who is equipped in knowledge and skill, rather than one who is animated exclusively by personal affection no matter how great his altruistic zeal. The political action of citizens of an organized community will not be morally satisfactory unless they have, individually, sympathetic dispositions. But the value of this sympathy is not as a direct dictator of conduct. Think of any complex political problem and you will realize how short a way unenlightened benevolence will carry you. It has a value, but this value consists in power to make us attend in a broad way to all the social ties which are involved in the formation and execution of policies. Regard for self and regard for others should not, in other words, be *direct* motives to overt action. They should be forces which lead us to *think* of objects and consequences that would otherwise escape notice. These objects and consequences then constitute the *interest* which is the proper motive of action. Their stuff and material are composed of the relations which men actually sustain to one another in concrete affairs.

Interest in the social whole of which one is a member necessarily carries with it interest in one's own self. Every member of the group has his own place and work; it is absurd to suppose that this fact is significant in other persons but of little account in one's own case. To suppose that social interest is incompatible with concern for one's own health, learning, advancement, power of judgment, etc., is, literally, nonsensical. Since each one of us is a member of social groups and since the latter have no existence apart from the selves who compose them, there can be no effective social interest unless there is at the same time an intelligent regard for our own well-being and development. Indeed, there is a certain *primary* responsibility placed upon each individual in respect to his own power and growth. No community more backward and ineffective *as* a community can be imagined than one in which every member neglected his own concerns in order to attend to the affairs of his neighbors. When selfhood is taken for what it is, something existing in relationships to others and not in unreal isolation, independence of judgment, personal insight, integrity and initiative, become indispensable excellencies from the social point of view.

There is too often current a conception of charity which illustrates the harm which may accrue when objective social relations are shoved into the background. The giving of a kindly hand to a human being in distress, to numbers caught in a common catastrophe, is such a natural thing that it should almost be too much a matter of course to need laudation as a virtue. But the theory which erects charity in and of itself into a supreme excellence is a survival of a feudally stratified society, that is, of conditions wherein a superior class achieved merit by doing things gratuitously for an inferior class. The objection to this conception of charity is that it too readily becomes an excuse for maintaining laws and social arrangements which ought themselves to be changed in the interest of fair play and justice. "Charity" may even be used as a means for administering a sop to one's social conscience while at the same time it buys off the resentment which might otherwise grow up in those who suffer from social injustice. Magnificent philanthropy may be employed to cover up brutal economic exploitation. Gifts to libraries, hospitals, missions, schools may be employed as a means of rendering existing institutions more tolerable, and of inducing immunity against social change.

Again, deliberate benevolence is used as a means of keeping others dependent and managing their affairs for them. Parents, for example, who fail to pay due heed to the growing maturity of their children, justify an unjustifiable interference in their affairs, on the ground of kindly parental feelings. They carry the habits of action formed when children were practically helpless into conditions in which children both want and need to help themselves. They pride themselves on conduct which creates either servile dependence or bitter resentment and revolt in their offspring. Perhaps no better test case of the contrast between regard for personality bound up with regard for the realities of a social situation and abstract "altruism" can be found than is afforded in such an instance as this. The moral is not that parents should become indifferent to the well-being of their children. It is that *intelligent* regard for this welfare realizes the need for growing freedom with growing maturity. It displays itself in a change of the habits formed when regard for welfare called for a different sort of conduct. If we generalize the lesson of this instance, it leads to the conclusion that overt acts of charity and benevolence are incidental phases of morals, demanded under certain emergencies, rather than its essential principle. This is found in a constantly expanding and changing sense of what the concrete realities of human relations call for.

One type of moral theory holds up self-realization as the ethical ideal. There is an ambiguity in the conception which will serve to illustrate what has been said about the self. Self-realization may be the end in the sense of being an outcome and limit of right action, without being the end-in-*view*. The *kind* of self which is formed through action which is faithful to relations with others will be a fuller and broader self than one which is cultivated in isolation from or in opposition to the purposes and needs of others. In contrast, the kind of self which results from generous breadth of interest may be said alone to constitute a development and fulfillment of self, while the other way of life stunts and starves selfhood by cutting it off from the connections necessary to its growth. But to make self-realization a conscious aim might and probably would prevent full attention to those very relationships which bring about the wider development of self.

The case is the same with the interests of the self as with its realization. The final happiness of an individual resides in the supremacy of certain interests in the makeup of character; namely, alert, sincere, enduring interests in the objects in which all can share. It is found in such interests rather than in the accomplishment of definite external results because this kind of happiness alone is not at the mercy of circumstances. No amount of outer obstacles can destroy the happiness that comes from lively and ever-renewed interest in others and in the conditions and objects which promote their development. To those in whom these interests are alive (and they flourish to some extent in all persons who have not already been warped) their exercise brings happiness because it fulfills the self. They are not, however, preferred and aimed at *because* they give greater happiness, but as expressing the kind of self which a person fundamentally desires to be they constitute a happiness unique in kind.

The final word about the place of the self in the moral life is, then, that the very problem of morals is to form an original body of impulsive tendencies into a voluntary self in which desires and affections center in the values which are common; in which interest focuses in objects that contribute to the enrichment of the lives of all. If we identify the interests of such a self with the virtues, then we shall say, with Spinoza, that happiness is not the reward of virtue, but is virtue itself. . . .

It is outside the scope of our discussion to look into the prospects of the reconstruction of face-to-face communities. But there is something deep within human nature itself which pulls toward settled relationships. Inertia and the tendency toward stability belong to emotions and desires as well as to masses and molecules. That happiness which is full of content and peace is found only in enduring ties with others, which reach to such depths that they go below the surface of conscious experience to form its undisturbed foundation. No one knows how much of the frothy excitement of life, of mania for motion, of fretful discontent, of need for artificial stimulation, is the expression of frantic search for something to fill the void caused by the loosening of the bonds which hold persons together in immediate community of experience. If there is anything in human psychology to be counted upon, it may be urged that when man is satiated with restless seeking for the remote which yields no enduring satisfaction, the human spirit will return to seek calm and order within itself. This, we repeat, can be found only in the vital, steady, and deep relationships which are present only in an immediate community. . . .

Over and over again, one point has recurred for criticism—the subordination of activity to a result outside itself. Whether that goal be thought of as pleasure, as virtue, as perfection, as final enjoyment of salvation, is secondary to the fact that the moralists who have asserted fixed ends have in all their differences from one another agreed in the basic idea that present activity is but a means. We have insisted that happiness, reasonableness, virtue, perfecting, are on the contrary parts of the present significance of present action. Memory of the past, observation of the present, foresight of the future are indispensable. But they are indispensable to a present liberation, an enriching growth of action. Happiness is fundamental in morals only because happiness is not something to be sought for, but is something now attained, even in the midst of pain and trouble, whenever recognition of our ties with nature and with fellowmen releases and informs our action. . . .

. . . Infinite relationships of man with his fellows and with nature already exist. The ideal means, as we have seen, a sense of these encompassing continuities with their infinite reach. This meaning even now attaches to present activities because they are set in a whole to which they belong and which belongs to them. Even in the midst of conflict, struggle and defeat a consciousness is possible of the enduring and comprehending whole.

To be grasped and held this consciousness needs, like every form of consciousness, objects, symbols. In the past men have sought many symbols which no longer serve, especially since men have been idolators worshiping symbols as things. Yet within these symbols which have so often claimed to be realities and which have imposed themselves as dogmas and intolerances, there has rarely been absent some trace of a vital and enduring reality, that of a community of life in which continuities of existence are consummated. Consciousness of the whole has been connected with reverences, affections, and loyalties which are communal. But special ways of expressing the communal sense have been established. They have been limited to a select social group; they have hardened into obligatory rites and been imposed as conditions of salvation. Religion has lost itself in cults, dogmas and myths. Consequently the office of religion as sense of community and one's place in it has been lost. In effect religion has been distorted into a possession—or burden—of a limited part of human nature, of a limited portion of humanity which finds no way to universalize religion except by imposing its own dogmas and ceremonies upon others; of a limited class within a partial group; priests, saints, a church. Thus other gods have been set up before the one God. Religion as a sense of the whole is the most individualized of all things, the most spontaneous, undefinable and varied. For individuality signifies unique connections in the whole. Yet it has been perverted into something uniform and immutable. It has been formulated into fixed and defined beliefs expressed in required acts and ceremonies. Instead of marking the freedom and peace of the individual as a member of an infinite whole, it has been petrified into a slavery of thought and sentiment, an intolerant superiority on the part of the few and an intolerable burden on the part of the many.

Yet every act may carry within itself a consoling and supporting consciousness of the whole to which it belongs and which in some sense belongs to it. With responsibility for the intelligent determination of particular acts may go a joyful emancipation from the burden for responsibility for the whole which sustains them, giving them their final outcome and quality. There is a conceit fostered by perversion of religion which assimilates the universe to our personal desires; but there is also a conceit of carrying the load of the universe from which religion liberates us. Within the flickering inconsequential acts of separate selves dwells a sense of the whole which claims and dignifies them. In its presence we put off mortality and live in the universal. The life of the community in which we live and have our being is the fit symbol of this relationship. The acts in which we express our perception of the ties which bind us to others are its only rites and ceremonies.

1. *Human Nature and Conduct*, pp. 17–19, 25–27, 39–41, 85–87, 91, 163–64, 21–22, 166–67. Heading provided by the editor.

2. *Art as Experience*, pp. 14–18. Heading provided by the editor.

3. The first three excerpts making up this selection are from *Human Nature and Conduct*, pp. 262–63, 266–67, and 242–49. The next two excerpts are from *Ethics*, pp. 340–42, 214–15. Heading provided by the editor.

4. *Human Nature and Conduct*, pp. 36–39, 130–31, 158–59, 182–84. Heading provided by the editor.

5. *Human Nature and Conduct*, pp. 122–23; *Democracy and Education* (New York: The Macmillan Company, 1916), pp. 288–91; *Human Nature and Conduct*, pp. 155, 138–39; *Ethics*, pp. 228–29. Heading provided by the editor.

6. *The Public and Its Problems* (New York: Henry Holt and Company, 1927), pp. 187–96. Heading provided by the editor. For an incisive analysis of the importance of clarifying the individual and the social, see Dewey's "The Crisis in Human History: The Danger of the Retreat to Individualism," *Commentary* I (March 1946): pp. 1–9.

7. *Human Nature and Conduct*, pp. 127–29; *Ethics*, pp. 331–36; *The Public and Its Problems*, pp. 213–14; *Human Nature and Conduct*, pp. 244, 300–02. Heading provided by the editor.

8. See *Experience and Nature*, p. 202.

9. New York: Henry Holt and Company, 1920. The quotation is from p. 211 of the enlarged edition of *Reconstruction in Philosophy* (Boston: The Beacon Press, 1948).

Value
and
Intelligence

5

Perhaps that part of Dewey's thought which is most misunderstood is his treatment of the relation of judgments of value to scientific inquiry.[1] He never supposed that value judgments are deduced from scientific propositions or from philosophic conclusions regarding the nature of experience, nature, society, etc. As the discussion in the introduction made clear, all such propositions and conclusions are morally important because they elucidate the conditions of unifications of value. They are, as well, the kinds of proposition that reliably bring to the attention of the agent the information pertinent to the determination of moral choice. The experimental use of intelligence in actual problematic situations is a necessary condition for converting them into consummatory experience. The aim of Dewey's inquiry is liberative, not prescriptive. Consistent with this aim, he regards a judgment of value to be a hypothesis specifying the conditions of consummatory experience in a given situation. Such a hypothesis is completely experimental; and it is its function in the problematic situation that renders it a judgment of value.

The first selection summarizes instrumentalism and its inherent connection with nature and value. By clarifying the origin, function, and test of scientific conceptions, Dewey eradicates the basis for assuming a dualism between science and experience, and hence between experimental intelligence and value.

As the passage on pp. 129–30 makes evident, Dewey—unlike James—was well aware of the distinction between what a proposition entails and what are the emotional consequences of believing a proposition to be true. Dewey's instrumentalism is wholly unsentimental: the liberating functions of ideas in conduct can only be realized when we unflinchingly recognize nature's instrumentalities and limitations. The scientific inquirer deals with problematic situations. He may seek a cure for cancer or the means to land a man on the moon. In any case, his problematic situation is not resolved until such ends-in-view are achieved.

Emotional satisfaction may well accompany the resolution of the problem, but it by no means constitutes a verification of the hypothesis in use. It is true, however, that the hypothesis is tested by further activity, or behavior, involving very careful observations and measurements. Hypotheses predict future activity in the unambiguous sense that they predict future interactions of the experimenter qua *experimenter with his subject matter. Dewey desires that the demonstrated powers of experimental inquiry be used in human situations to permit the persons involved in them to be as enlightened as possible in the determination of choice and the construction of consummatory values. Chapter 7 will show that he conceives this liberative process to be through and through social.*

INSTRUMENTALISM[2]

No mythology is more familiar than that which tells how labor is due to trespass of man upon divine prerogatives, an act that brought curse upon the earth and woe to man. Because of this primeval rebellion against God, men toil amid thorns to gain an uncertain livelihood, and women bring forth children in pain. The tale is touching evidence that man finds it natural that nature should support his activities, and unnatural that the burden of continued and hard endeavor should be placed upon him. Festivity is spontaneous; labor needs to be accounted for. There is a long distance between the birth of the old legend and the formulation of classic political economy; but the doctrine of the latter that labor which is the source of value signifies cost, onerous sacrifice of present consummation to attainment of later good, expresses the same human attitude.

Yet, in fact, it was not enjoyment of the apple but the enforced penalty of labor that made man as the gods, *knowing* good and evil instead of just having and enjoying them. The exacting conditions imposed by nature, that have to be observed in order that work be carried through to success, are the source of all noting and recording of nature's doings. They supply the discipline that chastens exuberant fancy into respect for the operation of events, and that effects subjection of thought to a pertinent order of space and time. While leisure is the mother of drama, sport and literary spellbinding, necessity is the mother of invention, discovery and consecutive reflection. . . .

That the sciences were born of the arts—the physical sciences of the crafts and technologies of healing, navigation, war and the working of wood, metals, leather, flax and wool; the mental sciences of the arts of political management—is, I suppose, an admitted fact. The distinctively intellectual attitude which marks scientific inquiry was generated in efforts at controlling persons and things so that consequences, issues, outcomes would be more stable and assured. The first step away from oppression by immediate things and events was taken when man employed tools and appliances for manipulating things so as to render them contributory to desired objects. In responding to things not in their immediate qualities but for the sake of ulterior results, immediate qualities are dimmed, while those features which are signs, indices of something else, are distinguished. A thing is more significantly what it makes possible than what it immediately is. The very conception of cognitive meaning, intellectual significance, is that things in their immediacy are subordinated to what they portend and give evidence of. An intellectual sign denotes that a thing is not taken immediately but is referred to something that may come in consequence of it. Intellectual meanings may themselves be appropriated, enjoyed and appreciated; but the character of intellectual meaning is instrumental. Fortunate for us is it that tools and their using can be directly enjoyed; otherwise all work would be drudgery. But this additive fact does not alter the definition of a tool; it remains a thing used as an agency for some concluding event.

The first groping steps in defining spatial and temporal qualities, in transforming purely immediate qualities of local things into generic relationships, were taken through the arts. The finger, the foot, the unit of walking were used to measure space; measurements of weight originated in the arts of commercial exchange and manufacture. Geometry, beginning as agricultural art, further emancipated space from being a localized quality of immediate extensity. But the radically different ways of conceiving geometry found in ancient and in modern science are evidence of the slowness of the process of emancipation of even geometrical forms from direct or esthetic traits. In Greek astronomy the intrinsic qualities of figures always dominated their instrumental significance in inquiry; they were forms to which phenomena had to conform instead of means of indirect measurements. Hardly till our own day did spatial relations get emancipated from esthetic and moral qualities, and become wholly intellectual and relational, abstracted from immediate qualifications, and thereby generalized to their limit.

Anything approaching a history of the growth of recognition of things in their intellectual or instrumental phase is far beyond our present scope. We can only point out some of its net results. In principle the step is taken whenever objects are so reduced from their status of complete objects as to be treated as signs or indications of other objects. Enter upon this road and the time is sure to come when the appropriate object-of-knowledge is stripped of all that is immediate and qualitative, of all that is final, self-sufficient. Then it becomes an anatomized epitome of just and only those traits which are of indicative or instrumental import. Abstraction is not a psychological incident; it is a following to its logical conclusion of interest in those phases of natural existence which are dependable and fruitful signs of other things; which are means of prediction by formulation in terms implying other terms.

Self-evidence ceases to be a characteristic trait of the fundamental objects of either sensory or noetic objects. Primary propositions are statements of objects in terms which procure the simplest and completest forming and checking of other propositions. Many systems of axioms and postulates are possible, the more the merrier, since new propositions as consequences are thus brought to light. Genuine science is impossible as long as the object esteemed for its own intrinsic qualities is taken as the object of knowledge. Its completeness, its immanent meaning, defeats its use as indicating and implying.

Said William James, "Many were the ideal prototypes of rational order: teleological and esthetic ties between things . . . as well as logical and mathematical relations. The most promising of these things at first were of course the richer ones, the more sentimental ones. The baldest and least promising were mathematical ones, but the history of the latter's application is a history of steadily advancing successes, while that of the sentimentally richer ones is one of relative sterility and failure. Take those aspects of phenomena which interest you as a human being most . . . and barren are all your results. Call the things of nature as much as you like by sentimental moral and esthetic names, no natural consequences follow from the naming. . . . But when you give the things mathematical and mechanical names and call them so many solids in just such positions, describing just such paths with just such velocities, all *is* changed. . . . Your 'things' realize the consequences of the names by which you classed them."*

A fair interpretation of these pregnant sentences is that as long as objects are viewed telically, as long as the objects of the truest knowledge, the most real forms of being, are thought of as ends, science does not advance. Objects are possessed and appreciated, but they are not *known*. To know, means that men have become willing to turn away from precious possessions; willing to let drop what they own, however precious, in behalf of a grasp of objects which they do not as yet own. Multiplied and secure ends depend upon letting go existent ends, reducing them to indicative and implying means. . . .

The net result of the new scientific method was conception of nature as a mathematical-mechanical object. If modern philosophy, reflecting the tendencies of the new science, abolished final causes from nature, it was because concern with qualitative ends, already existing objects of possession and enjoyment, blocked inquiry, discovery and control, and ended in barren dialectical disputes about definitions and classifications. A candid mind can hardly deny that sensory qualities, colors, moist and dry, hard and soft, light and heavy are genuine natural ends. In them the potentialities of the body are brought into functioning, while the activity of the body thus

*James, *Principles of Psychology*, Vol. II, pp. 605–06.

achieved brings in turn to completion potentialities in nature outside of the body. Nevertheless the theory that final objects are the appropriate objects of knowledge, in assimilating knowledge to esthetic contemplation had fatal consequences for science. All natural phenomena had to be known in terms of qualities. Hot and cold, wet and dry, up and down, light and heavy were things to know with and by. They were essential forms, active principles of nature. But Galileo and his scientific and philosophical followers (like Descartes and Hobbes) reversed the method by asserting that these sensory forms are things to be known, challenges to inquiry, problems, not solutions nor terms of solution. The assertion was a general one; it necessitated *search* for objects of knowledge. Dependable material with which to know was found in a different realm of being; in spatial relations, positions, masses, mathematically defined, and in motion as change of space having direction and velocity. Qualities were no longer things to do with; they were things already done, effects requiring to be known by statement and description in mathematical and mechanical relations. The only world which defines and explains was a world of masses in motion, arranged in a system of Cartesian coordinates.

When we view experientially this change, what occurs is the kind of thing that happens in the useful arts when natural objects, like crude ores, are treated as materials for getting something else. Their character ceases to lie in their immediate qualities, in just what they are and as directly enjoyed. Their character is now representative; some pure metal, iron, copper, etc., is their essence, which may be extracted as their "true" nature, their "reality." To get at this reality many existent constituents have to be got rid of. From the standpoint of the *object*, pure metal, these things to be eliminated are "false," irrelevant and obstructive. They stand in the way, and in the existent thing those qualities are alone significant which indicate the ulterior objective and which offer means for attaining it.

Modern science represents a generalized recognition and adoption of the point of view of the useful arts, for it proceeds by employment of a similar operative technique of manipulation and reduction. Physical science would be impossible without the appliances and procedures of separation and combination of the industrial arts. In useful arts, the consequence is increase of power, multiplication of ends appropriated and enjoyed, and an enlarged and varied flexibility and economy in means used to achieve ends. Metal can be put to thousands of uses, while the crude ore can only be beheld for whatever esthetic qualities it happens to present, or be hurled bodily at game or an enemy. Reduction of natural existences to the status of means thus presents nothing inherently adverse to possessed and appreciated ends, but rather renders the latter a more secure and extensive affair. . . .

. . . The objects of science, like the direct objects of the arts, are an order of relations which serve as tools to effect immediate havings and beings.

Goods, objects with qualities of fulfillment, are the natural fruition of the discovery and employment of means, when the connection of ends with a sequential order is determined. Immediate empirical things are just what they always were: endings of natural histories. Physical science does not set up another and rival realm of antithetical existence; it reveals the state or order upon which the occurrence of immediate and final qualities depends. It adds to casual having of ends an ability to regulate the date, place and manner of their emergence. . . .

. . . To follow the clews of experience is to see that the so-called sensible world is a world of immediate beginnings and endings; not at all an affair of cases of knowledge but a succession of qualitative events; while the so-called conceptual order is recognized to be the proper object of science, since it constitutes the scheme of constant relationships by means of which spare, scattered and casual events are bound together into a connected history. These emergent immediate events remain the beginning and the end of knowledge; but since their *occurrence* is one with their being sensibly, affectionally and appreciatively *had*, they are not themselves things known. That the qualities and characters of these immediate apparitions are tremendously modified when they are linked together by "physical objects"—that is, by means of the mathematical-mechanical objects of physics—is a fact of the same nature as that a steel watch-spring is a modification of crude iron ore. The objects of physics subsist precisely in order to bring about this transformation—to change, that is, casual endings into fulfillments and conclusions of an ordered series, with the development of meaning therein involved. . . . [3]

. . . Then . . . the foundation for value and the striving to realize it is found in nature, because when nature is viewed as consisting of events rather than substances, it is characterized by *histories*, that is, by continuity of change proceedings from beginnings to endings. Consequently, it is natural for genuine initiations and consummations to occur in experience. Owing to the presence of uncertain and precarious factors in these histories, attainment of ends, of goods, is unstable and evanescent. The only way to render them more secure is by ability to control the changes that intervene between the beginning and the end of a process. These intervening terms when brought under control are *means* in the literal and in the practical sense of the word. When mastered in actual experience they constitute tools, techniques, mechanisms, etc. Instead of being foes of purposes, they are means of execution; they are also tests for differentiating genuine aims from merely emotional and fantastic ideals.

The office of physical science is to discover those properties and relations of things in virtue of which they are capable of being used as instrumentalities; physical science makes claim to disclose not the inner nature of things

but only those connections of things with one another that determine outcomes and hence can be used as means. The *intrinsic* nature of events is
revealed in experience as the immediately felt qualities of things. The intimate
coordination and even fusion of these qualities with the regularities that form
the objects of knowledge, in the proper sense of the word "knowledge,"
characterizes intelligently directed experience, as distinct from mere casual
and uncritical experience. . . .[4]

. . . If we conceive of the world of immediately apparent things as an
emergence of peaks of mountains which are submerged except as to their
peaks or endings, and as a world of initial climbings whose subsequent
career emerges above the surface only here and there and by fits and starts;
and if we give attention to the fact that any ability of control whatever depends upon ability to unite these disparate appearances into a serial history,
and then give due attention to the fact that connection into a consecutive
history can be effected only by means of a scheme of constant relationships
(a condition met by the mathematical-logical-mechanical objects of physics),
we shall have no difficulty in seeing why it is that the immediate things
from which we start lend themselves to interpretation as signs or appearances
of the objects of physics; while we also recognize that it is only with respect
to the function of instituting connection that the objects of physics can be
said to be more "real." In the total situation in which they function, they
are means to weaving together otherwise disconnected beginnings and endings into a consecutive history. Underlying "reality" and surface "appearance" in this connection have a meaning fixed by the function of inquiry,
not an intrinsic metaphysical meaning. . . .[5]

The problem which is supposed to exist between two tables, one that of
direct perception and use and the other that of physics (to take the favorite
illustration of recent discussion) is thus illusory. The perceived and used
table is the only table, for it alone has both individuality of form—without
which nothing can exist or be perceived—and also includes within itself a
continuum of relations or interactions brought to a focus. We may perhaps
employ more instructively an illustration derived from the supposed contrast
between an object experienced in perception as it is rendered by a poet and
the same object described by a physicist. There is the instance of a body of
water where the movement of the wind over its surface is reflected in sun-
light. As an object of science, it is reported as follows: "Etherial vibrations
of various wave lengths, reflected at different angles from the disturbed inter-
face between air and water, reached our eyes and by photoelectric action
caused appropriate stimuli to travel along optic nerves to a brain center."
Such a statement, however, includes ordinary objects of individual perceptions; water, air, brain and nerves. Consequently, it must be reduced still

further; when so reduced it consists of mathematical functions between certain physical constants having no counterpart in ordinary perception.*...

The vogue of the philosophy that identifies the object of knowledge as such with the reality of the subject-matter of experience makes it advisable to carry the discussion further. Physical science submits the things of ordinary experience to specifiable operations. The result is objects of thought stated in numbers, where the numbers in question permit inclusion within complex systems of equations and other mathematical functions. In the physical object everything is ignored but the relations expressed by these numbers. It is safe to assert that no physicist *while at work* ever thought of denying the full reality of the things of ordinary, coarse experience. He pays no attention to their qualities except as they are signs of operations to be performed and of inference to relations to be drawn. But in these capacities he has to admit their full reality on pain of having, logically, to deny reality to the conclusions of his operative inferences. He takes the instruments he employs, including his own sensory-motor organs and measuring instruments, to be real in the ordinary sense of the word. If he denied the reality of these things as they are had in ordinary noncognitive perceptual experience, the conclusions reached by them would be equally discredited. Moreover, the numbers which define his metric object are themselves results of noting interactions or connections among perceived things. It would be the height of absurdity to assert the reality of these relations while denying the reality of the things between which they hold. If the latter are "subjective" what becomes of the former? Finally, observation is resorted to for verification. It is a strange world in which the conception of the real has to be corroborated by reference to that the reality of which is made dubious by the conception....[6]

It is characteristic of the inevitable moral prepossession of philosophy, together with the subjective turn of modern thought, that many critics take an "instrumental" theory of knowledge to signify that the value of knowing is instrumental to the knower. This is a matter which is as it may be in particular cases; but certainly in many cases the pursuit of science is sport, carried on, like other sports, for its own satisfaction. But "instrumentalism" is a theory not about personal disposition and satisfaction in knowing, but about the proper objects of science, what is "proper" being defined in terms of physics.

The distinction between tools (or things in their objectivities) and fulfilled products of the use of tools accounts for the distinction between known objects on one side and objects of appreciation and affection on the other. But the distinction primarily concerns objects themselves; only secondarily does it apply to attitudes, dispositions, motivations. Making and using tools

---

*The illustration is borrowed from Eddington, *The Nature of the Physical World*; see pp. 316–319. . . .

may be intrinsically delightful. Prior to the introduction of machinery for quantitative production and sale of commodities for profit, utensils were themselves usually works of art, esthetically satisfying. This fact does not however define them *as* utensils; it does not confer upon them their characteristic property. In like manner, the pursuit of knowledge is often an immediately delightful event; its attained products possess esthetic qualities of proportion, order, and symmetry. But these qualities do not mark off or define the characteristic and appropriate *objects* of science. The character of the object is like that of a tool, say a lever; it is an order of determination of sequential changes terminating in a foreseen consequence....

. . . In the practice of science, knowledge is an affair of *making* sure, not of grasping antecedently given sureties. What is already known, what is accepted as truth, is of immense importance; inquiry could not proceed a step without it. But it is held subject to use, and is at the mercy of the discoveries which it makes possible. It has to be adjusted to the latter and not the latter to it. When things are defined as instruments, their value and validity reside in what proceeds from them; consequences, not antecedents, supply meaning and verity. Truths already possessed may have practical or moral certainty, but logically they never lose a hypothetic quality. They are true *if*: if certain other things eventually present themselves; and when these latter things occur they in turn suggest further possibilities; the operation of doubt-inquiry-finding recurs. . . .[7]

. . . All general conceptions (ideas, theories, thought) are hypothetical. Ability to frame hypotheses is the means by which man is liberated from submergence in the existences that surround him and that play upon him physically and sensibly. It is the positive phase of abstraction. But hypotheses are conditional; they have to be tested by the consequences of the operations they define and direct. The discovery of the value of hypothetical ideas when employed to suggest and direct concrete processes, and the vast extension of this operation in the modern history of science, mark a great emancipation and correspondent increase of intellectual control. But their final value is not determined by their internal elaboration and consistency, but by the consequence they effect in existence as that is perceptibly experienced. Scientific conceptions are not a revelation of prior and independent reality. They are a system of hypotheses, worked out under conditions of definite test, by means of which our intellectual and practical traffic with nature is rendered freer, more secure and more significant.

Our discussion has been one-sided in that it has dealt with the matter of conceptions mainly in reference to the "rationalistic" tradition of interpretation. The reasons for this emphasis are too patent to need exposition. But before leaving the topic, it should be noted that traditional empiricism has also misread the significance of conceptions or general ideas. It has steadily opposed the doctrine of their *a priori* character; it has connected them with experience of the actual world. But even more obviously than the rationalism it has opposed, empiricism has connected the origin, content and measure of validity of general ideas with antecedent existence. According to it, concepts are formed by comparing particular objects, already perceived, with one another, and then eliminating the elements in which they disagree and retaining that which they have in common. Concepts are thus simply memoranda of identical features in objects already perceived; they are conveniences, bunching together a variety of things scattered about in concrete experience. But they have to be *proved* by agreement with the material of particular antecedent experiences; their value and function is essentially retrospective. Such ideas are dead, incapable of performing a regulative office in new situations. They are "empirical" in the sense in which the term is opposed to scientific —that is, they are mere summaries of results obtained under more or less accidental circumstances. . . .

. . . We conclude with a summary statement of the more important results reached in the present phase of discussion. First, the active and productive character of ideas, of thought, is manifest. The motivating desire of idealistic systems of philosophy is justified. But the constructive office of thought is empirical—that is, experimental. "Thought" is not a property of something termed intellect or reason apart from nature. It is a mode of directed overt action. Ideas are anticipatory plans and designs which take effect in concrete *reconstructions* of antecedent conditions of existence. They are not innate properties of mind corresponding to ultimate prior traits of Being, nor are they *a priori* categories imposed on sense in a wholesale, once-for-all way, prior to experience so as to make it possible. The active power of ideas is a reality, but ideas and idealisms have an operative force in concrete experienced situations; their worth has to be tested by the specified consequences of their operation. Idealism is something experimental not abstractly rational; it is related to experienced needs and concerned with projection of operations which remake the actual content of experienced objects.

Secondly, ideas and idealisms are in themselves hypotheses not finalities. Being connected with operations to be performed, they are tested by the consequences of these operations, not by what exists prior to them. Prior experience supplies the conditions which evoke ideas and of which thought has to take account, with which it must reckon. It furnishes both obstacles to attainment of what is desired and the resources that must be used to attain it. Conception and systems of conceptions, ends-in-view and plans, are constantly making and remaking as fast as those already in use reveal their weaknesses, defects and positive values. There is no predestined course they must follow. Human experience consciously guided by ideas evolves its own standards and measures and each new experience constructed by their means is an opportunity for new ideas and ideals.

In the third place, action is at the heart of ideas. The experimental practice of knowing, when taken to supply the pattern of philosophic doctrine of mind and its organs, eliminates the age-old separation of theory and practice. It discloses that knowing is itself a kind of action, the only one which progressively and securely clothes natural existence with realized meanings. For the outcome of experienced objects which are begot by operations which define thinking, take into themselves, as part of their own funded and incorporated meaning, the relation to other things disclosed by thinking. There are no sensory or perceived objects fixed in themselves. In the course of experience, as far as that is an outcome influenced by thinking, objects perceived, used and enjoyed take up into their own meaning the results of thought; they become ever richer and fuller of meanings. This issue constitutes the last significance of the philosophy of experimental idealism. Ideas direct operations; the operations have a result in which ideas are no longer abstract, mere ideas, but where they qualify sensible objects. The road from a perceptible experience which is blind, obscure, fragmentary, meager in meaning, to objects of sense which are also objects which satisfy, reward and feed intelligence is through ideas that are experimental and operative.

Our conclusion depends upon an analysis of what takes place in the experimental inquiry of natural science. It goes without saying that the wider scope of human experience, that which is concerned with distinctively human conditions and ends, does not comport, as it currently exists, with the result that the examination of natural science yields. The genuinely philosophic force, as distinct from a technical one, of the conclusion reached lies in precisely this incongruity. The fact that the most exacting type of experience has attained a marvelous treasury of working ideas that are used in control of objects is an indication of possibilities as yet unattained in less restricted forms of experience. Negatively, the result indicates the need of thoroughgoing revision of ideas of mind and thought and their connection with natural things that were formed before the rise of experimental inquiry; such is the critical task imposed on contemporary thought. Positively, the result achieved in science is a challenge to philosophy to consider the possibility of the extension of the method of operative intelligence to direction of life in other fields.[8]

. . . Experimental intelligence, conceived after the pattern of science, and used in the creation of social arts, . . . has something to do. It liberates man from the bondage of the past, due to ignorance and accident hardened into custom. It projects a better future and assists man in its realization. And its operation is always subject to test in experience. The plans which are formed, the principles which man projects as guides of reconstructive action, are not dogmas. They are hypotheses to be worked out in practice, and to be rejected, corrected and expanded as they fail or succeed in giving our present experience the guidance it requires. We may call them programs of action, but since they are to be used in making our future acts less blind, more directed, they are flexible. Intelligence is not something possessed once for all. It is in constant process of forming, and its retention requires constant alertness in observing consequences, an open-minded will to learn and courage in re-adjustment. . . .[9]

INTELLIGENCE AND MORALS[10]

. . . Lack of understanding of human nature is the primary cause of dis-regard for it. Lack of insight always ends in despising or else unreasoned admiration. When men had no scientific knowledge of physical nature they either passively submitted to it or sought to control it magically. What can-not be understood cannot be managed intelligently. It has to be forced into subjection from without. The opaqueness of human nature to reason is equivalent to a belief in its intrinsic irregularity. Hence a decline in the authority of social oligarchy was accompanied by a rise of scientific interest in human nature. This means that the makeup and working of human forces afford a basis for moral ideas and ideals. Our science of human nature in comparison with physical sciences is rudimentary, and morals which are concerned with the health, efficiency and happiness of a development of human nature are correpondingly elementary. . . .

The idea persists that there is something materialistic about natural science and that morals are degraded by having anything seriously to do with mate-rial things. If a sect should arise proclaiming that men ought to purify their lungs completely before they ever drew a breath it ought to win many ad-herents from professed moralists. For the neglect of sciences that deal specif-ically with facts of the natural and social environment leads to a side tracking of moral forces into an unreal privacy of an unreal self. It is impossible to say how much of the remediable suffering of the world is due to the fact that physical science is looked upon as merely physical. It is impossible to say how much of the unnecessary slavery of the world is due to the conception that moral issues can be settled within conscience or human sentiment apart from consistent study of facts and application of specific knowledge in industry, law and politics. Outside of manufacturing and transportation, sci-ence gets its chance in war. These facts perpetuate war and the hardest, most brutal side of modern industry. Each sign of disregard for the moral poten-tialities of physical science drafts the conscience of mankind away from con-cern with the interactions of man and nature which must be mastered if freedom is to be a reality. It diverts intelligence to anxious preoccupation with the unrealities of a purely inner life, or strengthens reliance upon out-bursts of sentimental affection. The masses swarm to the occult for assistance. The cultivated smile contemptuously. They might smile, as the saying goes, out of the other side of their mouths if they realized how recourse to the occult exhibits the practical logic of their own beliefs. For both rest upon a separation of moral ideas and feelings from knowable facts of life, man and the world.

It is not pretended that a moral theory based upon realities of human nature and a study of the specific connections of these realities with those of physical science would do away with moral struggle and defeat. It would not make the moral life as simple a matter as wending one's way along a well-lighted boulevard. All action is an invasion of the future, of the unknown. Conflict and uncertainty are ultimate traits. But morals based upon concern with facts and deriving guidance from knowledge of them would at least locate the points of effective endeavor and would focus available resources upon them. It would put an end to the impossible attempt to live in two unrelated worlds. It would destroy fixed distinction between the human and the physical, as well as that between the moral and the industrial and political. A morals based on study of human nature instead of upon disregard for it would find the facts of man continuous with those of the rest of nature and would thereby ally ethics with physics and biology. It would find the nature and activities of one person coterminous with those of other human beings and therefore link ethics with the study of history, sociology, law and economics.

Such a morals would not automatically solve moral problems nor resolve perplexities. But it would enable us to state problems in such forms that action could be courageously and intelligently directed to their solution. It would not assure us against failure, but it would render failure a source of instruction. It would not protect us against the future emergence of equally serious moral difficulties, but it would enable us to approach the always recurring troubles with a fund of growing knowledge which would add significant values to our conduct even when we overtly failed—as we should continue to do. Until the integrity of morals with human nature and of both with the environment is recognized, we shall be deprived of the aid of past experience to cope with the most acute and deep problems of life. Accurate and extensive knowledge will continue to operate only in dealing with purely technical problems. The intelligent acknowledgment of the continuity of nature, man and society will alone secure a growth of morals which will be serious without being fanatical, aspiring without sentimentality, adapted to reality without conventionality, sensible without taking the form of calculation of profits, idealistic without being romantic.

MORAL DELIBERATION AND EXPERIMENTAL LOGIC [11]

The Aristotelian logic as far as its spirit, instead of its letter, is concerned, is . . . both generically and specifically significant for what needs to be done in logic in the contemporary situation. Generically, the need is for logic to do for present science and culture what Aristotle did for the science and culture of his time. Specifically, his logic is significant for present logic in that it included in a single unified scheme the contents of both the common sense and the science of his day. The unification was effected in a way which is no longer possible. We can no longer take the contents and procedures of both common sense and science as inherently fixed, differing only in qualitative grade and rank in a qualitatively fixed hierarchy. The fixity of the contents and logical forms of both common sense and science in the Aristotelian scheme precluded the possibility of the reaction of science back into common sense and the possibility of the ever-continuing rise of new scientific problems and conceptions out of the material of common sense activities and materials. All that science could do was to accept what was given and established in common sense and formulate it in its relation to the fixed subjects of higher rational knowledge. The present need is for a unified logic that takes account of a two-way movement between common sense and science....

Science has ... affected the actual conditions under which men live, use, enjoy and suffer much more than (aside from material technologies) it has affected their habits of belief and inquiry. Especially is this true about the uses and enjoyments of final concern: religious, moral, legal, economic, political. The demand for reform of logic is the demand for a unified theory of inquiry through which the authentic pattern of experimental and operational inquiry of science shall become available for regulation of the habitual methods by which inquiries in the field of common sense are carried on; by which conclusions are reached and beliefs are formed and tested....

The previous chapter was devoted to enforcing the necessity of mediation in knowledge as warranted assertion. This necessity does not stand alone, for it is a necessary phase of the theory of inquiry and judgment that has been developed. It received separate development because of the traditional and still current doctrine of self-evident truths and self-grounded propositions. There is, however, another phase of our basic theory which stands equally (and possibly to a greater degree) in opposition to accepted logical theory, and which accordingly stands also in need of explicit treatment. For, contrary to current doctrine, the position here taken is that inquiry effects *existential* transformation and reconstruction of the material with which it deals; the result of the transformation, when it is grounded, being conversion of an indeterminate problematic situation into a determinate resolved one.

This emphasis upon requalification of antecedent existential material, and upon judgment as the resulting transformation, stands in sharp contrast with traditional theory. The latter holds that such modifications as may occur in even the best controlled inquiry are confined to states and processes of the knower—the one conducting the inquiry. They may, therefore, properly be

called "subjective," mental or psychological, or by some similar name. They
are without objective standing, and hence lack logical force and meaning.
The position that is here taken is to the contrary effect: namely, that beliefs
and mental states of the inquirer cannot be legitimately changed except as
existential operations, rooted ultimately in organic activities, modify and re-
qualify objective matter. Otherwise, "mental" changes are not only merely
mental (as the traditional theory holds) but are arbitrary and on the road
to fantasy and delusion.

The traditional theory in both its empiricistic and rationalistic forms
amounts to holding that all propositions are purely declaratory or enuncia-
tive of what antecedently exists or subsists, and that this declarative office
is complete and final in itself. The position here taken holds, on the contrary, that declarative propositions, whether of facts or of conceptions (principles and laws) are intermediary means or instruments (respectively material and procedural) of effecting that controlled transformation of subject-
matter which is the end-in-view (and final goal) of all declarative affirma-
tions and negations. It is not, be it noted, the *occurrence* of purely declarative propositions that is denied. On the contrary, as will be shown later in
detail, the existence of such propositions, setting forth relationships that obtain between factual data on one hand and between conceptual subject-matter
on the other hand, is expressly affirmed. The point at issue concerns not their
being but their function and interpretation.

The position may be stated in the following language: All controlled inquiry and all institution of grounded assertion necessarily contains a *practical*
factor; an activity of doing and making which reshapes antecedent existential
material which sets the problem of inquiry. That this view is not assumed
ad hoc, but represents what certainly occurs (or is a *vera causa*) in at least
some cases, will be shown by considering some forms of commonsense inquiry which aim at determining what is to be done in some practical predicament.

Inquiries of this type are neither exceptional nor infrequent. For the stock
and staple of commonsense inquiries and judgments are of this sort. The
deliberations of daily life concern in largest measure questions of what to
make or to do. Every art and every profession is faced with constantly recurring problems of this sort. To put their existence in doubt is equivalent to
denying that any element of intelligence enters into any form of practice; to
affirming that all decisions on practical matters are the arbitrary products of
impulse, caprice, blind habit, or convention. Farmer, mechanic, painter,
musician, writer, doctor, lawyer, merchant, captain of industry, administrator
or manager has constantly to inquire what it is better to do next. Unless
the decision reached is arrived at blindly and arbitrarily it is obtained by
gathering and surveying evidence appraised as to its weight and relevancy;

and by framing and testing plans of action in their capacity as hypotheses: that is, as ideas.

By description, the situations which *evoke* deliberation resulting in decision, are themselves indeterminate with respect to what might and should be done. They require that *something* should be done. But *what* action is to be taken is just the thing in question. The problem of *how* the uncertain situation should be dealt with is urgent. But as merely urgent, it is so emotional as to impede and often to frustrate wise decision. The intellectual question is what sort of action the *situation* demands in order that it may receive a satisfactory objective reconstruction. This question can be answered only, I repeat, by operations of observation, collection of data and of inference, which are directed by ideas whose material is itself examined through operations of ideational comparison and organization.

I did not include the scientist in the list of persons who have to engage in inquiry in order to make judgments upon matters of practice. But a slight degree of reflection shows that he has to decide what researches to engage in and how to carry them on—a problem that involves the issue of what observations to undertake, what experiments to carry on, what lines of reasoning and mathematical calculations to pursue. Moreover, he cannot settle these questions once and for all. He is continually having to judge what it is best to do next in order that his conclusion, no matter how abstract or theoretical it may be as a conclusion, shall be grounded when it is arrived at. In other words, the conduct of scientific inquiry, whether physical or mathematical, is a mode of *practice;* the working scientist is a practitioner above all else, and is constantly engaged in making practical judgments: decisions as to what to do and what means to employ in doing it.

The results of deliberation as to what it is *better to do* are, obviously, not identical with the final issue for the sake of which the deliberative inquiries are undertaken. For the final issue is some new situation in which the difficulties and troubles which elicited deliberation are done away with; in which they no longer *exist.* This objective end cannot be attained by conjuring with mental states. It is an end brought about only by means of existential changes. The question for deliberation is what to do in order to effect these changes. They are means to the required existential reconstruction; *a fortiori*, the inquiries and decisions which issue in performance of these acts are instrumental and intermediate. But what should be done depends upon the conditions that exist in the given situation and hence require a declarative or enunciatory proposition: "The actual conditions are so-and-so." These conditions are the ground of inference to a declarative proposition that such and such an act is the one best calculated to produce the desired issue under the factual conditions ascertained. Declarative propositions as to the state of facts involved set forth the obstacles and resources to be overcome and administered in reaching the intended goal. They state potentialities, positive and adverse. They function as instrumentalities. The propositions which set forth the way existing conditions should be dealt with stand in functional correlation with the enunciatory propositions which state existing conditions. The propositions as to procedure are not carriers of existential or factual materials. They are of the general form: "If such and such a course is adopted under the existing circumstances, such and such will be the probable result." Logically, the formation of these hypotheses as to methods of action involves reasoning, or a series of declarative propositions stating relationships of conceptual materials. For it is only rarely that the idea of the procedure which first suggests itself can be directly set to work. It has to be developed; this development constitutes rational discourse, which in scientific practice usually takes the form of mathematical calculation.

Preliminary to offering illustrations of what has been said, I shall summarize formally what is logically involved in every situation of deliberation and grounded decision in matters of practice. There is an existential situation such that (a) its constituents are changing so that in any case *something* different is going to happen in the future; and such that (b) just *what* will exist in the future depends in part upon introduction of *other* existential conditions interacting with those already existing, while (c) *what* new conditions are brought to bear depends upon what activities are undertaken, (d) the latter matter being influenced by the intervention of inquiry in the way of observation, inference and reasoning. . . .

Moral evaluations are . . . a case in point. The common, perhaps prevailing, assumption is that there are objects which are ends-in-themselves; that these ends are arranged in a hierarchy from the less to the more ultimate and have corresponding authority over conduct. It follows from this view that moral "judgment" consists simply in direct apprehension of an end-in-itself in its proper place in the scheme of fixed values. It is assumed that apart from this hierarchy of fixed ends, a moral agent has no alternative save to follow his desires as they come and go. According to the position here taken, ends as objective termini or as fulfillments function in judgment as representative of modes of operation that will resolve the doubtful situation which evokes and demands judgment. As *ends-in-view* they denote plans of action or purposes. The business of inquiry is to determine that mode of operation which will resolve the predicament in which the agent finds himself involved, in correspondence with the observations which determine just what the facts of the predicament are. . . .

Such evaluative judgments are clearly an instance of judgments of practice; or, more strictly, all judgments of practice are evaluations, being occupied with judging what to do on the basis of estimated consequences of conditions which, since they are existential, are going to operate in any case.

The more it is emphasized that direct enjoyment, liking, admiration, etc., are themselves emotional-motor in nature, the clearer is it that they are modes of action (of interaction). Hence a decision whether to engage or indulge in them in a given situation is a judgment of practice—of what should be done.

A point still more important for logical theory is that these evaluative judgments (as was brought out in the earlier discussion of judgment) enter into the formation of *all* final judgments. There is no inquiry that does not involve judgments of practice. The scientific worker has continually to appraise the information he gathers from his own observations and from the findings of others; he has to appraise its bearing upon what problems to undertake and what activities of observation, experimentation and calculation to carry out. While he "knows," in the sense of understanding, systems of conceptual materials, including laws, he has to estimate their relevancy and force as conditions of the particular inquiry undertaken. . . .

The net conclusion is that evaluations as judgments of practice are not a particular kind of judgment in the sense that they can be put over against other kinds, but are an inherent phase of judgment itself. In some cases, the immediate problem may so directly concern appraisal of existences in their capacity as means, positive–negative (resources and obstacles), and so directly concern appraisal of the relative importance of possible consequences that offer themselves as ends-in-view, that the evaluative aspect is the dominant one. In that case, there are judgments which in a *relative* sense may be called valuational in distinction from the subject-matter of other judgments where this aspect is subordinate. But since selection of existences to serve as subject-data and of ideas as predicate-possibilities (or ends-in-view) is necessarily involved in every judgment, the valuation operation is inherent in judgment as such. The more problematic the situation and the more thorough the inquiry that has to be engaged in, the more explicit becomes the valuational phase. The identity of valuational judgment with judgments of practice is implicitly recognized in scientific inquiry in the necessity of experiment for determination of data and for the use of ideas and conceptions—including principles and laws—as directive hypotheses. In substance, the present chapter is then a plea that logical theory be made to conform with the realities of scientific practice, since in the latter there are no grounded determinations without operations of doing and making.

DELIBERATION AND CHOICE [12]

The analysis of choice pertains of course to moral choice, as well as to any other kind of deciding. Choosing is a particular kind of response to one's situation. Accordingly, one's conduct need not be directed by moral exhortation. Liberative activity, indeed, is a product of determin-

ing how the values of a situation can be integrated. Choice has implica-
tions extending far beyond the success or failure of the moment, how-
ever. It will be evident that Dewey's characterization of deliberation and
choice is very much like that of Aristotle.

Our first problem is . . . to investigate the nature of ordinary judgments upon what it is best or wise to do, or, in ordinary language, the nature of deliberation. We begin with a summary assertion that deliberation is a dramatic rehearsal (in imagination) of various competing possible lines of action. It starts from the blocking of efficient overt action, due to that con- flict of prior habit and newly released impulse to which reference has been made. Then each habit, each impulse, involved in the temporary suspense of overt action takes its turn in being tried out. Deliberation is an experiment in finding out what the various lines of possible action are really like. It is an experiment in making various combinations of selected elements of habits and impulses, to see what the resultant action would be like if it were entered upon. But the trial is in imagination, not in overt fact. The experi- ment is carried on by tentative rehearsals in thought which do not affect physical facts outside the body. Thought runs ahead and foresees outcomes, and thereby avoids having to await the instruction of actual failure and disaster. An act overtly tried out is irrevocable, its consequences cannot be blotted out. An act tried out in imagination is not final or fatal. It is retrievable.

Each conflicting habit and impulse takes its turn in projecting itself upon the screen of imagination. It unrolls a picture of its future history, of the career it would have if it were given head. Although overt exhibition is checked by the pressure of contrary propulsive tendencies, this very inhibi- tion gives habit a chance at manifestation in thought. Deliberation means precisely that activity is disintegrated, and that its various elements hold one another up. While none has force enough to become the center of a redirected activity, or to dominate a course of action, each has enough power to check others from exercising mastery. Activity does not cease in order to give way to reflection; activity is turned from execution into intra- organic channels, resulting in dramatic rehearsal.

If activity were directly exhibited it would result in certain experiences, contacts with the environment. It would succeed by making environing objects, things and persons, copartners in its forward movement; or else it would run against obstacles and be troubled, possibly defeated. These experiences of contact with objects and their qualities give meaning, charac- ter, to an otherwise fluid, unconscious activity. We find out what seeing means by the objects which are seen. They constitute the significance of visual activity which would otherwise remain a blank. "Pure" activity is for consciousness pure emptiness. It acquires a content or filling of meanings only in static termini, what it comes to rest in, or in the obstacles which check its onward movement and deflect it. As has been remarked, the object is that which objects.

There is no difference in this respect between a visible course of conduct and one proposed in deliberation. We have no direct consciousness of what we purpose to do. We can judge its nature, assign its meaning, only by following it into the situations whither it leads, noting the objects against which it runs and seeing how they rebuff or unexpectedly encourage it. In imagination as in fact we know a road only by what we see as we travel on it. Moreover the objects which prick out the course of a proposed act until we can see its design also serve to direct eventual overt activity. Every object hit upon as the habit traverses its imaginary path has a direct effect upon existing activities. It reinforces, inhibits, redirects habits already working or stirs up others which had not previously actively entered in. In thought as well as in overt action, the objects experienced in following out a course of action attract, repel, satisfy, annoy, promote and retard. Thus deliberation proceeds. To say that at last it ceases is to say that choice, decision, takes place.

What then is choice? Simply hitting in imagination upon an object which furnishes an adequate stimulus to the recovery of overt action. Choice is made as soon as some habit, or some combination of elements of habits and impulse, finds a way fully open. Then energy is released. The mind is made up, composed, unified. As long as deliberation pictures shoals or rocks or troublesome gales as marking the route of a contemplated voyage, deliberation goes on. But when the various factors in action fit harmoniously together, when imagination finds no annoying hindrance, when there is a picture of open seas, filled sails and favoring winds, the voyage is definitely entered upon. This decisive direction of action constitutes choice. It is a great error to suppose that we have no preferences until there is a choice. We are always biased beings, tending in one direction rather than another. The occasion of deliberation is an *excess* of preferences, not natural apathy or an absence of likings. We want things that are incompatible with one another; therefore we have to make a choice of what we *really* want, of the course of action, that is, which most fully releases activities. Choice is not the emergence of preference out of indifference. It is the emergence of a unified preference out of competing preferences. Biases that had held one another in check now, temporarily at least, reinforce one another, and constitute a unified attitude. The moment arrives when imagination pictures an objective consequence of action which supplies an adequate stimulus and releases definitive action. All deliberation is a search for a way to act, not for a final terminus. Its office is to facilitate stimulation.

Hence there is reasonable and unreasonable choice. The object thought of may simply stimulate some impulse or habit to a pitch of intensity where it is temporarily irresistible. It then overrides all competitors and secures for itself the sole right of way. The object looms large in imagination; it swells to fill the field. It allows no room for alternatives; it absorbs us, enraptures us, carries us away, sweeps us off our feet by its own attractive force. Then choice is arbitrary, unreasonable. But the object thought of may be one which stimulates by unifying, harmonizing, different competing tendencies. It may release an activity in which all are fulfilled, not indeed, in their original form, but in a "sublimated" fashion, that is, in a way which modifies the original direction of each by reducing it to a component along with others in an action of transformed quality. . . .

As we have said, reflection when directed to practical matters, to determination of what to do, is called deliberation. A general deliberates upon the conduct of a campaign, weighing possible moves of the enemy and of his own troops, considering pros and cons; a businessman deliberates in comparing various modes of investment; a lawyer deliberates upon the conduct of his case, and so on. In all cases of deliberation, judgment of *value* enters; the one who engages in it is concerned to weigh values with a view to discovering the better and rejecting the worse. In some cases, the value of ends is thought of and in other cases the value of means. Moral deliberation differs from other forms not as a process of forming a judgment and arriving at knowledge but in the kind of value which is thought about. The value is technical, professional, economic, etc., as long as one thinks of it as something which one can aim at and attain by way of having, *possessing;* as something to be got or to be missed. Precisely the same object will have a moral value when it is thought of as making a difference in the *self,* as determining what one will *be,* instead of merely what one will *have.* Deliberation involves doubt, hesitation, the need of making up one's mind, of arriving at a decisive choice. The choice at stake in a moral deliberation or valuation is the worth of this and that kind of character and disposition. Deliberation is not then to be identified with calculation, or a quasi-mathematical reckoning of profit and loss. Such calculation assumes that the nature of the self does not enter into question, but only how much the self is going to *get* of this and that. Moral deliberation deals not with quantity of value but with quality. . . .

Now every such choice sustains a double relation to the self. It reveals the existing self and it forms the future self. That which is chosen is that which is found congenial to the desires and habits of the self as it already exists. Deliberation has an important function in this process, because each different possibility as it is presented to the imagination appeals to a different element in the constitution of the self, thus giving all sides of character a chance to play their part in the final choice. The resulting choice also shapes the self, making it, in some degree, a new self. This fact is especially marked at critical junctures . . . , but it marks every choice to some extent however slight. Not all are as momentous as the choice of a calling in life, or of a life-partner. But every choice is at the forking of the roads, and the path chosen shuts off certain opportunities and opens others. In committing one-self to a particular course, a person gives a lasting set to his own being. Consequently, it is proper to say that in choosing this object rather than that, one is in reality choosing what kind of person or self one is going to be. Superficially, the deliberation which terminates in choice is concerned with weighing the values of particular ends. Below the surface, it is a process of discovering what sort of being a person most wants to become. . . .

Consequences include effects upon character, upon confirming and weakening habits, as well as tangibly obvious results. To keep an eye open to these effects upon character may signify the most reasonable of precautions or one of the most nauseating of practices. It may mean concentration of attention upon personal rectitude in neglect of objective consequences, a practice which creates a wholly unreal rectitude. But it may mean that the survey of objective consequences is duly extended in time. An act of gambling may be judged, for example, by its immediate overt effects, consumption of time, energy, disturbance of ordinary monetary considerations, etc. It may also be judged by its consequences upon character, setting up an enduring love of excitement, a persistent temper of speculation, and a persistent disregard of sober, steady work. To take the latter effects into account is equivalent to taking a broad view of future consequences; for these dispositions affect future companionships, vocation and avocations, the whole tenor of domestic and public life. . . .

In short, the thing actually at stake in any serious deliberation is not a difference of quantity, but what kind of person one is to become, what sort of self is in the making, what kind of a world is making. This is plain enough in those crucial decisions where the course of life is thrown into widely different channels, where the pattern of life is rendered different and diversely dyed according as this alternative or that is chosen. Deliberation as to whether to be a merchant or a school teacher, a physician or a politician is not a choice of quantities. It is just what it appears to be, a choice of careers which are incompatible with one another, within each of which definitive inclusions and rejections are involved. With the difference in career belongs a difference in the constitution of the self, of habits of thought and feeling as well as of outward action. With it comes profound differences in all future objective relationships. Our minor decisions differ in acuteness and range, but not in principle. Our world does not so obviously hang upon any one of them; but put together they make the world what it is in meaning for each one of us. Crucial decisions can hardly be more than a disclosure of the cumulative force of trivial choices. . . .

THE NATURE OF PRINCIPLES [13]

Intelligence is concerned with foreseeing the future so that action may have order and direction. It is also concerned with principles and criteria of judgment. The diffused or wide applicability of habits is reflected in the *general* character of principles: a principle is intellectually what a habit is for direct action. As habits set in grooves dominate activity and swerve it from conditions instead of increasing its adaptability, so principles treated as fixed rules instead of as helpful methods take men away from experience. The more complicated the situation, and the less we really know about it, the more insistent is the orthodox type of moral theory upon the prior existence of some fixed and universal principle or law which is to be directly applied and followed. Ready-made rules available at a moment's notice for settling any kind of moral difficulty and resolving every species of moral doubt have been the chief object of the ambition of moralist. In the much less complicated and less changing matters of bodily health such pretensions are known as quackery. But in morals a hankering for certainty, born of timidity and nourished by love of authoritative prestige, has led to the idea that absence of immutably fixed and universally applicable readymade principles is equivalent to moral chaos.

In fact, situations into which change and the unexpected enter are a challenge to intelligence to create new principles. Morals must be a growing science if it is to be a science at all, not merely because all truth has not yet been appropriated by the mind of man, but because life is a moving affair in which old moral truth ceases to apply. Principles are methods of inquiry and forecast which require verification by the event; and the time-honored effort to assimilate morals to mathematics is only a way of bolstering up an old dogmatic authority, or putting a new one upon the throne of the old. But the experimental character of moral judgments does not mean complete uncertainty and fluidity. Principles exist as hypotheses with which to experiment. Human history is long. There is a long record of past experimentation in conduct, and there are cumulative verifications which give many principles a well-earned prestige. Lightly to disregard them is the height of foolishness. But social situations alter; and it is also foolish not to observe how old principles actually work under new conditions, and not to modify them so that they will be more effectual instruments in judging new cases. Many men are now aware of the harm done in legal matters by assuming the antecedent existence of fixed principles under which every new case may be brought. They recognize that this assumption merely puts an artificial premium on ideas developed under bygone conditions, and that their perpetuation in the present works inequity. Yet the choice is not between throwing away rules previously developed and sticking obstinately by them. The intelligent alternative is to revise, adapt, expand and alter them. The problem is one of continuous, vital readaptation.

The popular objection to casuistry is similar to the popular objection to the maxim that the end justifies the means. It is creditable to practical moral sense, but not to popular logical consistency. For recourse to casuistry is the only conclusion which can be drawn from belief in fixed universal principles, just as the Jesuit maxim is the only conclusion proper to be drawn from belief in fixed ends. Every act, every deed is individual. What is the sense in having fixed general rules, commandments, laws, unless they are such as to confer upon individual cases of action (where alone instruction is finally needed) something of their own infallible certainty? Casuistry, so-called, is simply the systematic effort to secure for particular instances of conduct the advantage of general rules which are asserted and believed in. By those who accept the notion of immutable regulating principles, casuistry ought to be lauded for sincerity and helpfulness, not dispraised as it usually is. Or else men ought to carry back their aversion to manipulation of particular cases, until they will fit into the procrustean beds of fixed rules, to the point where it is clear that all principles are empirical generalizations from the ways in which previous judgments of conduct have practically worked out. When this fact is apparent, these generalizations will be seen to be not fixed rules for deciding doubtful cases, but instrumentalities for their investigation, methods by which the net value of past experience is rendered available for present scrutiny of new perplexities. Then it will also follow that they are hypotheses to be tested and revised by their further working. . . .

. . . *Because* situations in which deliberation is evoked are new, and therefore unique, general principles are needed. Only an uncritical vagueness will assume that the sole alternative to fixed generality is absence of continuity. Rigid habits insist upon duplication, repetition, recurrence; in their case there are accordingly fixed principles. Only there is no *principle* at all, that is, no conscious intellectual rule, for thought is not needed. But all habit has *continuity*, and while a flexible habit does not secure in its operation bare recurrence nor absolute assurance neither does it plunge us into the hopeless confusion of the absolutely different. To insist upon change and the new is to insist upon alteration *of* the old. In denying that the meaning of any genuine case of deliberation can be exhausted by treating it as a mere case of an established classification the value of classification is not denied. It is shown where its value lies, namely, in directing attention to resemblances and differences in the new case, in economizing effort in foresight. To call a generalization a tool is not to say it is useless; the contrary is patently the case. A tool is something to use. Hence it is also something to be improved by noting how it works. The need of such noting and improving is indispensable if, as is the case with moral principles, the tool has to be used in unwonted circumstances. Continuity of growth, not atomism, is thus the alternative to fixity of principles and aims. This is no Bergsonian plea for dividing the universe into two portions, one all of fixed, recurrent habits, and the other all spontaneity of flux. Only in such a universe would reason in morals have to take its choice between absolute fixity and absolute looseness. . . .

THE CONSTRUCTION OF GOOD[14]

It is highly significant that Dewey characterized the subject matter of Chapter 10 of The Quest for Certainty *as the construction of good (not how to derive "ought" from "is"). The next selection consists of a substantial portion of this chapter. In a later publication, he elucidated the nature of the difference between de facto and de jure judgments, stressing that his aim was to distinguish notably different stages of inquiry pertinent to the transformation of the situation.[15] The difference between de facto and de jure is not the difference between is and ought, but between not having and having a hypothesis which indicates the means to consummatory experience. It was not Dewey's interest that conduct be guided by the force of so-called moral language, but by the individual's response to the real possibilities of his situation (see the earlier selection, "Deliberation and Choice," and Chapter 6, "Moral Language;" note also Dewey's emphasis and the sentence immediately following in "The Construction of Good," p. 153).*

Dewey's preoccupation in The Quest for Certainty *was to exhibit that values can be known and constructed by scientific means. He did not emphasize in this work that the intelligent construction of unifications of value must also be a social process. The social nature of value construction receives extensive attention in his works in social philosophy, which are represented in Chapter 7.*

We saw at the outset of our discussion that insecurity generates the quest for certainty. Consequences issue from every experience, and they are the source of our interest in what is present. Absence of arts of regulation diverted the search for security into irrelevant modes of practice, into rite and cult; thought was devoted to discovery of omens rather than of signs of what is to occur. Gradually there was differentiation of two realms, one higher, consisting of the powers which determine human destiny in all important affairs. With this religion was concerned. The other consisted of the prosaic matters in which man relied upon his own skill and his matter-of-fact insight. Philosophy inherited the idea of this division. Meanwhile in Greece many of the arts had attained a state of development which raised them above a merely routine state; there were intimations of measure, order and regularity in materials dealt with which give intimations of underlying rationality. Because of the growth of mathematics, there arose also the ideal of a purely rational knowledge, intrinsically solid and worthy and the means by which the intimations of rationality within changing phenomena could be comprehended within science. For the intellectual class the stay and consolation, the warrant of certainty, provided by religion was henceforth found in intellectual demonstration of the reality of the objects of an ideal realm.

With the expansion of Christianity, ethico-religious traits came to dominate the purely rational ones. The ultimate authoritative standards for regulation of the dispositions and purposes of the human will were fused with those which satisfied the demands for necessary and universal truth. The authority of ultimate Being was, moreover, represented on earth by the Church; that which in its nature transcended intellect was made known by a revelation of which the Church was the interpreter and guardian. The system endured for centuries. While it endured, it provided an integration of belief and conduct for the western world. Unity of thought and practice extended down to every detail of the management of life; efficacy of its operation did not depend upon thought. It was guaranteed by the most powerful and authoritative of all social institutions.

Its seemingly solid foundation was, however, undermined by the conclusions of modern science. They effected, both in themselves and even more in the new interests and activities they generated, a breach between what man is concerned with here and now and the faith concerning ultimate reality which, in determining his ultimate and eternal destiny, had previously given regulation to his present life. The problem of restoring integration and cooperation between man's beliefs about the world in which he lives and his beliefs about the values and purposes that should direct his conduct is the deepest problem of modern life. It is the problem of any philosophy that is not isolated from that life.

The attention which has been given to the fact that in its experimental procedure science has surrendered the separation between knowing and doing has its source in the fact that there is now provided within a limited, specialized and technical field the possibility and earnest, as far as theory is concerned, of effecting the needed integration in the wider field of collective human experience. Philosophy is called upon to be the theory of the practice, through ideas sufficiently definite to be operative in experimental endeavor, by which the integration may be made secure in actual experience. Its central problem is the relation that exists between the beliefs about the nature of things due to natural science to beliefs about values—using that word to designate whatever is taken to have rightful authority in the direction of conduct. A philosophy which should take up this problem is struck first of all by the fact that beliefs about values are pretty much in the position in which beliefs about nature were before the scientific revolution. There is either a basic distrust of the capacity of experience to develop its own regulative standards, and an appeal to what philosophers call eternal values, in order to ensure regulation of belief and action; or there is acceptance of enjoyments actually experienced irrespective of the method or operation by which they are brought into existence. Complete bifurcation between rationalistic method and an empirical method has its final and most deeply human significance in the ways in which good and bad are thought of and acted for and upon.

As far as technical philosophy reflects this situation, there is division of theories of values into two kinds. On the one hand, goods and evils, in every region of life, as they are concretely experienced, are regarded as characteristic of an inferior order of Being—intrinsically inferior. Just because they are things of human experience, their worth must be estimated by reference to standards and ideals derived from ultimate reality. Their defects and perversion are attributed to the same fact; they are to be corrected and controlled through adoption of methods of conduct derived from loyalty to the requirements of Supreme Being. This philosophic formulation gets actuality and force from the fact that it is a rendering of the beliefs of men in general as far as they have come under the influence of institutional religion. Just as rational conceptions were once superimposed upon observed and temporal phenomena, so eternal values are superimposed upon experienced goods. In one case as in the other, the alternative is supposed to be confusion and lawlessness. Philosophers suppose these eternal values are known by reason; the mass of persons that they are divinely revealed.

Nevertheless, with the expansion of secular interests, temporal values have enormously multipled; they absorb more and more attention and energy. The sense of transcendent values has become enfeebled; instead of permeating all things in life, it is more and more restricted to special times and acts. The authority of the church to declare and impose divine will and purpose has narrowed. Whatever men say and profess, their tendency in the presence of actual evils is to resort to natural and empirical means to remedy them. But in formal belief, the old doctrine of the inherently disturbed and unworthy character of the goods and standards of ordinary experience persists. This divergence between what men do and what they nominally profess is closely connected with the confusions and conflicts of modern thought.

It is not meant to assert that no attempts have been made to replace the older theory regarding the authority of immutable and transcendent values by conceptions more congruous with the practices of daily life. The contrary is the case. The utilitarian theory, to take one instance, has had great power. The idealistic school is the only one in contemporary philosophies, with the exception of one form of neo-realism, that makes much of the notion of a reality which is all one with ultimate moral and religious values. But this school is also the one most concerned with the conservation of "spiritual" life. Equally significant is the fact that empirical theories retain the notion that thought and judgment are concerned with values that are experienced independently of them. For these theories, emotional satisfactions occupy the same place that sensations hold in traditional empiricism. Values are constituted by liking and enjoyment; to be enjoyed and to be a value are two names for one and the same fact. Since science has extruded values from its objects, these empirical theories do everything possible to emphasize their purely subjective character of value. A psychological theory of desire and liking is supposed to cover the whole ground of the theory of values; in it, immediate feeling is the counterpart of immediate sensation.

I shall not object to this empirical theory as far as it connects the theory of values with concrete experiences of desire and satisfaction. The idea that there is such a connection is the only way known to me by which the pallid remoteness of the rationalistic theory, and the only too glaring presence of the institutional theory of transcendental values can be escaped. The objection is that the theory in question holds down value to objects *antecedently* enjoyed, apart from reference to the method by which they come into existence; it takes enjoyments which are casual because unregulated by intelligent operations to be values in and of themselves. Operational thinking needs to be applied to the judgment of values just as it has now finally been applied in conceptions of physical objects. Experimental empiricism in the field of ideas of good and bad is demanded to meet the conditions of the present situation.

The scientific revolution came about when material of direct and uncontrolled experience was taken as problematic; as supplying material to be transformed by reflective operations into known objects. The contrast between experienced and known objects was found to be a temporal one; namely, one between empirical subject-matters which were had or "given" prior to the acts of experimental variation and redisposition and those which succeeded these acts and issued from them. The notion of an act whether of sense or thought which supplied a valid measure of thought in immediate knowledge was discredited. Consequences of operations became the important thing. The suggestion almost imperatively follows that escape from the defects of transcendental absolutism is not to be had by setting up as values enjoyments that happen anyhow, but in defining value by enjoyments which are the consequences of intelligent action. Without the intervention of thought, enjoyments are not values but problematic goods, becoming values when they reissue in a changed form from intelligent behavior. The fundamental trouble with the current empirical theory of values is that it merely formulates and justifies the socially prevailing habit of regarding enjoyments as they are actually experienced as values in and of themselves. It completely sidesteps the question of regulation of these enjoyments. This issue involves nothing less than the problem of the directed reconstruction of economic, political and religious institutions.

There was seemingly a paradox involved in the notion that if we turned our backs upon the immediately perceived qualities of things, we should be enabled to form valid conceptions of objects, and that these conceptions could be used to bring about a more secure and more significant experience of them. But the method terminated in disclosing the connections or interactions upon which perceived objects, viewed as events, depend. Formal analogy suggests that we regard our direct and original experience of things liked and enjoyed as only *possibilities* of values to be achieved; that enjoyment becomes a value when we discover the relations upon which its presence depends. Such a causal and operational definition gives only a conception of a value, not a value itself. But the utilization of the conception in action results in an object having secure and significant value.

The formal statement may be given concrete content by pointing to the difference between the enjoyed and the enjoyable, the desired and the desirable, the satis*fying* and the satis*factory*. To say that something is enjoyed is to make a statement about a fact, something already in existence; it is not to judge the value of that fact. There is no difference between such a proposition and one which says that something is sweet or sour, red or black. It is just correct or incorrect and that is the end of the matter. But to call an object a value is to assert that it satisfies or fulfills certain conditions. Function and status in meeting conditions is a different matter from bare existence. The fact that something is desired only raises the *question* of its desirability; it does not settle it. Only a child in the degree of his immaturity thinks to settle the question of desirability by reiterated proclamation: "I want it, I want it, I want it." What is objected to in the current empirical theory of values is not connection of them with desire and enjoyment but failure to distinguish between enjoyments of radically different sorts. There are many common expressions in which the difference of the two kinds is clearly recognized. Take for example the difference between the ideas of "satisfying" and "satisfactory." To say that something satisfies is to report something as an isolated finality. To assert that it is satis*factory* is to define it in its connections and interactions. The fact that it pleases or is immediately congenial poses a problem to judgment. How shall the satisfaction be rated? Is it a value or is it not? Is it something to be prized and cherished, *to be* enjoyed? Not stern moralists alone but everyday experience informs us that finding satisfaction in a thing may be a warning, a summons to be on the lookout for consequences. To declare something satis*factory* is to assert that it meets specifiable conditions. It is, in effect, a judgment that the thing "will do." It involves a prediction; it contemplates a future in which the thing will continue to serve; it *will* do. It asserts a consequence the thing will actively institute; it will *do*. That it is satisfying is the content of a proposition of fact;

that it is satisfactory is a judgment, an estimate, an appraisal. It denotes an attitude *to be* taken, that of striving to perpetuate and to make secure.

It is worth notice that besides the instances given, there are many other recognitions in ordinary speech of the distinction. The endings "able," "worthy" and "ful" are cases in point. Noted and notable, noteworthy; remarked and remarkable; advised and advisable; wondered at and wonderful; pleasing and beautiful; loved and lovable; blamed and blameable, blameworthy; objected to and objectionable; esteemed and estimable; admired and admirable; shamed and shameful; honored and honorable; approved and approvable, worthy of approbation, etc. The multiplication of words adds nothing to the force of the distinction. But it aids in conveying a sense of the fundamental character of the distinction; of the difference between mere report of an already existent fact and judgment as to the importance and need of bringing a fact into existence; or, if it is already there, of sustaining it in existence. The latter is a genuine practical judgment, and marks the only type of judgment that has to do with the direction of action. Whether or no we reserve the term "value" for the latter, (as seems to me proper) is a minor matter; that the distinction be acknowledged as the key to understanding the relation of values to the direction of conduct is the important thing. . . .

The word "taste" has perhaps got too completely associated with arbitrary liking to express the nature of judgments of value. But if the word be used in the sense of an appreciation at once cultivated and active, one may say that the formation of taste is the chief matter wherever values enter in, whether intellectual, esthetic or moral. Relatively immediate judgments, which we call tact or to which we give the name of intuition, do not precede reflective inquiry, but are the funded products of much thoughtful experience. Expertness of taste is at once the result and the reward of constant exercise of thinking. Instead of there being no disputing about tastes, they are the one thing worth disputing about, if by "dispute" is signified discussion involving reflective inquiry. Taste, if we use the word in its best sense, is the outcome of experience brought cumulatively to bear on the intelligent appreciation of the real worth of likings and enjoyments. There is nothing in which a person so completely reveals himself as in the things which he judges enjoyable and desirable. Such judgments are the sole alternative to the domination of belief by impulse, chance, blind habit and self-interest. The formation of a cultivated and effectively operative good judgment or taste with respect to what is esthetically admirable, intellectually acceptable and morally approvable is the supreme task set to human beings by the incidents of experience.

Propositions about what is or has been liked are of instrumental value in reaching judgments of value, in as far as the conditions and consequences of the thing liked are thought about. In themselves they make no claims; they put forth no demand upon subsequent attitudes and acts; they profess no authority to direct. If one likes a thing he likes it; that *is* a point about which there can be no dispute—although it is not so easy to state just *what* is liked as is frequently assumed. A judgment about what is *to be* desired and enjoyed is, on the other hand, a claim on future action; it possesses *de jure* and not merely *de facto* quality. It is a matter of frequent experience that likings and enjoyments are of all kinds, and that many are such as reflective judgments condemn. By way of self-justification and "rationalization," an enjoyment creates a tendency to assert that the thing enjoyed is a value. This assertion of validity adds authority to the fact. It is a decision that the object has a right to exist and hence a claim upon action to further its existence.

The analogy between the status of the theory of values and the theory of ideas about natural objects before the rise of experimental inquiry may be carried further. The sensationalistic theory of the origin and test of thought evoked, by way of reaction, the transcendental theory of *a priori* ideas. For it failed utterly to account for objective connection, order and regularity in objects observed. Similarly, any doctrine that identifies the mere fact of being liked with the value of the object liked so fails to give direction to conduct when direction is needed that it automatically calls forth the assertion that there are values eternally in Being that are the standards of all judgments and the obligatory ends of all action. Without the introduction of operational thinking, we oscillate between a theory that, in order to save the objectivity of judgments of values, isolates them from experience and nature, and a theory that, in order to save their concrete and human significance, reduces them to mere statements about our own feelings.

Not even the most devoted adherents of the notion that enjoyment and value are equivalent facts would venture to assert that because we have once liked a thing we should go on liking it; they are compelled to introduce the idea that *some* tastes are to be cultivated. Logically, there is no ground for introducing the idea of cultivation; liking is liking, and one is as good as another. If enjoyments *are* values, the judgment of value cannot regulate the form which liking takes; it cannot regulate its own conditions. Desire and purpose, and hence action, are left without guidance, although the question of regulation of their formation is the supreme problem of practical life. Values (to sum up) may be connected inherently with liking, and yet not with *every* liking but only with those that judgment has approved, after examination of the relation upon which the object liked depends. A casual liking is one that happens without knowledge of how it occurs nor to what effect. The difference between it and one which is sought because of a judgment that it is worth having and is to be striven for, makes just the difference between enjoyments which are accidental and enjoyments that have value and hence a claim upon our attitude and conduct.

In any case, the alternative rationalistic theory does not afford the guidance for the sake of which eternal and immutable norms are appealed to. The scientist finds no help in determining the probable truth of some proposed theory by comparing it with a standard of absolute truth and immutable being. He has to rely upon definite operations undertaken under definite conditions—upon method. We can hardly imagine an architect getting aid in the construction of a building from an ideal at large, though we can understand his framing an ideal on the basis of knowledge of actual conditions and needs. Nor does the ideal of perfect beauty in antecedent Being give direction to a painter in producing a particular work of art. In morals, absolute perfection does not seem to be more than a generalized hypostatization of the recognition that there is a good to be sought, an obligation to be met—both being concrete matters. Nor is the defect in this respect merely negative. An examination of history would reveal, I am confident, that these general and remote schemes of value actually obtain a content definite enough and near enough to concrete situations as to afford guidance in action only by consecrating some institution or dogma already having social currency. Concreteness is gained, but it is by protecting from inquiry some accepted standard which perhaps is outworn and in need of criticism.

When theories of values do not afford intellectual assistance in framing ideas and beliefs about values that are adequate to direct action, the gap must be filled by other means. If intelligent method is lacking, prejudice, the pressure of immediate circumstance, self-interest and class-interest, traditional customs, institutions of accidental historic origin, are *not* lacking, and they tend to take the place of intelligence. Thus we are led to our main proposition: *Judgments about values are judgments about the conditions and the results of experienced objects; judgments about that which should regulate the formation of our desires, affections and enjoyments.* For whatever decides their formation will determine the main course of our conduct, personal and social.

If it sounds strange to hear that we should frame our judgments as to what has value by considering the connections in existence of what we like and enjoy, the reply is not far to seek. As long as we do not engage in this inquiry enjoyments (values if we choose to apply that term) are casual; they are given by "nature," not constructed by art. Like natural objects in their qualitative existence, they at most only supply material for elaboration in rational discourse. A *feeling* of good or excellence is as far removed from goodness in fact as a feeling that objects are intellectually thus and so is removed from their being actually so. To recognize that the truth of natural objects can be reached only by the greatest care in selecting and arranging directed operations, and then to suppose that values can be truly determined by the mere fact of liking seems to leave us in an incredible position. All the serious perplexities of life come back to the genuine difficulty of forming a judgment as to the values of the situation; they come back to a conflict of goods. Only dogmatism can suppose that serious moral conflict is between something clearly bad and something known to be good, and that uncertainty lies wholly in the will of the one choosing. Most conflicts of importance are conflicts between things which are or have been satisfying, not between good and evil. And to suppose that we can make a hierarchical table of values at large once for all, a kind of catalogue in which they are arranged in an order of ascending or descending worth, is to indulge in a gloss on our inability to frame intelligent judgments in the concrete. Or else it is to dignify customary choice and prejudice by a title of honor.

The alternative to definition, classification and systematization of satisfactions just as they happen to occur is judgment of them by means of the relations under which they occur. If we know the conditions under which the act of liking, of desire and enjoyment, takes place, we are in a position to know what are the consequences of that act. The difference between the desired and the desirable, admired and the admirable, becomes effective at just this point. Consider the difference between the proposition "That thing has been eaten," and the judgment "That thing is edible." The former statement involves no knowledge of any relation except the one stated; while we are able to judge of the edibility of anything only when we have a knowledge of its interactions with other things sufficient to enable us to foresee its probable effects when it is taken into the organism and produces effects there.

To assume that anything can be known in isolation from its connections with other things is to identify knowing with merely having some object before perception or in feeling, and is thus to lose the key to the traits that distinguish an object as known. It is futile, even silly, to suppose that some quality that is directly present constitutes the whole of the thing presenting the quality. It does not do so when the quality is that of being hot or fluid or heavy, and it does not when the quality is that of giving pleasure, or being enjoyed. Such qualities are, once more, effects, ends in the sense of closing termini of processes involving causal connections. They are something to be investigated, challenges to inquiry and judgment. The more connections and interactions we ascertain, the more we *know* the object in question. Thinking is search for these connections. Heat experienced as a consequence of directed operations has a meaning quite different from the heat that is casually experienced without knowledge of how it came about. The same is true of enjoyments. Enjoyments that issue from conduct directed by insight into relations have a meaning and a validity due to the way in which they are experienced. Such enjoyments are not repented of; they generate no aftertaste of bitterness. Even in the midst of direct enjoyment, there is a sense of validity, of authorization, which intensifies the enjoyment. There is solicitude for perpetuation of the *object* having value which is radically different from mere anxiety to perpetuate the *feeling* of enjoyment.

Such statements as we have been making are, therefore, far from implying that there are values apart from things actually enjoyed as good. To find a thing enjoy*able* is, so to say, a *plus* enjoyment. We saw that it was foolish to treat the scientific object as a rival to or substitute for the perceived object, since the former is intermediate between uncertain and settled situations and those experienced under conditions of greater control. In the same way, judgment of the value of an object to be experienced is instrumental to appreciation of it when it is realized. But the notion that every object that happens to satisfy has an equal claim with every other to be a value is like supposing that every object of perception has the same cognitive force as every other. There is no knowledge without perception; but objects perceived are *known* only when they are determined as consequences of connective operations. There is no value except where there is satisfaction, but there have to be certain conditions fulfilled to transform a satisfaction into a value.

The time will come when it will be found passing strange that we of this age should take such pains to control by every means at command the formation of ideas of physical things, even those most remote from human concern, and yet are content with haphazard beliefs about the qualities of objects that regulate our deepest interests; that we are scrupulous as to methods of forming ideas of natural objects, and either dogmatic or else driven by immediate conditions in framing those about values. There is, by implication, if not explicitly, a prevalent notion that values are already well known and that all which is lacking is the will to cultivate them in the order of their worth. In fact the most profound lack is not the will to act upon goods already known but the will to know what they are.

It is not a dream that it is possible to exercise some degree of regulation of the occurrence of enjoyments which are of value. Realization of the possibility is exemplified for example, in the technologies and arts of industrial life—that is, up to a definite limit. Men desired heat, light, and speed of transit and of communication beyond what nature provides of itself. These things have been attained not by lauding the enjoyment of these things and preaching their desirability, but by study of the conditions of their manifestation. Knowledge of relations having been obtained, ability to produce followed, and enjoyment ensued as a matter of course. It is, however, an old story that enjoyment of these things as goods is no warrant of their bringing only good in their train. As Plato was given to pointing out, the physician knows how to heal and the orator to persuade, but the ulterior knowledge of whether it is better for a man to be healed or to be persuaded to the orator's opinion remains unsettled. Here there appears the split between what are traditionally and conventionally called the values of the baser arts and the higher values of the truly personal and humane arts.

With respect to the former, there is no assumption that they can be had and enjoyed without definite operative knowledge. With respect to them it is also clear that the degree in which we value them is measurable by the pains taken to control the conditions of their occurrence. With respect to the latter, it is assumed that no one who is honest can be in doubt what they are; that by revelation, or conscience, or the instruction of others, or immediate feeling, they are clear beyond question. And instead of action in their behalf being taken to be a measure of the extent to which things *are* values to us, it is assumed that the difficulty is to persuade men to act upon what they already know to be good. Knowledge of conditions and consequences is regarded as wholly indifferent to judging what is of serious value, though it is useful in a prudential way in trying to actualize it. In consequence, the existence of values that are by common consent of a secondary and technical sort are under a fair degree of control, while those denominated supreme and imperative are subject to all the winds of impulse, custom and arbitrary authority. . . .

1. The most notable and systematic misunderstanding is embodied in Morton White's "Value and Obligation in Dewey and Lewis" (*The Philosophical Review* LVIII [1949]: pp. 321–29) and in chapter 13 of his *Social Thought in America* (New York: The Viking Press, 1949). In precisely the same vein, see Ernest Nagel, "Philosophy of Science and Educational Theory" (*Studies in Philosophy and Education* VII, no. 1 [1969]: pp. 16–27).

2. The sources of the material in this selection are given in notes 3–9. Heading provided by the editor.

3. *Experience and Nature*, pp. 121–40.

4. *Ibid.*, pp. xi–xii.

5. *Ibid.*, pp. 138–39.

6. *The Quest for Certainty*, pp. 240–42.

7. *Experience and Nature*, pp. 151–55.

8. *The Quest for Certainty*, pp. 165–69.

9. *Reconstruction in Philosophy* (enlarged edition), pp. 96–97.

10. *Human Nature and Conduct*, pp. 5, 11–13. Heading provided by the editor.

11. *Logic: The Theory of Inquiry* (New York: Holt, Rinehart, and Winston, 1938), pp. 95–96, 97–98, 159–63, 167–68, 174, 179–80. Heading provided by the editor.

12. *Human Nature and Conduct*, pp. 178–82; Ethics, pp. 302, 317; *Human Nature and Conduct*, pp. 45–46, 202. Heading provided by the editor.

   In contrast to the view that the agency of choice is an isolated faculty–such as will or reason or appetite, Dewey makes the following remarks about the coordinate functions of intelligence and desire (*Ibid.*, pp. 234–35, 238):

   "Analysis of desire . . . reveals the falsity of theories which magnify it at the expense of intelligence. Impulse is primary and intelligence is secondary and in some sense derivative. There should be no blinking of this fact. But recognition of it as a fact exalts intelligence. For thought is not the slave of impulse to do its bidding. Impulse does not know what it is after; it cannot give orders, not even if it wants to. It rushes blindly into any opening it chances to find. Anything that expends it, satisfies it. One outlet is like another to it. It is indiscriminate. . . . What intelligence has to do in the service of impulse is to act not as its obedient servant, but as its clarifier and liberator. And this can be accomplished only by a study of the conditions and causes, the workings and consequences of the greatest possible variety of desires and combinations of desire. Intelligence converts desire into plans, systematic plans based on assembling facts, reporting events as they happen, keeping tab on them and analyzing them.

". . . The separation of warm emotion and cool intelligence is the great moral tragedy. This division is perpetuated by those who deprecate science and foresight in behalf of affection, as it is by those who in the name of an idol labeled reason would quench passion. The intellect is always inspired by some impulse. . . . But an actuating impulse easily hardens into isolated habit. It is unavowed and disconnected. The remedy is not lapse of thought, but its quickening and extension to contemplate the continuities of existence, and restore the connection of the isolated desire to the companionship of its fellows. The glorification of 'will' apart from thought turns out either a commitment to blind action which serves the purpose of those who guide their deeds by narrow plans, or else a sentimental, romantic faith in the harmonies of nature leading straight to disaster."

13. *Ibid.*, pp. 220–22, 225–26.

14. *The Quest for Certainty*, pp. 254–69.

15. "The answer to the question I raised in my original list of 'Questions' as to whether the distinction between direct valuings and evaluations as judgments is one of separate kinds or one of emphasis is, accordingly, answered in the latter sense. I am the more bound to make this statement because in some still earlier writings I tended to go too far in the direction of separation. I still think the reason that actuated me is sound. In current discussion, traits distinctive of valuing are frequently indiscriminately transferred to valuation. But the resulting confusion can be escaped by noting the distinction to be one of phase in development." ("The Field of 'Value,'" in Ray Lepley [ed.], *Value: A Cooperative Inquiry* [New York: Columbia University Press, 1949], p. 75.)

Moral
Language

6

Language is defined functionally: it is whatever succeeds in creating a community of shared use and enjoyment. It is a product of the necessity to engage in cooperative social activity. The more effectively these functions are fulfilled, the better is the language.

Dewey was not particularly interested in analyzing the inherent logic of the English language. The implicit rules for the use of moral language were not of first concern to him. However, he found the meanings of moral terms to be especially vague and laden with inherited cultural bias. Language of this sort is ineffective in precise communication and making reliable inferences. He finally concluded that the values of human existence would be better discerned and enhanced if we eschewed the use of moral language altogether. Voluntary conduct is in any case a response to the values believed to be contingent upon a proposed action. It seems that the function of making the nature and relations of these contingent values perspicuous is best satisfied by making our language in such deliberations as scientific as possible.

Scientific language fulfills the functions of guiding conduct more effectively than moral language, which is often mere expletive—used to make emotional or sentimental appeals. Whatever the chances of human beings to solve their joint problems, adjust and unite their aims, and share in consummatory experience, choice must be a consequence of honest communication and the sharing of reliable knowledge.

THE NATURE AND FUNCTION OF LANGUAGE[1]

In this . . . discussion, language is taken in its widest sense, a sense wider than oral and written speech. It includes the latter. But it includes also not only gestures but rites, ceremonies, monuments and the products of industrial and fine arts. A tool or machine, for example, is not simply a simple or complex physical object having its own physical properties and effects, but is also a mode of language. For it *says* something, to those who understand it, about operations of use and their consequences. To the members of a primitive community a loom operated by steam or electricity says nothing. It is composed in a foreign language, and so with most of the mechanical devices of modern civilization. In the present cultural setting, these objects are so intimately bound up with interests, occupations and purposes that they have an eloquent voice.

The importance of language as the necessary, and, in the end, sufficient condition of the existence and transmission of nonpurely organic activities and their consequences lies in the fact that, on one side, it is a strictly biological mode of behavior, emerging in natural continuity from earlier organic activities, while, on the other hand, it compels one individual to take the standpoint of other individuals and to see and inquire from a standpoint that is not strictly personal but is common to them as participants or "parties" in a conjoint undertaking. It may be directed by and toward some physical existence. But it first has reference to some other person or persons with whom it institutes *communication*—the making of something common. Hence, to that extent its reference becomes general and "objective."

Language is made up of physical existences; sounds, or marks on paper, or a temple, statue, or loom. But these do not *operate* or function as mere physical things when they are media of communication. They operate in virtue of their *representative* capacity or *meaning*. The particular physical existence which has meaning is, in the case of speech, a conventional matter. But the convention or common consent which sets it apart as a means of recording and communicating meaning is that of agreement in *action*; of shared modes of responsive behavior and participation in their consequences. The physical sound or mark gets its meaning in and by conjoint community of functional use, not by any explicit convening in a "convention" or by passing resolutions that a certain sound or mark shall have a specified meaning. Even when the meaning of certain legal words is determined by a court, it is not the agreement of the judges which is finally decisive. For such assent does not finish the matter. It occurs for the sake of determining future agreements in associated *behavior*, and it is this subsequent behavior which finally settles the actual meaning of the words in question. Agreement in the proposition arrived at is significant only through this function in promoting agreement in action.

The reason for mentioning these considerations is that they prove that the meaning which a conventional symbol has is not itself conventional. For the meaning is established by agreements of different persons in existential activities having reference to existential consequences. The particular existential sound or mark that stands for *dog* or *justice* in different cultures is arbitrary or conventional in the sense that although it has *causes* there are no *reasons* for it. But *in so far* as it is a medium of communication, its meaning is common, because it is constituted by existential conditions. If a word varies in meaning in intercommunication between different cultural groups, then to that degree communication is blocked and misunderstanding results. Indeed, there ceases to be communication until variations of understanding can be translated, through the meaning of words, into a meaning that is the same to both parties. Whenever communication is blocked and yet is supposed to exist, misunderstanding, not merely absence of understanding, is the result. It is an error to suppose that the misunderstanding is about the meaning of the *word* in isolation, just as it is fallacious to suppose that because two persons accept the same dictionary meaning of a word they have therefore come to agreement and understanding. For agreement and disagreement are determined by the consequences of conjoint activities. Harmony or the opposite exists in the effects produced by the several activities that are occasioned by the words used.

Reference to concord of consequences as the determinant of the meaning of any sound used as a medium of communication shows that there is no such thing as a *mere* word or *mere* symbol. The physical existence that is the vehicle of meaning may as a particular be called *mere; the* recitation of such sounds or the stringing together of such marks may be called *mere* language. But in fact there is no word in the first case and no language in the second. The activities that occur and the consequences that result which are not determined by meaning, are, by description, only physical. A sound or mark of any physical existence is a part of *language* only in virtue of its *operational* force; that is, as it functions as a means of evoking different activities performed by different persons so as to produce consequences that are shared by all the participants in the conjoint undertaking. This fact is evident and direct in oral communication. It is indirect and disguised in written communication. Where written literature and literacy abound, the conception of language is likely to be framed upon their model. The intrinsic connection of language with community of action is then forgotten. Language is then supposed to be simply a means of expressing or communicating "thoughts"—a means of conveying ideas or meanings that are complete in themselves apart from communal operational force.

Much literature is read, moreover, simply for enjoyment, for esthetic purposes. In this case, language is a means of action only as it leads the reader to build up pictures and scenes to be enjoyed by himself. There ceases to be immediate inherent reference to conjoint activity and to consequences mutually participated in. Such is not the case, however, in reading to get at the meaning of the author; that is, in reading that is emphatically intellectual in distinction from esthetic. In the mere reading of a scientific treatise there is, indeed, no direct overt participation in action with another to produce consequences that are *common* in the sense of being immediately and personally shared. But there must be imaginative construction of the materials and operations which led the author to certain conclusions, and there must be agreement or disagreement with his conclusions as a consequence of following through conditions and operations that are imaginatively reinstated.

Connection with overt activities is in such a case indirect or mediated. But so far as definite grounded agreement or disagreement is reached, an attitude is formed which is a preparatory readiness to act in a responsive way when the conditions in question or others similar to them actually present themselves. The connection with action in question is, in other words, with *possible* ways of operation rather than with those found to be *actually* and immediately required. But preparation for *possible* action in situations not as yet existent in actuality is an essential condition of, and factor in, all intelligent behavior. When persons meet together in conference to plan in advance of actual occasions and emergencies what shall later be done, or when an individual deliberates in advance regarding his possible behavior in a possible future contingency, something occurs, but more directly, the same sort as happens in understanding intellectually the meaning of a scientific treatise.

I turn now to the positive implication of the fact that no sound, mark, product of art, is a word or part of language in isolation. Any word or phrase has the meaning which it has only as a member of a constellation of related meanings. Words as representatives are part of an inclusive code. The code may be public or private. A public code is illustrated in any language that is current in a given cultural group. A private code is one agreed upon by members of special groups so as to be unintelligible to those who have not been initiated. Between these two come argots of special groups in a community, and the technical codes invented for a restricted special purpose, like the one used by ships at sea. But in every case, a particular word has its meaning only in relation to the code of which it is one constituent. The distinction just drawn between meanings that are determined respectively in fairly direct connection with action in situations that are present or near at hand, and meanings determined for possible use in remote and contingent situations, provides the basis upon which language codes as systems may be differentiated into two main kinds.

While all language or symbol-meanings are what they are as parts of a system, it does not follow that they have been determined on the basis of their fitness to be such members of a system; much less on the basis of their membership in a comprehensive system. The system may be simply the language in common use. Its meanings hang together not in virtue of their examined relationship to one another, but because they are current in the same set of group habits and expectations. They hang together because of group activities, group interests, customs and institutions. Scientific language, on the other hand, is subject to a test over and above this criterion. Each meaning that enters into the language is expressly determined in its relation to other members of the language system. In all reasoning or ordered discourse this criterion takes precedence over that instituted by connection with cultural habits.

The resulting difference in the two types of language-meanings fundamentally fixes the difference between what is called common sense and what is called science. In the former cases, the customs, the *ethos* and spirit of a group is the decisive factor in determining the system of meanings in use. The system is one in a practical and institutional sense rather than in an intellectual sense. Meanings that are formed on this basis are sure to contain much that is irrelevant and to exclude much that is required for intelligent control of activity. The meanings are coarse, and many of them are inconsistent with each other from a logical point of view. One meaning is appropriate to action under certain institutional group conditions; another, in some other situation, and there is no attempt to relate the different situations to one another in a coherent scheme. In an intellectual sense, there are many languages, though in a social sense there is but one. This multiplicity of language-meaning constellations is also a mark of our existing culture. A word means one thing in relation to a religious institution, still another thing in business, a third thing in law, and so on. This fact is the real Babel of communication. There is an attempt now making to propagate the idea that education which indoctrinates individuals into some special tradition provides the way out of this confusion. Aside from the fact that there are in fact a considerable number of traditions and that selection of some one of them, even though that one be internally consistent and extensively accepted, is arbitrary, the attempt reverses the *theoretical* state of the case. Genuine community of language or symbols can be achieved only through efforts that bring about community of activities under existing conditions. The ideal of scientific-language is construction of a system in which meanings are related to one another in inference and discourse and where the symbols are such as to indicate the relation. . . .

The next two selections are concerned with a critique of the emotive theory of ethical language. In the first of them, Dewey argues that the context in which ethical language is used determines the meaning of such language. Accordingly, in actual situations of behavior, there are no purely emotive meanings. This argument is developed still further in the review article from which the second selection is taken. The portions reprinted, however, are concerned only with showing that insofar as moral language is emotive, it is dysfunctional.

MORAL EXPRESSIONS AS LANGUAGE[2]

Discussion will begin with consideration of the most extreme of the views which have been advanced. This view affirms that value-expressions cannot be constituents of propositions, that is, of sentences which affirm or deny, because they are purely ejaculatory. Such expressions as 'good,' 'bad,' 'right,' 'wrong,' 'lovely,' 'hideous,' etc., are regarded as of the same nature as interjections; or as phenomena like blushing, smiling, weeping; or/and as stimuli to move others to act in certain ways—much as one says "Gee" to oxen or "Whoa" to a horse. They do not say or state anything, not even about feelings; they merely evince or manifest the latter.

The following quotations represent this view: "If I say to some one, 'You acted wrongly in stealing that money,' I am not *stating* anything more than if I had simply said 'You stole that money,' . . . It is as if I had said 'You stole that money' in a peculiar tone of horror, or written it with the addition of some special exclamation marks. The tone . . . merely serves to show that the expression is attended by certain feelings in the speaker." And again: "Ethical terms do not serve only to express feelings. They are calculated also to arouse feeling and so to stimulate action. . . . Thus the sentence 'It is your duty to tell the truth' may be regarded both as the expression of a certain sort of ethical feeling about truthfulness and as the expression of the command 'Tell the truth.' . . . In the sentence 'It is good to tell the truth' the command has become little more than a suggestion." On what grounds the writer calls the terms and the "feelings" of which he speaks "ethical" does not appear. Nevertheless, applying this adjective to the feelings seems to involve some objective ground for discriminating and identifying them as of a certain kind, a conclusion inconsistent with the position taken. But, ignoring this fact, we pass on to a further illustration: "In saying 'tolerance is a virtue' I should not be making a statement about my own feelings or about anything else. I should simply be evincing my own feelings, which is not at all the same thing as saying that I have them." Hence "it is impossible to dispute about questions of value," for sentences that do not say or state anything whatever cannot, *a fortiori,* be incompatible with one another. Cases of apparent dispute or of opposed statements are, if they have any meaning at all, reducible to differences regarding the facts of the case—as there might be a dispute whether a man performed the particular action called stealing or lying. Our hope or expectation is that if "we can get an opponent to agree with us about the empirical facts of the case he will adopt the same moral attitude toward them as we do"—though once more it is not evident why the attitude is called "moral" rather than "magical," "belligerent," or any one of thousands of adjectives that might be selected at random.

Discussion will proceed, as has previously been intimated, by analyzing the facts that are appealed to and not by discussing the merits of the theory in the abstract. Let us begin with phenomena that admittedly say nothing, like the first cries of a baby, his first smiles, or his early cooings, gurglings, and squeals. When it is said that they "express feelings," there is a dangerous ambiguity in the words 'feelings' and 'express.' What is clear in the case of tears or smiles ought to be clear in the case of sounds involuntarily uttered. They are not in themselves expressive. They are constituents of a larger organic condition. They are facts of organic behavior and are *not* in any sense whatever value-expressions. They may, however, be taken by other persons as *signs* of an organic state, and, so taken, *qua* signs or treated as *symptoms*, they evoke certain responsive forms of behavior in these other persons. A baby cries. The mother takes the cry as a sign the baby is hungry or that a pin is pricking it, and so acts to change the organic condition inferred to exist by using the cry as an evidential sign.

Then, as the baby matures, it becomes aware of the connection that exists between a certain cry, the activity evoked, and the consequences produced in response to it. The cry (gesture, posture) is now made *in order* to evoke the activity and in order to experience the consequences of that activity. Just as with respect to the original response there is a difference between the activity that is merely *caused* by the cry as a stimulus (as the cry of a child may awaken a sleeping mother before she is even aware there is a cry) and an activity that is evoked by the cry interpreted as a *sign* or evidence of something, so there is a difference between the original cry—which may properly be called purely ejaculatory—and the cry made on purpose, that is, with the intent to evoke a response that will have certain consequences. The latter cry exists in the medium of language: it is a linguistic sign that not only says something but is intended to say, to convey, to tell.

What is it which is then told or stated? In connection with this question, a fatal ambiguity in the word 'feelings' requires notice. For perhaps the view will be propounded that at most all that is communicated is the existence of certain feelings along perhaps with a desire to obtain other feelings in consequence of the activity evoked in another person. But any such view (a) goes contrary to the obvious facts with which the account began and (b) introduces a totally superfluous not to say empirically unverifiable matter. (a) For what we started with was not a feeling but an organic condition of which a cry, or tears, or a smile, or a blush, is a constituent part. (b) The word 'feelings' is accordingly either a strictly behavioral term, a name for the total organic state of which the cry or gesture is a part, or it is a word which is introduced entirely gratuitously. The phenomena in question are events in the course of the life of an organic being, not differing from taking food or gaining weight. But just as a gain in weight may be taken as a sign or evidence of proper feeding, so the cry may be taken as a sign or evidence of some special occurrence in organic life.

The phrase 'evincing feeling,' whether or not 'evincing' is taken as a synonym of 'expressing,' has, then, no business in the report of what takes place. The original activity—crying, smiling, weeping, squealing—is, as we have seen, a part of a larger organic state, so the phrase does not apply to it. When the cry or bodily attitude is purposely made, it is not a feeling that is evinced or expressed. Overt linguistic behavior is undertaken so as to obtain a change in organic conditions—a change to occur as the result of some behavior undertaken by some other person. Take another simple example: A smacking of the lips is or may be part of the original behavioral action called taking food. In one social group the noise made in smacking the lips is treated as a sign of boorishness or of "bad manners." Hence as the young grow in power of muscular control, they are taught to inhibit this activity. In another social group smacking the lips and the accompanying noise are taken as a sign that a guest is properly aware of what the host has provided. Both cases are completely describable in terms of observable modes of behavior and their respectively observable consequences.

The serious problem in this connection is why the word 'feelings' is introduced in the theoretical account, since it is unnecessary in report of what actually happens. There is but one reasonable answer. The word is brought in from an alleged psychological theory which is couched in mentalistic terms, or in terms of alleged states of an inner consciousness or something of that sort. Now it is irrelevant and unnecessary to ask in connection with events before us whether there are in fact such inner states. For, even if there be such states, they are by description wholly private, accessible only to private inspection. Consequently, even if there were a legitimate introspectionist theory of states of consciousness or of feelings as purely mentalistic, there is no justification for borrowing from this theory in giving an account of the occurrences under examination. The reference to "feelings" is superfluous and gratuitous, moreover, because the important part of the account given is the use of "value-expressions" to influence the conduct of others by evoking certain responses from them. From the standpoint of an empirical report it is meaningless, since the interpretation is couched in terms of something not open to public inspection and verification. If there are "feelings" of the kind mentioned, there cannot be any assurance that any given word when used by two different persons even refers to the same thing, since the thing is not open to common observation and description.

Confining further consideration, then, to the part of the account that has an empirical meaning, namely, the existence of organic activities which evoke certain responses from others and which are capable of being employed with a view to evoking them, the following statements are warranted: (1) The phenomena in question are *social* phenomena where 'social' means simply that there is a form of behavior of the nature of an interaction or transaction between two or more persons. Such an interpersonal activity exists whenever one person—as a mother or nurse—treats a sound made by another person incidentally to a more extensive organic behavior *as a sign*, and responds to it in that capacity instead of reacting to it in its primary existence. The interpersonal activity is even more evident when the item of organic personal behavior in question takes place *for the sake of* evoking a certain kind of response from other persons. If, then, we follow the writer in locating value-expressions where he located them, we are led, after carrying out the required elimination of the ambiguity of 'expression' and the irrele-

vance of 'feeling,' to the conclusions that value-expressions have to do with
or are involved in the behavioral relations of persons to one another. (2)
Taken as signs (and, *a fortiori*, when used as signs) gestures, postures, and
words are linguistic symbols. They say something and are of the nature of
propositions. Take, for example, the case of a person who assumes the posture
appropriate to an ailing person and who utters sounds such as the latter person would ordinarily make. It is then a legitimate subject of inquiry whether
the person is genuinely ailing and incapacitated for work or is malingering.
The conclusions obtained as a result of the inquiries undertaken will certainly
"evoke" from other persons very different kinds of responsive behavior. The
investigation is carried on to determine what is the actual case of things that
are empirically observable; it is not about inner "feelings." Physicians have
worked out experimental tests that have a high degree of reliability. Every
parent and schoolteacher learns to be on guard against the assuming by a
child of certain facial "expressions" and bodily attitudes for the purpose of
causing inferences to be drawn which are the source of favor on the part of
the adult. In such cases (they could easily be extended to include more complex matters) the propositions that embody the inference are likely to be in
error when only a short segment of behavior is observed and are likely to be
warranted when they rest upon a prolonged segment or upon a variety of
carefully scrutinized data—traits that the propositions in question have in
common with all genuine physical propositions. (3) So far the question has
not been raised as to whether the propositions that occur in the course of
interpersonal behavioral situations are or are not of the nature of valuation-
propositions. The conclusions reached are hypothetical. *If* the expressions
involved are valuation-expressions, as this particular school takes them to be,
then it follows (i) that valuation-phenomena are social or interpersonal
phenomena and (ii) that they are such as to provide material for propositions about observable events—propositions subject to empirical test and verification or refutation. But so far the hypothesis remains a hypothesis. It
raises the question whether the statements which occur with a view to influencing the activity of others, so as to call out from them certain modes of
activity having certain consequences, are phenomena falling under the head
of valuation.

Take, for example, the case of a person calling "Fire!" or "Help!" There
can be no doubt of the intent to influence the conduct of others in order to
bring about certain consequences capable of observation and of statement in
propositions. The expressions, taken in their observable context, say something of a complex character. When analyzed, what is said is (i) that there
exists a situation that will have obnoxious consequences; (ii) that the person
uttering the expressions is unable to cope with the situation; and (iii) that
an improved situation is anticipated in case the assistance of others is obtained. All three of these matters are capable of being tested by empirical

evidence, since they all refer to things that are observable. The proposition in which the content of the last point (the anticipation) is stated is capable, for example, of being tested by observation of what happens in a particular case. Previous observations may substantiate the conclusion that in any case objectionable consequences are much less likely to happen if the linguistic sign is employed in order to obtain the assistance it is designed to evoke.

Examination shows certain resemblances between these cases and those previously examined which, according to the passage quoted, contain valuation-expressions. The propositions refer directly to an *existing* situation and indirectly to a future situation which it is intended and desired to produce. The expressions noted are employed as intermediaries to bring about the desired change from present to future conditions. In the set of illustrative cases that was first examined, certain valuation-words, like 'good' and 'right,' explicitly appear; in the second set there are no *explicit* value-expressions. The cry for aid, however, when taken in connection with its existential context, affirms in effect, although not in so many words, that the situation with reference to which the cry is made is "bad." It is "bad" in the sense that it is objected to, while a future situation which is *better* is anticipated, provided the cry evokes a certain response. The analysis may seem to be unnecessarily detailed. But, unless in each set of examples the existential context is made clear, the verbal expressions that are employed can be made to mean anything or nothing. When the contexts are taken into account, what emerges are propositions assigning a relatively negative value to existing conditions; a comparatively positive value to a prospective set of conditions; and intermediate propositions (which may or may not contain a valuation-expression) intended to evoke activities that will bring about a transformation from one state of affairs to another. There are thus involved (i) aversion to an existing situation and attraction toward a prospective possible situation and (ii) a *specifiable and testable relation between the latter as an end and certain activities as means for accomplishing it.* . . .

THE MORALITY OF EMOTIVE LANGUAGE[3]

Discussion of the topic indicated by the caption of this article centers about a particular thesis put forward by Professor Stevenson in his recent book.* Since my article is definitely critical as to this particular thesis, I feel the more bound to indicate at the outset certain points in which I think his book as a whole should command not only the attention but the support of students of ethical theory. Among points of agreement are the following: (i) There is great need for more attention to the language that characterizes specifically

Ethics and Language by Charles L. Stevenson, Yale University Press, 1944. . . .

ethical judgments or sentences. (ii) Ethical inquires should "draw from the *whole* of a man's knowledge," since the materials of such inquiries lend "themselves very poorly to specialization." (iii) Ethical inquiry has suffered from "quest for ultimate principles, definitively established"—a procedure that "not only hides the full complexity of moral issues, but puts static, other-worldly norms in the place of flexible, realistic ones." (iv) Finally since "ethical *issues* differ from scientific ones," there should be careful attention to the *way* in which they differ.*

There is such ambiguity in the word "issues" that grasp upon its double reference is indispensable. In one sense of the word, that moral and scientific issues differ is not just to be admitted as a concession, but is to be insisted upon as characteristic of ethical subject-matter and ethical sentences *qua* ethical. The sense in which *issues* differ, if not a commonplace, is commonly acknowledged in calling ethics a practical or "normative" subject. But in this sense "issue" is equivalent to office, function, use, force; it concerns the contextual "practical" reference, the *objective* of ethical sentences. As far as accomplishment of this function and use is intended on the part of those who engage in forming, accepting, or rejecting ethical sentences, a differential *interest* marks them off from sentences having what is conventionally called a scientific interest. While difference determines the specific facts *selected* as the distinctive content or subject-matter of ethical sentences, it does not constitute a component part of that subject-matter. It is one thing to say that, because of the differential use or function of ethical sentences, certain facts rather than others are selected and that they are arranged or organized in a given way rather than in some other way. A like proposition applies to differences that mark off the sciences from one another—physics, for example, from physiology. It is quite another thing to convert the difference in function and use into a differential component of the structure and contents of ethical sentences. This conversion marks, in effect, Stevenson's treatment.

I may further anticipate the tenor of the discussion which follows by saying that I do not see how it can be denied that the subject-matter which is selected as appropriate and required for sentences which will fulfill the proper office or function of ethical sentences is charged (and properly so) with facts designated by such names as greed-generosity, love-hate, sympathy-antipathy, reverence-indifference. It is usual to give such facts, taken collectively, the name "emotions," or, slightly more technically, the name "affective-motor." It is one thing to acknowledge (and insist) upon this feature of ethical sentences as one demanded by their function or the use they are put to. It is quite another thing to hold that this subject-matter is not capable of

*The quoted passages are all from page 336 of *Ethics and Language;* "*whole*" is italicized in the original text while "*issues*" and "*way*" are not. The reason why I have italicized these words is central in my discussion, as will appear as it proceeds.

and does not need *description,* and description of the kind belonging to sentences having "scientific" standing. I believe that examination of Stevenson's specific treatment of the "emotional" (or the "emotive" in his terminology) will show that he takes the fact that factually grounded reasons are employed in genuinely ethical sentences in order to modify affective-motor attitudes which influence and direct conduct, to be equivalent to the presence of an extra-cognitive constituent in the sentences in question. In short, the very fact that factual grounds (which are capable of description) are the means used in genuine ethical sentences to affect the springs of conduct and thereby to direct and redirect conduct, is employed as if it introduced into the specific subject-matter of ethical sentences a factor completely recalcitrant to intellectual or cognitive consideration. . . . One can agree fully that ethical sentences (as far as their end and use is concerned) "plead and advise" and speak "to the conative-affective natures of men."* Their use and intent is practical. But the point at issue concerns the means by which this result is accomplished. It is, I repeat, a radical fallacy to convert the end-in-view into an inherent constituent of the means by which, in genuinely moral sentences, the end is accomplished. To take the cases in which "emotional" factors *accompany* the giving of reasons as if this accompaniment factor were an inherent part of the judgment is, I submit, both a theoretical error and is, when widely adopted in practice, a source of moral weakness. . . .

. . . His general point of view is fairly presented in the following passage: "For the contexts that are most typical of normative ethics, the ethical terms have a function that is *both* emotive and descriptive."† In admitting the "descriptive," Stevenson goes beyond those writers who have denied all descriptive force to moral expressions. . . . In so far, Stevenson's treatment constitutes a decided advance upon them. I begin by stating what the point at issue is not. Stevenson says "Ethical terms cannot be taken as fully comparable to scientific ones. They have a quasi-imperative *function.*"* Now (as was said earlier) the point at issue does not concern the last of the two sentences quoted. Nor does it concern the correctness of the statement that "Both imperative and ethical sentences are *used* more for encouraging, altering, or redirecting people's aims and conduct than for simply describing them."† The point at issue is whether the facts of *use* and *function* render ethical terms and sentences not fully comparable with scientific ones as respects their subject-matter and content. As far as concerns *use* it would not, I believe, be going too far to say the word "more" in the above passage is not strong enough. Of ethical sentences as ordinarily used, it may be said, I believe, that their *entire* use and function of ethical sentences is directive or "practical." The point at issue concerns another matter: It concerns how this end

Op. cit., p. 13.
†*Op. cit.,* p. 84. . . .
Op. cit., p. 36; italics not in original.
†*Op. cit.,* p. 21; italics not in original text.

is to be accomplished if sentences are to possess distinctively and genuinely *ethical* properties. The theoretical view about ethical sentences which is an alternative to that put forward by Stevenson is, that as far as noncognitive, extra-cognitive, factors enter into the subject-matter or content of sentences purporting to be legitimately ethical, these sentences are by just that much deprived of the properties sentences should have in order to be genuinely *ethical*.

Let us note a somewhat analogous case. The practices, often resorted to by a skilled lawyer in defending a client charged with a criminal act, often contain noncognitive elements and these may sometimes be more influential, more directive, of what the jury does than evidence of the matter-of-fact or descriptive sort. Would one say in this case that these means, such as intonations, facial expressions, gestures, etc., are a *part* of legal propositions *qua* legal? If not in this case, why in the case of ethical propositions? And in this connection it is worth noting that in some cases at least (possibly in all cases) scientific propositions have a practical office and function. Such is assuredly the case in which a scientific theory is in current dispute because opposite views are entertained. Surely evidence adduced is *used* and is *intended* to be used so as to confirm, weaken, modify, redirect propositions accepted by others. But I doubt if one would hold that the *heat* that sometimes accompanies the putting forth of reasons for changing old views is a part of the *subject-matter* of the propositions *qua* scientific.

Extra-cognitive devices are without doubt employed to effect a result which in consequence is moral only in the sense in which the word "*im*moral" is included in the scope of "moral." Many propositions which are now taken to be immoral have had positive moral property ascribed to them at former times. There is here a strong indication that extra-rational factors played an undue part in forming the earlier propositions and in getting them accepted. It would be foolish to deny that partisanship, "wishful thinking," etc., plays today a great role in not only getting propositions accepted but in determining the *subject-matter* of *what* is accepted. But I should suppose it to be evident that such facts are "ethical" only in the sense in which that word covers the anti-ethical and the pseudo-ethical. If moral theory has any distinctive province and any important function it is, I would say, to criticize the language of the *mores* prevalent at a given time, or in given groups, so as to eliminate if possible this factor as a component of their subject-matter; to provide in its place sound matter-of-fact or "descriptive" grounds drawn from any relevant part of the *whole* knowledge possessed at the time. . . .

WHY NOT ABANDON MORAL LANGUAGE?[4]

One of the many obstructions in the way of satisfying the logical conditions of scientific method should receive special notice. Serious social troubles tend

to be interpreted in *moral* terms. That the situations themselves are profoundly moral in their causes and consequences, in the genuine sense of
moral, need not be denied. But conversion of the situations investigated into
definite problems, that can be intelligently dealt with, demands objective
intellectual formulation of conditions; and such a formulation demands in
turn complete abstraction from the qualities of sin and righteousness, of
vicious and virtuous motives, that are so readily attributed to individuals,
groups, classes, nations. There was a time when desirable and obnoxious
physical phenomena were attributed to the benevolence and malevolence of
overruling powers. There was a time when diseases were attributed to the
machinations of personal enemies. Spinoza's contention that the occurrence
of moral evils should be treated upon the same basis and plane as the occurrence of thunderstorms is justifiable on the ground of the requirements of
scientific method, independently of its context in his own philosophic system.
For each procedure is the only way in which they can be formulated objectively or in terms of selected and ordered conditions. And such formulation
is the sole mode of approach through which plans of remedial procedure can
be projected in objective terms. Approach to human problems in terms of
moral blame and moral approbation, of wickedness or righteousness, is probably the greatest single obstacle now existing to development of competent
methods in the field of social subject-matter.

When we turn from consideration of the methods of inquiry currently employed in political and many administrative matters, to the methods that are
adopted in the professed name of social science, we find quite an opposite
state of affairs. We come upon an assumption which if it were . . . explicitly
formulated would take some such shape as "The facts are out there and only
need to be observed, assembled and arranged to give rise to suitable and
grounded generalizations." Investigators of physical phenomena often speak
and write in similar fashion. But analysis of what they *do* as distinct from
what they *say* yields a very different result. Before, however, considering this
point I shall discuss a closely connected assumption, namely the assumption
that in order to base conclusions upon the facts and only the facts, all *evaluative* procedures must be strictly ruled out.

This assumption on the part of those engaged, in the name of science, in
social investigation derives in the minds of those who entertain it from a
sound principle. It springs, at least in large measure, from realization of the
harm that has been wrought by forming social judgments on the ground of
moral preconceptions, conceptions of what is right and wrong, vicious and
virtuous. As has just been stated, this procedure inevitably prejudices the
institution of relevant significant data, the statement of the problems that are
to be solved, and the methods by which they may be solved. The soundness
of the principle that moral condemnation and approbation should be excluded
from the operations of obtaining and weighing material data and from the

operations by which conceptions for dealing with the data are instituted, is, however, often converted into the notion that all evaluations should be excluded. This conversion is, however, effected only through the intermediary of a thoroughly fallacious notion; the notion, namely, that the moral blames and approvals in question *are* evaluative and that they exhaust the field of evaluation. For they are *not* evaluative in any logical sense of evaluation. They are not even judgments in the logical sense of judgment. For they rest upon some preconception of *ends* that *should* or *ought* to be attained. This preconception excludes ends (consequences) from the field of inquiry and reduces inquiry at its very best to the truncated and distorted business of finding out means for realizing objectives already settled upon. Judgment which is actually judgment (that satisfies the logical conditions of judgment) institutes means-consequences (ends) in *strict conjugate relation* to each other. Ends have to be adjudged (evaluated) on the basis of the available means by which they can be attained just as much as existential materials have to be adjudged (evaluated) with respect to their function as material means of effecting a resolved situation. For an end-in-view is itself a means, namely, a procedural means.

The idea that "the end justifies the means" is in as bad repute in moral theory as its adoption is a commonplace of political practice. The doctrine may be given a strictly logical formulation, and when so formulated its inherent defect becomes evident. From the logical standpoint, it rests upon the postulate that some end is already so fixedly given that it is outside the scope of inquiry, so that the only problem for inquiry is to ascertain and manipulate the materials by which the end may be attained. The hypothetical and directive function of ends-in-view as procedural means is thus ignored and a fundamental logical condition of inquiry is violated. Only an end-in-view that is treated as a *hypothesis* (by which discrimination and ordering of existential material is operatively effected) can by any logical possibility determine the existential materials that are means. In all fields but the social, the notion that the correct solution is already given and that it only remains to find the facts that prove it is so thoroughly discredited that those who act upon it are regarded as pretenders, or as cranks who are trying to impose some pet notion upon facts. But in social matters, those who claim that they are in possession of the one sure solution of social problems often set themselves up as being peculiarly scientific while others are floundering around in an "empirical" morass. Only recognition in both theory and practice that ends to be attained (ends-in-view) are of the nature of hypotheses and that hypotheses have to be formed and tested in strict correlativity with existential conditions as means can alter current habits of dealing with social issues.

What has been said indicates the valid meaning of evaluation in inquiry in general and also shows the necessity of evaluative judgments in social inquiry. The need for selective discrimination of certain existential or factual material to be data proves that an evaluative estimate is operating. The notion that evaluation is concerned only with *ends* and that, with the ruling out of moral ends, evaluative judgments are ruled out rests, then, upon a profound misconception of the nature of the logical conditions and constituents of all scientific inquiry. All competent and authentic inquiry demands that out of the complex welter of existential and potentially observable and recordable material, certain material be selected and weighed *as* data or the "facts of the case." This process is one of adjudgment, of appraisal or evaluation. On the other end, there is, as has been just stated, no evaluation when ends are taken to be already given. An idea of an end *to be* reached, an end-*in-view*, is logically indispensable in discrimination of existential material as the evidential and testing facts of the case. Without it, there is no guide for observation; without it, one can have no conception of what one should look for or even *is* looking for. One "fact" would be just as good as another—that is, good for nothing in control of inquiry and formation and in settlement of a problem. . . .

Before leaving this endeavor to clarify my position . . . , I shall mention a . . . matter which . . . is still more or less actively pursued in contemporary philosophical discussion. I refer here to the extraordinary contrast that exists beyond peradventure between the subject-matters that are known in science and those known in the course of our everyday and common living—common not only in the sense of the usual but of that which is shared by large numbers of human beings in the conduct of the affairs of their life. To avoid misunderstanding it should be observed that the word "practical" has a much fuller meaning when used to designate these affairs than it has when it is used in a narrow utilitarian way, since it includes the moral, the political, and the artistic. A simple but fairly typical example of the undeniable contrast between the subject-matters of this common life and the knowings that are appropriate to it, and the subject-matter and method of scientific knowing is found in the radical unlikeness of the water we drink, wash with, sail boats upon, use to extinguish fires, etc., etc., and the H_2O of scientific subject-matter. . . .

It seems pertinent at this point . . . to refer to that aspect of my theory of knowledge to which I gave the name "instrumentalism." For it was intended to deal with the problem just mentioned on the basis of the idea or hypothesis that scientific subject-matter grows out of and returns into the subject-matter of the everyday kind. . . . Moreover, new construction accrues to the subject-matter of physical science just because of its extreme unlikeness to the subject-matters which for the sake of brevity may be called those of common sense. There is presented in this unlikeness a striking example of the view of the function of thoroughgoing abstraction mentioned shortly

ago. The extreme remoteness of the subject-matter of physical science from
the subject-matter of everyday living is precisely that which renders the
former applicable to an immense variety of the occasions that present themselves in the course of everyday living. Today there is probably no case of
everyday living in which physical conditions hold a place that is beyond the
reach of being effectively dealt with on the ground of available *scientific*
subject-matter. A similar statement is now coming to hold regarding matters
which are specifically physiological! Note, in evidence, the revolution that is
taking place in matters relating to illness and health. Negative illustration,
if not confirmation, may be supplied by the backward state of both knowledge
and practice in matters that are distinctively human and moral. The latter in
my best judgment will continue to be matter of customs and of conflict of
customs until inquiry has found a method of abstraction which, because of
its degree of remoteness from established customs, will bring them into a
light in which their nature will be indefinitely more clearly seen than is
now the case. . . .

1. *Logic: The Theory of Inquiry*, pp. 46–51. See also chapter 5 of *Experience and Nature*. Heading provided by the editor.

2. *Theory of Valuation*, pp. 6–13. Quotations in the text are from A. J. Ayer's *Language, Truth and Logic*, chapter 6. Heading provided by the editor.

3. "Ethical Subject-Matter and Language," *The Journal of Philosophy* XLII (1945): pp. 701–12. Heading provided by the editor.

4. *Logic: The Theory of Inquiry*, pp. 494–97; excerpt from letter by Dewey to Albert G. A. Balz, printed in *The Journal of Philosophy* XLVI (1949): pp. 329–42. Heading provided by the editor.

Social Intelligence and Democracy

7

Dewey's intellectual achievement culminates in his philosophy of social intelligence, or democracy. As elucidated in the introduction, the philosophy of democracy embodies the ideals of social method, growth, freedom, and shared experience. Democratic behavior, as Dewey characterizes it, is the only realistic means by which human beings can share optimally in the most satisfactory modes of conduct.

Being democratic, however, is ineffectual unless the practice is widely shared. While many philosophers are concerned with determining the criteria for universalizing a prescription for conduct in a particular situation, Dewey, by contrast, is concerned with universalizing democratic habits of thought and action. When he says, for example, "The problem of bringing about an effective socialization of intelligence is probably the greatest problem of democracy today,"[1] he means that our social well-being depends above all on the widest possible currency of democratic habits. The democratic nature is not only intrinsically desirable, but it is the most effective way of behaving as part of the whole which can be shared in by all. That is, it is eminently universalizable. Accordingly, a principal goal of inquiry is to determine the conditions of democratic life.

Dewey's most fundamental recommendation for dealing with actual moral disputes is to submit them to the processes of social intelligence. Democratic behavior will not solve every specific moral problem with which it is confronted. As the history of moral thought abundantly illustrates, no such means is possessed by any ethical theory. Yet when the emphasis is placed on democratic social method, the opportunities for creating a voluntary and informed consensus are much greater than in any alternative means for dealing with conflict.[2]

The first selection below provides Dewey's argument that moral habits *are social both in origin and function. In this conviction his conclusions are remarkably like those of Aristotle: Intelligence affects moral habits primarily through the community. A community can be organized according to an intelligently conceived plan such that certain forms of behavior will be fostered. Experimental thinking is one such habit (more so for Dewey than for Aristotle); and this habit itself is conducive to consummatory experience. It not only determines the means of reconstructing situations, but at the same time it effects a reconstitution of desires by reconstituting the meaning of immediate or otherwise isolated actions. As the meaning of an object of desire is reconstituted, so is the desire; and choice and action are in some measure qualified.*[3]

MORALITY IS SOCIAL[4]

Intelligence becomes ours in the degree in which we use it and accept responsibility for consequences. It is not ours originally or by production. "It thinks" is a truer psychological statement than "I think." Thoughts sprout and vegetate; ideas proliferate. They come from deep unconscious sources. "I think" is a statement about voluntary action. Some suggestion surges from the unknown. Our active body of habits appropriates it. The suggestion then becomes an assertion. It no longer merely comes to us. It is accepted and uttered by us. We act upon it and thereby assume, by implication, its consequences. The stuff of belief and proposition is not originated by us. It comes to us from others, by education, tradition and the suggestion of the environment. Our intelligence is bound up, so far as its materials are concerned, with the community life of which we are a part. We know what it communicates to us, and know according to the habits it forms in us. Science is an affair of civilization not of individual intellect.

So with conscience. When a child acts, those about him re-act. They shower encouragement upon him, visit him with approval, or they bestow frowns and rebuke. What others do to us when we act is as natural a consequence of our action as what the fire does to us when we plunge our hands in it. The social environment may be as artificial as you please. But its action in response to ours is natural not artificial. In language and imagination we rehearse the responses of others just as we dramatically enact other consequences. We foreknow how others will act, and the foreknowledge is the beginning of judgment passed on action. We know *with* them; there is conscience. An assembly is formed within our breast which discusses and appraises proposed and performed acts. The community without becomes a forum and tribunal within, a judgment-seat of charges, assessments and exculpations. Our thoughts of our own actions are saturated with the ideas that others entertain about them, ideas which have been expressed not only in explicit instruction but still more effectively in reaction to our acts.

Liability is the beginning of responsibility. We are held accountable by others for the consequences of our acts. They visit their like and dislike of these consequences upon us. In vain do we claim that these are not ours; that they are products of ignorance not design, or are incidents in the execution of a most laudable scheme. Their authorship is imputed to us. We are disapproved, and disapproval is not an inner state of mind but a most definite act. Others say to us by their deeds we do not care a fig whether you did this deliberately or not. We intend that you *shall* deliberate before you do it again, and that if possible your deliberation shall prevent a repetition of this act we object to. The reference in blame and every unfavorable judgment is prospective, not retrospective. Theories about responsibility may become confused, but in practice no one is stupid enough to try to change the past. Approbation and disapprobation are ways of influencing the formation of habits and aims; that is, of influencing future acts. The individual is *held* accountable for what he *has* done in order that he may be responsive in what he is *going* to do. Gradually persons learn by dramatic imitation to hold themselves accountable, and liability becomes a voluntary deliberate acknowledgment that deeds are our own, that their consequences come from us.

These two facts, that moral judgment and moral responsibility are the work wrought in us by the social environment, signify that all morality is social; not because we *ought* to take into account the effect of our acts upon the welfare of others, but because of facts. Others *do* take account of what we do, and they respond accordingly to our acts. Their responses actually *do* affect the meaning of what we do. The significance thus contributed is as inevitable as is the effect of interaction with the physical environment. In fact as civilization advances the physical environment gets itself more and more humanized, for the meaning of physical energies and events becomes involved with the part they play in human activities. Our conduct *is* socially conditioned whether we perceive the fact or not.

The effect of custom on habit, and of habit upon thought is enough to prove this statement. When we begin to forecast consequences, the consequences that most stand out are those which will proceed from other people. The resistance and the cooperation of others is the central fact in the furtherance or failure of our schemes. Connections with our fellows furnish both the opportunities for action and the instrumentalities by which we take advantage of opportunity. All of the actions of an individual bear the stamp of his community as assuredly as does the language he speaks. Difficulty in reading the stamp is due to variety of impressions in consequence of membership in many groups. This social saturation is, I repeat, a matter of fact, not of what should be, not of what is desirable or undesirable. It does not guarantee the rightness or goodness of an act; there is no excuse for thinking of evil action as individualistic and right action as social. Deliberate unscrupulous pursuit of self-interest is as much conditioned upon social opportunities, training and assistance as is the course of action prompted by a beaming benevolence. The difference lies in the quality and degree of the perception of ties and interdependencies; in the use to which they are put. Consider the form commonly assumed today by self-seeking; namely command of money and economic power. Money is a social institution; property is a legal custom; economic opportunities are dependent upon the state of society; the objects aimed at, the rewards sought for are what they are because of social admiration, prestige, competition and power. If money-making is morally obnoxious it is because of the way these social facts are handled, not because a money-making man has withdrawn from society into an isolated selfhood or turned his back upon society. His "individualism" is not found in his original nature but in his habits acquired under social influences. It is found in his concrete aims, and these are reflexes of social conditions. Well-grounded moral objection to a mode of conduct rests upon the kind of social connections that figure, not upon lack of social aim. A man may attempt to utilize social relationships for his own advantage in an inequitable way; he may intentionally or unconsciously try to make them feed one of his own appetites. Then he is denounced as egoistic. But both his course of action and the disapproval he is subject to are facts *within* society. They are social phenomena. He pursues his unjust advantage as a social asset.

Explicit recognition of this fact is a prerequisite of improvement in moral education and of an intelligent understanding of the chief ideas or "categories" of morals. Morals is as much a matter of interaction of a person with his social environment as walking is an interaction of legs with a physical environment. The character of walking depends upon the strength and competency of legs. But it also depends upon whether a man is walking in a bog or on a paved street, upon whether there is a safeguarded path set aside or whether he has to walk amid dangerous vehicles. If the standard of morals is low it is because the education given by the interaction of the individual with his social environment is defective. Of what avail is it to preach unassuming simplicity and contentment of life when communal admiration goes to the man who "succeeds"—who makes himself conspicuous and envied because of command of money and other forms of power? If a child gets on by peevishness or intrigue, then others are his accomplices who assist in the habits which are built up. The notion that an abstract ready-made conscience exists in individuals and that it is only necessary to make an occasional appeal to it and to indulge in occasional crude rebukes and punishments, is associated with the causes of lack of definitive and orderly moral advance. For it is associated with lack of attention to social forces.

There is a peculiar inconsistency in the current idea that morals *ought* to be social. The introduction of the moral "ought" into the idea contains an implicit assertion that morals depend upon something apart from social relations. Morals *are* social. The question of ought, should be, is a question of better and worse *in* social affairs. The extent to which the weight of theories has been thrown against the perception of the place of social ties and connections in moral activity is a fair measure of the extent to which social forces work blindly and develop an accidental morality. The chief obstacle, for example, to recognizing the truth of a proposition frequently set forth in these pages to the effect that all conduct is potential, if not actual, matter of moral judgment is the habit of identifying moral judgment with praise and blame. So great is the influence of this habit that it is safe to say that every professed moralist when he leaves the pages of theory and faces some actual item of his own or others' behavior, first or "instinctively" thinks of acts as moral or nonmoral in the degree in which they are exposed to condemnation or approval. Now this kind of judgment is certainly not one which could profitably be dispensed with. Its influence is much needed. But the tendency to equate it with all moral judgment is largely responsible for the current idea that there is a sharp line between moral conduct and a larger region of nonmoral conduct which is a matter of expediency, shrewdness, success or manners.

Moreover this tendency is a chief reason why the social forces effective in shaping actual morality work blindly and unsatisfactorily. Judgment in which the emphasis falls upon blame and approbation has more heat than light. It is more emotional than intellectual. It is guided by custom, personal convenience and resentment rather than by insight into causes and consequences. It makes toward reducing moral instruction, the educative influence of social opinion, to an immediate personal matter, that is to say, to an adjustment of personal likes and dislikes. Fault-finding creates resentment in the one blamed, and approval, complacency, rather than a habit of scrutininzing conduct objectively. It puts those who are sensitive to the judgments of others in a standing defensive attitude, creating an apologetic, self-accusing and self-exculpating habit of mind when what is needed is an impersonal impartial habit of observation. "Moral" persons get so occupied with defending their conduct from real and imagined criticism that they have little time left to see what their acts really amount to, and the habit of self-blame inevitably extends to include others since it is a habit.

Now it is a wholesome thing for any one to be made aware that thoughtless, self-centered action on his part exposes him to the indignation and dislike of others. There is no one who can be safely trusted to be exempt from immediate reactions of criticism, and there are few who do not need to be braced by occasional expressions of approval. But these influences are immensely overdone in comparison with the assistance that might be given by the influence of social judgments which operate without accompaniments of praise and blame; which enable an individual to see for himself what he is doing, and which put him in command of a method of analyzing the obscure and usually unavowed forces which move him to act. We need a permeation of judgments on conduct by the method and materials of a science of human nature. Without such enlightenment even the best-intentioned attempts at the moral guidance and improvement of others often eventuate in tragedies of misunderstanding and division, as is so often seen in the relations of parents and children. . . .

At present we not only have no assured means of forming character except crude devices of blame, praise, exhortation and punishment, but the very meaning of the general notions of moral inquiry is matter of doubt and dispute. The reason is that these notions are discussed in isolation from the concrete facts of the interactions of human beings with one another—an abstraction as fatal as was the old discussion of phlogiston, gravity and vital force apart from concrete correlations of changing events with one another. Take for example such a basic conception as that of Right involving the nature of authority in conduct. There is no need here to rehearse the multitude of contending views which give evidence that discussion of this matter is still in the realm of opinion. We content ourselves with pointing out that this notion is the last resort of the antiempirical school in morals and that it proves the effect of neglect of social conditions.

In effect its adherents argue as follows: "Let us concede that concrete ideas about right and wrong and particular notions of what is obligatory have grown up within experience. But we cannot admit this about the idea of Right, of Obligation itself. Why does moral authority exist at all? Why is the claim of the Right recognized in conscience even by those who violate it in deed? Our opponents say that such and such a course is wise, expedient, better. But *why* act for the wise, or good, or better? Why not follow our own immediate devices if we are so inclined? There is only one answer: We have a moral nature, a conscience, call it what you will. And this nature responds directly in acknowledgment of the supreme authority of the Right over all claims of inclination and habit. We may not act in accordance with this acknowledgment, but we still know that the authority of the moral law, although not its power, is unquestionable. Men may differ indefinitely according to what their experience has been as to just *what* is Right, what its contents are. But they all spontaneously agree in recognizing the supremacy of the claims of whatever is thought of as Right. Otherwise there would be no such thing as morality, but merely calculations of how to satisfy desire."

Grant the foregoing argument, and all the apparatus of abstract moralism follows in its wake. A remote goal of perfection, ideals that are contrary in a wholesale way to what is actual, a free will of arbitrary choice; all of these conceptions band themselves together with that of a nonempirical authority of Right and a nonempirical conscience which acknowledges it. They constitute its ceremonial or formal train.

Why, indeed, acknowledge the authority of Right? That many persons do not acknowledge it in fact, in action, and that all persons ignore it at times, is assumed by the argument. Just what is the significance of an alleged recognition of a supremacy which is continually denied in fact? How much would be lost if it were dropped out, and we were left face to face with actual facts? If a man lived alone in the world there might be some sense in the question "Why be moral?" were it not for one thing: No such question would then arise. As it is, we live in a world where other persons live too. Our acts affect them. They perceive these effects, and react upon us in consequence. Because they are living beings they make demands upon us for certain things from us. They approve and condemn—not in abstract theory but in what they do to us. The answer to the question "Why not put your hand in the fire?" is the answer of fact. If you do your hand will be burnt. The answer to the question why acknowledge the right is of the same sort. For Right is only an abstract name for the multitude of concrete demands in action which others impress upon us, and of which we are obliged, if we would live, to take some account. Its authority is the exigency of their demands, the efficacy of their insistencies. There may be good ground for the contention that in theory the idea of the right is subordinate to that of the good, being a statement of the course proper to attain good. But in fact it signifies the totality of social pressures exercised upon us to induce us to think and desire in certain ways. Hence the right can in fact become the road to the good only as the elements that compose this unremitting pressure are enlightened, only as social relationships become themselves reasonable.

It will be retorted that all pressure is a nonmoral affair partaking of force, not of right; that right must be ideal. Thus we are invited to enter again the circle in which the ideal has no force and social actualities no ideal quality. We refuse the invitation because social pressure is involved in our own lives, as much so as the air we breathe and the ground we walk upon. If we had desires, judgments, plans, in short a mind, apart from social connections, then the latter would be external and their action might be regarded as that of a nonmoral force. But we live mentally as physically only *in* and *because* of our environment. Social pressure is but a name for the interactions which are always going on and in which we participate, living so far as we partake and dying so far as we do not. The pressure is not ideal but empirical, yet empirical here means only actual. It calls attention to the fact that considerations of right are claims originating not outside of life, but within it. They are "ideal" in precisely the degree in which we intelligently recognize and act upon them, just as colors and canvas become ideal when used in ways that give an added meaning to life.

Accordingly failure to recognize the authority of right means defect in effective apprehension of the realities of human association, not an arbitrary exercise of free will. This deficiency and perversion in apprehension indicates a defect in education—that is to say, in the operation of actual conditions, in the consequences upon desire and thought of existing interactions and interdependencies. It is false that every person has a consciousness of the supreme authority of right and then misconceives it or ignores it in action. One has such a sense of the claims of social relationships as those relationships enforce in one's desires and observations. The belief in a separate, ideal or transcendental, practically ineffectual Right is a reflex of the inadequacy with which existing institutions perform their educative office—their office in generating observation of social continuities. It is an endeavor to "rationalize" this defect. Like all rationalizations, it operates to divert attention from the real state of affairs. Thus it helps maintain the conditions which created it, standing in the way of effort to make our institutions more humane and equitable. A theoretical acknowledgment of the supreme authority of Right, of moral law, gets twisted into an effectual substitute for acts which would better the customs which now produce vague, dull, halting and evasive observation of actual social ties. We are not caught in a circle; we traverse a spiral in which social customs generate some consciousness of interdependencies, and this consciousness is embodied in acts which in improving the environment generate new perceptions of social ties, and so on forever. The relationships, the interactions are forever there as fact, but they acquire meaning only in the desires, judgments and purposes they awaken.

We recur to our fundamental propositions. Morals is connected with actualities of existence, not with ideals, ends and obligations independent of concrete actualities. The facts upon which it depends are those which arise out of active connections of human beings with one another, the consequences of their mutually intertwined activities in the life of desire, belief, judgment, satisfaction and dissatisfaction. In this sense conduct and hence morals are social: they are not just things which *ought* to be social and which fail to come up to the scratch. But there are enormous differences of better and worse in the quality of what is social. Ideal morals begin with the perception of these differences. Human interaction and ties are there, are operative in any case. But they can be regulated, employed in an orderly way for good only as we know how to observe them. And they cannot be observed aright, they cannot be understood and utilized, when the mind is left to itself to work without the aid of science. For the natural unaided mind means precisely the habits of belief, thought and desire which have been accidentally generated and confirmed by social institutions or customs. But with all their admixture of accident and reasonableness we have at last reached a point where social conditions create a mind capable of scientific outlook and inquiry. To foster and develop this spirit is the social obligation of the present because it is its urgent need. . . .

. . . There are still those who think they are in possession of codes and principles which settle finally and automatically the right and wrong of, say, divorce, the respective rights of capital and labor, the exact limits of private property, the extent to which legislation should go in deciding what individuals shall eat, drink, wear, etc. But there are also many other persons, an increasing number, who see that such questions as these cannot be settled by deduction from fixed premises, and that the attempt to decide them in that fashion is the road to the intolerant fanaticism, dogmatism, class strife, of the closed mind. Wars waged in the alleged interest of religion, or in defense of particular economic conceptions, prove the practical danger of carrying theoretical dogmatism into action. Since the right course is to bring the best intelligence we can command to bear upon such social problems, theory has a definite function in establishing the value of such intelligence and in promoting it by clarifying issues, proposing solutions, guiding the action which tests the worth of these proposals.

The foregoing remarks should make clear what is meant by that change from personal to social morality which has been referred to. It does *not* signify that morality becomes impersonal and collective; it remains and must remain personal in that social problems have to be faced by individuals, and decisions reached in the forum of individual minds have to be carried into effect by individual agents, who are in turn personally responsible for the consequences of their acts. Morals are personal because they spring from personal insight, judgment, and choice. Such facts as these, however, are wholly consistent with the fact that *what* men think and believe is affected by common factors, and that the thought and choice of one individual spreads to others. They do not militate against the fact that men have to act together, and that their conjoint action is embodied in institutions and laws; that unified action creates government and legislative policies, forms the family, establishes schools and churches, manifests itself in business corporations of vast extent and power, in clubs and fraternities for enjoyment and recreation, and in armies which set nation against nation. . . .

. . . In one sense the change to social morality makes morals more acutely personal than they were when custom ruled. It forces the need of more personal reflection, more personal knowledge and insight, more deliberate and steadfast personal convictions, more resolute personal attitudes in action— more personal in the sense of being more *conscious* in choice and more voluntary in execution. It would then be absurd to suppose that "social morals" meant a swallowing up of individuality in an anonymous mass, or an abdication of personal responsibility in decision and action. It signifies that the social conditions and social consequences of personal action (which always exist in any case), are now brought to explicit consciousness so that they require searching thought and careful judgment in a way practically unprecedented formerly. It indicates that reflection is morally indispensable. It points out the material of reflection: the sort of things to which moral inquiry and judgment must go out. . . .

. . . The idea of common good, general welfare, needs . . . careful interpretation. We may say of welfare what was said of the kindred idea of happiness, that we must beware of giving it a fixed meaning. Since it includes the harmonious fulfillment of all capacities, it grows as new potentialities are disclosed; it develops as social changes present new opportunities for personal development.

Such terms as "general" and "common" need, perhaps, even more careful interpretation. The words come easily to the tongue and too readily give a wrong impression. They do *not* mean a sacrifice of individuality; it would be a poor kind of society whose members were personally undeveloped. It does not mean the submergence of what is distinctive, unique, in different human beings; such submergence would produce an impoverishment of the social whole. The positive import of "common good" is suggested by the idea of sharing, participating—an idea involved in the very idea of *community*. Sharing a good or value in a way which makes it social in quality is not identical with dividing up a material thing into physical parts. To partake is to *take* part, to *play* a role. It is something active, something which engages the desires and aims of each contributing member. Its proper analogue is not physical division but taking part in a game, in conversation, in a drama, in family life. It involves diversification, not sameness and repetition. There could be no communication of feeling and idea in a conversation if each one parrotlike said the same sentence over and over, and there could be no game played if all made the same motions at the same time. Each contributes something distinctive from his own store of knowledge, ability, taste, while receiving at the same time elements of value contributed by others. What is contributed to each is, first, a support, a reinforcement, of his own action; thereby each receives from others the factors which give his own position greater *security*—a fact illustrated by the mutual aid given to one another by the partners, the partakers on the same side of a game. In the second place what is contributed is enjoyment of new meanings, new values. In a debate each debater on the same "side" tries to strengthen or reinforce the position of every other one on that side. But in a genuine conversation the ideas of one are corrected and changed by what others say; what is confirmed is not his previous notions, which may have been narrow and ill-formed, but his capacity to judge wisely. What he gains is an expansion of experience; he learns; even if previous ideas are in the main confirmed, yet in the degree in which there is genuine mutual give and take they are seen in a new light, deepened and extended in meaning, and there is the enjoyment of enlargement of experience, of growth of capacity.

What has been said helps to an understanding of the idea of equality as part of the social ideal. It does not mean sameness; it is not to be understood quantitatively, an interpretation which always ends in ideas of external and mechanical equality. Children gain enrichment of experience from parents precisely because of *disparity*. There is quantitative inequality—inequality in *possession* of skill, knowledge, but qualitative equality, for when children are *active*, when they give as well as receive, the lives of parents are fuller and richer because of what they receive from their children as well as because of what they put forth. There is a great deal of discussion of equality which is meaningless and futile because the conception is taken in a static instead of in a functional way. One person is morally equal to others when he has the same opportunity for developing his capacities and playing his part that others have, although his capacities are quite unlike theirs. When there is an equation in his *own* life and experience between what he contributes to the group activity and experience and what he receives in return in the way of stimulus and of enrichment of experience, he is *morally* equal. The equality is one of *values*, not of materials and quantities, and equality of value has on this account to be measured in terms of the intrinsic life and growth of each individual, not by mechanical comparisons. Each individual is incommensurable as an individual with every other, so that it is impossible to find an external measure of equality. Concretely, one person is superior in one particular respect and inferior in some other to many others. He is morally equal when his values with respect to his own possibilities of growth, whatever they are, are reckoned with in the social organization as scrupulously as those of every other. To employ a somewhat mechanical analogy, a violet and an oak tree are equal when one has the same opportunity to develop to the full as a violet which the other has as an oak.

The conception of community of good may be clarified by reference to attempts of those in fixed positions of superiority to confer good upon others. History shows that there have been benevolent despots who wished to bestow blessings on others. They have not succeeded except when their actions have taken the indirect form of changing the conditions under which those lived who were disadvantageously placed. The same principle holds of reformers and philanthropists when they try to do good to others in ways which leave passive those to be benefited. There is a moral tragedy inherent in efforts to further the common good which prevent the result from being either good or common—not good, because it is at the expense of the active growth of those to be helped, and not common because these have no share in bringing the result about. The social welfare can be advanced only by means which enlist the positive interest and active energy of those to be benefited or "improved." The traditional notion of the great man, of the hero, works harm. It encourages the idea that some "leader" is to show the way; others are to follow in imitation. It takes time to arouse minds from apathy and lethargy, to get them to thinking for themselves, to share in making plans, to take part in their execution. But without active cooperation both in forming aims and in carrying them out there is no possibility of a common good.

The other side of this picture is the fact that all special privilege narrows the outlook of those who possess it, as well as limits the possibilities of development of those not having it. A very considerable portion of what is regarded as the inherent selfishness of mankind is the product of an inequitable distribution of power—inequitable because it shuts out some from the conditions which evoke and direct their capacities, while it produces a one-sided growth in those who have privilege. Much of the alleged unchangeableness of human nature signifies only that as long as social conditions are static and distribute opportunity unevenly, it is absurd to expect change in men's desires and aspirations. Special privilege always induces a standpat and reactionary attitude on the part of those who have it; in the end it usually provokes a blind rage of destruction on the part of those who suffer from it. The intellectual blindness caued by privileged and monopolistic possession is made evident in "rationalization" of the misery and cultural degradation of others which attend its existence. These are asserted to be the fault of those who suffer; to be the consequence of their own improvidence, lack of industry, willful ignorance, etc. There is no favored class in history which has not suffered from distorted ideas and ideals, just as the deprived class has suffered from inertia and undevelopment.

The tenor of this discussion is that the conception of common good, of general well-being, is a criterion which demands the full development of individuals in their distinctive individuality, not a sacrifice of them to some alleged vague larger good under the plea that it is "social." Only when individuals have initiative, independence of judgment, flexibility, fullness of experience, can they act so as to enrich the lives of others and only in this way can a truly common welfare be built up. The other side of this statement, and of the moral criterion, is that individuals are free to develop, to contribute and to share, only as social conditions break down walls of privilege and of monopolistic possession.

The fallacies which most often lead to putting individual development in opposition to attainment of a common good are (a) restricting the number of individuals to be considered, and (b) taking these individuals statically instead of dynamically, that is, with reference to what they are at a given time instead of in connection with their possibilities of growth. The historic "Individualism" criticized in the last chapter went astray at both these points. It confined its outlook to a particular class of individual, the industrialists, leaving out of account the much greater number of men, women, and children who were employees attached to machinery. And it treated the latter as if their efficiency, skill, intelligence, and character could be determined by their existing status, without regard to the developments which would take place if institutions were changed. The moral criterion attaches more weight to what men and women are capable of becoming than to their actual attainments, to possibilities than to possessions, even though the possessions be intellectual or even moral. Generosity in judgment of others as distinct from narrowness is largely a matter of estimating what they can grow into instead of judging them on the basis of what conditions have so far made of them. . . .

PHILOSOPHIES OF FREEDOM[5]

The next article, reprinted in its entirety, presents an extraordinarily rich, lucid, and comprehensive analysis of freedom. Dewey contends that both individuality and powers of consummatory behavior are functions of the social order. The growth and freedom of the individual can only occur insofar as he is able to function effectively as part of the larger whole of associated life and nature. Intelligence is thus the chief instrumentality of these values, but—again—it must be social intelligence, democratic behavior being widely practiced.

A recent book on *Sovereignty* concludes a survey of various theories on that subject with the following words: "The career of the notion of sovereignty illustrates the general characteristics of political thinking. The various forms of the notion have been apologies for causes rather than expressions of the disinterested love of knowledge. The notion has meant many things at different times; and the attacks upon it have sprung from widely different sources and been directed toward a multiplicity of goals. The genesis of all political ideas is to be understood in terms of their utility rather than of their truth and falsity."* Perhaps the same thing may be said of moral notions; I do not think there is any doubt that freedom is a word applied to many things of varied plumage and that it owes much of its magic to association with a variety of different causes. It has assumed various forms as needs have varied; its "utility" has been its service in helping men deal with many predicaments.

Primary among the needs it has been employed to meet and the interests it has served to promote is the moral. A good deal is assumed in asserting that the center of this moral need and cause is the fact of choice. The desire to dignify choice, to account for its significance in human affairs, to magnify that significance by making it the center of man's moral struggles and achievements has been reflected in the idea of freedom. There is an inexpugnable feeling that choice *is* freedom and that man without choice is a puppet, and that man then has no acts which he can call his very own. Without genuine choice, choice that when expressed in action makes things different from what they otherwise would be, men are but passive vehicles through which external forces operate. This feeling is neither self-explanatory nor self-justificatory. But at least it contributes an element in the statement of the problem of freedom. Choice is one of the things that demands examination.

Sovereignty, by Paul Ward, p. 167.

The theoretical formulation for the justification of choice as the heart of freedom became, however, involved at an early time with other interests; and they rather than the unprejudiced examination of the fact of choice determined the form taken by a widely prevalent philosophy of freedom. Men are given to praise and blame; to reward and punishment. As civilization matured, definitive civil agencies were instituted for "trying" men for modes of conduct so that if found guilty they might be punished. The fact of praise and blame, of civil punishment, directed at men on account of their behavior, signifies that they are held liable or are deemed responsible. The fact of punishment called attention, as men became more inquiring, to the ground of liability. Unless men were responsible for their acts, it was unjust to punish them; if they could not help doing what they did, what was the justice in holding them responsible for their acts, and blaming and punishing them? Thus a certain philosophy of the nature of choice as freedom developed as an apologia for an essentially legal interest: liability to punishment. The outcome was the doctrine known as freedom of will: the notion that a power called will, lies back of choice as its author, and is the ground of liability and the essence of freedom. This will has the power of indifferent choice; that is, it is equally free to choose one way or another unmoved by any desire or impulse, just because of a causal force residing in will itself. So established did this way of viewing choice become, that it is still commonly supposed that choice and the arbitrary freedom of will are one and the same thing.*

It is then worth while to pause in our survey while we examine more closely the nature of choice in relation to this alleged connection with free will, free here meaning unmotivated choice. Analysis does not have to probe to the depths to discover two serious faults in the theory. It is a man, a human being in the concrete, who is held responsible. If the act does not proceed from the man, from the human being in his concrete makeup of habits, desires and purposes, why should *he* be held liable and be punished? Will appears as a force outside of the individual person as he actually is, a force which is the real ultimate cause of the act. *Its* freedom to make a choice arbitrarily thus appears no ground for holding the human being as a concrete being responsible for its choice. Whatever else is to be said or left unsaid, choice must have some closer connection with the actual makeup of disposition and character than this philosophy allows.

We may seem then to be in a hopeless dilemma. If the man's nature, ori-

---

*Doubt may be felt as to the assertion that this interpretation of freedom developed in connection with the legal motif. The historic connecting link is found in the invasion of moral ideas by legal considerations that grew up in the Roman Empire. The association was perpetuated by the influence of Roman law and modes of moral thought, and even more by the incorporation of the latter in the theology and practices of the Christian Church, the nurse of morals in Europe.

ginal and acquired, makes him do what he does, how does his action differ from that of a stone or tree? Have we not parted with any ground for responsibility? When the question is looked at in the face of facts rather than in a dialectic of concepts it turns out not to have any terrors. Holding men to responsibility may make a decided difference in their *future* behavior; holding a stone or tree to responsibility is a meanlingless performance; it has no consequences; it makes no difference. If we locate the ground of liability in future consequences rather than in antecedent causal conditions, we moreover find ourselves in accord with actual practice. Infants, idiots, the insane, those completely upset, are not held to liability; the reason is that it is absurd—meaningless to do so, for it has no effect on their further actions. A child as he grows older finds responsibilities thrust upon him. This is surely not because freedom of the will has suddenly been inserted in him, but because his assumption of them is a necessary factor in his *further* growth and movement.

Something has been accomplished, I think, in transferring the issue from the past to the future, from antecedents to consequences. Some animals, dogs and horses, have their future conduct modified by the way they are treated. We can imagine a man whose conduct is changed by the way in which he is treated, so that it becomes different from what it would have been, and yet like the dog or horse, the change may be due to purely external manipulation, as external as the strings that move a puppet. The whole story has not then been told. There must be some practical participation from within to make the change that is effected significant in relation to choice and freedom. From *within*—that fact rules out the appeal, so facilely made, to will as a cause. Just what is signified by that participation by the human being himself in a choice that makes it really a choice?

In answering this question, it is helpful to go, apparently at least, far afield. Preferential action in the sense of selective behavior is a universal trait of all things, atoms and molecules as well as plants, animals and man. Existences, universally as far as we can tell, are cold and indifferent in the presence of some things and react energetically in either a positive or negative way to other things. These "preferences" or differential responses of behavior, are due to their own constitution; they "express" the nature of the things in question. They mark a distinctive contribution to what takes place. In other words, while changes in one thing may be described on the basis of changes that take place in other things, the *existence* of things which make certain changes having a certain quality and direction occur cannot be so explained. Selective behavior is the evidence of at least a rudimentary individuality or uniqueness in things. Such preferential action is not exactly what makes choice in the case of human beings. But unless there is involved in choice at least something continuous with the action of other things in nature, we could impute genuine reality to it only by isolating man from nature and thus treating him as in some sense a supra-natural being in the literal sense. Choice is more than just selectivity in behavior but it is also *at least* that.

What is the more which is involved in choice? Again, we may take a circuitous course. As we ascend in the range of complexity from inanimate things to plants, and from plants to animals and from other animals to man, we find an increasing variety of selective responses, due to the influence of life-history, or experiences already undergone. The manifestation of preferences becomes a "function" of an entire history. To understand the action of a fellowman we have to know something of the *course* of his life. A man is susceptible, sensitive, to a vast variety of conditions and undergoing varied and opposed experiences—as lower animals do not. Consequently a man in the measure of the scope and variety of his past experiences carries in his present capacity for selective response a large set of varied possibilities. That life-history of which his present preference is a function is complex. Hence the possibility of continuing diversification of behavior: in short, the distinctive *educability* of men. This factor taken by itself does not cover all that is included within the change of preference into genuine choice, but it has a bearing on that individual participation and individual contribution that is involved in choice as a mode of freedom. It is a large factor in our strong sense that we are not pushed into action from behind as are inanimate things. For that which is "behind" is so diversified in its variety and so intimately a part of the present self that preference becomes hesitant. Alternative preferences simultaneously manifest themselves.

Choice, in the distinctively human sense, then presents itself as one preference among and out of preferences; not in the sense of one preference already made and stronger than others, but as the formation of a new preference out of a conflict of preferences. If we can say upon what the formation of this new and determinate preference depends, we are close to finding that of which we are in search. Nor does the answer seem far to seek nor hard to find. As observation and foresight develop, there is ability to form signs and symbols that stand for the interaction and movement of things, without involving us in their actual flux. Hence the new preference may reflect this operation of mind, especially of forecast of the consequences of acting upon the various competing preferences. If we sum up, pending such qualification or such confirmation as further inquiry may supply, we may say that a stone has its preferential selections set by a relatively fixed, a rigidly set, structure and that no anticipation of the results of acting one way or another enter into the matter. The reverse is true of human action. Insofar as a variable life-history and intelligent insight and foresight enter into it, choice signifies a capacity for deliberately changing preferences. The hypothesis that is suggested is that in these two traits we have before us the

essential constituents of choice as freedom: the factor of individual participation.

Before that idea is further examined, it is, however, desirable to turn to
another philosophy of freedom. For the discussion thus far has turned about
the fact of choice alone. And such an exclusive emphasis may well render
some readers impatient. It may seem to set forth an idea of freedom which
is too individual, too "subjective." What has this affair to do with the freedom for which men have fought, bled and died: freedom from oppression
and despotism, freedom of institutions and laws? This question at once
brings to mind a philosophy of freedom which shifts the issue from choice
to action, action in an overt and public sense. This philosophy is sufficiently
well presented for our purposes in the idea of John Locke, the author, one
may say, of the philosophy of Liberalism in its classic sense. Freedom is
power to act in accordance with choice. It is actual ability displayed to carry
desire and purpose into operation, to *execute* choices when they are made.
Experience shows that certain laws and institutions prevent such operation
and execution. This obstruction and interference constitutes what we call
oppression, enslavement. Freedom, in fact, the freedom worth fighting for, is
secured by abolition of these oppressive measures, tyrannical laws and modes
of government. It is liberation, emancipation; the possession and active
manifestation of *rights*, the right to self-determination in action. To many
minds, the emphasis which has been put upon the formation of choice in
connection with freedom will appear an evasion, a trifling with metaphysical
futilities in comparison with this form of freedom, a desire for which has
caused revolutions, overthrown dynasties, and which as it is attained supplies the measure of human progress in freedom.

Before, however, we examine further into this notion in its relation to the
idea of choice already set forth, it will be well to consider another factor
which blended with the political *motif* just mentioned in forming the classic
philosophy of Liberalism. This other factor is the economic. Even in Locke
the development of property, industry and trade played a large part in
creating the sense that existing institutions were oppressive, and that they
should be altered to give men power to express their choices in action. About
a century after Locke wrote this implicit factor became explicit and dominant. In the later eighteenth century, attention shifted from power to
execute choice to power to carry *wants* into effect, by means of free—that is,
unimpeded—labor and exchange. The test of free institutions was then the
relation they bore to the unobstructed play of wants in industry and commerce and to the enjoyment of the fruits of labor. This notion blended with
the earlier political idea to form the philosophy of Liberalism so influential
in a large part of the nineteenth century. It led to the notion that all positive
action of government is oppressive; that its maxim should be Hands Off; and

that its action should be limited as far as possible to securing the freedom of behavior of one individual against interference proceeding from the exercise of similar freedom on the part of others; the theory of *laissez-faire* and the limitation of government to legal and police functions.

In the popular mind, the same idea has grown up in a noneconomic form, and with the substitution of instincts or impulses for wants. This phase has the same psychological roots as the economic philosophy of freedom, and is a large part of the popular philosophy of "self-expression." In view of this community of intellectual basis and origin, there is irony in the fact that the most ardent adherents of the idea of "self-expression" as freedom in personal and domestic relations are quite often equally ardent opponents of the idea of a like freedom in the region of industry and commerce. In the latter realm, they are quite aware of the extent in which the "self-expression" of a few may impede, although manifested in strict accordance with law, the self-expression of others. The popular idea of personal freedom as consisting in "free" expression of impulses and desire—free in the sense of unrestricted by law, custom and the inhibitions of social disapprovals—suggests the fallacy inhering in the wider economic concept, suggests it in a more direct way than can readily be derived from the more technical economic concept.

Instincts and impulses, however they may be defined, are part of the "natural" constitution of man; a statement in which "natural" signifies "native," original. The theory assigns a certain intrinsic rightness in this original structure, rightness in the sense of conferring upon them a title to pass into direct action, except when they directly and evidently interfere with similar self-manifestation in others. The idea thus overlooks the part played by interaction with the surrounding medium, especially the social, in generating impulses and desires. They are supposed to inhere in the "nature" of the individual when that is taken in a primal state, uninfluenced by interaction with an environment. The latter is thus thought of as purely external to an individual, and as irrelevant to freedom except when it interferes with the operation of native instincts and impulses. A study of history would reveal that this notion, like its theoretically formulated congeners in economic and political Liberalism, is a "faint rumor" left on the air of morals and politics by disappearing theological dogmas, which held that "nature" is thoroughly good as it comes from the creative hand of God, and that evil is due to corruption through artificial interference and oppression exercised by external or "social" conditions.

The point of this statement is that it suggests the essential fallacy in the elaborate political and economic theories of freedom entertained by classic Liberalism. They thought of individuals as endowed with an equipment of fixed and ready-made capacities, the operation of which if unobstructed by external restrictions would be freedom, and a freedom which would almost automatically solve political and economic problems. The difference between the theories is that one thought in terms of natural rights and the other in terms of natural wants as original and fixed. The difference is important with respect to special issues, but it is negligible with respect to the common premise as to the nature of freedom.

The liberalistic movement in each of its phases accomplished much practically. Each was influential in supplying inspiration and direction to reforming endeavors that modified institutions, laws and arrangements that *had* become oppressive. They effected a great and needed work of liberation. What were taken to be "natural" political rights and "natural" demands of human beings (natural being defined as inherent in an original and native fixed structure, moral or psychological) marked in fact the sense of new potentialities that were possessed by rather limited classes because of changes in social life due to a number of causes. On the political side, there was the limited class that found their activities restricted by survivals of feudal institutions; on the economic side, there was the rise of a manufacturing and trading class that found its activities impeded and thwarted by the fact that these same institutions worked to protect property interests connected with land at the expense of property interests growing out of business and commerce. Since the members of the two classes were largely identical, and since they represented the new moving forces, while their opponents represented interests vested and instituted in a past that knew nothing of these forces, political and economic liberalism fused as time went on, and in their fusion performed a necessary work of emancipation.

But the course of historic events has sufficiently proved that they emancipated the *classes* whose special interests they represented rather than human beings impartially. In fact, as the newly emancipated forces gained momentum, they actually imposed new burdens and subjected to new modes of oppression the mass of individuals who did not have a privileged economic status. It is impossible to justify this statement by an adequate assemblage of evidence. Fortunately it is not necessary to attempt the citation of relevant facts. Practically everyone admits that there is a new social problem, one that everywhere affects the issues of politics and law; and that this problem, whether we call it the relation of capital to labor, or individualism versus socialism, or the emancipation of wage earners, has an economic basis. The facts here are sufficient evidence that the ideals and hopes of the earlier liberal school have been frustrated by events; the universal emancipation and the universal harmony of interests they assumed are flagrantly contradicted by the course of events. The common criticism is that the liberal school was too "individualistic"; it would be equally pertinent to say that it was not "individualistic" enough. Its philosophy was such that it assisted the emancipation of individuals having a privileged antecedent status, but promoted no general liberation of all individuals.

The real objection to classic Liberalism does not hinge then upon concepts of "individual" and "society."

The real fallacy lies in the notion that individuals have such a native or original endowment of rights, powers and wants that all that is required on the side of institutions and laws is to eliminate the obstructions they offer to the "free" play of the natural equipment of individuals. The removal of obstructions did have a liberating effect upon such individuals as were antecedently possessed of the means, intellectual and economic, to take advantage of the changed social conditions. But it left all others at the mercy of the new social conditions brought about by the freed powers of those advantageously situated. The notion that men are equally free to act if only the same legal arrangements apply equally to all—irrespective of differences in education, in command of capital, and that control of the social environment which is furnished by the institution of property—is a pure absurdity, as facts have demonstrated. Since actual, that is, effective, rights and demands are products of interactions, and are not found in the original and isolated constitution of human nature, whether moral or psychological, mere elimination of obstructions is not enough. The latter merely liberates force and ability as that happens to be distributed by past accidents of history. This "free" action operates disastrously as far as the many are concerned. The only possible conclusion, both intellectually and practically, is that the attainment of freedom conceived as power to act in accord with choice depends upon positive and constructive changes in social arrangements.

We now have two seemingly independent philosophies, one finding freedom in choice itself, and the other in power to *act* in accord with choice. Before we inquire whether the two philosophies must be left in a position of mutual independence, or whether they link together in a single conception, it will be well to consider another track followed by another school of thinkers who also in effect identify freedom with operative power in action. This other school had a clear consciousness of the dependence of this power to act upon social conditions, and attempted to avoid and correct the mistakes of the philosophy of classic Liberalism. It substituted a philosophy of institutions for a philosophy of an original moral or psychological structure of individuals. This course was first charted by Spinoza, the great thinker of the seventeenth century. Although the philosophy of Liberalism had not as yet taken form, his ideas afford in anticipation an extraordinarily effective means of criticizing it. To Spinoza freedom was power. The "natural" rights of an individual consist simply in freedom to do whatever he *can* do—an idea probably suggested by Hobbes. But what *can* he do? The answer to that question is evidently a matter of the amount of the power he actually possesses. The whole discussion turns on this point. The answer in effect is that man in his original estate possesses a very limited amount of power. Men as "natural," that is, as native, beings are but parts, almost infinitesimally small fractions, of the whole of Nature to which they belong. In Spinoza's phraseology, they are "modes" not substances. As merely a part, the action of any part is limited on every hand by the action and counteraction of other parts. Even if there is power to initiate an act—a power inhering in any natural thing, inanimate as well as human—there is no power to carry it through; an action is immediately caught in an infinite and intricate network of *inter*-actions. If a man acts upon his private impulse, appetite or want and upon his private judgment about the aims and measures of conduct, he is just as much a subjected part of an infinitely complex whole as is a stock or stone. What he actually does is conditioned by equally blind and partial action of other parts of nature. Slavery, weakness, dependence, is the outcome, not freedom, power and independence.

There is no freedom to be reached by this road. Man has however intellect, capacity of thought. He is a mode not only of physical existence but of mind. Man is free only as he has power, and he can possess power only as he acts in accord with the whole, being reinforced by its structure and momentum. But in being a mode of mind he has a capacity for understanding the order of the whole to which he belongs, so that through development and use of intellect he may become cognizant of the order and laws of the whole, and insofar align his action with it. Insofar he shares the power of the whole and is free. Certain definite political implications follow from this identification of freedom with reason in operation. No individual can overcome his tendencies to act as a mode or mere part in isolation. Theoretic insight into the constitution of the whole is neither complete nor firm; it gives way under the pressure of immediate circumstances. Nothing is of as much importance to a reasonable creature in sustaining effectively his actual —or forceful—reasonableness as another reasonable being. We are bound together as parts of a whole, and only as others are free, through enlightenment as to the nature of the whole and its included parts, can any one be free. Law, government, institutions, all social arrangements must be informed with a rationality that corresponds to the order of the whole, which is true Nature or God, to the end that power of unimpeded action can be found anywhere. It would be difficult to imagine a more complete challenge to the philosophy of Locke and the Liberalistic school. Not power but impotency, not independence but dependence, not freedom but subjection is the natural estate of man—in the sense in which this school conceived "the natural." Law, however imperfect and poor, is at least a recognition of the universal, of the interconnection of parts, and hence operates as a schoolmaster to bring men to reason, power and freedom. The worst government is better than none, for some recognition of law, of universal relationship, is an absolute prerequisite. Freedom is not obtained by mere abolition of law and institutions, but by the progressive saturation of all laws and institutions with greater and greater acknowledgment of the necessary laws governing the constitution of things.

It can hardly be said that Spinoza's philosophy either in its general form or in its social aspect had any immediate effect—unless it was to render Spinoza a figure of objurgation. But some two centuries later a phase of reaction against the philosophy of Liberalism and all the ideas and practices associated with it arose in Germany; and Spinoza's ideas were incorporated indeed in a new metaphysical scheme and took on new life and significance. This movement may be called institutional idealism, Hegel being selected as its representative. Hegel substituted a single substance, called Spirit, for the two-faced substance of Spinoza, and restated the order and law of the whole in terms of an evolutionary or unfolding development instead of in terms of relations conceived upon a geometrical pattern. This development is intrinsically timeless or logical, after the manner of dialectic as conceived by Hegel. But from the outside this inner logical development of a whole is manifested serially or temporally in history. Absolute spirit embodies itself, by a series of piecemeal steps, in law and institutions; they are objective reason, and an individual becomes rational and free by virtue of participation in the life of these institutions, since in that participation he absorbs their spirit and meaning. The institutions of property, criminal and civil law, the family and above all the national state are the instrumentalities of rationality in outward action and hence of freedom. History is the record of the development of freedom through development of institutions. The philosophy of history is the understanding of this record in terms of the progressive manifestation of the objective form of absolute mind. Here we have instead of an anticipatory criticism and challenge of the classic liberal notion of freedom, a deliberate reflective and reactionary one. Freedom is a growth, an attainment, not an original possession, and it is attained by idealization of institutions and law and the active participation of individuals in their loyal maintenance, not by abolition or reduction in the interests of personal judgments and wants.

We now face what is admittedly the crucial difficulty in framing a philosophy of freedom: What is the connection or lack of connection between freedom defined in terms of choice and freedom defined in terms of power in action? Do the two ways of conceiving freedom have anything but the name in common? The difficulty is the greater because we have so little material to guide us in dealing with it. Each type of philosophy has been upon the whole developed with little consideration of the point of view of the other. Yet it would seem that there must be some connection. Choice would hardly be significant if it did not take effect in outward action, and if it did not when expressed in deeds make a difference in things. Action as power would hardly be prized if it were power like that of an avalanche or an earthquake. The power, the ability to command issues and consequences, that forms freedom must, it should seem, have some connection with that something in personality that is expressed in choice. At all events, the essential problem of freedom, is, it seems to me, the problem of the relation of choice and unimpeded effective action to each other.

I shall first give the solution to this problem that commends itself to me, and then trust to the further discussion not indeed to prove it but to indicate the reasons for holding it. There is an intrinsic connection between choice as freedom and power of action as freedom. A choice which intelligently manifests individuality enlarges the range of action, and this enlargement in turn confers upon our desires greater insight and foresight, and makes choice more intelligent. There is a circle, but an enlarging circle, or, if you please, a widening spiral. This statement is of course only a formula. We may perhaps supply it with meaning by first considering the matter negatively. Take for example an act following from a blind preference from an impulse not reflected upon. It will be a matter of luck if the resulting action does not get the one who acts into conflict with surrounding conditions. Conditions go against the realization of his preference; they cut across it, obstruct it, deflect its course, get him into new and perhaps more serious entanglements. Luck may be on his side. Circumstances may happen to be propitious or he may be endowed with native force that enables him to brush aside obstructions and sweep away resistances. He thus gets a certain freedom, judged from the side of power-to-do. But this result is a matter of favor, of grace, of luck; it is not due to anything in himself. Sooner or later he is likely to find his deeds at odds with conditions; an accidental success may only reinforce a foolhardy impulsiveness that renders a man's future subjection the more probable. Enduringly lucky persons are exceptions.

Suppose, on the other hand, our hero's act exhibits a choice expressing a preference formed after consideration of consequences, an intelligent preference. Consequences depend upon an interaction of what he starts to perform with his environment, so he must take the latter into account. No one can foresee all consequences because no one can be aware of all the conditions that enter into their production. Every person builds better or worse than he knows. Good fortune or the favorable cooperation of environment is still necessary. Even with his best thought, a man's proposed course of action may be defeated. But in as far as his act was truly a manifestation of intelligent choice, he learns something—as in a scientific experiment an inquirer may learn through his experimentation, his intelligently directed action, quite as much or even more from a failure than from a success. He finds out at least a little as to what was the matter with his prior choice. He can choose better and *do* better next time; "better choice" meaning a more reflective one, and "better doing" meaning one better coordinated with the conditions that are involved in realizing his purpose. Such control or power is never complete; luck or fortune, the propitious support of circumstances not fore-seeable is always involved. But at least such a person forms the habit of choosing and acting with conscious regard to the grain of circumstance, the run of affairs. And what is more to the point, such a man becomes able to turn frustration and failure to account in his further choices and purposes. Everything insofar serves his purpose—to be an intelligent human being. This gain in power or freedom can be nullified by no amount of external defeats.

In a phrase just used, it was implied that intelligent choice may operate on different levels or in different areas. A man may, so to speak, specialize in intelligent choices in the region of economic or political affairs; he may be shrewd, politic, within the limit of these conditions, and insofar attain power in action or be free. Moralists have always held that such success is not success, such power not power, such freedom not freedom, in the ultimate sense.

One does not need to enter upon hortatory moralization in order to em-ploy this contention of the great moral teachers for the sake of eliciting two points. The first is that there are various areas of freedom, because there is a plural diversity of conditions in our environment, and choice, intelligent choice, may select the special area formed by one special set of conditions —familial and domestic, industrial, pecuniary, political, charitable, scientific, ecclesiastical, artistic, etc. I do not mean of course that these areas are sharply delimited or that there is not something artificial in their segregation. But within limits, conditions are such that specialized types of choice and kinds of power or freedom develop. The second (and this is the one empha-sized by moral teachers in drawing a line between true and false power and freedom), is that there *may* be—these moral idealists insist there *is*— one area in which freedom and power is always attainable by anyone, no matter how much he may be blocked in other fields. This of course is the area they call *moral* in a distinctive sense. To put it roughly but more con-cretely: Anyone can be kind, helpful to others, just and temperate in his choices, and insofar be sure of achievement and power in action. It would take more rashness than I possess to assert that there is not an observation of reality in this insight of the great teachers of the race. But without taking up that point, one may venture with confidence upon a hypothetical statement. If and inasfar as this idea is correct, there is one way in which the force of fortunate circumstance and lucky original endowment is re-duced in comparison with the force of the factor supplied by personal individuality itself. Success, power, freedom in *special* fields is relatively in a maximum degree at the mercy of external conditions. But against kindness and justice there is no law: that is, no counteracting grain of things nor run of affairs. With respect to such choices, there may be freedom and power, no matter what the frustrations and failures in other modes of action. Such is the virtual claim of moral prophets.

An illustration drawn from the denial of the idea that there is an intimate connection of the two modes of freedom, namely, intelligent choice and power in action, may aid in clearing up the idea. The attitude and acts of other persons is of course one of the most important parts of the conditions involved in bringing the manifestation of preference to impotency or to power in action. Take the case of a child in a family where the environment formed by others is such as to humor all his choices. It is made easy for him to do what he pleases. He meets a minimum of resistance; upon the whole others cooperate with him in bringing his preferences to fulfillment. Within this region he seems to have free power of action. By description he is unimpeded, even aided. But it is obvious that as far as he is concerned, this is a matter of luck. He is "free" merely because his surrounding conditions happen to be of the kind they are, a mere happening or accident as far as his makeup and his preferences are concerned. It is evident in such a case that there is *no growth* in the intelligent exercise of preferences. There is rather a conversion of blind impulse into regular habits. Hence his attained freedom is such only in appearance: it disappears as he moves into other social conditions.

Now consider the opposite case. A child is balked, inhibited, interfered with and nagged pretty continuously in the manifestation of his spontaneous preferences. He is constantly "disciplined" by circumstances adverse to his preferences—as discipline is not infrequently conceived. Does it follow then that he develops in "inner" freedom, in thoughtful preference and purpose? The question answers itself. Rather is some pathological condition the outcome. "Discipline" is indeed necessary as a preliminary to any freedom that is more than unrestrained outward power. But our dominant conception of discipline is a travesty; there is only one genuine discipline, namely, that which takes effect in producing habits of observation and judgment that ensure intelligent desires. In short, while men do not think about and gain freedom in conduct unless they run during action against conditions that resist their original impulses, the secret of education consists in having that blend of check and favor which influences thought and foresight, and that takes effect in outward action through this prior modification of disposition and outlook.

I have borrowed the illustration from the life of a child at home or in school, because the problem is familiar and easily recognizable in those settings. But there is no difference when we consider the adult in industrial, political and ecclesiastic life. When social conditions are such as to prepare a prosperous career for a man's spontaneous preferences in advance, when things are made easy by institutions and by habits of admiration and approval, there is precisely the same kind of outward freedom, of relatively unimpeded action, as in the case of the spoiled child. But there is hardly more of freedom on the side of varied and flexible capacity of choice; preferences are restricted to the one line laid down, and in the end the individual becomes the slave of his successes. Others, vastly more in number, are in the state of the "disciplined" child. There is hard sledding for their spontaneous preferences; the grain of the environment, especially of existing economic arrangements, runs against them. But the check, the inhibition to the immediate operation of their native preferences no more confers on them the quality of intelligent choice than it does with the child who never gets a fair chance to try himself out. There is only a crushing that results in apathy and indifference; a deflection into evasion and deceit; a compensatory overresponsiveness to such occasions as permit untrained preferences to run riot—and all the other consequences which the literature of mental and moral pathology has made familiar.

I hope these illustrations may at least have rendered reasonably clear what is intended by our formula; by the idea that freedom consists in a trend of conduct such as causes choices to be more diversified and flexible, more plastic and more cognizant of their own meaning, while it enlarges their range of unimpeded operation. There is an important implication in this idea of freedom. The orthodox theory of freedom of the will and the classic theory of Liberalism both define freedom on the basis of something antecedently given, something already possessed. Unlike in content as are the imputation of unmotivated liberty of choice and of natural rights and native wants, the two ideas have an important element in common. They both seek for freedom in something already there, given in advance. Our idea compels us on the other hand to seek for freedom in something which comes to be, in a certain kind of growth; in consequences, rather than in antecedents. We are free not because of what we statically are, but inasfar as we are becoming different from what we have been. Reference to another philosophy of freedom, that of Immanuel Kant, who is placed chronologically in the generation preceding that of Hegel and institutional idealism, may aid in developing this idea. If we ignore the cumbrous technicalities of Kant, we may take him as one who was impressed by the rise of natural science and the role played in science by the idea of causation, this being defined as a necessary, universal or invariant connection of phenomena. Kant saw that in all consistency this principle applies to human phenomena as well as to physical; it is a law of all phenomena. Such a chain of linked phenomena left no room for freedom. But Kant believed in duty and duty postulates freedom. Hence in his moral being, man is not a phenomenon but a member of a realm of noumena to which as things-in-themselves free causality may be ascribed. It is with the problem rather than the solution we are concerned. How one and the same act can be, naturalistically speaking, causally determined while transcendentally speaking it is free from any such determination is so high a mystery that I shall pass it by.

But the *problem* as Kant stated it has the form in which it weighs most heavily on contemporary consciousness. The idea of a reign of law, of the inclusion of all events under law, has become almost omnipresent. No freedom seems to be left save by alleging that man is somehow supra-natural in his makeup—an idea of which Kant's noumenal and transcendental man is hardly more than a translation into a more impressive phraseology.

This way of stating the problem of freedom makes overt, explicit, the assumption that either freedom is something antecedently possessed or else it is nothing at all. The idea is so current that it seems hopeless to question its value. But suppose that the origin of every thought I have had and every word I have uttered is in some sense causally determined, so that if anybody knew enough he could explain the origin of each thought and each word just as the scientific inquirer ideally hopes to explain what happens physically. Suppose also—the argument is hypothetical and so imagination may be permitted to run riot—that my words had the effect of rendering the future choices of some one of my hearers more thoughtful; more cognizant of possible alternatives, and thereby rendering his future choices more varied, flexible and apt. Would the fact of antecedent causality deprive those future preferences of their actual quality? Would it take away their reality and that of their operation in producing their distinctive effects? There is no superstition more benumbing, I think, than the current notion that things are not what they are, and do not do what they are seen to do, because these things have themselves come into being in a causal way. Water is what it *does* rather than what it is caused by. The same is true of the fact of intelligent choice. A philosophy which looks for freedom in antecedents and one which looks for it in consequences, in a developing course of action, in becoming rather than in static being, will thus have very different notions about it.

Yet we cannot separate power to become from consideration of what already and antecedently is. Capacity to become different, even though we define freedom by it, must be a present capacity, something in some sense present. At this point of the inquiry, the fact that all existences whatever possess selectivity in action recurs with new import. It may sound absurd to speak of electrons and atoms exhibiting preference, still more perhaps to attribute bias to them. But the absurdity is wholly a matter of the words used. The essential point is that they have a certain opaque and irreducible individuality which shows itself in what they do; in the fact that they behave in certain ways and not in others. In the description of causal sequences, we still have to start with and from existences, things that are individually and uniquely just what they are. The fact that we can reduce changes that occur to certain uniformities and regularities does not eliminate this original element of individuality, of preference and bias. On the contrary, the statement of laws presupposes just this capacity. We cannot escape this fact by an attempt to treat each thing as an effect of other things. That merely pushes individuality back into those other things. Since we have to admit individuality no matter how far we carry the chase, we might as well forgo the labor and start with the unescapable fact.

In short, anything that is has something unique in itself, and this unique something, enters into what it does. Science does not concern itself with the individualities of things. It is concerned with their *relations*. A law or statement of uniformity like that of the so-called causal sequence tells us nothing about a thing inherently; it tells us only about an invariant relation sustained in behavior of that thing with that of other things. That this fact implies contingency as an ultimate and irreducible trait of existence is something too complicated to go into here. But evidence could be stated from many contemporary philosophers of science, not writing with any thought of freedom in mind, but simply as interpreters of the methods and conclusions of science, to the effect that the laws leave out of account the inner being of things, and deal only with their relations with other things. Indeed, if this were the place and if I only knew enough, it could be shown, I think, that the great change now going on in the physical sciences, is connected with this idea. Older formulas were in effect guilty of confusion. They took knowledge of the relations that things bear to one another as if it were knowledge of the things themselves. Many of the corrections that are now being introduced into physical theories are due to recognition of this confusion.

The point needs an elaboration that cannot here be given if its full import for the idea and fact of freedom is to be clearly perceived. But the connection is there and its general nature may be seen. The fact that all things show bias, preference or selectivity of reaction, while not itself freedom, is an indispensable condition of any human freedom. The present tendency among scientific men is to think of laws as statistical in nature—that is, as statements of an "average" found in the behavior of an enormous number of things, no two of which are exactly alike. If this line of thought be followed out, it implies that the existence of laws or uniformities and regularities among natural phenomena, human acts included, does not in the least exclude the item of choice as a distinctive fact having its own distinctive consequences. No law does away with individuality of existence, each having its own particular way of operating; for a law is concerned with relations and hence presupposes the being and operation of individuals. If choice is found to be a distinctive act, having distinctive consequences, then no appeal to the authority of scientific law can militate in any way against its reality. The problem reduces itself to one of fact. Just what *is* intelligent choice and just what does it effect in human life? I cannot ask you to retraverse the ground already gone over. But I do claim that the considerations already adduced reveal that what men actually cherish under the name of freedom is that power of varied and flexible growth, of change of disposition and character, that springs from intelligent choice, so there is a sound basis for the commonsense practical belief in freedom, although theories in justification of this belief have often taken an erroneous and even absurd form.

We may indeed go further than we have gone. Not only is the presence of uniform relations of change no bar to the reality of freedom, but these are, *when known*, aids to the development of that freedom. Take the suppositious case already mentioned. That my ideas have causes signifies that their *rise*, their *origin* (not their nature), is a change connected with other changes. If I only knew the connection, my power over getting certain ideas would be that much increased. The same thing holds good of any effect my idea may have upon the ideas and choices of someone else. Knowledge of the conditions under which a choice *arises* is the same as potential ability to guide the formation of choices intelligently. This does not eliminate the distinctive quality of choice; choice is still choice. But it is now an intelligent choice instead of a dumb and stupid one, and thereby the probability of its leading to freedom in unimpeded action is increased.

This fact explains the strategic position occupied in our social and political life by the issue of freedom of thought and freedom of speech. It is unnecessary to dwell by way of either laudation or exhortation upon the importance of this freedom. If the position already taken—namely, that freedom resides in the development of preferences into intelligent choices—is sound, there is an explanation of the central character of this particular sort of freedom. It has been assumed, in accord with the whole theory of Liberalism, that all that is necessary to secure freedom of thought and expression, is removal of external impediments: take away artificial obstructions and thought will operate. This notion involves all the errors of individualistic psychology. Thought is taken to be a native capacity or faculty; all it needs to operate is an outer chance. Thinking, however, is the most difficult occupation in which man engages. If the other arts have to be acquired through ordered apprenticeship, the power to think requires even more conscious and consecutive attention. No more than any other art is it developed internally. It requires favorable objective conditions, just as the art of painting requires paint, brushes and canvas. The most important problem in freedom of thinking is whether social conditions obstruct the development of judgment and insight or effectively promote it. We take for granted the necessity of special opportunity and prolonged education to secure ability to think in a special calling, like mathematics. But we appear to assume that ability to think effectively in social, political and moral matters is a gift of God, and that the gift operates by a kind of spontaneous combustion. Few would perhaps defend this doctrine thus boldly stated; but upon the whole we act as if that were true. Even our deliberate education, our schools, are conducted so as to promote habits of thought. If that is true of them, what is not true of the other social institutions as to their effect upon thought?

This state of things accounts, to my mind, for the current indifference to what is the very heart of actual freedom: freedom of thought. It is considered to be enough to have certain legal guarantees of its possibility. Encroachment upon even the nominal legal guarantees appears to arouse less and less resentment. Indeed, since the mere absence of legal restrictions may take effect only in stimulating the expression of half-baked and foolish ideas, and since the effect of their expression may be idle or harmful, popular sentiment seems to be growing less and less adverse to the exercise of even overt censorship. A genuine energetic interest in the cause of human freedom will manifest itself in a jealous and unremitting care for the influence of social institutions upon the attitudes of curiosity, inquiry, weighing and testing of evidence. I shall begin to believe that we care more for freedom than we do for imposing our own beliefs upon others in order to subject them to our will, when I see that the main purpose of our schools and other institutions is to develop powers of unremitting and discriminating observation and judgment.

The other point is similar. It has often been assumed that freedom of speech, oral and written, is independent of freedom of thought—but you cannot take the latter away in any case, since it goes on inside of them where it cannot be got at. No idea could be more mistaken. Expression of ideas in communication is one of the indispensable conditions of the awakening of thought not only in others, but in ourselves. If ideas when aroused cannot be communicated they either fade away or become warped and morbid. The open air of public discussion and communication is an indispensable condition of the birth of ideas and knowledge and of other growth into health and vigor.

I sum up by saying that the possibility of freedom is deeply grounded in our very beings. It is one with our individuality, our being uniquely what we are and not imitators and parasites of others. But like all other possibilities, this one has to be actualized; and, like all others, it can only be actualized through interaction with objective conditions. The question of political and economic freedom is not an addendum or afterthought, much less a deviation or excrescence, in the problem of personal freedom. For the conditions that form political and economic liberty are required in order to realize the potentiality of freedom each of us carries with him in his very structure. Constant and uniform relations in change and a knowledge of them in "laws," are not a hindrance to freedom, but a necessary factor in coming to be effectively that which we have the capacity to grow into. Social conditions interact with the preferences of an individual (that *are* his individuality) in a way favorable to actualizing freedom only when they develop intelligence, not abstract knowledge and abstract thought, but power of vision and reflection. For these take effect in making preference, desire and purpose more flexible, alert, and resolute. Freedom has too long been thought of as an indeterminate power operating in a closed and ended world. In its reality, freedom is a resolute will operating in a world in some respects indeterminate, because open and moving toward a new future.

INTELLIGENCE AND DEMOCRATIC INSTITUTIONS[6]

In a misleading choice of words, Dewey uses "democratic theory" to refer to the inquiry into the conditions of democratic life. But the inquiry is of the utmost moral significance nonetheless.

Discussion up to this point has been intended to elicit two principles. One of them is that the views about human nature that are popular at a given time are usually derived from contemporary social currents: currents so conspicuous as to stand out or else less marked and less effective social movements which a special group believes *should* become dominant—as for example, in the case of the legislative reason with Plato, and of competitive love of gain with classical economists. The other principle is that reference to components of original human nature, even if they actually exist, explains no social occurrence whatever and gives no advice or direction as to what policies it is better to adopt. This does not mean that reference to them must necessarily be of a "rationalizing" concealed apologetic type. It means that whenever it occurs with practical significance it has *moral* not psychological import. For, whether brought forward from the side of conserving what already exists or from that of producing change, it is an expression of valuation, and of purpose determined by estimate of values. When a trait of human nature is put forward on this basis, it is in its proper context and is subject to intelligent examination.

The prevailing habit, however, is to assume that a social issue does not concern values to be preferred and striven for, but rather something predetermined by the constitution of human nature. This assumption is the source of serious social ills. Intellectually it is a reversion to the type of explanation that governed physical science until say, the seventeenth century: a method now seen to have been the chief source of the long-continued retardation of natural science. For this type of theory consists of appeal to general forces to "explain" what happens.

Natural science began to progress steadily only when general forces were banished and inquiry was directed instead to ascertaining correlations that exist between observed changes. Popular appeal to, say, electricity, light or heat, etc., as a force to account for some particular event still exists, as to electricity to explain storms attended by thunder and lightning. Scientific men themselves often talk in similar words. But such general terms are in their case shorthand expressions. They stand for uniform relations between events that are observed to occur; they do not mark appeal to something be-hind what happens and which is supposed to produce it. If we take the case of the lightning flash and electricity, Franklin's identification of the former as of the electrical kind brought it into connection with things from which it had been formerly isolated, and knowledge about them was available in dealing with it. But instead of electricity being an explanatory force, knowl-edge that lightning is an electrical phenomenon opened a number of special problems, some of which are still unsolved.

If the analogy between the relatively sterile condition of natural science when this method prevailed and the present state of the social "sciences" is not convincing, the misdirection of inquiry that results may be cited in evi-dence. There is an illusion of understanding, when in reality there is only a general word that conceals lack of understanding. Social ideas are kept in the domain of glittering generalities. Opinion as distinct from knowledge breeds controversy. Since what is regarded as a cause is that which is used as an agency or instrumentality of production, there is no controlled method of bringing anything into existence and of preventing the occurrence of that not wanted, save as there is knowledge of the conditions of its occurrence. When men knew that a certain kind of friction produced fire, they had at command at least one means, rubbing of sticks together, for producing fire when they wanted it. And it goes without saying that greater acquaintance with causal conditions has multiplied men's practical ability to have fire when needed, and to use it for an increased number of ends. The principle applies to the relation of social theory and social action.

Finally theories supposed to explain the course of events are used to urge and justify certain practical policies. Marxism is, of course, a striking in-stance. But it is so far from being the only instance that non-Marxian and anti-Marxian social theories often exemplify the principle. Utilitarianism used the idea that pleasure and pain are the sole determinant of human action to advance a sweeping theory of legislation, judicial and penal procedure; namely, that they be directed to secure the greatest happiness of the greatest number. Explanation of events on the basis of free, unimpeded manifestation of wants was used on the practical side as active propaganda for an open-market economic regime with all political and legal measures adapted to it. Belief in the general character of the alleged "force" rendered it unnecessary to keep track of actual events so as to check the theory. If things happened that obviously went contrary to the creed, the inconsistency was not taken as a reason for examining it, but as the cue for alleging special reasons for the failure, so that the truth of the principle could be kept intact.

Mere general ideas can be argued for and against without the necessity of recourse to observation. The arguments are saved from being a mere matter of words only because there are certain emotional attitudes involved. When general ideas are not capable of being continuously checked and revised by observation of what actually takes place, they are, as a mere truism, in the field of opinion. Clash of opinions is in that case the occasion for controversy, not, as is now the case in natural science, a location of a problem and an occasion for making further observations. If any generalization can be safely laid down about intellectual matters and their consequences, it is that the reign of opinion, and of controversial conflicts, is a function of absence of methods of inquiry which bring new facts to light and by so doing establish the basis for consensus of beliefs.

Social events are sufficiently complex in any case so that the development of effective methods of observation, yielding generalization about correlation of events, is difficult. The prevailing type of theory adds the further handicap of making such observation unnecessary—save as this and that arbitrarily selected event is used in argumentative controversy. The prime necessity is to frame general ideas, first, to promote search for problems—as against the assumption of a ready-made solution in view of which there are no problems; and, secondly, to solve these problems by generalizations that state interactions between analytically observed events.

I return to the particular social philosophy which associates the economic regime actuated by effort to make private profit with the essential conditions of free and democratic institutions. It is not necessary to go back to the theory in its early English formulation at the hands of laissez-faire liberals. For in spite of the discrediting of the philosophy by events, efforts put forth in this country to establish so-called social control of business has led at present to its revival in an extremely naked form. One does not need to endorse the measures for control that are used to be aware of the fallacy of the theory upon which current objections to them are based. The theory is that capitalism, interpreted as the maximum range of free personal opportunity for production and exchange of goods and services is the Siamese twin of democracy. For the former is identical, so it is claimed, with the personal qualities of initiative, independence, vigor, that are the basic conditions of free political institutions. Hence, so it is argued, the check given to the operation of these personal qualities by governmental regulation of business activities is at the same time an attack upon the practical and moral conditions for the existence of political democracy.

I am not concerned here with the merits of the special arguments put forth in behalf and against the measures employed. The point is that appeal to certain alleged human motivations in a wholesale way, such as "initiative, independence, enterprise" at large, obscures the need for observation of events in the concrete. If and when special events are observed, interpretation of them is predestined instead of growing out of what is observed. By keeping the issues in the realm of opinion, appeal to equally general wholesale views on the other side is promoted. Then we get a kind of head-on conflict between something called "individualism" on one side and "socialism" on the other.

Examination of concrete conditions might disclose certain specifiable conditions under which both of the methods vaguely pointed at by these words would operate to advantage.

The current use of the word *enterprise* as an honorific term is especially instructive with regard to the attempt to draw support for policies from a reference to general inherent traits of human nature. For the only legitimate signification of "enterprise" is a neutral one, an *undertaking* the desirability of which is a matter of actual results produced, which accordingly need to be studied in the concrete. But *enterprise* is given the significance of a certain desirable trait of human nature, so that the issue is taken out of the field of observation into that of opinion plus a eulogistic emotion. "Enterprise" like "initiative" and like "industry" can be exerted in behalf of an indefinite number of objects; the words may designate the activities of an Al Capone or a racketeering labor union as well as a socially useful industrial undertaking.

The case is cited in some detail because it provides a striking example, first, of the conversion of an existing mode of social behavior into a psychological property of human nature; and, secondly, conversion of an alleged matter of psychological fact into a principle of value—a moral matter. Social problems that are set by conditions having definite spatial and temporal boundaries—which have to be determined by observation—are made into matters capable of absolute determination without reference to conditions of place and date. Hence they become matters of opinion and controversial argument—and as the latter decides nothing, the final tendency is to appeal to force as the ultimate arbiter.

The theory of the components of human nature used by the intellectual radicals of Great Britain to justify popular government and freedom included more than the self-interest motivation. It was officially held that sympathy with the gains and losses, the pleasures and pains of others, is a native part of the human endowment. The two components, self-interest and sympathy, opposite in quality, were ingeniously linked together in the complete doctrine—occasionally with explicit reference to the supposedly analogous centripetal and centrifugal components of Newtonian celestial mechanics. The self-interest phase supplied the foundation of the theory of public and governmental action; the sympathetic phase took care of the relations of individuals to one another in their private capacities. The doctrine taught that if political institutions were reformed to do away with special privileges and unfair favoritisms, the sympathetic motive would have a vastly enlarged field of effective and successful operation, since bad institutions were the chief cause that led men to find their personal advantage in acts injurious to others.

The theory was even more important in the reaction it called out than in itself. For "organic idealistic" philosophies developed in Germany during the nineteenth century and now form the theoretical background and justification of totalitarianism. They took their clew and point of departure from the weaknesses of the theories that based politics and morals, in theory and in practice, upon alleged components of human nature. An adequate account of the form and substance of the reaction would take us into matters which cannot be set forth without going into technicalities. But its basis is simple.

The attempt to locate the source of authority of politics and morals in human nature was regarded as the source of anarchy, disorder, and conflict— an attempt to build social institutions and personal relationships upon the most unstable of shifting quicksands. At the same time, the philosophers who formulated the new view were Protestants and Northerners. Hence their reaction did not move them to urge acceptance of the doctrines of the Roman Church as the bulwark against the dissolving tendencies of ultra-individualistic ideas and policies.

The French Revolution, with its excesses, was uniformly regarded in German thought as the logical outcome of the attempt to locate authority where nothing binding could be found. It was thus taken to be a practical large-scale demonstration of the weakness inherent in the position. The most that could be said for the doctrine was what could be said in defense of the French Revolution—it helped to get rid of abuses that had grown up. As a positive and constructive principle, it was a tragic delusion. The statement of the Rights of Man setting forth the official creed of the Revolution was said to be a summary of the false doctrines that had produced all the characteristic evils of the age. The protest, as just said, refused to accept the doctrines of the Church as the basis for its criticisms and for the constructive measures it proposed. It was itself too deeply influenced by the conditions which had produced the individualism against which it revolted. The extent of this influence is why the movement is criticized by representatives of the Hellenic-medieval ideas as itself intensely "subjectivistic." It found the way to "reconcile" freedom and authority, individuality and law, by setting up an Absolute Self, Mind, Spirit, of which human beings are individually partial manifestations, a "truer" and fuller manifestation being found in social institutions, the state and the course of history. Since history is the final court of judgment and since it represents the movement of absolute Spirit, appeal to force to settle issues between nations is not "really" an appeal to force, but rather to the ultimate logic of absolute reason. The individualistic movement was a necessary transitional movement to bring men to recognition of the primacy and ultimacy of Spirit and Personality in the constitution of nature, man, and society. German organic idealism was to save all that is true in the movement, while eliminating its errors and dangers by lifting it up to the plane of absolute Self and Spirit. There is much that is technical in the movement; much of its detail can be explained only on the ground of special intellectual events. But its heart and core is found in its attempt to find a "higher" justification for individuality and freedom where the latter are merged with law and authority, which *must* be rational since they are manifestations of Absolute Reason. Contemporary totalitarianism has no difficulty in discovering that the Germanic racial spirit embodied in the German state is an adequate substitute, for all practical purposes, for the Hegelian Absolute Spirit.

Rousseau is usually, and in many respects properly, regarded as the prophet and intellectual progenitor of the French Revolution. But by one of those ironies with which history abounds he was also a stepfather of the theory that came to full expression in Germany. He served in this capacity partly indirectly by his attack on culture which, as previously said, was the challenge that resulted in glorification of culture over against human nature. But he also acted positively and directly. For in his political writings he advanced the idea that a Common Will is the source of legitimate political institutions; that freedom and law are one and the same thing in the operations of the Common Will, for it must act for the Common Good and hence for the "real" or true Good of every individual.

If the latter set up their purely personal desires against the General Will, it was accordingly legitimate (indeed necessary) to *"force* them to be free." Rousseau intended his theory to state the foundation of self-governing institutions and majority rule. But his premise was employed to prove that the Common—or Universal—Will and Reason was embodied in the national state. Its most adequate incarnation was in those states in which the authority of law, order, and discipline had not been weakened by democratic heresies—a view which was used in Germany after the Napoleonic conquest to create an aggressive national spirit in that country, one which provided the basis for systematic depreciation of French "materialistic" civilization as over against German *Kultur*—a depreciation later extended to condemnation of democratic institutions in any country.

While this brief exposition of the reaction against the individualistic theory of human nature suggests the ground pattern of National Socialism, it also throws some light upon the predicament in which democratic countries find themselves. The fact that the individualistic theory was used a century and more ago to justify political self-government and then aided promotion of its cause does not constitute the theory a present trustworthy guide of democratic action. It is profitable to read today the bitterly vivid denunciations of Carlyle on the theory as it was originally put forth. He denounced with equal fierceness the attempt to erect political authority upon the basis of self-interest and private morals upon the exercise of sympathy. The latter was sentimentalism run riot and the former was "Anarchy plus the Constable"—the latter being needed to preserve even a semblance of outward order. His plea for discipline and order included even a plea for leadership by select persons.

The present predicament may be stated as follows: Democracy does involve a belief that political institutions and law be such as to take fundamental account of human nature. They must give it freer play than any nondemocratic institutions. At the same time, the theory, legalistic and moralistic, about human nature that has been used to expound and justify this reliance upon human nature has proved inadequate. Upon the legal and political side, during the nineteenth century it was progressively overloaded with ideas and practices which have more to do with business carried on for profit than with democracy. On the moralistic side, it has tended to substitute emotional exhortation to act in accord with the Golden Rule for the discipline and the control afforded by incorporation of democratic ideals into *all* the relations of life. Because of lack of an adequate theory of human nature in its relations to democracy, attachment to democratic ends and methods has tended to become a matter of tradition and habit—an excellent thing as far as it goes, but when it becomes routine is easily undermined when change of conditions changes other habits. . . .

The impact of the humanist view of democracy upon all forms of culture, upon education, science and art, morals and religion, as well as upon industry and politics, saves it from the criticism passed upon moralistic exhortation. For it tells us that we need to examine every one of the phases of human activity to ascertain what effects it has in release, maturing and fruition of the potentialities of human nature. It does not tell us to "rearm morally" and all social problems will be solved. It says, Find out how all the constituents of our existing culture are operating and then see to it that whenever and wherever needed they be modified in order that their workings may release and fulfill the possibilities of human nature. . . .

INTELLIGENCE AS SOCIAL[7]

Effective intelligence is a social affair. This means not only that the growth of knowledge and the confirmation of hypotheses are social processes; it also means that the intelligence of any particular individual is enhanced in its effectiveness by virtue of participating in these processes of inquiry and criticism. Even more fundamentally, when intelligent modes of behavior are embodied in social practice, the habits of intelligent conduct are acquired as a matter of normal growth.

Dewey's principal criticism of prevailing theories of inquiry was that they uniformly neglected the creative functions of intelligence. In assuming that ideas are merely summaries of antecedently existing phenomena, or copies of antecedently existing structures, such theories never recognized that a hypothesis predicts future events which are contingent upon a proposed reconstruction of present events. Hypotheses indicate ways in which circumstances of nature can be reordered to produce novel outcomes. They are of the greatest use, therefore, in the practical context of directing conduct to consummatory ends by reconstructing problematic situations.

Liberalism has to assume the responsibility for making it clear that intelligence is a social asset and is clothed with a function as public as is its origin, in the concrete, in social cooperation. It was Comte who, in reaction against the purely individualistic ideas that seemed to him to underlie the French Revolution, said that in mathematics, physics and astronomy there is no right of private conscience. If we remove the statement from the context of actual scientific procedure, it is dangerous because it is false. The individual inquirer has not only the right but the duty to criticize the ideas, theories and "laws" that are current in science. But if we take the statement in the context of scientific method, it indicates that he carries on this criticism in virtue of a socially generated body of knowledge and by means of methods that are not of private origin and possession. He uses a method that retains public validity even when innovations are introduced in its use and application.

Henry George, speaking of ships that ply the ocean with a velocity of five or six hundred miles a day, remarked, "There is nothing whatever to show that the men who today build and navigate and use such ships are one whit superior in any physical or mental quality to their ancestors, whose best vessel was a coracle of wicker and hide. The enormous improvement which these ships show is not an improvement of human nature; it is an improvement of society—it is due to a wider and fuller union of individual efforts in accomplishment of common ends." This single instance, duly pondered, gives a better idea of the nature of intelligence and its social office than would a volume of abstract dissertation. Consider merely two of the factors that enter in and their social consequences. Consider what is involved in the production of steel, from the first use of fire and then the crude smelting of ore, to the processes that now effect the mass production of steel. Consider also the development of the power of guiding ships across trackless wastes from the day when they hugged the shore, steering by visible sun and stars, to the appliances that now enable a sure course to be taken. It would require a heavy tome to describe the advances in science, in mathematics, astronomy, physics, chemistry, that have made these two things possible. The record would be an account of a vast multitude of cooperative efforts, in which one individual uses the results provided for him by a countless number of other individuals, and uses them so as to add to the common and public store. A survey of such facts brings home the actual social character of intelligence as it actually develops and makes its way. Survey of the consequences upon the ways of living of individuals and upon the terms on which men associate together, due to the new method of transportation would take us to the wheat farmer of the prairies, the cattle raiser of the plains, the cotton grower of the South; into a multitude of mills and factories, and to the counting-room of banks, and what would be seen in this country would be repeated in every country of the globe.

It is to such things as these, rather than to abstract and formal psychology that we must go if we would learn the nature of intelligence: in itself, in its origin and development, and its uses and consequences. At this point, I should like to recur to an idea put forward in the preceding chapter. I then referred to the contempt often expressed for reliance upon intelligence as a social method, and I said this scorn is due to the identification of intelligence with native endowments of individuals. In contrast to this notion, I spoke of the power of individuals to appropriate and respond to the intelligence, the knowledge, ideas and purposes that have been integrated in the medium in which individuals live. Each of us knows, for example, some mechanic of ordinary native capacity who is intelligent within the matters of his calling. He has lived in an environment in which the cumulative intelligence of a multitude of cooperating individuals is embodied, and by the use of his native capacities he makes some phase of this intelligence his own. Given a social medium in whose institutions the available knowledge, ideas and art of humanity were incarnate, and the average individual would rise to undreamed heights of social and political intelligence.

The rub, the problem, is found in the proviso. Can the intelligence actually existent and potentially available be embodied in that institutional medium in which an individual thinks, desires and acts? Before dealing directly with this question, I wish to say something about the operation of intelligence in our present political institutions, as exemplified by current practices of democratic government. I would not minimize the advance scored in substitution of methods of discussion and conference for the method of arbitrary rule. But the better is too often the enemy of the still better. Discussion, as the manifestation of intelligence in political life, stimulates publicity; by its means sore spots are brought to light that would otherwise remain hidden. It affords opportunity for promulgation of new ideas. Compared with despotic rule, it is an invitation to individuals to concern themselves with public affairs. But discussion and dialectic, however indispensable they are to the elaboration of ideas and policies after ideas are once put forth, are weak reeds to depend upon for systematic origination of comprehensive plans, the plans that are required if the problem of social organization is to be met. There was a time when discussion, the comparison of ideas already current so as to purify and clarify them, was thought to be sufficient in discovery of the structure and laws of physical nature. In the latter field, the method was displaced by that of experimental observation guided by comprehensive working hypotheses, and using all the resources made available by mathematics.

But we still depend upon the method of discussion, with only incidental scientific control, in politics. Our system of popular suffrage, immensely valuable as it is in comparison with what preceded it, exhibits the idea that intelligence is an individualistic possession, at best enlarged by public discussion. Existing political practice, with its complete ignoring of occupational groups and the organized knowledge and purposes that are involved in the existence of such groups, manifests a dependence upon a summation of individuals quantitatively, similar to Bentham's purely quantitative formula of the greatest sum of pleasures of the greatest possible number. The formation of parties or, as the eighteenth-century writers called them, factions, and the system of party government is the practically necessary counterweight to a numerical and atomistic individualism. The idea that the conflict of parties will, by means of public discussion, bring out necessary public truths is a kind of political watered-down version of the Hegelian dialectic, with its synthesis arrived at by a union of antithetical conceptions. The method has nothing in common with the procedure of organized cooperative inquiry which has won the triumphs of science in the field of physical nature. . . .

. . . Grateful recognition is due early liberals for their valiant battle in behalf of freedom of thought, conscience, expression and communication. The civil liberties we possess, however precariously today, are in large measure the fruit of their efforts and those of the French liberals who engaged in the same battle. But their basic theory as to the nature of intelligence is such as to offer no sure foundation for the permanent victory of the cause they espoused. They resolved mind into a complex of external associations among atomic elements, just as they resolved society itself into a similar compound of external associations among individuals, each of whom has his own independently fixed nature. Their psychology was not in fact the product of impartial inquiry into human nature. It was rather a political weapon devised in the interest of breaking down the rigidity of dogmas and of institutions that had lost their relevancy. Mill's own contention that psychological laws of the kind he laid down were prior to the laws of men living and communicating together, acting and reacting upon one another, was itself a political instrument forged in the interest of criticism of beliefs and institutions that he believed should be displaced. The doctrine was potent in exposure of abuses; it was weak for constructive purposes. Bentham's assertion that he introduced the method of experiment into the social sciences held good as far as resolution into atoms acting externally upon one another, after the Newtonian model, was concerned. It did not recognize the place in experiment of comprehensive social ideas as working hypotheses in direction of action.

The practical consequence was also the logical one. When conditions had changed and the problem was one of constructing social organization from individual units that had been released from old social ties, liberalism fell upon evil times. The conception of intelligence as something that arose from the association of isolated elements, sensations and feelings left no room for farreaching experiments in construction of a new social order. It was definitely hostile to everything like collective social planning. The doctrine of laissez-faire was applied to intelligence as well as to economic action, although the conception of experimental method in science demands a control by comprehensive ideas, projected in possibilities to be realized by action. Scientific method is as much opposed to go-as-you-please in intellectual matters as it is to reliance upon habits of mind whose sanction is that they were formed by "experience" in the past. The theory of mind held by the early liberals advanced beyond dependence upon the past but it did not arrive at the idea of experimental and constructive intelligence.

The dissolving atomistic individualism of the liberal school evoked by way of reaction the theory of organic objective mind. But the effect of the latter theory embodied in idealistic metaphysics was also hostile to intentional social planning. The historical march of mind, embodied in institutions, was believed to account for social changes—all in its own good time. A similar conception was fortified by the interest in history and in evolution so characteristic of the later nineteenth century. The materialistic philosophy of Spencer joined hands with the idealistic doctrine of Hegel in throwing the burden of social direction upon powers that are beyond deliberate social foresight and planning. The economic dialectic of history, substituted by Marx for the Hegelian dialectic of ideas, as interpreted by the social-democratic party in Europe, was taken to signify an equally inevitable movement toward a predestined goal. . . .

. . . Decline in the prestige of suffrage and of parliamentary government are intimately associated with the belief, manifest in practice even if not expressed in words, that intelligence is an individual possession to be reached by means of verbal persuasion.

This fact suggests, by way of contrast, the genuine meaning of intelligence in connection with public opinion, sentiment and action. The crisis in democracy demands the substitution of the intelligence that is exemplified in scientific procedure for the kind of intelligence that is now accepted. The need for this change is not exhausted in the demand for greater honesty and impartiality, even though these qualities be now corrupted by discussion carried on mainly for purposes of party supremacy and for imposition of some special but concealed interest. These qualities need to be restored. But the need goes further. The social use of intelligence would remain deficient even if these moral traits were exalted, and yet intelligence continued to be identified simply with discussion and persuasion, necessary as are these things. Approximation to use of scientific method in investigation and of the engineering mind in the invention and projection of far-reaching social plans is demanded. The habit of considering social realities in terms of cause and effect and social policies in terms of means and consequences is still inchoate. The contrast between the state of intelligence in politics and in the physical control of nature is to be taken literally. What has happened in this latter is the outstanding demonstration of the meaning of organized intelligence. The combined effect of science and technology has released more productive energies in a bare hundred years than stands to the credit of prior human history in its entirety. Productively it has multiplied nine million times in the last generation alone. The prophetic vision of Francis Bacon of subjugation of the energies of nature through change in methods of inquiry has well-nigh been realized. The stationary engine, the locomotive, the dynamo, the motor car, turbine, telegraph, telephone, radio and moving picture are not the products of either isolated individual minds nor of the particular economic regime called capitalism. They are the fruit of methods that first penetrated to the working causalities of nature and then utilized the resulting knowledge in bold imaginative ventures of invention and construction.

We hear a great deal in these days about class conflict. The past history of man is held up to us as almost exclusively a record of struggles between classes, ending in the victory of a class that had been oppressed and the transfer of power to it. It is difficult to avoid reading the past in terms of the contemporary scene. Indeed, fundamentally it is impossible to avoid this course. With a certain proviso, it is highly important that we are compelled to follow this path. For the past as past is gone, save for esthetic enjoyment and refreshment, while the present is with us. Knowledge of the past is significant only as it deepens and extends our understanding of the present. Yet there is a proviso. We must grasp the things that are most important in the present when we turn to the past and not allow ourselves to be misled by secondary phenomena no matter how intense and immediately urgent they are. Viewed from this standpoint, the rise of scientific method and of technology based upon it is the genuinely active force in producing the vast complex of changes the world is now undergoing, not the class struggle whose spirit and method are opposed to science. If we lay hold upon the causal force exercised by this embodiment of intelligence we shall know where to turn for the means of directing further change. . . .

It is easy to exaggerate the amount of intelligence and ability demanded to render such judgments fitted for their purpose.[8] In the first place, we are likely to form our estimate on the basis of present conditions. But indubitably one great trouble at present is that the data for good judgment are lacking; and no innate faculty of mind can make up for the absence of facts. Until secrecy, prejudice, bias, misrepresentation, and propaganda as well as sheer ignorance are replaced by inquiry and publicity, we have no way of telling how apt for judgment of social policies the existing intelligence of the masses may be. It would certainly go much further than at present. In the second place, *effective* intelligence is not an original, innate endowment. No matter what are the differences in native intelligence (allowing for the moment that intelligence can be native), the actuality of mind is dependent upon the education which social conditions effect. Just as the specialized mind and knowledge of the past is embodied in implements, utensils, devices and technologies which those of a grade of intelligence which could not produce them can now intelligently use, so it will be when currents of public knowledge blow through social affairs.

The level of action fixed by *embodied* intelligence is always the important thing. In savage culture a superior man will be superior to his fellows, but his knowledge and judgment will lag in many matters far behind that of an inferiorly endowed person in an advanced civilization. Capacities are limited by the objects and tools at hand. They are still more dependent upon the prevailing habits of attention and interest which are set by tradition and institutional customs. Meanings run in the channels formed by instrumentalities of which, in the end, language, the vehicle of thought as well as of communication, is the most important. A mechanic can discourse of ohms and amperes as Sir Isaac Newton could not in his day. Many a man who has tinkered with radios can judge of things which Faraday did not dream of. It is aside from the point to say that if Newton and Faraday were now here, the amateur and mechanic would be infants beside them. The retort only brings out the point: the difference made by different objects to think of and by different meanings in circulation. A more intelligent state of social affairs, one more informed with knowledge, more directed by intelligence, would not improve original endowments one whit, but it would raise the level upon which the intelligence of all operates. The height of this level is much more important for judgment of public concerns than are differences in intelligence quotients. . . .

. . . It is said that the average citizen is not endowed with the degree of intelligence that the use of it as a method demands. This objection, supported by alleged scientific findings about heredity and by impressive statistics concerning the intelligence quotients of the average citizen, rests wholly upon the old notion that intelligence is a ready-made possession of individuals. The last stand of oligarchical and antisocial seclusion is perpetuation of this purely individualistic notion of intelligence. The reliance of liberalism is not upon the mere abstraction of a native endowment unaffected by social relationships, but upon the fact that native capacity is sufficient to enable the average individual to respond to and to use the knowledge and the skill that are embodied in the social conditions in which he lives, moves and has his being. There are few individuals who have the native capacity that was required to invent the stationary steam engine, locomotive, dynamo or telephone. But there are none so mean that they cannot intelligently utilize these embodiments of intelligence once they are a part of the organized means of associated living.

The indictments that are drawn against the intelligence of individuals are in truth indictments of a social order that does not permit the average individual to have access to the rich store of the accumulated wealth of mankind in knowledge, ideas and purposes. There does not now exist the kind of social organization that even permits the average human being to share the potentially available social intelligence. Still less is there a social order that has for one of its chief purposes the establishment of conditions that will move the mass of individuals to appropriate and use what is at hand. Back of the appropriation by the few of the material resources of society lies the appropriation by the few in behalf of their own ends of the cultural, the spiritual, resources that are the product not of the individuals who have taken possession but of the cooperative work of humanity. It is useless to talk about the failure of democracy until the source of its failure has been grasped and steps are taken to bring about that type of social organization that will encourage the socialized extension of intelligence. . . .

As the two preceding excerpts show, Dewey does not suppose that democracy requires uniformly high native intelligence in a community. It requires intelligent institutions and habits of thought. In the following excerpts he considers whether experimental habits of thought can have widespread efficacy in determining our valuations. He also points out that art can provide a great impetus to a free culture—not by direct intent, but by liberating the imagination from the bondage of fixed beliefs.[9]

That the popular esteem of science is largely due to the aid it has given to men for attainment of things they wanted independently of what they had learned from science is doubtless true. Russell has stated in a vivid way the sort of thing that has enabled science to displace beliefs that had previously been held: "The world ceased to believe that Joshua caused the sun to stand still, because Copernican astronomy was useful in navigation; it abandoned Aristotle's physics, because Galileo's theory of falling bodies made it possible to calculate the trajectory of a cannonball. It rejected the theory of the flood because geology is useful in mining and so on."* That the quotation expresses the sort of thing that gave the conclusions of the new science prestige and following at a time when it badly needed some outside aid in getting a hearing can hardly be doubted. As illustrative material it is especially impressive

*Bertrand Russell, *Power*, p. 138.

because of the enormous authority enjoyed by the doctrines of Aristotle and of the Church. If even in the case where all the advantage was on the side of old doctrines, the demonstrated serviceability of science gave it the victory, we can easily judge the enhancement of the esteem in which science was held in matters where it had no such powerful foe to contend with.

Quite apart from the antagonism to science displayed by entrenched institutional interests that had previously obtained a monopoly over beliefs in, say, astronomy, geology and some fields of history, history proves the existence of so much indifference on the part of mankind to the quality of its beliefs, and such lethargy toward methods that disturb old beliefs, that we should be glad that the new science has had such powerful adventitious aid. But it leaves untouched the question as to whether scientific knowledge has power to modify the ends which men prize and strive to attain. Is it proved that the findings of science—the best authenticated knowledge we have—add only to our power to realize desires already in existence? Or is this view derived from some previous theory about the constitution of human nature? Can it be true that desires and knowledge exist in separate noncommunicating compartments? Do the facts which can undoubtedly be cited as evidence, such as the use of scientific knowledge indifferently to heal disease and prolong human life and to provide the instruments for wholesale destruction of life, really prove the case? Or are they specially selected cases that support a doctrine that originated on other grounds than the evidence of facts? Is there such a complete separation of human ends from human beliefs as the theory assumes?

The shock given old ideas by the idea that knowledge is incapable of modifying the quality of desires (and hence cannot affect the formation of ends and purposes) is not of course in itself a ground for denying it is sound. It may be that the old view is totally false. Nevertheless, the point is worth discussion. We do not have to refer to the theory of Plato that knowledge, or what passes as knowledge, is the sole final determinant of men's ideas of the Good and hence of their actions. Nor is it needful to refer to Bacon's vision of the organization of scientific knowledge as the prospective foundation of future social policies directed exclusively to the advance of human well-being. The simple fact is that all the deliberately liberal and progressive movements of modern times have based themselves on the idea that action is determined by ideas, up to the time when Hume said that reason was and should be the "slave of the passions"; or, in contemporary language, of the emotions and desires. Hume's voice was a lonely one when he uttered the remark. The idea is now echoed and reechoed from almost every quarter. The classic economic school made wants the prime motors of human action, reducing reason to a power of calculating the means best fitted to satisfy the wants. The first effect of biology upon psychology was to emphasize the primacy of appetites and instincts. Psychiatrists have enforced the same conclusion by showing that intellectual disturbances originate in emotional maladjustments, and by exhibiting the extent of dictation of belief by desire.

It is one thing, however, to recognize that earlier theories neglected the importance of emotions and habits as determinants of conduct and exaggerated that of ideas and reason. It is quite another thing to hold that ideas (especially those warranted by competent inquiry) and emotions (with needs and desires) exist in separate compartments so that no interaction between them exists. When the view is as baldly stated it strikes one as highly improbable that there can be any such complete separation in the constitution of human nature. And while the idea must be accepted if the evidence points that way, no matter into what plight human affairs are forever plunged, the implications of the doctrine of complete separation of desire and knowledge must be noted. The assumption that desires are rigidly fixed is not one on its face consistent with the history of man's progress from savagery through barbarism to even the present defective state of civilization. If knowledge, even of the most authenticated kind, cannot influence desires and aims, if it cannot determine what is of value and what is not, the future outlook as to formation of desires is depressing. Denial that they can be influenced by knowledge points emphatically to the nonrational and antirational forces that will form them. One alternative to the power of ideas is habit or custom, and then when the rule of sheer habit breaks down—as it has done at the present time—all that is left is competition on the part of various bodies and interests to decide which shall come out ahead in a struggle, carried on by intimidation, coercion, bribery, and all sorts of propaganda, to shape the desires which shall predominantly control the ends of human action. The prospect is a black one. It leads one to consider the possibility that Bacon, Locke, and the leaders of the Enlightenment—typified by the act of Condorcet, writing, while imprisoned and waiting for death, about the role of science in the future liberation of mankind—were after all quite aware of the actual influence of appetite, habit, and blind desire upon action, but were engaged in holding up another and better way as the alternative to follow in the future.

That the course they anticipated has not come to fruition is obvious without argument. Bacon's action in using his own knowledge as a servant of the Crown in strengthening Great Britain in a military way against other nations now seems more prophetic of what has happened than what he put down in words. The power over Nature which he expected to follow the advance of science has come to pass. But in contradiction to his expectations, it has been largely used to increase, instead of reduce, the power of Man over Man. Shall we conclude that the early prophets were totally and intrinsically wrong? Or shall we conclude that they immensely underestimated the obduracy of institutions and customs antedating the appearance of science on

the scene in shaping desires in their image? Have events after all but accentuated the problem of discovering the means by which authenticated
beliefs shall influence desires, the formation of ends, and thereby the course
of events? Is it possible to admit the power of propaganda to shape ends
and deny that of science?

Looked at from one angle, the question brings us back to our fundamental
issue: the relation of culture and human nature. For the fact which is decisive in answering the question whether verified knowledge is or is not
capable of shaping desires and ends (as well as means) is whether the
desires that are effective in settling the course of action are innate and
fixed, or are themselves the product of a certain culture. If the latter is the
case, the practical issue reduces itself to this: Is it possible for the scientific
attitude to become such a weighty and widespread constituent of culture that,
through the medium of culture, it may shape human desires and purposes?

To state the question is a long way from ability to answer it. But it is
something to have the issue before us in its actual instead of in its factitious
form. The issue ceases to be the indeterminate one of the relation of knowledge and desires in the native psychological constitution of man—indeterminate, among other reasons, because it is disputable whether there is any
such thing as the latter apart from native biological constitution. It becomes
the determinate one of the institution of the kind of culture in which scientific method and scientific conclusions are integrally incorporated.

The problem stated in this way puts in a different light the esteem gained
by science because of its serviceability. That there are individuals here and
there who have been influenced to esteem science because of some obvious
contribution to satisfaction of their merely personal desires may well be a
fact. That there are groups similarly influenced must be admitted. But the
reasons why men have been willing to accept conclusions derived from
science in lieu of older ideas are not exclusively or even mainly those of
direct personal and class benefit. Improvements in navigation and mining
have become part of the state of culture. It is in this capacity they have
tended to displace beliefs that were congenial to an earlier state of culture.
By and large the same thing is true of the application of physics and
chemistry in more effective satisfaction of wants and in creation of new
wants. While their application to produce increased efficiency in carrying on
war has doubtlessly recommended those sciences to persons like rulers and
generals, who otherwise would have been indifferent, the mass of persons
have been moved to an attitude of favorable esteem by what has happened
in the arts of peace. The decisive factor would seem to be whether the arts
of war or of peace are to be in the future the ones that will control culture,
a question that involves the need of discovering why war is such an important constituent of present culture.

I should be on controversial ground if I held up as evidence the belief that the technologies, which are the practical correlates of scientific theories, have now reached a point in which they can be used to create an era of abundance instead of the deficit-economies that existed before natural science developed, and that with an era of abundance and security the causes of conflict would be reduced. It may be mentioned as a hypothetical illustration. The kind of serviceability which is capable of generating high esteem for science *may* possibly be serviceability for general and shared, or "social," welfare. If the economic regime were so changed that the resources of science were employed to maintain security for all, the present view about the limitation of science might fade away. I imagine there are not many who will deny that esteem for science, even when placed upon the ground of serviceability alone, is produced at least in part by an admixture of general with private serviceability. If there is a skeptic let him consider the contribution made by science both actually and still more potentially to agriculture, and the social consequences of the change in production of foods and raw materials, thereby effected.

The other side of the ledger is marked by such a debit entry as the following from the English chemist Soddy: "So far the pearls of science have been cast before swine, who have given us in return millionaires and slums, armaments and the desolation of war." The contrast is real. If its existence seems to support the doctrine that science only supplies means for more efficient execution of already existing desires and purposes, it is because it points to the division which exists in our culture. The war that mobilizes science for wholesale destruction mobilizes it, also, for support of life and for healing the wounded. The desires and ends involved proceed not from native and naked human nature but from modifications it has undergone in interaction with a complex of cultural factors of which science is indeed one, but one which produces social consequences only as it is affected by economic and political traditions and customs formed before its rise.

For in any case, the influence of science on both means and ends is not exercised directly upon individuals but indirectly through incorporation within culture. In this function and capacity it is that scientific beliefs have replaced earlier unscientific beliefs. The position stated at its worst is that science operates as a part of folklore, not just as science. Even when put in this way, attention is invited to differences in folklore and to differences of the consequences that are produced by different folklores. And when it is admitted that the folklore may be one of aggressive nationalism, where the consequences of science as part of the prevailing folklore is war of the present destructive scope, we at least have the advantage of clear knowledge as to the location of the problem.

We have been considering science as a body of conclusions. We have ignored science in its quality of an attitude embodied in habitual will to employ certain methods of observation, reflection, and test rather than others.

When we look at science from this point of view, the significance of science as a constituent of culture takes on a new color. The great body of scientific inquirers would deny with indignation that they are actuated in *their* esteem for science by its material serviceability. If they use words sanctioned by long tradition, they say they are moved by love of the truth. If they use contemporary phraseology, less grandiloquent in sound but of equivalent meaning, they say they are moved by a controlling interest in inquiry, in discovery, in following where the evidence of discovered facts points. Above all they say that this kind of interest excludes interest in reaching any conclusion not warranted by evidence, no matter how personally congenial it may be.

In short, it is a fact that a certain group of men, perhaps relatively not very numerous, have a "disinterested" interest in scientific inquiry. This interest has developed a morale having its own distinctive features. Some of its obvious elements are willingness to hold belief in suspense, ability to doubt until evidence is obtained; willingness to go where evidence points instead of putting first a personally preferred conclusion; ability to hold ideas in solution and use them as hypotheses to be tested instead of as dogmas to be asserted; and (possibly the most distinctive of all) enjoyment of new fields for inquiry and of new problems.

Every one of these traits goes contrary to some human impulse that is naturally strong. Uncertainty is disagreeable to most persons; suspense is so hard to endure that assured expectation of an unfortunate outcome is usually preferred to a long-continued state of doubt. "Wishful thinking" is a comparatively modern phrase; but men upon the whole have usually believed what they wanted to believe, except as very convincing evidence made it impossible. Apart from a scientific attitude, guesses, with persons left to themselves, tend to become opinions and opinions dogmas. To hold theories and principles in solution, awaiting confirmation, goes contrary to the grain. Even today questioning a statement made by a person is often taken by him as a reflection upon his integrity, and is resented. For many millennia opposition to views widely held in a community was intolerable. It called down the wrath of the deities who are in charge of the group. Fear of the unknown, fear of change and novelty, tended, at all times before the rise of scientific attitude, to drive men into rigidity of beliefs and habits; they entered upon unaccustomed lines of behavior—even in matters of minor moment—with qualms which exacted rites of expiation. Exceptions to accepted rules have either been ignored or systematically explained away when they were too conspicuous to ignore. Baconian idols of the tribe, the cave, the theater, and den have caused men to rush to conclusions, and then to use all their powers to defend from criticism and change the conclusions arrived at. The connection of common law with custom and its resistance to change are familiar facts. Even religious beliefs and rites which were at first more or less heretical deviations harden into modes of action it is impious to question, after once they have become part of the habits of a group.

If I mention such familiar considerations it is in part to suggest that we may well be grateful that science has had undeniable social serviceability, and that to some extent and in some places strong obstructions to adoption of changed beliefs have been overcome. But the chief reason for calling attention to them is the proof they furnish that in some persons and to some degree science has already created a new morale—which is equivalent to the creation of new desires and new ends. The existence of the scientific attitude and spirit, even upon a limited scale, is proof that science is capable of developing a distinctive type of disposition and purpose: a type that goes far beyond provision of more effective means for realizing desires which exist independently of any effect of science.

It is not becoming, to put it moderately, for those who are themselves animated by the scientific morale to assert that other persons are incapable of coming into possession of it and being moved by it.

Such an attitude is saved from being professional snobbery only when it is the result of sheer thoughtlessness. When one and the same representative of the intellectual class denounces any view that attaches inherent importance to the consequences of science, claiming the view is false to the spirit of science—and also holds that it is impossible for science to do anything to affect desires and ends, the inconsistency demands explanation.

A situation in which the fundamental dispositions and ends of a few are influenced by science while that of most persons and most groups is not so influenced proves that the issue is cultural. The difference sets a social problem: what are the causes for the existence of this great gap, especially since it has such serious consequences? If it is possible for persons to have their beliefs formed on the ground of evidence, procured by systematic and competent inquiry, nothing can be more disastrous socially than that the great majority of persons should have them formed by habit, accidents of circumstance, propaganda, personal and class bias. The existence, even on a relatively narrow scale, of a morale of fairmindedness, intellectual integrity, of will to subordinate personal preference to ascertained facts and to share with others what is found out, instead of using it for personal gain, is a challenge of the most searching kind. Why don't a great many more persons have this attitude?

The answer given to this challenge is bound up with the fate of democracy. The spread of literacy, the immense extension of the influence of the press in books, newspapers, periodicals, make the issue peculiarly urgent for a democracy. The very agencies that a century and a half ago were looked upon as those that were sure to advance the cause of democratic freedom are those which now make it possible to create pseudo-public opinion and to undermine democracy from within. Callousness due to continuous reiteration may produce a certain immunity to the grosser kinds of propaganda. But in the long run negative measures afford no assurance. While it would be absurd to believe it desirable or possible for every one to become a scientist when science is defined from the side of subject matter, the future of democracy is allied with spread of the scientific attitude. It is the sole guarantee against wholesale misleading by propaganda. More important still, it is the only assurance of the possibility of a public opinion intelligent enough to meet present social problems.

To become aware of the problem is a condition of taking steps toward its solution. The problem is in part economic. The nature of control of the means of publicity enters directly; sheer financial control is not a favorable sign. The democratic belief in free speech, free press and free assembly is one of the things that exposes democratic institutions to attack. For representatives of totalitarian states, who are the first to deny such freedom when they are in power, shrewdly employ it in a democratic country to destroy the foundations of democracy. Backed with the necessary financial means, they are capable of carrying on a work of continuous sapping and mining. More dangerous, perhaps, in the end is that fact that all economic conditions tending toward centralization and concentration of the means of production and distribution affect the public press, whether individuals so desire or not. The causes which require large corporate capital to carry on modern business, naturally influence the publishing business.

The problem is also an educative one. A book instead of a paragraph could be given to this aspect of the topic. That the schools have mostly been given to imparting information ready-made, along with teaching the tools of literacy, cannot be denied. The methods used in acquiring such information are not those which develop skill in inquiry and in test of opinions. On the contrary, they are positively hostile to it. They tend to dull native curiosity, and to load powers of observation and experimentation with such a mass of unrelated material that they do not operate as effectively as they do in many an illiterate person. The problem of the common schools in a democracy has reached only its first stage when they are provided for everybody. Until what shall be taught and how it is taught is settled upon the basis of formation of the scientific attitude, the so-called educational work of schools is a dangerously hit-or-miss affair as far as democracy is concerned. . . .

To say that the issue is a moral one is to say that in the end it comes back to personal choice and action. From one point of view everything which has been said is a laboring of the commonplace that democratic government is a function of public opinion and public sentiment. But identification of its formation in the democratic direction with democratic extension of the scientific morale till it is part of the ordinary equipment of the ordinary individual indicates the issue is a moral one. It is individual persons who need to have this attitude substituted for pride and prejudice, for class and personal interest, for beliefs made dear by custom and early emotional associations. It is only by the choice and the active endeavor of many individuals that this result can be effected.

A former president of the United States once made a political stir by saying that "Public office is a public trust." The saying was a truism although one that needed emphasis. That possession of knowledge and special skill in intellectual methods is a public trust has not become a truism even in words. Scientific morale has developed in some persons to a point where it is a matter of course that what is found out is communicated to other persons who are also engaged in specialized research. But it has not developed to the point where wider responsibility for communication is acknowledged. Circumstances which have attended the historic growth of modern science explain why this is so, although they do not justify its continuance. Internal and external circumstances have brought about a social seclusion of science which from a certain standpoint is analogous to an earlier monastic seclusion.

The external circumstance was the opposition scientific men had to overcome before it was possible for them to carry on their work free from dictation or persecution. The internal circumstance was in part the need for extreme specialization of inquiries which necessarily accompanied the novelty of the new method; in part, it was a self-protective policy for maintaining the purity of a new, still immature and struggling attitude from contamination that proceeded from taking sides in practical affairs. This attitude had the blessing of the old and ingrained tradition of the "purity" of science as an exclusively theoretical subject; a subject aloof from practice, since reason and theory were so high above practice, which was, according to tradition, only material and utilitarian. The danger of loss of the impartiality of the scientific spirit through affiliation with some partisan and partial interest seemed to give significance to the established tradition about "purity," which, like traditional feminine chastity, needed all kinds of external safeguards to hedge it about. The need is not that scientific men become crusaders in special practical causes. Just as the problem with art is to unite the inherent integrity of the artist with imaginative and emotional appeal of ideas, so the present need is recognition by scientific men of social responsibility for contagious diffusion of the scientific attitude: a task not to be accomplished without abandoning once for all the belief that science is set apart from all other social interests as if possessed of a peculiar holiness.

Extension of the qualities that make up the scientific attitude is quite a different matter than dissemination of the results of physics, chemistry, biology and astronomy, valuable as the latter may be. The difference is the reason why the issue is a moral one. The question of whether science is capable of influencing the formation of ends for which men strive or is limited to increasing power of realizing those which are formed independently of it is the question whether science has intrinsic moral potentiality. Historically, the position that science is devoid of moral quality has been held by theologians and their metaphysical allies. For the position points unmistakably to the necessity for recourse to some other source of moral guidance. That a similar position is now taken in the name of science is either a sign of a confusion that permeates all aspects of culture, or is an omen of ill for democracy. If control of conduct amounts to conflict of desires with no possibility of determination of desire and purpose by scientifically warranted beliefs, then the practical alternative is competition and conflict between unintelligent forces for control of desire. The conclusion is so extreme as to suggest that denial in the name of science of the existence of any such things as moral facts may mark a transitional stage thoughtlessly taken to be final. It is quite true that science cannot affect moral values, ends, rules, principles as these were once thought of and believed in, namely, prior to the rise of science. But to say that that there are no such things as moral facts because desires control formation and valuation of ends is in truth but to point to desires and interests as themselves moral facts requiring control by intelligence equipped with knowledge. Science through its physical technological consequences is now determining the relations which human beings, severally and in groups, sustain to one another. If it is incapable of developing moral techniques which will also determine these relations, the split in modern culture goes so deep that not only democracy but all civilized values are doomed. Such at least is the problem. A culture which permits science to destroy traditional values but which distrusts its power to create new ones is a culture which is destroying itself. . . .

The theories that attribute direct moral effect and intent to art fail because they do not take account of the collective civilization that is the context in which works of art are produced and enjoyed. I would not say that they tend to treat works of art as a kind of sublimated Æsop's fables. But they all tend to extract particular works, regarded as especially edifying, from their milieu and to think of the moral function of art in terms of a strictly personal relation between the selected works and a particular individual. Their whole conception of morals is so individualistic that they miss a sense of the *way* in which art exercises its humane function.

Matthew Arnold's dictum that "poetry is criticism of life" is a case in point. It suggests to the reader a moral intent on the part of the poet and a moral judgment on the part of the reader. It fails to see or at all events to state *how* poetry is a criticism of life; namely, not directly, but by disclosure, through imaginative vision addressed to imaginative experience (not to set judgment) of possibilities that contrast with actual conditions. A sense of possibilities that are unrealized and that might be realized are when they are put in contrast with actual conditions, the most penetrating "criticism" of the latter that can be made. It is by a sense of possibilities opening before us that we become aware of constrictions that hem us in and of burdens that oppress.

Mr. Garrod, a follower of Matthew Arnold in more senses than one, has wittily said that what we resent in didactic poetry is not that it teaches, but that it does not teach, its incompetency. He added words to the effect that poetry teaches as friends and life teach, by being, and not by express intent. He says in another place, "Poetical values are, after all, values in a human life. You cannot mark them off from other values, as though the nature of man were built in bulkheads." I do not think that what Keats has said in one of his letters can be surpassed as to the way in which poetry acts. He asks what would be the result if every man spun from his imaginative experience "an airy citadel" like the web the spider spins, "filling the air with a beautiful circuiting." For, he says, "man should not dispute or assert, but whisper results to his neighbor, and thus, by every germ of spirit sucking the sap from mold etherial, every human being might become great, and Humanity instead of being a wide heath of Furze and briars with here and there a remote Pine or Oak, would become a grand democracy of Forest Trees!"

It is by way of communication that art becomes the incomparable organ of instruction, but the way is so remote from that usually associated with the idea of education, it is a way that lifts art so far above what we are accustomed to think of as instruction, that we are repelled by any suggestion of teaching and learning in connection with art. But our revolt is in fact a reflection upon education that proceeds by methods so literal as to exclude the imagination and one not touching the desires and emotions of men. Shelley said, "The imagination is the great instrument of moral good, and poetry administers to the effect by acting upon the causes." Hence it is, he goes on to say, "a poet would do ill to embody his own conceptions of right and wrong, which are usually those of his own time and place, in his poetical creations. . . . By the assumption of this inferior office . . . he would resign participation in the cause"—the imagination. It is the lesser poets who "have frequently affected a moral aim, and the effect of their poetry is diminished in exact proportion as they compel us to advert to this purpose." But the power of imaginative projection is so great that he calls poets "the founders of civil society."

The problem of the relation of art and morals is too often treated as if the problem existed only on the side of art. It is virtually assumed that morals are satisfactory in idea if not in fact, and that the only question is whether and in what ways art should conform to a moral system already developed. But Shelley's statement goes to the heart of the matter. Imagination is the chief instrument of the good. It is more or less a commonplace to say that a person's ideas and treatment of his fellows are dependent upon his power to put himself imaginatively in their place. But the primacy of the imagination extends far beyond the scope of direct personal relationships. Except where "ideal" is used in conventional deference or as a name for a sentimental reverie, the ideal factors in every moral outlook and human loyalty are imaginative. The historic alliance of religion and art has its roots in this common quality. Hence it is that art is more moral than moralities. For the latter either are, or tend to become, consecrations of the *status quo,* reflections of custom, reinforcements of the established order. The moral prophets of humanity have always been poets even though they spoke in free verse or by parable. Uniformly, however, their vision of possibilities has soon been converted into a proclamation of facts that already exist and hardened into semipolitical institutions. Their imaginative presentation of ideals that should command thought and desire have been treated as rules of policy. Art has been the means of keeping alive the sense of purposes that outrun evidence and of meanings that transcend indurated habit.

Morals are assigned a special compartment in theory and practice because they reflect the divisions embodied in economic and political institutions. Wherever social divisions and barriers exist, practices and ideas that correspond to them fix metes and bounds, so that liberal action is placed under restraint. Creative intelligence is looked upon with distrust; the innovations that are the essence of individuality are feared, and generous impulse is put under bonds not to disturb the peace. Were art an acknowledged power in human association and not treated as the pleasuring of an idle moment or as a means of ostentatious display, and were morals understood to be identical with every aspect of value that is shared in experience, the "problem" of the relation of art and morals would not exist.

The idea and the practice of morality are saturated with conceptions that stem from praise and blame, reward and punishment. Mankind is divided into sheep and goats, the vicious and virtuous, the law-abiding and criminal, the good and bad. To be beyond good and evil is an impossibility for man, and yet as long as the good signifies only that which is lauded and rewarded, and the evil that which is currently condemned or outlawed, the ideal factors of morality are always and everywhere beyond good and evil. Because art is wholly innocent of ideas derived from praise and blame, it is looked upon with the eye of suspicion by the guardians of custom, or only the art that is itself so old and "classic" as to receive conventional praise is grudgingly admitted, provided, as with, say, the case of Shakespeare, signs of regard for conventional morality can be ingeniously extracted from his work. Yet this indifference to praise and blame because of preoccupation with imaginative experience constitutes the heart of the moral potency of art. From it proceeds the liberating and uniting power of art.

Shelley said, "The great secret of morals is love, or *a going out of our nature* and the identification of ourselves with the beautiful which exists in thought, action, or person, not our own. A man to be greatly good must imagine intensely and comprehensively." What is true of the individual is true of the whole system of morals in thought and action. While perception of the union of the possible with the actual in a work of art is itself a great good, the good does not terminate with the immediate and particular occasion in which it is had. The union that is presented in perception persists in the remaking of impulsion and thought. The first intimations of wide and large redirections of desire and purpose are of necessity imaginative. Art is a mode of prediction not found in charts and statistics, and it insinuates possibilities of human relations not to be found in rule and precept, admonition and administration. . . .

THE TASKS OF SOCIAL INTELLIGENCE[10]

Dewey attempts to diagnose the ills of American democracy and to propose the main requisites to its renewal. The institutions of American life are largely survivals of a preindustrial order. Consequently, they are inappropriate to meet the demands and possibilities of contemporary conditions. Above all, they are impediments to the invigoration of social intelligence. It should be especially noted that social intelligence, in Dewey's conception, is anything but technocracy.

Associated behavior directed toward objects which fulfill wants not only produces those objects, but brings customs and institutions into being. The indirect and unthought-of consequences are usually more important than the direct. The fallacy of supposing that the new industrial regime would produce just and for the most part only the consequences consciously forecast and aimed at was the counterpart of the fallacy that the wants and efforts characteristic of it were functions of "natural" human beings. They arose out of institutionalized action and they resulted in institutionalized action. The disparity between the results of the industrial revolution and the conscious intentions of those engaged in it is a remarkable case of the extent to which indirect consequences of conjoint activity outweigh, beyond the possibility of reckoning, the results directly contemplated. Its outcome was the development of those extensive and invisible bonds, those "great impersonal concerns, organizations," which now pervasively affect the thinking, willing and doing of everybody, and which have ushered in the "new era of human relationships."[11]

Equally undreamed of was the effect of the massive organizations and complicated interactions upon the state. Instead of the independent, self-moved individuals contemplated by the theory, we have standardized interchangeable units. Persons are joined together, not because they have voluntarily chosen to be united in these forms, but because vast currents are running which bring men together. Green and red lines, marking out political boundaries, are on the maps and affect legislation and jurisdiction of courts, but railways, mails and telegraph-wires disregard them. The consequences of the latter influence more profoundly those living within the legal local units than do boundary lines. The forms of associated action characteristic of the present economic order are so massive and extensive that they determine the most significant constituents of the public and the residence of power. Inevitably they reach out to grasp the agencies of government; they are controlling factors in legislation and administration. Not chiefly because of deliberate and planned self-interest, large as may be its role, but because they are the most potent and best organized of social forces. In a word, the new forms of combined action due to the modern economic regime control present polities, much as dynastic interests controlled those of two centuries ago. They affect thinking and desire more than did the interests which formerly moved the state. . . .

We thus reach our conclusion. The same forces which have brought about the forms of democratic government, general suffrage, executives and legislators chosen by majority vote, have also brought about conditions which halt the social and humane ideals that demand the utilization of government as the genuine instrumentality of an inclusive and fraternally associated public. "The new age of human relationships" has no political agencies worthy of it. The democratic public is still largely inchoate and unorganized . . . (*PIP*, pp. 106–109).

. . . Indirect, extensive, enduring and serious consequences of conjoint and interacting behavior call a public into existence having a common interest in controlling these consequences. But the machine age has so enormously expanded, multiplied, intensified and complicated the scope of the indirect consequences, have formed such immense and consolidated unions in action, on an impersonal rather than a community basis, that the resultant public cannot identify and distinguish itself. And this discovery is obviously an antecedent condition of any effective organization on its part. Such is our thesis regarding the eclipse which the public idea and interest have undergone. There are too many publics and too much of public concern for our existing resources to cope with. The problem of a democratically organized public is primarily and essentially an intellectual problem, in a degree to which the political affairs of prior ages offer no parallel . . . (*ibid.*, p. 126).

. . . The local face-to-face community has been invaded by forces so vast, so remote in initiation, so far-reaching in scope and so complexly indirect in operation, that they are, from the standpoint of the members of local social units, unknown. Man, as has been often remarked, has difficulty in getting on either with or without his fellows, even in neighborhoods. He is not more successful in getting on with them when they act at a great distance in ways invisible to him. An inchoate public is capable of organization only when indirect consequences are perceived, and when it is possible to project agencies which order their occurrence. At present, many consequences are felt rather than perceived; they are suffered, but they cannot be said to be known, for they are not, by those who experience them, referred to their origins. It goes, then, without saying that agencies are not established which canalize the streams of social action and thereby regulate them. Hence the publics are amorphous and unarticulated.

There was a time when a man might entertain a few general political principles and apply them with some confidence. A citizen believed in states' rights or in a centralized federal government; in free trade or protection. It did not involve much mental strain to imagine that by throwing in his lot with one party or another he could so express his views that his belief would count in government. For the average voter today the tariff question is a complicated medley of infinite detail, schedules of rates specific and *ad valorem* on countless things, many of which he does not recognize by name, and with respect to which he can form no judgment. Probably not one voter in a thousand even reads the scores of pages in which the rates of toll are enumerated and he would not be much wiser if he did. The average man gives it up as a bad job. At election time, appeal to some timeworn slogan may galvanize him into a temporary notion that he has convictions on an important subject, but except for manufacturers and dealers who have some interest at stake in this or that schedule, belief lacks the qualities which attach to beliefs about matters of personal concern. Industry is too complex and intricate . . . (*ibid.*, pp. 131–2).

Political apathy, which is a natural product of the discrepancies between actual practices and traditional machinery, ensues from inability to identify one's self with definite issues. These are hard to find and locate in the vast complexities of current life. When traditional war-cries have lost their import in practical policies which are consonant with them, they are readily dismissed as bunk. Only habit and tradition, rather than reasoned conviction, together with a vague faith in doing one's civic duty, send to the polls a considerable percentage of the fifty per cent who still vote. And of them it is a common remark that a large number vote against something or somebody rather than for anything or anybody, except when powerful agencies create a scare. The old principles do not fit contemporary life as it is lived, however well they may have expressed the vital interests of the times in which they arose. Thousands feel their hollowness even if they cannot make their feeling articulate. The confusion which has resulted from the size and ramifications of social activities has rendered men skeptical of the efficiency of political action. Who is sufficient unto these things? Men feel that they are caught in the sweep of forces too vast to understand or master. Thought is brought to a stand-still and action paralyzed. Even the specialist finds it difficult to trace the chain of "cause and effect"; and even he operates only after the event, looking backward, while meantime social activities have moved on to effect a new state of affairs . . . (*ibid.*, pp. 134–35).

. . . The ramification of the issues before the public is so wide and intricate, the technical matters involved are so specialized, the details are so many and so shifting, that the public cannot for any length of time identify and hold itself. It is not that there is no public, no large body of persons having a common interest in the consequences of social transactions. There is too much public, a public too diffused and scattered and too intricate in composition. And there are too many publics, for conjoint actions which have indirect, serious and enduring consequences are multitudinous beyond comparison, and each one of them crosses the others and generates its own group of persons especially affected with little to hold these different publics together in an integrated whole . . . (*ibid.*, p. 137).

The new era of human relationships in which we live is one marked by mass production for remote markets, by cable and telephone, by cheap printing, by railway and steam navigation. Only geographically did Columbus discover a new world. The actual new world has been generated in the last hundred years. Steam and electricity have done more to alter the conditions under which men associate together than all the agencies which affected human relationships before our time. There are those who lay the blame for all the evils of our lives on steam, electricity and machinery. It is always convenient to have a devil as well as a savior to bear the responsibilities of humanity. In reality, the trouble springs rather from the ideas and absence of ideas in connection with which technological factors operate. Mental and moral beliefs and ideals change more slowly than outward conditions. If the ideals associated with the higher life of our cultural past have been impaired, the fault is primarily with them. Ideals and standards formed without regard to the means by which they are to be achieved and incarnated in flesh are bound to be thin and wavering. Since the aims, desires and purposes created by a machine age do not connect with tradition, there are two sets of rival ideals, and those which have actual instrumentalities at their disposal have the advantage. Because the two are rivals and because the older ones retain their glamor and sentimental prestige in literature and religion, the newer ones are perforce harsh and narrow. For the older symbols of ideal life still engage thought and command loyalty. Conditions have changed, but every aspect of life, from religion and education to property and trade, shows that nothing approaching a transformation has taken place in ideas and ideals. Symbols control sentiment and thought, and the new age has no symbols consonant with its activities. Intellectual instrumentalities for the formation of an organized public are more inadequate than its overt means. The ties which hold men together in action are numerous, tough and subtle. But they are invisible and intangible. We have the physical tools of communication as never before. The thoughts and aspirations congruous with them are not communicated, and hence are not common. Without such communication the public will remain shadowy and formless, seeking spasmodically for itself, but seizing and holding its shadow rather than its substance. Till the Great Society is converted into a Great Community, the Public will remain in eclipse. Communication can alone create a great community. Our Babel is not one of tongues but of the signs and symbols without which shared experience is impossible (*ibid.*, pp. 141–42).

. . . The prime difficulty, as we have seen, is that of discovering the means by which a scattered, mobile and manifold public may so recognize itself as to define and express its interests. This discovery is necessarily precedent to any fundamental change in the machinery. We are not concerned therefore to set forth counsels as to advisable improvements in the political forms of democracy. Many have been suggested. It is no derogation of their relative worth to say that consideration of these changes is not at present an affair of primary importance. The problem lies deeper; it is in the first instance an intellectual problem: the search for conditions under which the Great Society may become the Great Community. When these conditions are brought into being they will make their own forms. Until they have come about, it is somewhat futile to consider what political machinery will suit them.

In a search for the conditions under which the inchoate public now extant may function democratically, we may proceed from a statement of the nature of the democratic idea in its generic social sense.* From the standpoint of the individual, it consists in having a responsible share according to capacity in forming and directing the activities of the groups to which one belongs and in participating according to need in the values which the groups sustain. From the standpoint of the groups, it demands liberation of the potentialities of members of a group in harmony with the interests and goods which are common. Since every individual is a member of many groups, this specification cannot be fulfilled except when different groups interact flexibly and fully in connection with other groups. A member of a robber band may express his powers in a way consonant with belonging to that group and be directed by the interest common to its members. But he does so only at the cost of repression of those of his potentialities which can be realized only through membership in other groups. The robber band cannot interact flexibly with other groups; it can act only through isolating itself. It must prevent the operation of all interests save those which circumscribe it in its separateness. But a good citizen finds his conduct as a member of a political group enriching and enriched by his participation in family life, industry, scientific and artistic associations. There is a free give-and-take: fullness of integrated

---

*The most adequate discussion of this ideal with which I am acquainted is T. V. Smith's "The Democratic Way of Life."

personality is therefore possible of achievement, since the pulls and responses of different groups reinforce one another and their values accord.

Regarded as an idea, democracy is not an alternative to other principles of associated life. It is the idea of community life itself. It is an ideal in the only intelligible sense of an ideal: namely, the tendency and movement of some thing which exists carried to its final limit, viewed as completed, perfected. Since things do not attain such fulfillment but are in actuality distracted and interfered with, democracy in this sense is not a fact and never will be. But neither in this sense is there or has there ever been anything which is a community in its full measure, a community unalloyed by alien elements. The idea or ideal of a community presents, however, actual phases of associated life as they are freed from restrictive and disturbing elements, and are contemplated as having attained their limit of development. Wherever there is conjoint activity whose consequences are appreciated as good by all singular persons who take part in it, and where the realization of the good is such as to effect an energetic desire and effort to sustain it in being just because it is a good shared by all, there is insofar a community. The clear consciousness of a communal life, in all its implications, constitutes the idea of democracy.

Only when we start from a community as a fact, grasp the fact in thought so as to clarify and enhance its constituent elements, can we reach an idea of democracy which is not utopian. The conceptions and shibboleths which are traditionally associated with the idea of democracy take on a veridical and directive meaning only when they are construed as marks and traits of an association which realizes the defining characteristics of a community. Fraternity, liberty and equality isolated from communal life are hopeless abstractions. Their separate assertion leads to mushy sentimentalism or else to extravagant and fanatical violence which in the end defeats its own aims. Equality then becomes a creed of mechanical identity which is false to facts and impossible of realization. Effort to attain it is divisive of the vital bonds which hold men together; as far as it puts forth issue, the outcome is a mediocrity in which good is common only in the sense of being average and vulgar. Liberty is then thought of as independence of social ties, and ends in dissolution and anarchy. It is more difficult to sever the idea of brotherhood from that of a community, and hence it is either practically ignored in the movements which identify democracy with Individualism, or else it is a sentimentally appended tag. In its just connection with communal experience, fraternity is another name for the consciously appreciated goods which accrue from an association in which all share, and which give direction to the conduct of each. Liberty is that secure release and fulfillment of personal potentialities which take place only in rich and manifold association with others: the power to be an individualized self making a distinctive contribution and enjoying in its own way the fruits of association. Equality denotes the unhampered share which each individual member of the community has in the consequences of associated action. It is equitable because it is measured only by need and capacity to utilize, not by extraneous factors which deprive one in order that another may take and have. A baby in the family is equal with others, not because of some antecedent and structural quality which is the same as that of others, but insofar as his needs for care and development are attended to without being sacrificed to the superior strength, possessions and matured abilities of others. Equality does not signify that kind of mathematical or physical equivalence in virtue of which any one element may be substituted for another. It denotes effective regard for whatever is distinctive and unique in each, irrespective of physical and psychological inequalities. It is not a natural possession but is a fruit of the community when its action is directed by its character as a community.

Associated or joint activity is a condition of the creation of a community. But association itself is physical and organic, while communal life is moral, that is, emotionally, intellectually, consciously sustained. Human beings combine in behavior as directly and unconsciously as do atoms, stellar masses and cells; as directly and unknowlingly as they divide and repel. They do so in virtue of their own structure, as man and woman unite, as the baby seeks the breast and the breast is there to supply its need. They do so from external circumstances, pressure from without, as atoms combine or separate in presence of an electric charge, or as sheep huddle together from the cold. Associated activity needs no explanation; things are made that way. But no amount of aggregated collective action of itself constitutes a community. For beings who observe and think, and whose ideas are absorbed by impulses and become sentiments and interests, "we" is as inevitable as "I." But "we" and "our" exist only when the consequences of combined action are perceived and become an object of desire and effort, just as "I" and "mine" appear on the scene only when a distinctive share in mutual action is consciously asserted or claimed. Human associations may be ever so organic in origin and firm in operation, but they develop into societies in a human sense only as their consequences, being known, are esteemed and sought for. Even if "society" were as much an organism as some writers have held, it would not on that account be society. Interactions, transactions, occur *de facto* and the results of interdependence follow. But participation in activities and sharing in results are additive concerns. They demand *communication* as a prerequisite.

Combined activity happens among human beings; but when nothing else happens it passes as inevitably into some other mode of interconnected activity as does the interplay of iron and the oxygen of water. What takes place is wholly describable in terms of energy, or, as we say in the case of human interactions, of force. Only when there exist *signs* or *symbols* of activities and of their outcome can the flux be viewed as from without, be arrested for consideration and esteem, and be regulated. Lightning strikes and rives a tree or rock, and the resulting fragments take up and continue the process of interaction, and so on and on. But when phases of the process are represented by signs, a new medium is interposed. As symbols are related to one another, the important relations of a course of events are recorded and are preserved as meanings. Recollection and foresight are possible; the new medium facilitates calculation, planning, and a new kind of action which intervenes in what happens to direct its course in the interest of what is foreseen and desired.

Symbols in turn depend upon and promote communication. The results of conjoint experience are considered and transmitted. Events cannot be passed from one to another, but meanings may be shared by means of signs. Wants and impulses are then attached to common meanings. They are thereby transformed into desires and purposes, which, since they implicate a common or mutually understood meaning, present new ties, converting a conjoint activity into a community of interest and endeavor. Thus there is generated what, metaphorically, may be termed a general will and social consciousness: desire and choice on the part of individuals in behalf of activities that, by means of symbols, are communicable and shared by all concerned. A community thus presents an order of energies transmuted into one of meanings which are appreciated and mutually referred by each to every other on the part of those engaged in combined action. "Force" is not eliminated but is transformed in use and direction by ideas and sentiments made possible by means of symbols.

The work of conversion of the physical and organic phase of associated behavior into a community of action saturated and regulated by mutual interest in shared meanings, consequences which are translated into ideas and desired objects by means of symbols, does not occur all at once nor completely. At any given time, it sets a problem rather than marks a settled achievement. We are born organic beings associated with others, but we are not born members of a community. The young have to be brought within the traditions, outlook and interests which characterize a community by means of education: by unremitting instruction and by learning in connection with the phenomena of overt association. Everything which is distinctively human is learned, not native, even though it could not be learned without native structures which mark man off from other animals. To learn in a human way and to human effect is not just to acquire added skill through refinement of original capacities.

To learn to be human is to develop through the give-and-take of communication an effective sense of being an individually distinctive member of a community; one who understands and appreciates its beliefs, desires and methods, and who contributes to a further conversion of organic powers into human resources and values. But this translation is never finished. The old Adam, the unregenerate element in human nature, persists. It shows itself

wherever the method obtains of attaining results by use of force instead of
by the method of communication and enlightenment. It manifests itself more
subtly, pervasively and effectually when knowledge and the instrumentalities
of skill which are the product of communal life are employed in the service
of wants and impulses which have not themselves been modified by reference
to a shared interest. To the doctrine of "natural" economy which held that
commercial exchange would bring about such an interdependence that harmony would automatically result, Rousseau gave an adequate answer in advance. He pointed out that interdependence provides just the situation which
makes it possible and worthwhile for the stronger and abler to exploit others
for their own ends, to keep others in a state of subjection where they can be
utilized as animated tools. The remedy he suggested, a return to a condition
of independence based on isolation, was hardly seriously meant. But its desperateness is evidence of the urgency of the problem. Its negative character
was equivalent to surrender of any hope of solution. By contrast it indicates
the nature of the only possible solution: the perfecting of the means and
ways of communication of meanings so that genuinely shared interest in the
consequences of interdependent activities may inform desire and effort and
thereby direct action.

This is the meaning of the statement that the problem is a moral one dependent upon intelligence and education. We have in our prior account sufficiently emphasized the role of technological and industrial factors in creating the Great Society. What was said may even have seemed to imply acceptance of the deterministic version of an economic interpretation of history
and institutions. It is silly and futile to ignore and deny economic facts. They
do not cease to operate because we refuse to note them, or because we smear
them over with sentimental idealizations. As we have also noted, they generate as their result overt and external conditions of action and these are
known with various degrees of adequacy. What actually happens in consequence of industrial forces is dependent upon the presence or absence of
perception and communication of consequences, upon foresight and its effect
upon desire and endeavor. Economic agencies produce one result when they
are left to work themselves out on the merely physical level, or on that level
modified only as the knowledge, skill and technique which the community has
accumulated are transmitted to its members unequally and by chance. They
have a different outcome in the degree in which knowledge of consequences
is equitably distributed, and action is animated by an informed and lively
sense of a shared interest. The doctrine of economic interpretation as usually
stated ignores the transformation which meanings may effect; it passes over
the new medium with communication may interpose between industry and
its eventual consequences. It is obsessed by the illusion which vitiated the
"natural economy": an illusion due to failure to note the difference made
in action by perception and publication of its consequences, actual and pos-

sible. It thinks in terms of antecedents, not of the eventual; of origins, not fruits.

We have returned, through this apparent excursion, to the question in which our earlier discussion culminated: What are the conditions under which it is possible for the Great Society to approach more closely and vitally the status of a Great Community, and thus take form in genuinely democratic societies and state? What are the conditions under which we may reasonably picture the Public emerging from its eclipse?

The study will be an intellectual or hypothetical one. There will be no attempt to state how the required conditions might come into existence, nor to prophesy that they will occur. The object of the analysis will be to show that *unless* ascertained specifications are realized, the Community cannot be organized as a democratically effective Public. It is not claimed that the conditions which will be noted will suffice, but only that at least they are indispensable. In other words, we shall endeavor to frame a hypothesis regarding the democratic state to stand in contrast with the earlier doctrine which has been nullified by the course of events.

Two essential constituents in that older theory, as will be recalled, were the notions that each individual is of himself equipped with the intelligence needed, under the operation of self-interest, to engage in political affairs; and that general suffrage, frequent elections of officials and majority rule are sufficient to ensure the responsibility of elected rulers to the desires and interests of the public. As we shall see, the second conception is logically bound up with the first and stands or falls with it. At the basis of the scheme lies what Lippmann has well called the idea of the "omnicompetent" individual: competent to frame policies, to judge their results; competent to know in all situations demanding political action what is for his own good, and competent to enforce his idea of good and the will to effect it against contrary forces. Subsequent history has proved that the assumption involved illusion. Had it not been for the misleading influence of a false psychology, the illusion might have been detected in advance. But current philosophy held that ideas and knowledge were functions of a mind or consciousness which originated in individuals by means of isolated contact with objects. But in fact, knowledge is a function of association and communication; it depends upon tradition, upon tools and methods socially transmitted, developed and sanctioned. Faculties of effectual observation, reflection and desire are habits acquired under the influence of the culture and institutions of society, not ready-made inherent powers. The fact that man acts from crudely intelligized emotion and from habit rather than from rational consideration, is now so familiar that it is not easy to appreciate that the other idea was taken seriously as the basis of economic and political philosophy. The measure of truth which it contains was derived from observation of a relatively small group of shrewd businessmen who regulated their enterprises by calculation and accounting, and of citizens of small and stable local communities who were so intimately acquainted with the persons and affairs of their locality that they could pass competent judgment upon the bearing of proposed measures upon their own concerns.

Habit is the mainspring of human action, and habits are formed for the most part under the influence of the customs of a group. The organic structure of man entails the formation of habit, for, whether we wish it or not, whether we are aware of it or not, every act effects a modification of attitude and set which directs future behavior. The dependence of habit-forming upon those habits of a group which constitute customs and institutions is a natural consequence of the helplessness of infancy. . . .

The influence of habit is decisive because all distinctively human action has to be learned, and the very heart, blood and sinews of learning is creation of habitudes. Habits bind us to orderly and established ways of action because they generate ease, skill and interest in things to which we have grown used and because they instigate fear to walk in different ways, and because they leave us incapacitated for the trial of them. Habit does not preclude the use of thought, but it determines the channels within which it operates. Thinking is secreted in the interstices of habits. The sailor, miner, fisherman and farmer think, but their thoughts fall within the framework of accustomed occupations and relationships. We dream beyond the limits of use and wont, but only rarely does revery become a source of acts which break bounds; so rarely that we name those in whom it happens demonic geniuses and marvel at the spectacle. Thinking itself becomes habitual along certain lines; a specialized occupation. Scientific men, philosophers, literary persons, are not men and women who have so broken the bonds of habits that pure reason and emotion undefiled by use and wont speak through them. They are persons of a specialized infrequent habit. Hence the idea that men are moved by an intelligent and calculated regard for their own good is pure mythology. Even if the principle of self-love actuated behavior, it would still be true that the *objects* in which men find their love manifested, the objects which they take as constituting their peculiar interests, are set by habits reflecting social customs . . . (*ibid.*, pp. 146–61).

. . . The prime condition of a democratically organized public is a kind of knowledge and insight which does not yet exist. In its absence, it would be the height of absurdity to try to tell what it would be like if it existed. But some of the conditions which must be fulfilled if it is to exist can be indicated. We can borrow that much from the spirit and method of science even if we are ignorant of it as a specialized apparatus. An obvious requirement is freedom of social inquiry and of distribution of its conclusions. The notion that men may be free in their thought even when they are not in its expression and dissemination has been sedulously propagated. It had its origin in the idea of a mind complete in itself, apart from action and from objects. Such a consciousness presents in fact the spectacle of mind deprived of its normal functioning, because it is baffled by the actualities in connection with which alone it is truly mind, and is driven back into secluded and impotent revery.

There can be no public without full publicity in respect to all consequences which concern it. Whatever obstructs and restricts publicity, limits and distorts public opinion and checks and distorts thinking on social affairs. Without freedom of expression, not even methods of social inquiry can be developed. For tools can be evolved and perfected only in operation; in application to observing, reporting and organizing actual subject-matter; and this application cannot occur save through free and systematic communication. The early history of physical knowledge, of Greek conceptions of natural phenomena, proves how inept become the conceptions of the best endowed minds when those ideas are elaborated apart from the closest contact with the events which they purport to state and explain. The ruling ideas and methods of the human sciences are in much the same condition today. They are also evolved on the basis of past gross observations, remote from constant use in regulation of the material of new observations.

The belief that thought and its communication are now free simply because legal restrictions which once obtained have been done away with is absurd. Its currency perpetuates the infantile state of social knowledge. For it blurs recognition of our central need to possess conceptions which are used as tools of directed inquiry and which are tested, rectified and caused to grow in actual use. No man and no mind was ever emancipated merely by being left alone. Removal of formal limitations is but a negative condition; positive freedom is not a state but an act which involves methods and instrumentalities for control of conditions. Experience shows that sometimes the sense of external oppression, as by censorship, acts as a challenge and arouses intellectual energy and excites courage. But a belief in intellectual freedom where it does not exist contributes only to complacency in virtual enslavement, to sloppiness, superficiality and recourse to sensations as a substitute for ideas: marked traits of our present estate with respect to social knowledge. On one hand, thinking deprived of its normal course takes refuge in academic specialism, comparable in its way to what is called scholasticism. On the other hand, the physical agencies of publicity which exist in such abundance are utilized in ways which constitute a large part of the present meaning of publicity: advertising, propaganda, invasion of private life, the "featuring" of passing incidents in a way which violates all the moving logic of continuity, and which leaves us with those isolated intrusions and shocks which are the essence of "sensations."

It would be a mistake to identify the conditions which limit free communication and circulation of facts and ideas, and which thereby arrest and pervert social thought or inquiry, merely with overt forces which are obstructive. It is true that those who have ability to manipulate social relations for their own advantage have to be reckoned with. They have an uncanny instinct for detecting whatever intellectual tendencies even remotely threaten to encroach upon their control. They have developed an extraordinary facility in enlisting upon their side the inertia, prejudices and emotional partisanship of the masses by use of a technique which impedes free inquiry and expression. We seem to be approaching a state of government by hired promoters of opinion called publicity agents. But the more serious enemy is deeply concealed in hidden entrenchments.

Emotional habituations and intellectual habitudes on the part of the mass of men create the conditions of which the exploiters of sentiment and opinion only take advantage. Men have got used to an experimental method in physical and technical matters. They are still afraid of it in human concerns. The fear is the more efficacious because like all deep-lying fears it is covered up and disguised by all kinds of rationalizations. One of its commonest forms is a truly religious idealization of, and reverence for, established institutions; for example in our own politics, the Constitution, the Supreme Court, private property, free contract and so on. The words "sacred" and "sanctity" come readily to our lips when such things come under discussion. They testify to the religious aureole which protects the institutions. If "holy" means that which is not to be approached nor touched, save with ceremonial precautions and by specially anointed officials, then such things are holy in contemporary political life. . . (*ibid.*, pp. 166–70).

At present, the application of physical science is rather *to* human concerns than *in* them. That is, it is external, made in the interests of its consequences for a possessing and acquisitive class. Application *in* life would signify that science was absorbed and distributed; that it was the instrumentality of that common understanding and thorough communication which is the precondition of the existence of a genuine and effective public. The use of science to regulate industry and trade has gone on steadily. The scientific revolution of the seventeenth century was the precursor of the industrial revolution of the eighteenth and nineteenth. In consequence, man has suffered the impact of an enormously enlarged control of physical energies without any corresponding ability to control himself and his own affairs. Knowledge divided against itself, a science to whose incompleteness is added an artificial split, has played its part in generating enslavement of men, women and children in factories in which they are animated machines to tend inanimate machines. It has maintained sordid slums, flurried and discontented careers, grinding poverty and luxurious wealth, brutal exploitation of nature and man in times of peace and high explosives and noxious gases in times of war. Man, a child in understanding of himself, has placed in his hands physical tools of incalculable power. He plays with them like a child, and whether they work harm or good is largely a matter of accident. The instrumentality becomes a master and works fatally as if possessed of a will of its own—not because it has a will but because man has not.

The glorification of "pure" science under such conditions is a rationalization of an escape; it marks a construction of an asylum of refuge, a shirking of responsibility. The true purity of knowledge exists not when it is uncontaminated by contact with use and service. It is wholly a moral matter, an affair of honesty, impartiality and generous breadth of intent in search and communication. The adulteration of knowledge is due not to its use, but to vested bias and prejudice, to one-sidedness of outlook, to vanity, to conceit of possession and authority, to contempt or disregard of human concern in its use. Humanity is not, as was once thought, the end for which all things were formed; it is but a slight and feeble thing, perhaps an episodic one, in the vast stretch of the universe. But for man, man is the center of interest and the measure of importance. The magnifying of the physical realm at the cost of man is but an abdication and a flight. To make physical science a rival of human interests is bad enough, for it forms a diversion of energy which can ill be afforded. But the evil does not stop there. The ultimate harm is that the understanding by man of his own affairs and his ability to direct them are sapped at their root when knowledge of nature is disconnected from its human function.

It has been implied throughout that knowledge is communication as well as understanding. I well remember the saying of a man, uneducated from the standpoint of the schools, in speaking of certain matters: "Sometime they will be found out and not only found out, but they will be known." The schools may suppose that a thing is known when it is found out. My old friend was aware that a thing is fully known only when it is published, shared, socially accessible. Record and communication are indispensable to knowledge. Knowledge cooped up in a private consciousness is a myth, and knowledge of social phenomena is peculiarly dependent upon dissemination, for only by distribution can such knowledge be either obtained or tested. A fact of community life which is not spread abroad so as to be a common possession is a contradiction in terms. Dissemination is something other than scattering at large. Seeds are sown, not by virtue of being thrown out at random, but by being so distributed as to take root and have a chance of growth. Communication of the results of social inquiry is the same thing as the formation of public opinion. This marks one of the first ideas framed in the growth of political democracy as it will be one of the last to be fulfilled. For public opinion is judgment which is formed and entertained by those who constitute the public and is about public affairs. Each of the two phases imposes for its realization conditions hard to meet.

Opinions and beliefs concerning the public presuppose effective and organized inquiry. Unless there are methods for detecting the energies which are at work and tracing them through an intricate network of interactions to their consequences, what passes as public opinion will be "opinion" in its derogatory sense rather than truly public, no matter how widespread the opinion is. The number who share error as to fact and who partake of a false belief measures power for harm. Opinion casually formed and formed under the direction of those who have something at stake in having a lie believed can be *public* opinion only in name. Calling it by this name, acceptance of the name as a kind of warrant, magnifies its capacity to lead action astray. The more who share it, the more injurious its influence. Public opinion, even if it happens to be correct, is intermittent when it is not the product of methods of investigation and reporting constantly at work. It appears only in crises. Hence its "rightness" concerns only an immediate emergency. Its lack of continuity makes it wrong from the standpoint of the course of events. It is as if a physician were able to deal for the moment with an emergency in disease but could not adapt his treatment of it to the underlying conditions which brought it about. He may then "cure" the disease—that is, cause its present alarming symptoms to subside—but he does not modify its causes; his treatment may even affect them for the worse. Only continuous inquiry, continuous in the sense of being connected as well as persistent, can provide the material of enduring opinion about public matters.

There is a sense in which "opinion" rather than knowledge, even under the most favorable circumstances, is the proper term to use—namely, in the sense of judgment, estimate. For in its strict sense, knowledge can refer only to what *has* happened and been done. What is still *to be* done involves a forecast of a future still contingent, and cannot escape the liability to error in judgment involved in all anticipation of probabilities. There may well be honest divergence as to policies to be pursued, even when plans spring from knowledge of the same facts. But genuinely public policy cannot be generated unless it be informed by knowledge, and this knowledge does not exist except when there is systematic, thorough, and well-equipped search and record . . . (*ibid.*, pp. 174–79).

We have but touched lightly and in passing upon the conditions which must be fulfilled if the Great Society is to become a Great Community; a society in which the ever-expanding and intricately ramifying consequences of associated activities shall be known in the full sense of that word, so that an organized, articulate Public comes into being. The highest and most difficult kind of inquiry and a subtle, delicate, vivid and responsive art of communication must take possession of the physical machinery of transmission and circulation and breathe life into it. When the machine age has thus perfected its machinery it will be a means of life and not its despotic master. Democracy will come into its own, for democracy is a name for a life of free and enriching communion. It had its seer in Walt Whitman. It will have its consummation when free social inquiry is indissolubly wedded to the art of full and moving communication (*ibid.*, p. 184).

The strongest point to be made in behalf of even such rudimentary political forms as democracy has already attained, popular voting, majority rule and so on, is that to some extent they involve a consultation and discussion which uncover social needs and troubles. This fact is the great asset on the side of the political ledger. De Tocqueville wrote it down almost a century ago in his survey of the prospects of democracy in the United States. Accusing a democracy of a tendency to prefer mediocrity in its elected rulers, and admitting its exposure to gusts of passion and its openness to folly, he pointed out in effect that popular government is educative as other modes of political regulation are not. It forces a recognition that there are common interests, even though the recognition of *what* they are is confused; and the need it enforces of discussion and publicity brings about some clarification of what they are. The man who wears the shoe knows best that it pinches and where it pinches, even if the expert shoemaker is the best judge of how the trouble is to be remedied. Popular government has at least created public spirit even if its success in informing that spirit has not been great.

A class of experts is inevitably so removed from common interests as to become a class with private interests and private knowledge, which in social matters is not knowledge at all. The ballot is, as often said, a substitute for bullets. But what is more significant is that counting of heads compels prior recourse to methods of discussion, consultation and persuasion, while the essence of appeal to force is to cut short resort to such methods. Majority rule, just as majority rule, is as foolish as its critics charge it with being. But it never is *merely* majority rule. As a practical politician, Samuel J. Tilden, said a long time ago: "The means by which a majority comes to be a majority is the more important thing": antecedent debates, modification of views to meet the opinions of minorities, the relative satisfaction given the latter by the fact that it has had a chance and that next time it may be successful in becoming a majority. Think of the meaning of the "problem of minorities" in certain European states, and compare it with the status of minorities in countries having popular government. It is true that all valuable as well as new ideas begin with minorities, perhaps a minority of one. The important consideration is that opportunity be given that idea to spread and to become the possession of the multitude. No government by experts in which the masses do not have the chance to inform the experts as to their needs can be anything but an oligarchy managed in the interests of the few. And the enlightenment must proceed in ways which force the administrative specialists to take account of the needs. The world has suffered more from leaders and authorities than from the masses.

The essential need, in other words, is the improvement of the methods and conditions of debate, discussion and persuasion. That is *the* problem of the public. We have asserted that this improvement depends essentially upon freeing and perfecting the processes of inquiry and of dissemination of their conclusions. Inquiry, indeed, is a work which devolves upon experts. But their expertness is not shown in framing and executing policies, but in discovering and making known the facts upon which the former depend. They are technical experts in the sense that scientific investigators and artists manifest *expertise*. It is not necessary that the many should have the knowledge and skill to carry on the needed investigations; what is required is that they have the ability to judge of the bearing of the knowledge supplied by others upon common concerns . . . (*ibid.*, pp. 206–09).

As far as any actual American is true to the type that is proclaimed to be *the* American, he should be thrilled by the picture that is drawn of him. For we are told that the type is a genuine mutation in the history of culture; that it is new, the product of the last century, and that it is stamped with success. It is transforming the external conditions of life and thereby reacting on the psychical content of life; it is assimilating other types of itself and recoining them. No world-conquest, whether that of Rome or Christendom, compares with that of "Americanism" in extent or effectiveness. If success and quantity are in fact the standards of the "American," here are admissions that will content his soul. From the standpoint of the type depicted, he is approved; and what do adverse criticisms matter?

But either the type is not yet so definitely fixed as is represented, or else there are individual Americans who deviate from type. For there are many who will have reserves in their admiration of the picture that is presented. Of course the dissenters may be, as the European critics say, impotent sports, fish out of water and affected with nostalgia for the European tradition. Nevertheless, it is worthwhile to raise the question as to whether the American type, supposing there is to be one, has as yet taken on definitive form. First, however, what are alleged to be the characteristics of the type?

Fundamentally, they spring from impersonality. The roots of the intellect are unconscious and vital, in instincts and emotions. In America, we are told, this subconsciousness is disregarded; it is suppressed or is subordinated to conscious rationality, which means that it is adapted to the needs and conditions of the external world. We have "intellect," but distinctly in the Bergsonian sense; mind attuned to the conditions of action upon matter, upon the world. Our emotional life is quick, excitable, undiscriminating, lacking in individuality and in direction by intellectual life. Hence the "externality and superficiality of the American soul"; it has no ultimate inner unity and uniqueness—no true personality.

The marks and signs of this "impersonalization" of the human soul are quantification of life, with its attendant disregard of quality; its mechanization and the almost universal habit of esteeming technique as an end, not as a means, so that organic and intellectual life is also "rationalized"; and, finally, standardization. Differences and distinctions are ignored and overridden; agreement, similarity, is the ideal. There is not only absence of social discrimination but of intellectual; critical thinking is conspicuous by its absence. Our pronounced trait is mass suggestibility. The adaptability and flexibility that we display in our practical intelligence when dealing with external conditions have found their way into our souls. Homogeneity of thought and emotion has become an ideal.

Quantification, mechanization and standardization: these are then the marks of the Americanization that is conquering the world. They have their good side; external conditions and the standard of living are undoubtedly improved. But their effects are not limited to these matters; they have invaded mind and character, and subdued the soul to their own dye. The criticism is familiar; it is so much the burden of our own critics that one is never quite sure how much of the picture of foreign critics is drawn from direct observation and how much from native novels and essays that are not complacent with the American scene. This fact does not detract from the force of the indictment; it rather adds to it, and raises the more insistently the question of what our life means . . . (*ION*, pp. 22–25).

Until the issue is met, the confusion of a civilization divided against itself will persist. The mass development, which our European critics tell us has submerged individuality, *is* the product of a machine age; in some form it will follow in all countries from the extension of a machine technology. Its immediate effect has been, without doubt, a subjection of certain types of individuality. As far as individuality is associated with aristocracy of the historic type, the extension of the machine age will presumably be hostile to individuality in its traditional sense all over the world. But the strictures of our European critics only define the issue touched upon in the previous chapter. The problem of constructing a new individuality consonant with the objective conditions under which we live is the deepest problem of our times.

There are two "solutions" that fail to solve. One of these is the method of avoidance. This course is taken as far as it is assumed that the only valid type of individuality is that which holds over from the ages that anteceded machine technology and the democratic society it creates. The course that is complementary to the method of escape springs from assumption that the present situation is final; that it presents something inherently ultimate and fixed. Only as it is treated as transitive and moving, as material to be dealt with in shaping a later outcome, only, that is, as it is treated as a *problem*, is the idea of any solution genuine and relevant. We may well take the formula advanced by European critics as a means of developing our consciousness of some of the conditions of the problem. So regarded, the problem is seen to be essentially that of creation of a new individualism as significant for modern conditions as the old individualism at its best was for its day and place. The first step in further definition of this problem is realization of the collective age which we have already entered. When that is apprehended, the issue will define itself as utilization of the realities of a corporate civilization to validate and embody the distinctive moral element in the American version of individualism: Equality and freedom expressed not merely externally and politically but through personal participation in the development of a shared culture (*ibid.*, pp. 32–34).

There are, I suppose, those who fancy that the emphasis which I put upon the corporateness of existing society in the United States is in effect, even if not in the writer's conscious intent, a plea for greater conformity than now exists. Nothing could be further from the truth. Identification of society with a level, whatever it be, high as well as low, of uniformity is just another evidence of that distraction because of which the individual is lost. Society is, of course, but the relations of individuals to one another in this form and that. And all relations are interactions, not fixed molds. The particular interactions that compose a human society include the give and take of participation, of a sharing that increases, that expands and deepens, the capacity and significance of the interacting factors. Conformity is a name for the absence of vital interplay; the arrest and benumbing of communication. As I have been trying to say, it is the artificial substitute used to hold men together in lack of associations that are incorporated into inner dispositions of thought and desire. I often wonder what meaning is given to the term "society" by those who oppose it to the intimacies of personal intercourse, such as those of friendship. Presumably they have in their minds a picture of rigid institutions or some set and external organization. But an institution that is other than the structure of human contact and intercourse is a fossil of some past society; organization, as in any living organism, is the cooperative consensus of multitudes of cells, each living in exchange with others . . . (*ibid.*, pp. 85–86).

A point which concerns us in conclusion passes beyond the field of intellectual method, and trenches upon the question of practical re-formation of social conditions. In its deepest and richest sense a community must always remain a matter of face-to-face intercourse. This is why the family and neighborhood, with all their deficiences, have always been the chief agencies of nurture, the means by which dispositions are stably formed and ideas acquired which laid hold on the roots of character. The Great Community, in the sense of free and full intercommunication, is conceivable. But it can never possess all the qualities which mark a local community. It will do its final work in ordering the relations and enriching the experience of local associations. The invasion and partial destruction of the life of the latter by outside uncontrolled agencies is the immediate source of the instability, disintegration and restlessness which characterize the present epoch. Evils which are uncritically and indiscriminately laid at the door of industrialism and democracy might, with greater intelligence, be referred to the dislocation and unsettlement of local communities. Vital and thorough attachments are bred only in the intimacy of an intercourse which is of necessity restricted in range.

Is it possible for local communities to be stable without being static, progressive without being merely mobile? Can the vast, innumerable and intricate currents of trans-local associations be so banked and conducted that they will pour the generous and abundant meanings of which they are potential bearers into the smaller intimate unions of human beings living in immediate contact with one another? Is it possible to restore the reality of the lesser communal organizations and to penetrate and saturate their members with a sense of local community life? There is at present, at least in theory, a movement away from the principle of territorial organization to that of "functional," that is to say, occupational, organization. It is true enough that older forms of territorial association do not satisfy present needs. It is true that ties formed by sharing in common work, whether in what is called industry or what are called professions, have now a force which formerly they did not possess. But these ties can be counted upon for an enduring and stable organization, which at the same time is flexible and moving, only as they grow out of immediate intercourse and attachment. The theory, as far as it relies upon associations which are remote and indirect, would if carried into effect soon be confronted by all the troubles and evils of the present situation in a transposed form. There is no substitute for the vitality and depth of close and direct intercourse and attachment . . . (*PIP*, pp. 211–13).

Whatever the future may have in store, one thing is certain. Unless local communal life can be restored, the public cannot adequately resolve its most urgent problem: to find and identify itself. But if it be reestablished, it will manifest a fullness, variety and freedom of possession and enjoyment of meanings and goods unknown in the contiguous associations of the past. For it will be alive and flexible as well as stable, responsive to the complex and world-wide scene in which it is enmeshed. While local, it will not be isolated. Its larger relationships will provide an inexhaustible and flowing fund of meanings upon which to draw, with assurance that its drafts will be honored. Territorial states and political boundaries will persist; but they will not be barriers which impoverish experience by cutting man off from his fellows; they will not be hard and fast divisions whereby external separation is converted into inner jealously, fear, suspicion and hostility. Competition will continue, but it will be less rivalry for acquisition of material goods, and more an emulation of local groups to enrich direct experience with appreciatively enjoyed intellectual and artistic wealth. If the technological age can provide mankind with a firm and general basis of material security, it will be absorbed in a humane age. It will take its place as an instrumentality of shared and communicated experience. But without passage through a machine age, mankind's hold upon what is needful as the precondition of a free, flexible and many-colored life is so precarious and inequitable that competitive scramble for acquisition and frenzied use of the results of acquisition for purposes of excitation and display will be perpetuated.

We have said that consideration of this particular condition of the generation of democratic communities and an articulate democratic public carries us beyond the question of intellectual method into that of practical procedure. But the two questions are not disconnected. The problem of securing diffused and seminal intelligence can be solved only in the degree in which local communal life becomes a reality. Signs and symbols, language, are the means of communication by which a fraternally shared experience is ushered in and sustained. But the wingèd words of conversation in immediate intercourse have a vital import lacking in the fixed and frozen words of written speech. Systematic and continuous inquiry into all the conditions which affect association and their dissemination in print is a precondition of the creation of a true public. But it and its results are but tools after all. Their final actuality is accomplished in face-to-face relationships by means of direct give and take. Logic in its fulfillment recurs to the primitive sense of the word: dialogue. Ideas which are not communicated, shared, and reborn in expression are but soliloquy, and soliloquy is but broken and imperfect thought. It, like the acquisition of material wealth, marks a diversion of the wealth created by associated endeavor and exchange to private ends. It is more genteel, and it is called more noble. But there is no difference in kind.

In a word, that expansion and reinforcement of personal understanding and judgment by the cumulative and transmitted intellectual wealth of the community which may render nugatory the indictment of democracy drawn on the basis of the ignorance, bias and levity of the masses, can be fulfilled only in the relations of personal intercourse in the local community. The connections of the ear with vital and outgoing thought and emotion are immensely closer and more varied than those of the eye. Vision is a spectator; hearing is a participator. Publication is partial and the public which results is partially informed and formed until the meanings it purveys pass from mouth to mouth. There is no limit to the liberal expansion and confirmation of limited personal intellectual endowment which may proceed from the flow of social intelligence when that circulates by word of mouth from one to another in the communications of the local community. That and that only gives reality to public opinion. We lie, as Emerson said, in the lap of an immense intelligence. But that intelligence is dormant and its communications are broken, inarticulate and faint until it possesses the local community as its medium (*ibid.*, pp. 216–19).

THE METHOD OF SOCIAL INTELLIGENCE[12]

Democracy as Dewey conceives it is not a passive registration of prefer-ences. It is an active and continuing mode of social behavior; and nothing is more foreign to it than what Dewey calls the absolutistic mode of thought and action. The members of a genuinely democratic community are aware that they can achieve the most in growth, free-dom, and shared experience by mutual willingness to embrace the democratic method of decision and action. The experience from which such decision issues would involve communication of existing values and purposes, sharing the knowledge of the interactions and consum-mations which the situation might provide, and a commitment to the preservation and enrichment of the conditions of intelligent social method. Dewey's philosophy of democracy does not rest on such archaic notions as a general will or an implicit identity of interests. Rather, it insists on acknowledging that there is clash and conflict of values. It proposes a method for dealing with such conflict. Inclusive interests are something to be constructed, to be brought into existence by means of the method.

. . . The controversy between believers in private and in public action is manifested in every issue which concerns the extent and area of govern-mental action. . . .

The attempt to settle these issues in our discussion of ethics would ob-viously involve an exhibition of partisanship. But, what is more important, it would involve the adoption of a method which has been expressly criticized and repudiated. It would assume the existence of final and unquestionable knowledge upon which we can fall back in order to settle automatically every moral problem. It would involve the commitment to a dogmatic theory of morals. The alternative method may be called experimental. It implies that reflective morality demands observation of particular situations, rather than fixed adherence to *a priori* principles; that free inquiry and freedom of publi-cation and discussion must be encouraged and not merely grudgingly tolerated; that opportunity at different times and places must be given for trying different measures so that their effects may be capable of observation and of comparison with one another. It is, in short, the method of democracy, of a positive toleration which amounts to sympathetic regard for the intelligence and personality of others, even if they hold views opposed to ours, and of scientific inquiry into facts and testing of ideas.

The opposed method, even when we free it from the extreme traits of forcible suppression, censorship, and intolerant persecution which have often historically accompanied it, is the method of appeal to authority and to precedent. The will of divine beings, supernaturally revealed; of divinely ordained rulers; of so-called natural law, philosophically interpreted; of private conscience; of the commands of the state, or the constitution; of common consent; of a majority; of received conventions; of traditions coming from a hoary past; of the wisdom of ancestors; of precendents set up in the past, have at different times been the authority appealed to. The common feature of the appeal is that there is some voice so authoritative as to preclude the need of inquiry. The logic of the various positions is that while an open mind may be desirable in respect to physical truths, a completely settled and closed mind is needed in moral matters.

Adoption of the experimental method does not signify that there is no place for authority and precedent. On the contrary, precedent is, as we noted in another connection, a valuable *instrumentality*. . . . But precedents are to be *used* rather than to be implicitly followed; they are to be used as tools of analysis of present situations, suggesting points to be looked into and hypotheses to be tried. . . .

To some persons it may seem an academic matter whether their attitude and the method they follow in judging the ethical values of social institutions, customs, and traditions, be experimental or dogmatic and closed; whether they proceed by study of consequences, of the working of condition, or by an attempt to dispose of all questions by reference to preformed absolute standards. There is, however, no opening for application of scientific method in social morals unless the former procedure is adopted. There is at least a presumption that the development of methods of objective and impartial inquiry in social affairs would be as significant there as it has proved in physical matters. The alternative to organic inquiry is reliance upon prejudice, partisanship, upon tradition accepted without questioning, upon the varying pressures of immediate circumstance. Adoption of an experimental course of judgment would work virtually a moral revolution in social judgments and practice. It would eliminate the chief causes of intolerance, persecution, fanaticism, and the use of differences of opinion to create class wars. It is for such reasons as these that it is claimed that, at the present time, the question of method to be used in judging existing customs and policies proposed is of greater moral significance than the particular conclusion reached in connection with any one controversy.

It is frequently asserted that the method of experimental intelligence can be applied to physical facts because physical nature does not present conflicts of class interests, while it is inapplicable to society because the latter is so deeply marked by incompatible interests. It is then assumed that the "experimentalist" is one who has chosen to ignore the uncomfortable fact of conflicting interests. Of course, there *are* conflicting interests; otherwise there would be no social problems. The problem under discussion is precisely *how* conflicting claims are to be settled in the interest of the widest possible contribution to the interests of all—or at least of the great majority. The method of democracy—in as far as it is that of organized intelligence—is to bring these conflicts out into the open where their special claims can be seen and appraised, where they can be discussed and judged in the light of more inclusive interests than are represented by either of them separately. There is, for example, a clash of interests between munition manufacturers and most of the rest of the population. The more the respective claims of the two are publicly and scientifically weighed, the more likely it is that the public interest will be disclosed and be made effective. There is an undoubted objective clash of interests between finance-capitalism that controls the means of production and whose profit is served by maintaining relative scarcity, and idle workers and hungry consumers. But what generates violent strife is failure to bring the conflict into the light of intelligence where the conflicting interests can be adjudicated in behalf of the interest of the great majority. Those most committed to the dogma of inevitable force recognize the need for intelligently discovering and expressing the dominant social interest up to a certain point and then draw back. The "experimentalist" is one who would see to it that the method depended upon by all in some degree in every democratic community be followed through to completion. . . .

When we say that thinking and beliefs should be experimental, not absolutistic, we have then in mind a certain logic of method, not, primarily, the carrying on of experimentation like that of laboratories. Such a logic involves the following factors: First, that those concepts, general principles, theories and dialectical developments which are indispensable to any systematic knowledge be shaped and tested as tools of inquiry. Secondly, that policies and proposals for social action be treated as working hypotheses, not as programs to be rigidly adhered to and executed. They will be experimental in the sense that they will be entertained subject to constant and well-equipped observation of the consequences they entail when acted upon, and subject to ready and flexible revision in the light of observed consequences. . . .

These considerations suggest a brief discussion of the effect of the present absolutistic logic upon the method and aims of education, not just in the sense of schooling but with respect to all the ways in which communities attempt to shape the disposition and beliefs of their members. Even when the processes of education do not aim at the unchanged perpetuation of existing institutions, it is assumed that there must be a mental picture of some desired end, personal and social, which is to be attained, and that this conception of a fixed determinate end ought to control educative processes. Reformers share this conviction with conservatives. The disciples of Lenin and Mussolini vie with the captains of capitalistic society in endeavoring to bring about a formation of dispositions and ideas which will conduce to a preconceived goal. . . . If there is a difference, it is that the former proceed more consciously. An experimental social method would probably manifest itself first of all in surrender of this notion. Every care would be taken to surround the young with the physical and social conditions which best conduce, as far as freed knowledge extends, to release of personal potentialities. The habits thus formed would have entrusted to them the meeting of future social requirements and the development of the future state of society. Then and then only would all social agencies that are available operate as resources in behalf of a bettered community life. . . .

Neither the past nor the present afford . . . any ground for expecting that the adjustment of authority and freedom, stability and change, will be achieved by following old paths. The idea that any solution at all can ever be attained may seem to some romantic and utopian. But the most fantastically unrealistic of all notions is the widely prevalent belief that we can attain enduring stable authority by employing or by reexhuming the institutional means tried in the past; equally fantastic is the belief that the assured freedom of individuals can be secured by pitting individuals against one another in a pitiless struggle for material possessions and economic power. The issue, in my judgment, can be narrowed down to this question: Are there resources that have not as yet been tried out in the large field of human relations, resources that are available and that carry with them the potential promise of successful application?

In raising this question I am aware that it is almost inevitable that what I have said about the human necessity for some kind of collective authority to give individuals direction in their relations with one another and to give them the support that comes from a sense of solidarity, will appear to be a plea for a return to some kind of social control brought about through, and perpetuated by, external institutional means. If my question is so taken, then the criticism I have made of the alliance that has taken place between the principle of individual freedom and private initiative and enterprise in economic matters will necessarily also seem to be merely an argument for social control by means of a collective planned economy—put forward, of course, with some change in vocabulary. However, the argument in fact cuts in both directions. It indicates that while movements in the direction of collective, planned economy may cure evils from which we are now suffering, it will in the end go the way of all past attempts at organization of authoritative power unless some hitherto untried means are utilized on a large and systematic scale for bringing into life the desired organic coordination. Otherwise we shall finally find ourselves repeating on a different plane the old struggle between social organization and individual freedom, with the oscillation from one principle to the other that has so characteristically marked the past.

The resource that has not yet been tried on any large scale in the broad field of human, social relationships is the utilization of organized intelligence, the manifold benefits and values of which we have substantial evidence in the narrower field of science.

Within a limited area, the collective intelligence which is exemplified in the growth and application of scientific method has already become authoritative. It is authoritative in the field of beliefs regarding the structure of nature and relevant to our understanding of physical events. To a considerable extent, the same statement holds true of beliefs about historical personages and historical events—especially with those that are sufficiently remote from the present time. When we turn to the practical side, we see that the same method is supreme in controlling and guiding our active dealings with material things and physical energies. To a large and significant extent, the Baconian prophecy that knowledge is power of control has been realized in this particular, somewhat narrowly circumscribed, area. To be sure, it cannot be said that intelligence, operating by the methods that constitute science, has as yet completely won undisputed right and authority to control beliefs even in the restricted physical field. But organized intelligence has made an advance that is truly surprising when we consider the short time in which it has functioned and the powerful foes against which it had to make its way: the foes of inertia, of old, long-established traditions and habits—inertia, traditions and habits all of them entrenched in forms of institutional life that are effulgent with the prestige of time, that are enveloped in the glamor of imaginative appeal and that are crowned, severally and collectively, with an emotional halo made of values that men most prize.

The record of the struggle that goes by the name of "conflict between science and religion" or, if you please, "conflict between theology and science" was essentially a conflict of claims to exercise social authority. It was not just a conflict between two sets of theoretical beliefs, but between two alignments of social forces—one which was old and had institutional power that it did not hesitate to use and one which was new and striving and craving for recognition against gigantic odds.

What is pertinent, what is deeply significant to the theme of the *relation* between collective authority and freedom, is that the progress of intelligence —as exemplified in this summary story of scientific advance—exhibits their organic, effective union. Science has made its way by releasing, not by suppressing, the elements of variation, of invention and innovation, of novel creation in individuals. It is as true of the history of modern science as it is of the history of painting or music that its advances have been initiated by individuals who freed themselves from the bonds of tradition and custom whenever they found the latter hampering their own powers of reflection, observation and construction.

In spite of science's dependence for its development upon the free initiative, invention and enterprise of individual inquirers, the authority of science issues from and is based upon collective activity, cooperatively organized. Even when, temporarily, the ideas put forth by individuals have sharply diverged from received beliefs, the method used in science has been a public and open method which succeeded and could succeed only as it tended to produce agreement, unity of belief among all who labored in the same field. Every scientific inquirer, even when he deviates most widely from current ideas, depends upon methods and conclusions that are a common possession and not of private ownership, even though all the methods and conclusions may at some time have been initially the product of private invention. The contribution the scientific inquirer makes is collectively tested and developed. In the measure that it is cooperatively confirmed, it becomes a part of the common fund of the intellectual commonwealth.

One can most easily recognize the difference between the aim and operation of the free individual in the sphere of science and in that of current individualistic economic enterprise, by stretching the fancy to the point of imagining a scientific inquirer adopting the standards of the business entrepreneur. Imagine the scientific man who should say that his conclusion was scientific and, in so saying, maintain that it was also the product of his wants and efforts goading him on to seek his private advantage. The mere suggestion of such an absurdity vividly discloses the gap that divides the manifestations of individual freedom in these two areas of human activity. The suggestion brings into bold relief the kind of individual freedom that is both supported by collective, organic authority and that in turn changes and is encouraged to change and develop, by its own operations, the authority upon which it depends.

The thesis that the operation of cooperative intelligence as displayed in science is a working model of the union of freedom and authority does not slight the fact that the method has operated up to the present in a limited and relatively technical area. On the contrary, it emphasizes that fact. If the method of intelligence had been employed in any large field in the comprehensive and basic area of the relations of human beings to one another in social life and institutions, there would be no present need for our argument. The contrast between the restricted scope of its use and the possible range of its application to human relations—political, economic and moral— is outstanding enough to be depressing. It is this very contrast that serves to define the great problem that lies before us.

No consideration of the problem is adequate that does not take into account one fact about the development of the modern individualistic movement in industry and business. There is a suppressed premise in all the claims and reasonings of the individualistic school. All the beneficial changes that have been produced are attributed to the free play of individuals seeking primarily their own profit as isolated individuals. But in fact, the entire modern industrial development is the fruit of the technological applications of science. By and large, the economic changes of recent centuries have been parasitic upon the advances made in natural science. There is not a single process involved in the production and distribution of goods that is not dependent upon the utilization of results which are the consequences of the method of collective, organic intelligence working in mathematics, physics and chemistry. To speak baldly, it is a plain falsehood that the advances which the defenders of the existing regime point to as justification for its continuance are due to mere individualistic initiative and enterprise. Individualistic initiative and enterprise have sequestrated and appropriated the fruits of collective cooperative intelligence. Without the aid and support of organized intelligence they would have been impotent—perhaps even in those activities in which they have shown themselves to be socially most powerful.

In sum, the great weakness of the historic movement that has laid claim to the title of liberalism and that has proclaimed its operating purpose to be that of securing and protecting the freedom of individuals—the great weakness of this movement has been its failure to recognize that the true and final source of change has been, and now is, the corporate intelligence embodied in science. The principle, as I have already said, cuts in two directions. Insofar as the attempts that are now being made in the direction of organized social control and planned economy ignore the role of scientific intelligence; insofar as these attempts depend upon and turn for support to external institutional changes effected for the most part by force, just so far are they reinstating reliance upon the method of external authority that has always broken down in the past. For a time, while in need of security and a sense and feeling of solidarity, men will submit to authority of this kind. But if history shows anything, it shows that the variable factors in individuals cannot be permanently suppressed or completely eradicated. The principle of individual freedom expressed in the modern individualistic movement is deeply rooted in the constitution of human beings. The truth embodied in it cannot die, no matter how much force is brought down upon it. The tragedy of the movement is that it misconceived and misplaced the source and seat of this principle of freedom. But the attempt to eliminate this principle on behalf of the assurance of security and attainment of solidarity by means of external authority is doomed to ultimate defeat no matter what its temporary victories.

There is no need to dwell upon the enormous obstacles that stand in the way of extending from its limited field to the larger field of human relations the control of organized intelligence, operating through the release of individual powers and capabilities. There is the weight of past history on the side of those who are pessimistic about the possibility of achieving this humanly desirable and humanly necessary task. I do not predict that the extension will ever be effectively actualized. But I do claim that the problem of the relation of authority and freedom, of stability and change, if it can be solved, will be solved in this way. The failure of other methods and the desperateness of the present situation will be a spur to some to do their best to make the extension actual. They know that to hold in advance of trial that success is impossible is a way of condemning humanity to that futile and destructive oscillation between authoritative power and unregulated individual freedom to which we may justly attribute most of the sorrows and defeats of the past. They are aware of the slow processes of history and of the unmeasured stretch of time that lies ahead of mankind. They do not expect any speedy victory in the execution of the most difficult task human beings ever set their hearts and minds to attempt. They are, however, buoyed by the assurance that no matter how slight the immediate effect of their efforts, they are themselves, in their trials, exemplifying one of the first principles of the method of scientific intelligence. For they are experimentally projecting into events a large and comprehensive idea by methods that correct and mature the method and the idea in the very process of trial. The very desperateness of the situation is, for such as these, but a spur to sustained, courageous effort.

IDEALS OF SOCIAL INTELLIGENCE[13]

Read in the context of his humane insights into the nature of human good and his thoroughly elaborated moral philosophy, Dewey's summary statement of his democratic creed is genuinely moving.

. . . Democracy is much broader than a special political form, a method of conducting government, of making laws and carrying on governmental administration by means of popular suffrage and elected officers. It is that, of course. But it is something broader and deeper than that. The political and governmental phase of democracy is a means, the best means so far found, for realizing ends that lie in the wide domain of human relationships and the development of human personality. It is, as we often say, though perhaps without appreciating all that is involved in the saying, a way of life, social and individual. The keynote of democracy as a way of life may be expressed, it seems to me, as the necessity for the participation of every mature human being in formation of the values that regulate the living of men together:

which is necessary from the standpoint of both the general social welfare and the full development of human beings as individuals.

Universal suffrage, recurring elections, responsibility of those who are in political power to the voters, and the other factors of democratic government are means that have been found expedient for realizing democracy as the truly human way of living. They are not a final end and a final value. They are to be judged on the basis of their contribution to that end. It is a form of idolatry to erect means into the end which they serve. Democratic political forms are simply the best means that human wit has devised up to a special time in history. But they rest back upon the idea that no man or limited set of men is wise enough or good enough to rule others without their consent; the positive meaning of this statement is that all those who are affected by social institutions must have a share in producing and managing them. The two facts that each one is influenced in what he does and enjoys and in what he becomes by the institutions under which he lives, and that therefore he shall have, in a democracy, a voice in shaping them, are the passive and active sides of the same fact.

The development of political democracy came about through substitution of the method of mutual consultation and voluntary agreement for the method of subordination of the many to the few enforced from above. Social arrangements which involve fixed subordination are maintained by coercion. The coercion need not be physical. There have existed, for short periods, benevolent despotisms. But coercion of some sort there has been; perhaps economic, certainly psychological and moral. The very fact of exclusion from participation is a subtle form of suppression. It gives individuals no opportunity to reflect and decide upon what is good for them. Others who are supposed to be wiser and who in any case have more power decide the question for them and also decide the methods and means by which subjects may arrive at the enjoyment of what is good for them. This form of coercion and suppression is more subtle and more effective than is overt intimidation and restraint. When it is habitual and embodied in social institutions, it seems the normal and natural state of affairs. The mass usually become unaware that they have a claim to a development of their own powers. Their experience is so restricted that they are not conscious of restriction. It is part of the democratic conception that they as individuals are not the only sufferers, but that the whole social body is deprived of the potential resources that should be at its service. The individuals of the submerged mass may not be very wise. But there is one thing they are wiser about than anybody else can be, and that is where the shoe pinches, the troubles they suffer from.

The foundation of democracy is faith in the capacities of human nature; faith in human intelligence and in the power of pooled and cooperative experience. It is not belief that these things are complete but that, if given a

show, they will grow and be able to generate progressively the knowledge
and wisdom needed to guide collective action. Every autocratic and authoritarian scheme of social action rests on a belief that the needed intelligence is
confined to a superior few, who because of inherent natural gifts are endowed with the ability and the right to control the conduct of others; laying
down principles and rules and directing the ways in which they are carried out. It would be foolish to deny that much can be said for this point
of view. It is that which controlled human relations in social groups for
much the greater part of human history. The democratic faith has emerged
very, very recently in the history of mankind. Even where democracies now
exist, men's minds and feelings are still permeated with ideas about leadership imposed from above, ideas that developed in the long early history of
mankind. After democratic political institutions were nominally established,
beliefs and ways of looking at life and of acting that originated when men
and women were externally controlled and subjected to arbitrary power,
persisted in the family, the church, business, and the school; and experience
shows that as long as they persist there, political democracy is not secure.

Belief in equality is an element of the democratic credo. It is not, however, belief in equality of natural endowments. Those who proclaimed the
idea of equality did not suppose they were enunciating a psychological doctrine, but a legal and political one. All individuals are entitled to equality
of treatment by law and in its administration. Each one is affected equally in
quality if not in quantity by the institutions under which he lives and has an
equal right to express his judgment, although the weight of his judgment
may not be equal in amount when it enters into the pooled result to that of
others. In short, each one is equally an individual and entitled to equal
opportunity of development of his own capacities, be they large or small in
range. Moreover, each has needs of his own, as significant to him as those
of others are to them. The very fact of natural and psychological inequality
is all the more reason for establishment by law of equality of opportunity,
since otherwise the former becomes a means of oppression of the less gifted.

While what we call intelligence be distributed in unequal amounts, it is the
democratic faith that it is sufficiently general so that each individual has
something to contribute, whose value can be assessed only as it enters into
the final pooled intelligence constituted by the contributions of all. Every
authoritarian scheme, on the contrary, assumes that its value may be assessed
by some *prior* principle, if not of family and birth or race and color or
possession of material wealth, then by the position and rank a person occupies in the existing social scheme. The democratic faith in equality is the
faith that each individual shall have the chance and opportunity to contribute whatever he is capable of contributing and that the value of his
contribution be decided by its place and function in the organized total of

similar contributions, not on the basis of prior status of any kind whatever. . . .

Under present circumstances I cannot hope to conceal the fact that I have managed to exist eighty years. Mention of the fact may suggest to you a more important fact—namely, that events of the utmost significance for the destiny of this country have taken place during the past four-fifths of a century, a period that covers more than half of its national life in its present form. For obvious reasons I shall not attempt a summary of even the more important of these events. I refer here to them because of their bearing upon the issue to which this country committed itself when the nation took shape—the creation of democracy, an issue which is now as urgent as it was a hundred and fifty years ago when the most experienced and wisest men of the country gathered to take stock of conditions and to create the political structure of a self-governing society.

For the net import of the changes that have taken place in these later years is that ways of life and institutions which were once the natural, almost the inevitable, product of fortunate conditions have now to be won by conscious and resolute effort. Not all the country was in a pioneer state eighty years ago. But it was still, save perhaps in a few large cities, so close to the pioneer stage of American life that the traditions of the pioneer, indeed of the frontier, were active agencies in forming the thoughts and shaping the beliefs of those who were born into its life. In imagination at least the country was still having an open frontier, one of unused and unappropriated resources. It was a country of physical opportunity and invitation. Even so, there was more than a marvelous conjunction of physical circumstances involved in bringing to birth this new nation. There was in existence a group of men who were capable of readapting older institutions and ideas to meet the situations provided by new physical conditions—a group of men extraordinarily gifted in political inventiveness.

At the present time, the frontier is moral, not physical. The period of free lands that seemed boundless in extent has vanished. Unused resources are now human rather than material. They are found in the waste of grown men and women who are without the chance to work, and in the young men and young women who find doors closed where there was once opportunity. The crisis that one hundred and fifty years ago called out social and political inventiveness is with us in a form which puts a heavier demand on human creativeness.

At all events this is what I mean when I say that we now have to re-create by deliberate and determined endeavor the kind of democracy which in its origin one hundred and fifty years ago was largely the product of a fortunate combination of men and circumstances. We have lived for a long time upon the heritage that came to us from the happy conjunction of men and events in an earlier day. The present state of the world is more than a reminder that we have now to put forth every energy of our own to prove worthy of our heritage. It is a challenge to do for the critical and complex conditions of today what the men of an earlier day did for simpler conditions.

If I emphasize that the task can be accomplished only by inventive effort and creative activity, it is in part because the depth of the present crisis is due in considerable part to the fact that for a long period we acted as if our democracy were something that perpetuated itself automatically; as if our ancestors had succeeded in setting up a machine that solved the problem of perpetual motion in politics. We acted as if democracy were something that took place mainly at Washington and Albany—or some other state capital—under the impetus of what happened when men and women went to the polls once a year or so—which is a somewhat extreme way of saying that we have had the habit of thinking of democracy as a kind of political mechanism that will work as long as citizens were reasonably faithful in performing political duties.

Of late years we have heard more and more frequently that this is not enough; that democracy is a way of life. This saying gets down to hard pan. But I am not sure that something of the externality of the old idea does not cling to the new and better statement. In any case we can escape from this external way of thinking only as we realize in thought and act that democracy is a *personal* way of individual life; that it signifies the possession and continual use of certain attitudes, forming personal character and determining desire and purpose in all the relations of life. Instead of thinking of our own dispositions and habits as accommodated to certain institutions we have to learn to think of the latter as expressions, projections, and extensions of habitually dominant personal attitudes.

Democracy as a personal, an individual, way of life involves nothing fundamentally new. But when applied it puts a new practical meaning in old ideas. Put into effect it signifies that powerful present enemies of democracy can be successfully met only by the creation of personal attitudes in individual human beings; that we must get over our tendency to think that its defense can be found in any external means whatever, whether military or civil, if they are separated from individual attitudes so deep-seated as to constitute personal character.

Democracy is a way of life controlled by a working faith in the possibilities of human nature. Belief in the Common Man is a familiar article in the democratic creed. That belief is without basis and significance save as it means faith in the potentialities of human nature as that nature is exhibited in every human being irrespective of race, color, sex, birth, and family, of material or cultural wealth. This faith may be enacted in statutes, but it is only on paper unless it is put in force in the attitudes which human beings display to one another in all the incidents and relations of daily life. To denounce Naziism for intolerance, cruelty and stimulation of hatred amounts to fostering insincerity if, in our personal relations to other persons, if, in our daily walk and conversation, we are moved by racial, color, or other class prejudice; indeed, by anything save a generous belief in their possibilities as human beings, a belief which brings with it the need for providing conditions which will enable these capacities to reach fulfillment. The democratic faith in human equality is belief that every human being, independent of the quantity or range of his personal endowment, has the right to equal opportunity with every other person for development of whatever gifts he has. The democratic belief in the principle of leadership is a generous one. It is universal. It is belief in the capacity of every person to lead his own life free from coercion and imposition by others provided right conditions are supplied.

Democracy is a way of personal life controlled not merely by faith in human nature in general but by faith in the capacity of human beings for intelligent judgment and action if proper conditions are furnished. I have been accused more than once and from opposed quarters of an undue, a utopian, faith in the possibilities of intelligence and in education as a correlate of intelligence. At all events, I did not invent this faith. I acquired it from my surroundings as far as those surroundings were animated by the democratic spirit. For what is the faith of democracy in the role of consultation, of conference, of persuasion, of discussion, in formation of public opinion, which in the long run is self-corrective, except faith in the capacity of the intelligence of the common man to respond with common sense to the free play of facts and ideas which are secured by effective guarantees of free inquiry, free assembly, and free communication? I am willing to leave to upholders of totalitarian states of the right and the left the view that faith in the capacities of intelligence is utopian. For the faith is so deeply embedded in the methods which are intrinsic to democracy that when a professed democrat denies the faith he convicts himself of treachery to his profession.

When I think of the conditions under which men and women are living in many foreign countries today, fear of espionage, with danger hanging over the meeting of friends for friendly conversation in private gatherings, I am inclined to believe that the heart and final guarantee of democracy is in free gatherings of neighbors on the street corner to discuss back and forth what is read in uncensored news of the day, and in gatherings of friends in the living rooms of houses and apartments to converse freely with one another. Intolerance, abuse, calling of names because of differences of opinion about religion or politics or business, as well as because of differences of race, color, wealth, or degree of culture, are treason to the democratic way of life. For everything which bars freedom and fullness of communication sets up barriers that divide human beings into sets and cliques, into antagonistic sects and factions, and thereby undermines the democratic way of life. Merely legal guarantees of the civil liberties of free belief, free expression, free assembly are of little avail if in daily life freedom of communication, the give and take of ideas, facts, experiences, is choked by mutual suspicion, by abuse, by fear and hatred. These things destroy the essential condition of the democratic way of living even more effectually than open coercion, which—as the example of totalitarian states proves—is effective only when it succeeds in breeding hate, suspicion, intolerance in the minds of individual human beings.

Finally, given the two conditions just mentioned, democracy as a way of life is controlled by personal faith in personal day-by-day working together with others. Democracy is the belief that even when needs and ends or consequences are different for each individual, the habit of amicable cooperation—which may include, as in sport, rivalry and competition—is itself a priceless addition to life. To take as far as possible every conflict which arises—and they are bound to arise—out of the atmosphere and medium of force, of violence as a means of settlement, into that of discussion and of intelligence, is to treat those who disagree—even profoundly—with us as those from whom we may learn, and in so far, as friends. A genuinely democratic faith in peace is faith in the possibility of conducting disputes, controversies, and conflicts as cooperative undertakings in which both parties learn by giving the other a chance to express itself, instead of having one party conquer by forceful suppression of the other—a suppression which is none the less one of violence when it takes place by psychological means of ridicule, abuse, intimidation, instead of by overt imprisonment or in concentration camps. To cooperate by giving differences a chance to show themselves because of the belief that the expression of difference is not only a right of the other persons but is a means of enriching one's own life-experience, is inherent in the democratic personal way of life.

If what has been said is charged with being a set of moral commonplaces, my only reply is that that is just the point in saying them. For to get rid of the habit of thinking of democracy as something institutional and external and to acquire the habit of treating it as a way of personal life is to realize that democracy is a moral ideal and so far as it becomes a fact is a moral fact. It is to realize that democracy is a reality only as it is indeed a commonplace of living.

Since my adult years have been given to the pursuit of philosophy, I shall ask your indulgence if in concluding I state briefly the democratic faith in the formal terms of a philosophic position. So stated, democracy is belief in the ability of human experience to generate the aims and methods by which further experience will grow in ordered richness. Every other form of moral and social faith rests upon the idea that experience must be subjected at some point or other to some form of external control; to some "authority" alleged to exist outside the processes of experience. Democracy is the faith that the process of experience is more important than any special result attained, so that special results achieved are of ultimate value only as they are used to enrich and order the ongoing process. Since the process of experience is capable of being educative, faith in democracy is all one with faith in experience and education. All ends and values that are cut off from the ongoing process become arrests, fixations. They strive to fixate what has been gained instead of using it to open the road and point the way to new and better experiences.

If one asks what is meant by experience in this connection, my reply is that it is that free interaction of individual human beings with surrounding conditions, especially the human surroundings, which develops and satisfies need and desire by increasing knowledge of things as they are. Knowledge of conditions as they are is the only solid ground for communication and sharing; all other communication means the subjection of some persons to the personal opinion of other persons. Need and desire—out of which grow purpose and direction of energy—go beyond what exists, and hence beyond knowledge, beyond science. They continually open the way into the unexplored and unattained future.

Democracy as compared with other ways of life is the sole way of living which believes wholeheartedly in the process of experience as end and as means; as that which is capable of generating the science which is the sole dependable authority for the direction of further experience and which releases emotions, needs, and desires so as to call into being the things that have not existed in the past. For every way of life that fails in its democracy limits the contacts, the exchanges, the communications, the interactions by which experience is steadied while it is also enlarged and enriched. The task of this release and enrichment is one that has to be carried on day by day. Since it is one that can have no end till experience itself comes to an end, the task of democracy is forever that of creation of a freer and more humane experience in which all share and to which all contribute.

1. *Ethics*, p. 408.

2. An irremediable futility attends the attempt to universalize prescriptions, because there is not agreement on criteria for universalization, and situations are always more or less unrepeatable (see "The Nature of Principles," above, pp. 144–46). The most baneful effect of philosophies that deal with universalizing prescriptions, however, is not that they are futile, but that they persist in focusing the problem of moral choice on the isolated individual, who asks *himself* what he can universalize. In a social method the individual consults with other individuals to attempt to determine with them what mode of conduct they can share in—*Ed.*

3. See my *John Dewey's Philosophy of Value*, chapter 7: "Intelligence and Value"—*Ed.*

4. *Human Nature and Conduct*, pp. 287–93, 296–300; *Ethics*, pp. 350–51, 353, 382–87. Heading is taken from the indicated portion of *Human Nature and Conduct*.

5. In *Freedom in the Modern World*, edited by Horace M. Kallen (New York: Coward-McCann, 1928), pp. 236–71.

6. *Freedom and Culture* (New York: G. P. Putnam's Sons, 1939), pp. 113–30. Heading provided by the editor.

7. *Liberalism and Social Action* (New York: G. P. Putnam's Sons, 1935), pp. 67–71, 42–44, 72–74; *The Public and Its Problems*, pp. 209–11; *Liberalism and Social Action*, pp. 52–53. Heading provided by the editor.

8. Dewey refers to judgments about the bearing of technical knowledge on common concerns—*Ed.*

9. *Freedom and Culture*, pp. 137–50, 151–54; *Art as Experience*, pp. 346–49.

10. Most of the excerpts comprising this section are from *The Public and Its Problems*, but material is also used from *Individualism Old and New* (New York: Minton, Balch and Co., 1930). At the end of each excerpt the source and pages are given in parentheses, *The Public and Its Problems* abbreviated as *PIP* and *Individualism Old and New* as *ION*. Heading provided by the editor.

11. Dewey is quoting from Woodrow Wilson's *The New Freedom*—*Ed.*

12. *Ethics*, pp. 364–65, 375–76; *Liberalism and Social Action*, pp. 79–80; *The Public and Its Problems*, pp. 202–03, 200–01; and "Authority and Resistance to Social Change," *School and Society* XLIV (1936): pp. 457–66. "Authority and Resistance to Social Change" was reprinted in *Problems of Men* (New York: Philosophical Library, 1946), pp. 93–110. Selection is from *Problems of Men*, pp. 104–110. Heading provided by the editor.

13. From "Democracy and Educational Administration," *School and Society* XLV (1937): pp. 457–62, and, in its entirety, "Creative Democracy—The Task Before Us." The former was reprinted in *Problems of Men*, pp. 57–69; selection is pp. 57–60 in *Problems of Men*. The latter is from *The Philosopher of the Common Man: Essays in Honor of John Dewey to Celebrate His Eightieth Birthday*, ed. S. Ratner (New York: G. P. Putnam's Sons, 1940), pp. 220–28. Heading provided by the editor.

INDEX

INDEX

Absolutes, moral: Dewey's wariness of, xix; as reflecting social bias, xxii, xlii, liii

Activity: and environment, 73; and fixed ends, 120; good of, 95–96, 98; relation of future to present, 96–98; dependent upon social behavior, 177

Aims: *See* Ends, Ends-in-view, Value

Altruism: 118. *See also* Egoism

American culture: traits of, 246–47

Aristotle: 4; quoted, 81, 134–35

Art: moral value of, 227–30; its moral effects, and culture, 227; as criticism of life, 227–28; and morals, interaction between, 228–29

Associated behavior: and society, 110; unexpected consequences of, 230–31; and the public, 231; distinguished from community, 236

Augustine, Saint: 4

Authority: moral, li; coercive, 254, 257

Ayer, A. J.: quoted, xlvii, 163

Being: as fixed and unchanging, 25, 33

Benevolence: 118

Change: as organic to time, 33–34; inseparable from novelty and individuality, 34–35; physical, 37–38; qualitative, 39; and fixed ends, 40; and freedom, 40–41; and insecurity, 58. *See also* Process, Time

Character formation: need for knowledge of, 180. *See also* Human nature

Charity: 117–18

Choice: nature of, xxxiv; and the formation of the self, xxxv–xxxvi, 142–43; and unification of preferences, 141–42; need for understanding of, 187–88; and free will, 188–89; and preferential behavior, 189–90; as formation of preference, 190;

and educability, 190. *See also* Deliberation, Freedom

Choice, ethical: conceived by Dewey as concerning conflict of goods, ix–x. *See also* Morality

Coercion: as exclusion from social participation, 259

Common good: undergoes expansion, xxiii, 184; and individuality, 184, 186; not conceived paternalistically, 185; and privilege, 185–86

Communication: and the mental, 47; need to perfect means of, 238. *See also* Community, Social intelligence

Community: xxviii, xli, xlv; as religious, 114, 120–21; and self-interest, 117; as face-to-face association, 231, 248–49; and democracy, 235, 236; product of communication and sharing, 236–37; and individual development, 237–38. *See also* Shared experience, Social

Comte: 212

Conscience: as social product, 177

Consummatory experience: nature of, xx, 75–79; and unified situations, xxx–xxxi; as reconstruction of natural processes, xxxi; understanding of requires theory of the nature of nature, xxxi; distinguished from ends-in-view, 74; organic to situations, 74–75; unifying quality of, 76–77; and aesthetic experience, 77–79; and fixed ends, 79; and labor, 80; and formation of habit, 108–109; and the social order, 109

Crisis of value: liii; philosophic sources of, liii–liv; social sources of, liv; philosophic approach to, liv–lv

Darwin: Dewey's use of his theory of evolution, xxvi; influence on philosophy, 24

Darwinism: principal impact scientific, not religious, 24–25; as criticism of static

of, 90; and growth, 90; and ends, 100; and conflicting environments, 105

Happiness: and consummatory experience, 93; and present activity, 95–96, 120; and the self, 99–100; and character, 119; and shared interest, 119; and shared experience, 119–20. *See also* Growth

Hegel: xlii, 196

Human nature: outcome of interaction of organism and environment, xxvi; native differences in, xxvii, 217–18, 260; some traits of destructive, xl; functional analysis of, 23–24; obscurity of traditional language concerning, 47–48; unity of, 48; and dualisms, 48; inclusive of processes external to the organism, 49–51; and the human environment, 51–54; unification of, 53–54; as inherently active, 94; and society, 113–14; importance of knowledge of, 133; and morals, 133–34; without predetermined form, 205; conceptions of determined by moral bias, 205; original components of give no direction to social policy, 205; meaningless explanations of, 205–206, 207–208; need for scientific inquiry into, 206–207; and culture, 221. *See also* Habit, Self

Hume: xxix, xlii, 21, 219

Idealism: conception of society in, xxvii; as reaction to classical liberalism, 208–209; political philosophy reflecting fear of human nature, 209; conception of moral authority in, 209–210; as response to individualism, 215

Ideal values: and the human environment, 53

Ideas: and behavior, xxxii–xxxiii; as predictive, xxxii–xxxiii; as guides to conduct, xxxiii–xxxiv; and reconstitution of valuations, xxxiv; as having reference to antecedent reality in empiricism and rationalism, xxxiv, 130–31; as used in social intelligence, xliii; as instrumental, 10–11, 16–17, 126–33 *passim*; as plans for reconstructing situations, 211–12; and emotions, interaction between, 220, *See also* Inquiry, Instrumentalism, Science

Impulse: not preestablished form of behavior, xxvi, 192–93, 194; and habit, xxvi, 103; meaning of, 87; flexibility of,

88; and social environment, 88; and custom, 103; and intelligence, 156–57n12

Individual: determined by context, 109–10; and associated activity, 110–11; and the social, 110–12

Individualism: of modern moral philosophy, xli–xlii; and moral disagreement, xlii; and moral absolutism, xlii; of modern moral philosophy, sources of, xlii; and collectivism, 112–13; and collectivism, as untenable alternatives, 207–210. *See also* Intelligence, Liberalism, classical

Individuality: and freedom, xxxvi; and fixed ends, xxxvi; as mode of social interaction, xl, 184; genuineness of, 37–39; common to the physical and the human, 38–39; as unique connections in the whole, 120–21; and preferential behavior, 189–90; and causal law, 201–203; in America, 247–48; in a collective age, 248. *See also* Time

Industrial revolution: indirect consequences of, 230–31

Industrial society: need for shared perception of consequences of, 238–39; beneficial effects from science, 257

Inquiry: nature of, xxxii–xxxiv; as creative, xxxiii; as transforming existential subject matter, 135–36; and practical activity, 136–37; and transformation of situations, 136–38; and deliberation, 137; and judgments of practice, 138. *See also* Logical theory, Science

Instinct: and social control, 108. *See also* Impulse

Instrumentalism: distinguished from James's pragmatism, xxxv, 122–23, 129–30; and labor, 60, 123; characterized, 122–23; and science, 122–23; and qualities, 124–25; and personal satisfaction, 129–30; as showing inseparability of science and common sense, 173–74. *See also* Ideas, Inquiry, Science

Intellectualism: 15–16

Intelligence: and nature, xxviii; as method, xxxv; as object of contempt, lv; as alternative to dogmatism and absolutism, lv, 182–83; and ends, 72; and activity, 73; and means-ends, 81–82; and art, 81–82, 92; and consummatory experience, 81–82; and habit, 88–89, 240; and the